For the Common Good

A Critical Examination of Law and Social Control

For the Common Good

A Critical Examination of Law and Social Control

Edited by

R. Robin Miller, Ph.D.
Drury University

Sandra Lee Browning, Ph.D.
University of Cincinnati

Carolina Academic Press
Durham, North Carolina

ISBN 0-89089-223-7
LCCN 2003116522

Carolina Academic Press
700 Kent Street
Durham, North Carolina 27701
Telephone (919) 489-7486
Fax (919) 493-5668
E-mail: cap@cap-press.com
www.cap-press.com

Printed in the United States of America.

Dedication

R.R.M

To both my family and my Drury family.
I appreciate your support more than I can possibly express.

S.L.B

To Avery, the joy of my life.

Contents

Acknowledgments

To begin, we wish to express our heartfelt appreciation to our many and wonderful contributors! They generously shared their insights and original research to further our understanding of and appreciation for a critical perspective on law; this perspective is so needed. We must also thank them for their incredible patience on a project which lasted just over two years. It was a long haul, but a fruitful one. This anthology would not have been possible without the support and guidance of our families—so a special thanks to our families for putting up with us! And a special thanks to Jo Miller—the fastest reader in the West! Our thanks also to a fantastic group of people at Carolina Academic Press who helped immensely in the production of the book: Sue Johnson for her help in editing; Jay Stallings for his help with production; and Tim Colton for his patience and help with everything. Finally, a hearty thanks to both Marline Ritter and Kay Lowder, support staff at Drury. You two are amazing!

For the Common Good

A Critical Examination of Law and Social Control

INTRODUCTION

INTRODUCING A CRITICAL EXAMINATION OF LAW AND SOCIAL CONTROL

"A Critical Examination of Law and Social Control: Introductory Remarks"

R. Robin Miller
DRURY UNIVERSITY

Sandra Lee Browning
UNIVERSITY OF CINCINNATI

Introduction

On October 25, 2001, President George Bush signed into law the Provide Appropriate Tools Required to Intercept and Obstruct Terrorism legislation, now known as the Patriot's Act. The ostensible purpose of this policy initiative is to give to national and international law enforcement officers the ability to ably pursue terrorists like the ones responsible for the September 11, 2001 Trade Center towers attacks.

By expanding the range of common tools of surveillance, namely: wiretaps, search warrants, pen/trap orders and subpoenas, government agents may now track Americans who enter certain "suspicious" words on their computers without showing cause, nor must they demonstrate that the person under surveillance is the target of some investigation. Agents may now use roving wiretaps that allow them to go from phone to phone or computer to computer, also without demonstrating that the person under surveillance is the target of some specific investigation.

The Act also provides for the expansion of the definition of domestic terrorism, which quite reasonably heightens concerns about how legitimate protest activities and actors will be handled in the future. For instance, if the World Trade Organization protest which occurred in Seattle were to occur in the near future, would the powers that be decide to prosecute activists on terrorism charges?

The ways in which this initiative serves to threaten personal freedoms and citizens rights are glaringly obvious. And did the freedoms we had as American citizens from the unlawful and unprovoked spying of law enforcement officials actually give rise to the terrorist acts in the first place? Writing as someone who was heretofore reticent of posting students' grades, even by their personal school identification numbers, lest I violate the (completely necessary) Family Privacy Act of 1974, to be told by university administration that any one of us will now be forced to release private student information to any governmental official who asks (with or without pretense of cause) is more than a bit disturbing.

It seems that the state, by claiming that they are increasing our "collective security" through these broader powers, is in actuality, operating against the common good. More than anything else, recent events highlight the need for texts such as this.

The Necessity of Critical Perspectives on Law

It is understandably difficult to put forth a definitive statement about what does and does not constitute a critical perspective. Many other scholars have tried and failed to delineate the element(s) which must be included to ably define this perspective. However, it can be boldly stated that critical perspectives in the Western tradition include predominately European influences from the Frankfurt school like Marcuse (1960), Horkheimer (1974), and Habermas (1971). Thinkers from this perspective were to move from a strict Marxian focus on the material conditions of reality and economy to "...the cultural system, which it came to see as the major force in modern capitalist society... This was consistent with, but an extension of, the position taken earlier by Hegelian Marxists..." (Ritzer, 1996: 67). It may even be stated that a history of critical theory is a history of its various definitions. An inclusive articulation of all that critical theory encompases is of course well beyond the scope of this text. Therefore, for the purposes of this anthology, the critical perspective on law tends to include Marxist and neo-Marxist elements—whether they be focused on the importance of material conditions in society or states of consciousness. Obviously, not all contributors to this text will write from the same ideological vantage point. Nor is that singular focus strictly necessary for readers to gain a better understanding of the myriad ways we are controlled through law.

This anthology is necessary for so many reasons. Examining the structure and influence of law has long been something that social scientists have done. Social philosophers dealing with the influences of the law and polity are many and a few of them have been mentioned previously. Emile Durkheim (1897/1951) wrote of institutional structures which served to bind individuals more firmly to the social fabric and in so doing served as forces of social control. Of course, he addressed the influence of law more explicitly in *Division of Labor in Society* (1893/1964).

Karl Marx is, arguably, our first and most influential theorist to deal critically with the influences of law and the political order. Furthermore, many of these theoretical precursors have been previously mentioned. And while there have been theorists and researchers who have hastened us toward a critical perspective (as detailed earlier in this essay), surprisingly, the study of law and society at least through the texts that have been written and studied in the last decade continue to be dominated by a less critical perspective. In 1999, A. Javier Trevino conducted a comparative review of nine law and society and sociology of law texts. Only one of them had the economic order as a key element. Less than half of these texts included a critical examination of legal case studies. And finally, only two of these nine texts had a critical theoretical focus according to Trevino (1999).

What has been the difficulty of advancing a critical approach to reality including issues like law and social control? Marvin Harris (1974) would name these factors: that there has been ignorance of cultural and societal alternatives; that there is a fear which causes some to cleave to a false consciousness; and that there are the powerful in society who would seek to control and exploit others through the manipulation of reality, so that, "these inequalities are as much disguised, mystified, and lied about as old age and death" (Harris, 1974: 3). Given this paucity of perspective in recent years on the one hand and our long and varied history of critically examining law and social control on the other, it appears that we need to refocus our energies in this direction. This anthology serves in this capacity.

A Brief Explication of Terms

A critical perspective has been previously addressed, but what of "law"? What of "social control"? And what of the "common good"? I firmly believe that it is both necessary and good to study closely both law and social control.

If social control is the normative, or expected, element of social reality, then law can be understood as "governmental social control" (Radcliffe-Brown, 1933/1965) over the citizenry. It is in this way that law is so powerful. Law is a structural force that, at least theoretically, reaches everyone. It can be powerful in its scope, its frequency, and its intensity. Law is not divorced from the public over which it is exercised but is, again, some reflection of the normative order which reigns. And a law that is not commonly accepted by the people still has the power to shape behavior through sheer force of the punishments handed down for violations of it.

However, Donald Black (1976) states, "law itself is social control, but many other kinds of social control also appear in social life, in families, friendships, neighborhoods, villages, tribes, occupations, organizations, and groups of all kinds" (1976: 6). Because law is only one form of social control it would be an obvious and regrettable mistake to focus only on the behaviors of governmental bodies. Consequently, the reader will find a variety of processes explored with this text.

A brief review of the concepts touched on by the works of this anthology would be incomplete without some mention of the socially constructed nature of both reality and social control. The construction of social reality and the creation of deviance are processes about which much has been written and on which many of the works of this anthology indirectly depend. While this approach has developed over more than the last century in philosophy and the social sciences, we may more specifically begin our look with the work of W.I. Thomas who suggested that the powerful have, quite literally, the power to define the situation. Furthermore, Berger and Luckman (1967) believe that we must be most concerned with "...the processes by which any body of 'knowledge' comes to be socially established as 'reality'" (1966: 3). Richard Quinney in *The Social Reality of Crime* (1970) states that, "the social reality of crime is constructed on conflict in our society..." and further asks the question, How do persons and behaviors become criminal? He will point us toward a society's social, economic and political structure to answer that question. More specifically, our capitalist order must be examined to understand the forces which underlie the social construction of crime and deviance. But the constructionist approach to law and social control predates the work of Quinney. Howard Becker's (1963) idea that "social groups create deviance" (1963: 5) more than implies that deviance is a social construct that simply does not exist if the rules and norms of society are not constructed and maintained. And Edwin Shur (1984), following in the path of Becker, will suggest that even the statuses one holds in society (e.g. gender) can be defined as deviant as easily as overt behaviors. There is a long, rich tradition of examining law and social control from a social constructionist perspective, and to end, nearly every paper in this anthology speaks, at least tangentially, from this constructionist view of reality.

Finally, what of the "common good"? I regret the fact that a common understanding of this term is largely assumed but so rarely articulated. At its most basic, the good of all is meant. From the enlightenment thinkers, we gain the sense that the "public interest" in its most general sense is intended. From John Locke's notion of the liberties of citizens which must be protected, to the utilitarian James Mill who suggested that we seek "the greatest good of the greatest number," to his son, John Stuart Mill, who apparently believed that the common good should be promoted through public welfare programs (Mill, 1859/1978), the term, "common good" has been quite laden with value. At least implied in many of the works included here is this last, more visionary, meaning. It is our responsibility as citizens to be critical in our examination of the forces of law and social control.

Conclusion

Times of national crises seem to often give rise to increased prejudice and scapegoating—processes which rob citizens of individual rights. Our system of law, as reflective of the normative order, mostly operates to maintain this system. Nowhere is this more apparent than the executive branch. As case in point, since the implementation of the Freedom of Information Act (FOIA) in the 1970s, four attorneys general have issued memorandums regarding this Act to the heads of all departments in the executive branch. On October 12, 2001, shortly following the September 11, 2001 terrorist attacks Attorney General John Ashcroft released his own memorandum. This memorandum made only a glancing nod of recognition to our need of maintaining an open system of government that is accountable to the people. Instead, his memorandum was a call for the staunch defense of national security—suggesting that our need to stop terrorism overrides all other concerns we may have as a nation. He writes:

> The Department of Justice and this Administration are equally committed to protecting other fundamental values that are held by our society. Among them are safeguarding our national security, enhancing the effectiveness of our law enforcement agencies, protecting sensitive business information and, not least, preserving personal privacy...When you carefully consider FOIA requests and decide to withhold records, in whole or in part, you can be assured that the

> Department of Justice will defend your decisions.... (U.S. Department of Justice Freedom of Information website, 2001)

Ashcroft speaks of our national interest to maintain a government that is "fully functional and efficient." Apparently, allowing citizens to make themselves aware of the various daily actions of governmental agencies simply slows the efficiency of these governmental agencies and there is no time to be lost in catching terrorists.

It is these actions and others like them that call most strongly for a critical perspective on law and the processes of social control. Quite simply, our close and judicious examination of these processes may stand as the only true safeguard of the common good.

References

Becker, H. (1963). The Outsiders: Studies in the Sociology of Deviance. New York: The Free Press.

Berger, P. and T. Luckman. (1967). The Social Construction of Reality. Garden City, NY: Anchor Press.

Black, D. (1976). The Behavior of Law. New York: The Academic Press.

Durkheim, Emile. (1897/1951). Suicide. New York: The Free Press.

_______. (1893/1964). The Division of Labor in Society. New York: The Free Press.

Habermas, J. (1971). Knowledge and Human Interests. Boston: Beacon Press.

Harris, M. (1974). Cows, Pigs, Wars and Witches: The Riddles of Culture. New York: Vintage Books.

Horkheimer, M. (1974). Eclipse of reason. New York: Seabury Press.

Marcuse, H. (1960). Reason and Revolution. Boston: Beacon Press.

Mill, J.S. (1859/1978). On Liberty. Indianapolis, IN: Hackett Publishing Company, Inc.

Quinney, R. (1970). The Social Reality of Crime. Boston: Little and Brown.

Radcliffe-Brown, A.R. (1933/1965). Structure and Function in Primitive Society: Essays and Addresses. New York: The Free Press.

Ritzer, G. (1996). Contemporary Sociological Theory. Fourth Edition. New York: McGraw Hill, Inc.

Shur, E. (1984). Labeling Women Deviant: Gender, Stigma, and Social Control. New York: McGraw Hill, Inc.

Trevino, A.J. (1999). "Nine Law and Society/Sociology of Law Textbooks and Readers for the 1990s: a Comparative Review." *Teaching Sociology*, 26: 354–380.

United States Department of Justice Freedom of Information website, 2001.

Section 1

Race and the Social Control of Law

"The New American Apartheid: The Incarceration of African-Americans"

Randall G. Shelden,
Department of Criminal Justice,
University of Nevada-Las Vegas

William B. Brown,
Department of Criminal Justice,
Western Oregon University

Shelley Johnson Listwan,
Department of Criminal Justice,
University of Nevada-Las Vegas

Introduction

It appears obvious that African-Americans, especially males, are superfluous and expendable in American society (that is, not really needed for corporate profits). With the constant corporate downsizing and deindustrialization during the past couple of decades came the elimination of millions of occupations that used to lift minorities out of poverty. Thus, some form of social control has been needed. The criminal justice system currently fills this need (Parenti, 1999). As the data brought forth in this paper will show, a new form of apartheid has thus been created. Consider these facts:

- whereas in 1985, 5.2 percent of all African-Americans were either in jail or in prison (versus only 1.2 percent of all whites), in 1995 (the latest figures available) this percentage stood at 9.3 percent (versus only 2.0 percent of all whites) (Maguire and Pastore, 1998: 464);

- the total incarceration rate (per 100,000) for African-American males in 1985 stood at 3,544 (versus 528 for white males); African-American females had a rate of 183 (versus 27 for white females); in 1996 the rate for African-American males was 6,607 and for females it was 456 (versus 944 for white males and 73 for white females) (Kurki, 1999);
- in 1990 one in four black males in their 20s was under some form of control within the criminal justice system; in 1995 the percentage had increased to one-third (Mauer, 1995);
- the jail incarceration rate for African-Americans stood at 368 in 1985 (73 for whites); in 1997 the rate had doubled to 725 (138 for whites) (Bureau of Justice Statistics, 1999);
- the number of African-Americans incarcerated for drug offenses alone increased by 799% between 1986 and 1997, versus a more modest increase of 205% for whites (Kurki, 1999);
- a Human Rights Watch report noted that the rate of incarceration for African-American men for drug offenses is 482 per 100,000, compared to only 36 per 100,000 for white men. Put somewhat differently, that is one out of every 207 African-American men, versus one out of every 2778 white men; the report also noted that nationally, 62 percent of all imprisoned drug offenders are African-American males. In some states these percentages go as high as 80 or 90! This is despite the well-publicized fact that there are few racial differences as far as illegal drug use is concerned (Human Rights Watch, 2000);
- 13% of all adult African-American men are disenfranchised as a result of a felony conviction (1.4 million; one-third of all disenfranchised adults); in some states the percentage is more than 30 (e.g., Alabama and Florida), while in many more states over 20% are disenfranchised (The Sentencing Project/Human Rights Watch, 1998).

These are just some of the horrendous numbers that describe the plight of African-Americans in this country. While the "old" apartheid of residential segregation (Massey and Denton, 1993) continues unabated, a "new" apartheid has risen along side of it. The criminal justice system has been engaged in a systematic attack on African-Americans. The remaining pages of this paper will explore this phenomenon more fully.

The Growing American Prison Population and the Drug War

At yearend 2000, there were 2,071,686 adults in jails and prisons in America. This translated to an incarceration rate of 699 per 100,000 population, up from a rate of 458 in 1990 (Beck and Harrison, 2001). We are way ahead of other industrial democracies, whose incarceration rates tend to cluster in a range from around 55 to 120 per 100,000 population, with some well below that figure, like Japan's rate of 36, with an average incarceration rate for *all countries of the world* around 80. Thus, America's incarceration rate is around nine times greater than the average country (Currie, 1998: 15). And it should be noted that these figures do not include all of those in various community-based facilities (e.g., work-release centers) and incarcerated juveniles.

Table 1 shows changes in America's prison system during the past 75 plus years. Note that the most significant increases have occurred since 1975, roughly coinciding with the onset of the "war on drugs." This "war on drugs," which has targeted mostly the poor and racial minorities, in turn has helped to create what many are calling a "prison-industrial complex." This in turn is the result of an economic system driven by a "free market" philosophy that places profits above people (Shelden, 2001; Parenti, 1999).

Table 1. The Growing Prison Population, 1925–2000 (rates per 100,000 in state and federal prison)

Year	Number	Rate
1925	91,669	79
1935	144,180	113
1945	133,649	98
1955	185,780	112
1965	210,895	108
1975	240,593	111
1985	480,568	202
1995	1,085,363	411
1999	1,302,019	461
2000	1,381,892	478

Source: Maguire and Pastore, 1997: 518; Gilliard, 1999; Irwin and Austin, 2001: 2–4; Beck and Harrison, 2001.

There has been a dramatic increase in the number and percentage of African-Americans who are incarcerated in America's prisons, amply documented in numerous sources (Currie, 1998, 1993; Donziger, 1996; Higginbotham, 1996; Miller, 1996; Tonry, 1995; Mauer, 1999). Perhaps equally disturbing is the increase in the probability of young African-American males who will, at some point in time in their lives, be sentenced to jail or to prison. African-American prison admissions passed white admissions in 1986, and by 1993 the proportion of those sentenced to prison who were African-American had increased to 55% compared to 27% for whites (Miller, 1996: 55; Gilliard and Beck, 1998: 9). We suppose that this is largely a result of the insanity of the continuing drug war in American society. On the other hand, given the fact the drug war has been going on since at least the early 1980s, we are concerned that the reason for the increase in the number of African-Americans incarcerated is more sinister than simply the result of a failing drug war, and questionable racist laws (e.g., crack v. powder cocaine). It may be plausible to argue that the "war on drugs" (and the "war on gangs") has actually been a "success" if the aim was to control the surplus population, especially African-Americans.[1] We are suggesting that this apparent onslaught may actually be attributed to institutional segregation or apartheid practices.

How do we explain this phenomenal growth? One of the main culprits has to be the "war on drugs," which began in the early 1970s and really "took off" during the mid-1980s. This "war" began to have its effects on jail and prison populations by the late 1980s and early 1990s (Baum, 1997; Miller, 1996; Reinarman and Levine, 1997; Currie, 1993). A recent estimate is that convictions for drugs accounted for almost *one-half* of the increase in state prison inmates during the 1980s and early 1990s (Beck and Brien, 1995: 54).[2]

---

1. Noam Chomsky, among others, has argued that the war on drugs has been "successful" for the reasons stated here. For a good summary of this view see recently published interviews he did with David Barsamian (Chomsky, 1994,1996, 1998). Parenti (1999) has made a similar argument. Concerning the "war on gangs" and how it has concentrated on African-Americans and Hispanics, see Shelden, et al. (2001) and Klein (1995).

2. It should be emphasized that the "war on gangs" could easily be included in this analysis, however space does not permit such an inclusion. However, it is certainly no coincidence that the "gang problem" emerged as a "law enforcement" problem as well as a "media problem" during the mid-1980s, almost exactly the time that the "crack epidemic" emerged. Shelden, Tracy and Brown noted that newspaper and magazine coverage of gangs went from a mere 33 articles in 1984 to 159 in 1985 and thereafter underwent dramatic increases: to 249 in 1988, 403 in 1989, 533 in 1990 and up as high as 1,313 in 1994—an increase of almost 4,000 percent! Similarly, the actual *number* of "gangs" and "gang members" shot up almost as dramatically, despite the fact that there never has been a consensus among even law enforcement experts on what constitutes a "gang" and a "gang member." Not too surprisingly, in every major city the number of gangs and gang members has consistently risen since the mid-1980s, along with federal funding for special "gang units" within police departments. Also, not coincidentally, in every urban area the vast majority (as high as 90%) of "gang members" are racial minorities. See Shelden, Tracy and Brown (2001).

Data on court commitments to state prisons during the 1980s and early 1990s clearly show the dramatic changes for drug offenses. Between 1980 and 1992 sentences on drug charges increased by more than 1000 percent! In contrast, there was a more modest increase of 51 percent for violent offenses. Race played a key role in these increases, especially during the late 1980s and early 1990s as the number of African-Americans sentenced to prison for drug charges increased by over 90 percent, almost three times greater than white offenders (Maguire and Pastore, 1996: 550). Between 1985 and 1995 the number of African-American inmates who had been sentenced for drug crimes increased by 700 percent! (Currie, 1998: 12–13).

Not only were more African-Americans sentenced for drug crimes, but the *severity* of their sentences increased compared to whites. In 1992, in the federal system, the average sentence length for African-American drug offenders was about 107 months, compared to 74 months for white drug offenders. There has been a huge discrepancy when comparing powder and crack cocaine sentences in the federal system. In 1995, for instance, African-Americans constituted a phenomenal 88 percent of those sentenced for crack cocaine, compared to less than 30 percent of those sentenced for powder cocaine (Maguire and Pastore, 1996: 492).

Sentencing in the federal system for drug offenses shows some startling changes during the past half century. Between 1945 and 1995, the proportion of those going to prison for all offenses rose from 47 percent to 69 percent, compared to a decrease of those granted probation (from 40 percent to 24 percent), while the average sentence has risen by over 300 percent. The changes in the sentences for drug law violations are most dramatic. Whereas, in 1945 the percentage of drug offenders going to prison was high enough at 73 percent, by 1995 fully 90 percent were going to prison! And the average sentence for drug cases went from only 22 months in 1945 to almost 90 months in 1995, an increase of 300 percent! Finally, while in 1980 the most serious offense for those admitted to federal prison was a violent crime in about 13 percent of the cases and a drug offense in just over one-fourth of the cases, by 1992 in almost half of the cases (48.8%) the most serious offense was drugs, compared to a violent crime in less than eight percent of the cases. In the meantime, *the average maximum sentence declined for violent crimes (from 125 months to 88 months) and almost doubled for drug offenses (from 47 months to 82 months)* (Beck and Brien, 1995: 59). Incidentally, on any given day, almost 60 percent (58.6%) of all federal prisoners are serving time for drug offenses; of these 40 percent are African-American (Maguire and Pastore, 1996: 468, 472, 576).

One of the most recent sources of data on court cases comes from a U.S. Department of Justice report which examined felony defendants in the largest

75 counties in 1994 (Reaves, 1998). Here we can see the effects of the "war on drugs" and its impact on the nation's court system; we also can clearly see the effects of race. The most serious charge in just over one-third (34.6 percent) of the cases was a drug offense, with non-trafficking drug offenses being the most common (58 percent of all drug charges), followed closely by a property crime (31.1 percent), with about one-fourth (25.7 percent) being violent offenses, mostly assaults (constituting 45 percent of all the violent crimes).

Not surprisingly, race figured prominently in these cases. African-Americans constituted over half (56 percent) of all defendants and 62 percent of those charged with drug offenses. Another study noted that almost *all* (99 percent) drug trafficking defendants between 1985 and 1987 were African-Americans (Baum, 1997: 249). In some cities, the proportion of felony defendants who were African-American was quite high. For example, African-Americans constituted 93 percent of all felony defendants in Wayne County (Detroit), 90 percent in Baltimore and 85 percent in Cook County (Chicago) and Kings County (Seattle), but only 14 percent in Maricopa County (Phoenix) and nine percent in Honolulu (Reaves, 1998: 43).

The New American Apartheid

Apartheid is a policy that produces systematic racial segregation or discrimination and is usually associated with pre-Mandella South Africa. The word apartheid was introduced to the world by South Africa in 1948.[3] This term stems from the Dutch "apart" (which has the same English connotation), and "heid" (which translates as hood). The term was adopted to soften the image of the harsh racial segregation polices practiced by the South African government. World attention had focused on South Africa's segregation practices, and it was thought that through the substitution of the word apartheid for segregation, world attention would be diverted from their discriminatory practices. Soon after the adoption of that term, however, the world realized that nothing had actually changed in respect to the treatment of blacks in South Africa.

---

3. In 1948, the same year that the Nationalist Party came to power in South Africa and instituted apartheid, the Mississippi Supreme Court, in *Murray v. State*, decided that segregated seating in courtrooms was not a constitutional violation. Rather, the court argued that such seating arrangements were actually grounded firmly in community custom. It was not until 1963, in *Johnson v. Virginia*, that the United States Supreme Court ruled that segregated seating in a courtroom constituted a denial of equal protection (Higginbotham 1996).

There seems to be a pattern of contradictions by the United States concerning what is professed to be policy direction and what is actually supported by the U.S. government. America has always been a country that professes to place high value on children. However, in 1989, the United States refused to support G.A. Resolution 44/25, which was a product of the Convention on the Rights of the Child. This resolution was for the adoption of basic rights of children, such as the right to life (Henkin, Pugh, Schachter and Smit, 1993). As further evidence that the United States tends to differentiate between its public posture and its global voting record, the United States claims to be in favor of policing international criminals. Yet America refused to ratify the United Nations' recent attempt to create an International Criminal Court in Rome (United Nations Press Release, 1998). In fact, prior to the call for votes, the United States requested a non-recorded vote on the matter of adopting the Statute establishing an International Criminal Court. More specifically, speaking to the issue of apartheid, in 1973, The International Convention on the Suppression and Punishment of the Crime of Apartheid debated the issue of apartheid as a crime against humanity, and therefore argued that apartheid should be treated as a crime against humanity-an international crime. To date, the United States has not yet ratified this resolution (Lillich and Hannum, 1995).

Racial segregation is now a characteristic of many of America's inner cities. Central cities now contain 80 percent of the urban non-white population, and one-third of the African-American urban population resides in the nation's ten largest central cities (Piven and Cloward, 1997). There have been "symbolic" attempts to reduce racial segregation in American cities. We use the term "symbolic" because these attempts have often been either politicized and skewed to serve the interests of the elite or these attempts have been grossly under-funded to insure their failure (Handler and Hasenfeld, 1997; Wilson, 1987; Massey and Denton, 1993; Harrington, 1962, 1984). To illustrate, the Housing Acts of 1949, 1954, and 1965, provided federal funding to local authorities to acquire slum property and begin redevelopment of that property. In order to qualify for federal funds, local governments had to insure that affordable living accommodations would be provided for displaced families living in the redevelopment zones. The process used was commonly known as urban renewal, and sometimes referred to as "negro removal." The solution was high-density public housing. Today, these public housing projects are often referred to as the "projects." Raising slum areas and the construction of public housing often resulted in an overall reduction in living accommodations (Massey and Denton, 1993). In a study of African-American youth gangs in Detroit, it was noted that for that city there was a net loss of 31,500 homes between 1980 and 1987. Today, many African-Americans find themselves once again involved in a "negro removal" program—but rather than removed from one inner city slum area to a more high-density slum area, they find themselves removed from the inner cities entirely, and compartmentalized in America's prison industry (Brown, 1998).

It is obvious from the examination of arrest and prison data that the groups being targeted by the criminal justice system are disproportionately drawn from the most marginalized populations. African-Americans, particularly males, are especially vulnerable. For example, in 1995, according to the Sentencing Project in Washington, D.C., about one-third of all African-American males between the ages of 20 and 29 were, on any given day, either in jail, prison, on probation or on parole, a percentage that was up from 25 percent 1990. In some cities these percentages were even higher, such as Washington, D.C., where the figure was about 60 percent (Donziger, 1996; Miller, 1996). For comparison purposes, African-American males are far more likely to be in prison or jail than in college! In California, African-Americans are imprisoned at a rate of 1,951 per 100,000, compared to only 215 for whites (Koetting and Schiraldi, 1994).

Part of the methods of controlling the surplus population is through legislation, which defines what is a "crime" and, moreover, through sentencing structures, define what crimes are "serious." Many sentencing structures have a built-in class and racial bias.

A case in point are the drug laws, especially "crack" cocaine. The penalty for possession and/or sale of crack cocaine is far greater than for the powdered variety of cocaine. It just so happens that crack is far more likely to be associated with African-Americans. Little wonder that the enforcement of drug laws have been one of the major reasons the prison population has increased so rapidly in recent years (Irwin and Austin, 2001).

Indeed, a most persuasive argument can be made suggesting a close correlation between the "war on drugs" (and on "gangs") and the growth of the prison industrial complex. This "war" was officially launched by President Reagan in the mid-1980s when he promised that the police would attack the drug problem "with more ferocity than ever before." What he did *not* say, however, was that the enforcement of the new drug laws "would focus almost exclusively on low-level dealers in minority neighborhoods." Indeed, the police found such dealers in these areas mainly because *that is precisely where they looked for them*, rather than, say, on college campuses.[4] The results were im-

---

4. A Delaware prosecutor is quoted as follows: "Sure, it's true we prosecute a high percentage of minorities for drugs. The simple fact is, if you have a population, minority or not, that is conducting most of their illegal business on the street, those cases are easy pick-

mediate: the arrest rates for African-Americans on drug charges shot dramatically upward in the late 1980s and well into the 1990s. In fact, while African-Americans constitute only around 12 percent of the U.S. population and about 13 percent of all monthly drug users (and their rate of illegal drug use is roughly the same as for whites), they represent 35 percent of those arrested for drug possession and 74 percent of those sentenced to prison on drug charges. The evidence of racial disproportionality in the drug war is overwhelming. For instance, arrest rates for minorities went from under 600 per 100,000 in 1980 to over 1500 in 1990, while for whites they essentially remained the same. As far as prison sentences go, studies of individual states are telling. For instance, in North Carolina between 1980 and 1990, the rate of admissions to prison for nonwhites jumped from around 500 per 100,000 to almost 1,000, while in Pennsylvania, nonwhite males and females sentenced on drug offenses increased by 1613 percent and 1750 percent respectively; in Virginia the percentage of commitments for drug offenses for minorities went from just under 40 in 1983 to about 65 in 1989, while for whites the percentage actually *decreased* from just over 60 percent in 1983 to about 30 percent in 1989 (Donziger, 1996: 115; Tonry, 1995; Mauer, 1999; Cole, 1999).

The rate of incarceration for African-Americans exceeds that for whites by a ratio of 8 to 1; the odds of an African-American male going to prison is more than one in four (28.5 percent), compared to about one in twenty-five for white males (see Table 2) (Maguire and Pastore, 1998: 480). Moreover, a recent study found that while two percent of *all* adults have been disenfranchised because of a felony conviction (mostly drug convictions), *about 13 percent of all black men have been!* In six states the percentage of black men disenfranchised is 25 percent or more, *going higher than 30 percent in Alabama and Florida* (Fellner and Mauer, 1998).

Table 2. Chances of Going to State or Federal Prison at Some Time During the Rest of Life, as of 1991

Percent Expected to go to State or Federal Prison during rest of life among persons not previously incarcerated, by age

	Birth	20	25	30	35	40
Total	5.1	4.5	3.1	2.1	1.4	.9
Sex:						
Male	9.0	7.9	5.5	3.7	2.5	1.6
Female	1.1	1.0	.8	.6	.3	.2

ings for the police" (Mauer, 1999: 142). An excellent history of the war on drugs is provided by Baum (1997).

Race:							
White:	2.5	2.3	1.7	1.2	.9	.6	
Male		4.4	4.1	3.0	2.1	1.5	1.1
Female	.5	.5	.4	.3	.2	.1	
Black:		16.2	14.1	9.6	6.0	3.6	2.0
Male		28.5	25.3	17.3	10.8	6.5	3.6
Female	3.6	3.5	2.8	1.9	1.1	.6	
Hispanic:	9.4	8.7	6.4	4.9	3.8	2.3	
Male		16.0	14.8	11.1	8.6	6.8	4.3
Female	1.5	1.5	1.2	.9	.6	.4	

Source: Proband, 1997b: 22.

We need not elaborate the obvious any further, for the fact remains that the "war on crime" and the "war on drugs" targets disproportionately racial minorities, who find themselves in alarmingly increasing numbers behind bars and generally subjected to the efforts of the criminal justice system. The situation is not likely to improve, especially as long as federal, state and local governments continue to increase the money used for the crime control industry, instead of for prevention. With increasing attention given to our *reaction* to crime, the attention given to the ultimate *sources* of crime will decrease, only exacerbating the problem further.[5]

Modern prisoners occupy the lowest rungs on the social class ladder, and they always have.[6] The modern prison system (along with local jails) is a sort of *ghetto or poorhouse*[7] reserved primarily for the unskilled, the uneducated, the powerless and, in increasing numbers it is being reserved for racial mi-

---

5. An even more alarming trend comes from another piece of legislation that clearly targets African-Americans, namely the recent "Three Strikes" law in California. As reported by the Center on Juvenile and Criminal Justice, the results of this law is part of what they have called the "new apartheid." Their analysis of data on cases after the enactment of this law show that while African-Americans make up only 7% of the California population, they constitute 23% of all felony arrests, but have so far constituted 43% of the state's "Three Strikes" prisoners (a rate that was 13 times that of whites). A detailed analysis of three strikes prosecutions in the counties of Los Angeles, San Diego and Sacramento show that 90% of the cases were African-Americans! The rate (per 100,000 population) for African-Americans was 43.6, compared to only 2.6 for whites (Davis et al., 1996; Hewitt et al., 1992; Schichor and Sechrest, 1996).

6. This view hardly needs referencing, since it is common knowledge (or should be) among academics. For those who question this assertion, see the works already cited, but especially Currie (1998), Donziger (1996), Irwin and Austin (1997) and Tonry (1995).

7. For more detailed treatment of the notion of jails and prisons as "poorhouses" see Morris and Rothman (1995).

norities, especially African-Americans, which is why we are calling this system the *New American Apartheid.* This is the same segment of American society that have seen their incomes drastically reduced and have become more involved in drugs and the subsequent violence that extends from the lack of legitimate means of goal attainment (Fowles and Merva, 1996).

As already noted, the overall incarceration rate (prisons and jails combined) as of 1997 was 6,838 for African-American males (a ratio of 7 to 1 over white males); for African-American females the rate was 491 (a ratio of 6.5 to 1 over white females) (Maguire and Pastore, 2000). Between 1985 and 1997, the overall incarceration rate for white males increased by 79 percent, compared to an increase of 86 percent for African-American males. For women, the increases were even greater: the incarceration rate for white females went up by 170 percent, compared to an increase of 159 percent for African-American females (Kurki, 1999: 3).

What is often overlooked in the discussion of these recent trends is the impact these "get tough" policies and the "war on drugs" had on women. In the next section we will review some rather disturbing trends in the incarceration of women offenders.

The Growing Incarceration of African-American Women

One thing that cannot be overlooked in any analysis of women, crime and criminal justice is the interrelationship between class and race. Indeed, the vast majority of female offenders, especially those who end up in prison, are drawn from the lower class and are racial minorities (Daly, 1992; Miller, 1996; Chesney-Lind, 1997).

One specific example of the role of class and race is demonstrated in a very detailed and sophisticated study by Daly of a sample of women offenders in a court system in New Haven, Connecticut. From a larger sample of 397 cases, this study focused in depth on a smaller sample of 40 men and 40 women who were sentenced to prison (that is, they went through all of the stages of the criminal justice process). Of the forty women, twenty-four (60%) were African-American, five (12%) were Puerto Rican and the remainder (28%) were white. Half of the women were raised in single-parent families, and only two of the women were described as growing up in "middle class households." Most of these women were described by Daly as having grown up in families "whose economic circumstances were precarious," while in about two-thirds of the cases their biological fathers were "out of the picture" while they were growing up. Only one-third completed high school or the equivalent GED (General Education Diploma). Two-thirds "had either a sporadic or no paid employment record" and over 80 percent were unemployed at the time of their most recent arrest (Daly, 1992: 23–24).

It has often been claimed that the main reason so few women end up in prison is because the criminal justice system practices "chivalry." Chivalry, however, is largely a racist and classist concept in that such lenient treatment is typically reserved for white women from the higher social classes. Moreover, any "lenient" treatment granted to women is due largely to the fact that their crimes are so minor compared to men and the criminal careers are not nearly as lengthy as men, two variables that are highly predictive of treatment in the criminal justice system (Moyer, 1992). Additional support for the argument that African-American female offenders are treated more harshly came from a study in California of a sample of all felony cases in 1980 where it was found that the odds of women being arrested ranged from a high of 1 in 42 for African-American females in their 20s to a low of 1 in 667 for white females 70 years or older (Wilbanks, 1986). Finally, as of 1998, roughly 60 percent of the women on probation were white, however, nearly two-thirds confined in prisons and jails were minority group members (Greenfeld and Snell, 1999).

The most dramatic illustrations of the lack of chivalry toward African-American and other minority women comes from examining who gets sentenced to prison. And this has been, in recent years, a direct result of the "war on drugs." Indeed, there is no way we can separate the phenomenal growth in prison populations from the "war on drugs," a war that has targeted huge numbers of African-Americans. While there is little relationship between race and illicit drug use, African-Americans are far more likely to be arrested and sent to prison. For women, the poor in general and African-Americans in particular have been singled out.

If this is not bad enough, a large percentage of women sentenced to prison on parole violations have not committed any new crimes, but rather were returned for not passing their urine tests. Moreover, sentences to federal prisons have zoomed upward because of drug offenses. In 1989, 44.5 percent of women in federal prison were in for drugs, and this figure went up to 68 percent in just two years. (More than one-third of the women doing time in prison on drug charges had been convicted of drug *possession.*) About twenty years ago approximately two-thirds of women convicted of felonies in federal court were given probation, but in 1991 only 28 percent were. Further, the average time served for women on drug offenses went from 27 months in 1984 to 67 months in 1990 (Chesney-Lind, 1997: 147–148).

Overall, the proportion of women offenders in prison because of drug offenses went from 12 percent in 1986 to 32.8 percent in 1991. In fact, the percentage increase in women sentenced to prison for drugs has been much greater than for men sentenced for drugs. For instance, between 1987 and 1989 in the state of New York the number of women sentenced for drugs increased by 211 percent, compared to only an 82 percent increase for men. In Florida, during the 1980s admissions to prison for drugs increased by a whopping 1,825 percent; but for female offenders this increase was an astounding 3,103 percent! (Donziger, 1996: 151).

Much of the increase in women prisoners comes from the impact of *mandatory sentencing* laws, passed during the 1980s crackdown on crime. Under many of these laws, mitigating circumstances (e.g., having children, few or no prior offenses, non-violent offenses) are rarely allowed. One recent survey found that just over half (51%) of women in state prisons had only one prior offense, compared to 39 percent of the male prisoners (Donziger, 1996: 152).

Thus, this society's recent efforts to "get tough" on crime has had a most negative impact on female offenders, as more and more are finding their way into the nation's prison system. As a matter of fact, largely because of the war on drugs, the number of new women's prisons has dramatically increased in recent years. Whereas between 1940 and the end of the 1960s only 12 new women's prisons were built, in the 1970s a total of 17 were built, and 34 new prisons were built in the 1980s (Donziger, 1996: 148).

While women constitute around 20 percent of all those arrested and only about six percent of those in prison, their numbers and their rate of incarceration has been dramatically increasing during the past twenty years. As of yearend 2000, there were a total of 91,612 (compared to only 8,850 in 1976) women in federal and state prisons, constituting 6.6 percent (versus 3.6 percent in 1976) of all prisoners (Beck and Harrison, 2001; Maguire and Pastore, 1996; Shelden, 1982: 347). These latest figures represent an incredible numerical increase of 935% and their proportion increased by 83% during the past 20 years. Moreover, the incarceration *rate* of women went from 8 per 100,000 in 1975 to 59 per 100,000 in 2000, for an increase of 638% (Beck and Harrison, 2001; Maguire and Pastore, 1996).

These increases do not match the increases in women's crime as measured by arrests, except if we consider the impact of the "war on drugs" along with greater attention to domestic violence. During this period of time there has been a very dramatic change in the criminal justice system's response to female drug use, as it has for all illegal drug use, as well as domestic violence. In the latter case, such increased attention to domestic violence has led to an increase in arrests of women for both aggravated assault and "other assaults" (Chesney-Lind, 1997).

Table 3. Rate of Female Adults Held in State or Federal Prisons or Local Jails, by Race, 1985–1997

Year	Black	White	Ratio
1985	183	27	6.8:1
1986	189	29	6.5:1
1987	216	35	6.2:1
1988	257	41	6.3:1
1989	321	47	6.8:1
1990	329	48	6.9:1
1991	346	51	6.8:1
1992	356	53	6.7:1
1993	393	55	7.1:1
1994	426	61	7.0:1
1995	456	65	7.0:1
1996	474	73	6.5:1
1997	491	76	6:5:1
% increase 1985–1997	168.3	181.5	

Source: Kurki, 1999; Maguire and Pastore, 2000.

A more detailed view of women's incarceration rate and the role of race is seen in Table 3, which includes jail prisoners. As indicated here, the incarceration rate for African-American women has consistently been around seven times greater than for white women, although the rate for white women has increased the most during the period shown here. As for women in state and federal prisons, as of 1997 the overall rate was 53 per 100,000. Table 4 shows these data, as of 1997, according to age and race. As shown here, the rate for African-American women is far greater than both whites and Hispanics, regardless of age.

Table 4. Rate of Sentenced Female Prisoners Under State or Federal Jurisdiction, by Race, Hispanic Origin and Age, 2000

Age	Total	White	Black	Hispanic
Total	59	34	205	60
18–19	29	23	83	21
20–24	83	55	216	86
25–29	159	88	486	148
30–34	210	125	722	169
35–39	162	96	573	147
40–44	89	49	331	96
45–54	44	27	143	69
55 or older	6	5	21	9

Source: Beck and Harrison, 2001.

The Impact on African-American Families

Although precise data are hard to come by, we can easily infer from the above discussion that recent developments have had a negative impact on African-American communities in general and families in particular. The inner-cities of America have been the most negatively affected by these changes. The movement of capital out of the inner cities ("capital flight") corresponded to the phenomenon of "white flight" and the exodus of many middle class minorities, the decline of the tax base for these areas and the increasing concentration of the poor were left behind. There has also been a corresponding decline in federal funding for social programs, particularly those targeting the urban underclass. This largely occurred during the 1980s with the dawn of a "privatization" movement, a system aiming to replace federal assistance with private sector methods of solving urban problems. Among the specific types of programs that suffered included aid to disadvantaged school districts, housing assistance, financial aid to the poor, legal assistance to the poor and social services in urban areas in general (Cummings and Monti, 1993: 306).

There has been a marked decline in job opportunities, especially for minorities. Many jobs have shifted to the suburbs, as have many basic services and the tax base as well. It used to be common for many minority youth to be able to find unskilled and semi-skilled jobs. Today these jobs are disappearing and being replaced by either low-wage service jobs or high-wage jobs requiring advanced skills and education.

A closely related development has been described as the *feminization of poverty*. This refers to the increase in female-headed households that are most likely to be living in poverty. This has been especially true for African-American women for according to the 1990 census 43 percent of all African-American families are headed by women and 45 percent of these families are living under the poverty level (U.S. Bureau of the Census, 1990; Zopf, 1989). Within inner-cities these percentages are even greater (Wilson, 1987, 1996). The number of children living in "extreme poverty" (family incomes less than one-half the official poverty level) doubled from 1975 to 1993 (from 5 to 10 percent). In 1996 (the latest figures available) about 40 percent of all African-American children lived in poverty (of the African-American children under 6, 45 percent live in poverty). International comparisons show the United States ranked number one in terms of the overall child poverty rate among industrialized nations, with an overall rate of 25 percent.[8]

---

8. Child poverty rates taken from Miringoff and Miringoff (1999: 83–84).

The "welfare reform" movement ushered in during the Clinton Administration in 1996 significantly reduced the number of citizens on the welfare rolls. Specifically, as of 1999 about 7 million were receiving welfare, compared to just over 12 million in 1996. There has been a negative impact, however, as millions of single mothers who have left welfare are working at poverty wages. One study found that the average wage of these mothers was $6.60 per hour. More than one-fourth were working nights, while two-thirds have jobs without health insurance. Also, more than half of them are having trouble getting decent and affordable child care and paying for such necessities as food and rent. Still another report noted that whites were leaving welfare at a much faster pace than minorities. One example was in Ohio, where in 1995 just over half of the welfare recipients (54%) were white and 42% were African-American, by 1999 theses percentages were reversed: 53% African-American and 42% white. Research has also shown that it has been much easier to leave welfare for those living away from the inner cities, which obviously helps whites since they are most likely to live in the suburbs (Associated Press, 1999).

The declining social and economic position of African-Americans, especially as this relates to young African-American males whom one author has called an "endangered species." is significant (Gibbs, 1988). The impact on one particular city, Louisville, is described by Cummings and Monti. They describe the underclass in this city as being "comprised largely of minorities who are increasingly marginal to the city's economy. The neighborhoods populated by the underclass are characterized by high rates of crime, institutional instability, and impoverished households headed by females... Louisville's new urban poverty is exacerbated by severe dislocations in the manufacturing and industrial sectors of its regional economy." The unemployment rates among African-Americans in Louisville rose from 6.9 percent in 1970 to more than 20 percent by the end of the 1980s. Also, in 1970 45 percent of births by African-American women were out of wedlock, whereas in 1988 the percentage was 70 (Cummings and Monti, 1993: 312–313).

It is not very difficult to lay part of the blame of the devastation of poor, African-American communities on the shoulders of the criminal justice system and those who design the policies. A recent study by one of the co-authors of this paper underscores this point. Brown (1998) interviewed some of the families of gang members in Detroit to identify some of the effects of not only participation in gang life, but the impact on the family when a gang member goes to prison. All of these families are African-American, mostly poor (including many "working poor").

The families in Brown's study had no "material" luxuries. One father of four, wearing the scars of rejection and humiliation, stated:

> We ain't got much of anything anymore, but maybe we're luckier than some I guess. I worked at Chrysler for eight years, but they laid me off four years ago. They never did hire none of us back. I tried finding another job like that one but I never did get one. There just weren't none to be had. Now I'm just good for laboring I guess.

Holding his wife's hand (she works in a laundry for minimum wage), he looked up and said, "Me and this old woman is about wore down now." His wife in an attempt to lighten the subject and offer inspiration for her husband, said, "When they build that new stadium [Detroit Tigers' baseball stadium] here you can make some money then. Well," he replied, "they is just going to hire us niggers for the laboring jobs, so don't go counting on that new stadium to help us none."

The father of another gang member has two full-time, minimum-wage jobs. His wife works part-time. They have three children. "I've tried to get me a full-time job," she stated, "but they ain't none around here. We only got one car, and he's [husband] got to use it because his other job is a long way from the shop."

One mother of four, whose husband had abandoned her and the children several years earlier, lives in a deteriorating two-bedroom apartment with an inefficient heating system. During one visit, Brown heard gun shots very close by, and quickly moved his head toward the window. Obviously accustomed to the sound, she never moved. They began talking about the subject of "hope." This woman revealed,

> I used to think about the future all the time; that was before my husband lost his job. He started drinking heavy when he couldn't find no work. Then one day he just got up and left me and these kids. I used to think someday I'd have me a house and plant a garden. I love fresh tomatoes. I wanted my kids to get what I never got—a house of their own and a good education. Well, those times is gone now. I don't think much about what they ain't got because the biggest trouble is just feeding them mouths and having them a place to sleep...We manage though, but it sure ain't easy none. I ask the Lord for some help everyday. Guess He is listening because we still got a roof over our head and something to eat.

Thus, there is a sense of resignation, and a feeling that her life could be worse. When asked why she never left the neighborhood. She answered,

> Where do you want me to go live? I ain't got no other place to live. I ain't got no skills to get no job—at least one that can pay the bills.

> The only real job I ever had was working downtown once, but downtown is all gone now. Do you know someone who's going to help some old black woman with no education and has four kids? I sure don't. I live here because this is all there is.

Ten gang members live in households where a grandparent is the primary breadwinner. In eight of these cases, most of the family income comes from social security and/or very modest retirement benefits. Rather than the elderly being assisted by their children, many grandparents find themselves in a position where they must raise a second family. One elderly woman, who has lived in the same neighborhood for more than 40 years, shares her two-bedroom house with her daughter-in-law, three grandchildren, and "Boots," the family feline. Rags are stuffed around the windows to fill gaps that run her heating bill "through the ceiling." The middle step leading to the front door is broken. She leans back in an overstuffed chair, once belonging to her husband who died more than ten years ago, and started to talk about her "boys" who are both in prison.

> Both my boys is in prison, and Bobby's[9] [name of one son] wife and kids stay here with me because they can't live no other place. What they going to do? I can't work no more because I got a bad leg, and besides, who's going to hire an old black woman anyhow? I get my check [social security]. Kathy gets some money from the state; it sure ain't much. She can't work because she's got these kids to take care of. I help take care of them, but I'm old and can't do it by myself. Besides there ain't no jobs around here and we ain't got no car. We are doing the best we can do. I don't know what's going to happen to us. Engler [governor of Michigan] say he's going to cut welfare some more. If he do then I don't know what's going to happen. Sometimes I think that dying is about all that's left to do. But who is going to help Kathy with them kids if I ain't here? That oldest boy is a handful now. He's good to me and his mother though. He runs wild but I understand. He ain't got much else to do. There ain't no jobs for him. I worry about him all the time. He going to end up like his daddy—in prison some day. It's going to happen I tell you.

Bobby, who once was a member of a gang in this neighborhood, was prosecuted and convicted on auto theft and drug charges. He received 5 years and 15 years (consecutive) sentences. The women was asked about her husband and she responded as follows:

---

9. The names of all individuals quoted here have been disguised.

> Them boys' daddy was a good man. He bought this house for us when he worked at General Motors. We had a real good life then. Well, he killed himself off working all kinds of jobs when he got laid off from the plant. He managed to pay for this house before he died—God bless him. My boys was always mad about what happened to their daddy. Now I see Johnny mad about his daddy being taken away from him. He's running with the same crowd his daddy ran with.

All adult family members Brown interviewed expressed concern about their children's, or grandchildren's, involvement in youth gangs. Most attempted to control their children's activities. "I tell him all the time to stay away from them kind of kids," says one mother. A father stated, "I don't like him running wild out there, but we [including his wife] both got jobs. We just can't watch him all the time." Another concerned parent said,

> I do the best that I can do to get him to stay in school. I work hard, but, as you can see, I don't seem to get nowhere. He's not dumb. He can see that this family is never going to get ahead. He respects me and his little sister, but he knows that what I am doing ain't getting his family nowhere.

One father admitted, "I beat the hell out of him when I found out he was banging. But he keeps right on doing it. I can't just keep beating him—then they'll come and arrest me." Another father stated, "I try to tell him that he's going to end up dead or in prison some day. He just won't listen. I want him to get a job, but there ain't none around. I'm lucky to be working myself." One grandmother said,

> I know he is in a gang. I ain't dumb. But I also know that until all them kids lay down them guns then he's got to protect himself somehow. The police sure ain't going to protect him none. Those who is blaming the parents for these here gangs don't know much about life down here. We have to survive however we can. Them kids is surviving the only way they knows how to survive. They're just kids you know.

Some Concluding Thoughts

We live in times of great uncertainty as millions just barely eke out a living while a small minority become richer and richer, despite proclamations from politicians and the media about the "economic recovery" and the booming stock market (Piven and Cloward, 1997). We find more and more of our citizens relegated to the ranks of what Marx once described as the "surplus population," a population rendered unneeded or "superfluous" as far as creating profits are concerned. Along with more and more corporate "downsizing" there is the ominous disappearance of semi-skilled and unskilled jobs once filled by urban minorities, especially African-American males. But this group is still very much with us and, from the point of view of those in power, they need to be "managed" in some way. One way that has been used to manage or control this population is to confine them to inner city ghettos, while another way is to use the prison system as a mechanism of this form of "management."

It is especially ironic that we are experiencing what politicians are calling the "end of welfare as we know it." This is true. We previously had a welfare system that patronized the poor, we now have a welfare system that can be described in a single word—*mean.* The irony is that a component of this new form of welfare is called the prison system. And since there has not been a significant rise in the kinds of crimes that have historically resulted in prison sentences (burglaries, larcenies, robberies, murder, etc.), and we cannot use the crude techniques of control common in totalitarian societies (e.g., torture), we have invented new "crimes" and new "criminals" to justify prison expansion, namely drugs. But of course only certain kinds of drugs, used by certain classes of people are targeted (Gordon, 1994; Reinarman and Levine, 1997).

More and more women are finding themselves completely left out of the recent "economic upturn" American society has experienced. Like earlier generations, minority women have suffered the most, as they find themselves mired in poverty with the sole responsibility of child rearing. Even among women who are working, times are getting harder and harder.[10] Given the continuous "war on drugs" along with efforts to "end welfare as we know it," women, especially minority women, are going to continue to experience being processed by the criminal justice system.

The "war on drugs" and the "war on gangs" have intentionally targeted the most marginalized Americans.[11] Is this not also a form of slow genocide and

---

10. Between 1970 and 1990 there was a 500 percent increase in the number of women who held more than one job. Most of these jobs have been in the lowest paying sectors of society: service and retail trade. Women suffer the most as a result of a divorce: while men realize an average increase in income of 43 percent, women's income drops by an average of 73 percent. Only one out of six divorced women receive alimony and only 13 percent with preschool children receive child support. The majority of single-parent households are run by women and the majority of these are living at or near the poverty level (Parenti, 1994: 146–148).

11. Drug laws have historically targeted racial and ethnic minorities in particular and the poor in general. For documentation see Musto (1973) and Helmer (1975).

a disenfranchisement of urban minorities and a form of "ethnic cleansing"? Have we not created a new, more modern form of apartheid? To do this it is necessary to use certain scientific-sounding labels, like "sociopath" or "criminal personality." Of course the traditional, gut-level terms are also used, like "dangerous classes," "predators," "thugs," "gangs" and the like. It is not "our kind" that are being sent to prison, it is "them," "those people," etc. This way we can wash our hands of any responsibility (Miller, 1996).[12]

References

Associated Press. (1999). Whites Leaving Welfare Faster than Minorities, Survey Reveals. March 30.

Baum, D. (1997). *Smoke and Mirrors: The War on Drugs and The Politics of Failure.* Boston: Little Brown/Back Bay Books.

Beck, A. J. (2000). "Prison and Jail Inmates at Midyear 1999." Washington, D.C.: Bureau of Justice Statistics, Office of Justice Programs.

Beck, A. J. and P. M. Brien. (1995). Trends in the U. S. Correctional Populations: Recent Findings from the Bureau of Justice Statistics. In Haas, K. C. and G. P. Alpert (eds). *The Dilemmas of Corrections* (3rd ed.). Project Heights, IL: Waveland Press.

Beck, A. J. and P.M. Harrison. (2001). Prisoners in 2000. *Bureau of Justice Statistics, Bulletin.* Washington, D.C.: U.S. Department of Justice, August.

Brown, W.B. (1998). The Fight for Survival: African-American Gang Members and Their Families in a Segregated Society. *Juvenile and Family Court Journal* 49, 2: 1–14.

Bureau of Justice Statistics. (1999). The Rate of Jail Incarceration for Blacks is Five Times Higher Than the Rate for Whites. Washington, D.C.: U. S. Department of Justice, Bureau of Justice Statistics, home page http://www.ojp.usdoj.gov/bjs/glance/jailrair.htm/.

Chesney-Lind, M. (1997). *The Female Offender.* Thousand Oaks, CA: Sage.

Chomsky, N. (1987). On the Responsibility of Intellectuals. In E. Peck (ed.), *The Chomsky Reader.* New York: Pantheon Books.

_______. (1994). *Keeping the Rabble in Line.* Monroe, ME: Common Courage Press.

_______. (1996). *Class Warfare.* Monroe, ME: Common Courage Press.

_______. (1998). *The Common Good.* Monroe, ME: Odonian Press.

_______. (1999). "Crisis in the Balkans." *Z Magazine*, May.

Cole, D. (1999). *No Equal Justice: Race and Class in the American Criminal Justice System.* New York: The New Press.

Cummings, S., and D. J. Monti, eds. (1993). *Gangs: The Origins and Impact of Contemporary Youth Gangs in the United States.* Albany, N.Y.: SUNY Press.

Currie, E. (1998). *Crime and Punishment in America.* New York: Metropolitan Books.

_______. (1993). *Reckoning: Drugs, the Cities, and the American Future.* New York: Hill and Wang.

---

12. A classic statement about the responsibilities that we as academics have to expose such oppression was made by Noam Chomsky back in the late 1960s (Chomsky, 1987).

Daly, K. (1992). Women's Pathways to Felony Court: Feminist Theories of Lawbreaking and Problems of Representation. *Southern California Review of Law and Women's Studies* 2: 11–52.

Davis, C., R. Estes, and V. Schiraldi. (1996). *"Three Strikes": The New Apartheid.* San Francisco Center on Juvenile and Criminal Justice, March.

Donziger, S. R. (1996). *The Real War On Crime: The Report of the National Criminal Justice Commission.* New York: Harper Perennial.

Fellner, J. and M. Mauer. (1998). Nearly 4 Million Americans Denied Vote Because of Felony Convictions. *Overcrowded Times* 9, 5 (October).

Fowles, R. and M. Merva. (1996). Wage Inequality and Criminal Activity: An Extreme Bounds Analysis for the United States. *Criminology* 34: 163–182.

Gilliard, D. K. (1999). Prison and Jail Inmates at Midyear 1998. Bureau of Justice Statistics, Bulletin. Washington, D.C.: U.S. Department of Justice, August.

_______ and A. J. Beck. (1998). Prisoners in 1997. Bureau of Justice Statistics, Bulletin. Washington, D.C.: U.S. Department of Justice, August.

Gibbs, J. T., ed. (1988). *Young, Black, and Male in America: An Endangered Species.* Dover, MA: Andover House.

Gordon, D. (1994). *The Return of the Dangerous Classes: Drug Prohibition and Policy Politics.* New York: W. W. Norton

Greenfeld, L. A. and T. L. Snell. (1999). *Women Offenders.* Bureau of Justice Statistics, Special Report. Washington, D.C.: U.S. Department of Justice, December.

Handler, J. F. and Y. Hasenfeld. (1997). *We the Poor People: Work, Poverty, and Welfare.* New Haven, C.T.: Yale University Press.

Harrington, M. (1962). *The Other America.* New York: MacMillan.

_______. (1984). *The New American Poverty.* New York: Penguin Books.

Helmer, J. (1975). *Drugs and Minority Oppression.* New York: Seabury Press.

Henkin, L., R.C. Pugh, O. Schachter, and H. Smit. (1993). *International Law: Cases and Materials* (3rd Ed.). St. Paul, Minn.: West Publishing Company.

Hewitt, C., K. Kubota, and V. Schiraldi. (1992). *Race and Incarceration in San Francisco: Localizing Apartheid.* San Francisco: Center on Juvenile and Criminal Justice.

Higginbotham, A. L., Jr. (1996). *Shades of Freedom: Racial Politics and Presumptions of the American Legal Process.* New York: Oxford University Press.

Human Rights Watch. (2000). *Punishment and Prejudice.* New York: Human Rights Watch.

Irwin, J. and J. Austin. (2001). *It's About Time: America's Incarceration Binge.* 3rd ed. Belmont, CA: Wadsworth.

Klein, M. (1995). *The American Street Gang.* New York: Oxford University Press.

Koetting, M. and V. Schiraldi. (1994). *Singapore West: The Incarceration of 200,000 Californians.* San Francisco: Center on Juvenile and Criminal Justice (July).

Kurki, L. (1999). Racial Incarceration Disparities High, but Decreasing. *Overcrowded Times 10,* 6: 3–6.

Lillich, R.B and H. Hannum. (1995). *International Human Rights: Problems of Law, Policy, and Practice. New York: Little, Brown, and Company.*

Maguire, K. and A. L. Pastore, eds. (2000). *Sourcebook of Criminal Justice Statistics—1999.* Washington, D. C.: U. S. Department of Justice, Bureau of Justice Statistics.

_______. (1998). *Sourcebook on Criminal Justice Statistics—1997.* Washington, D.C.: Department of Justice, Bureau of Justice Statistics.

_______. (1997). *Sourcebook on Criminal Justice Statistics—1996.* Washington, D.C.: Department of Justice, Bureau of Justice Statistics.

_______. (1996). *Sourcebook on Criminal Justice Statistics—1995.* Washington, D.C.: Department of Justice, Bureau of Justice Statistics.

Massey, D. and N. Denton. (1993). *The American Apartheid: Segregation and the Making of the Underclass.* Cambridge: Harvard University Press.

Mauer, M. (1995). *Young Black Americans and the Criminal Justice System: Five Years Later.* Washington, D.C.: The Sentencing Project.

_______. (1999). *Race to Incarcerate.* New York: The New Press.

Mays, G. L. and L. T. Winfree, Jr. (1998). *Contemporary Corrections.* Belmont, CA: Wadsworth.

Miller, J. (1996). *Search and Destroy: African-American Males in the Criminal Justice System.* New York: Cambridge University Press.

Miringoff, M. and M. Miringoff. (1999). *The Social Health of the Nation.* New York: Oxford University Press.

Morris, N. and D. J. Rothman (eds.) (1995). *The Oxford History of the Prison.* New York: Oxford University Press.

Moyer, I. L. (1992). Police/Citizen Encounters: Issues of Chivalry, Gender, and Race. In I. L. Moyer (ed.), *The Changing Roles of Women in the Criminal Justice System.* (2nd ed.). Prospect Heights, IL: Waveland Press.

Musto, D. F. (1973). *The American Disease: Origins of Narcotic Control.* New Haven, CT: Yale University Press.

Parenti, C. (1999). *Lockdown America: Police and Prisons in the Age of Crisis.* New York: Verso.

Parenti, M. (1994). *Land of Idols: Political Mythology in America.* New York: St. Martin's Press.

Piven, F. F. and R. A. Cloward. (1997). *The Breaking of the American Social Compact.* New York: The New Press.

Proband, S. C. (1997a). Jail and Prison Populations Continue to Grow in 1996. *Overcrowded Times* 8 (4).

_______. (1997b). Black Men Face 29 Percent Lifetime Chance of Prison. *Overcrowded Times* 8, 1.

Reaves, B. A. (1998). *Felony Defendants in Large Urban Counties, 1994.* Washington, D.C.: U.S. Department of Justice, Bureau of Justice Statistics.

Reinarman, C. and H. G. Levine (eds.). (1997). *Crack in America: Demon Drugs and Social Justice.* Berkeley, C.A.: University of California Press.

Schichor, D. and D. K. Sechrest (eds.). (1996). *Three Strikes and You're Out: Vengeance as Public Policy.* Thousand Oaks, C.A.: Sage.

Schiraldi, V. and J. Ziedenberg (1999). *The Punishing Decade: Prison and Jail Estimates at the Millennium.* Washington, D.C.: Justice Policy Institute.

Sentencing Project/Human Rights Watch (1998). *Losing the Vote: The Impact of Felony Disenfranchisement Laws in the Unites States.* Washington, D.C.: The Sentencing Project.

Shelden, R. G. (1982). *Criminal Justice in America: A Sociological Approach.* Boston: Little Brown.

_______. (2001). *Controlling the Dangerous Classes: A Critical Introduction to the History of Criminal Justice.* Boston: Allyn and Bacon.

Shelden, R. G., S. Tracy and W. B. Brown. (2001). *Youth Gangs in American Society.* 2nd ed. Belmont, C.A.: Wadsworth.

Tonry, M. (1995). *Malign Neglect: Race, Crime, and Punishment in America.* New York: Oxford University Press.

United Nations Press Release. (1998). *UN Diplomatic Conference Concludes in Rome with Decision to Establish Permanent International Criminal Court.* July 17.

U.S. Bureau of the Census. (1990). *1990 Census, Summary Tape, File 3C.* Washington, DC: U.S. Government Printing Office.

Wilbanks, W. (1986). Are Female Felons Treated More Leniently by the Criminal Justice System? *Justice Quarterly* 3: 517–529.

Wilson, W. J. (1987). *The Truly Disadvantaged.* Chicago: University of Chicago Press.

_______. (1996). *When Work Disappears: The World of the New Urban Poor.* New York: Vintage.

Ziedenberg, J. and V. Schiraldi. (2000). Texas Leads U.S. in Incarceration Growth. Washington, D.C.: Justice Policy Institute.

Zopf, P. E., Jr. (1989). *American Women in Poverty.* New York: Greenwood Press.

"Racial Prejudice and Public Attitudes About the Punishment of Criminals"

Steven F. Cohn,
University of Maine

Steven E. Barkan,
University of Maine

Abstract

During the last few decades the United States has adopted a "get tough" approach to crime emphasizing the quick apprehension of criminals and more certain and severe punishment. This trend stems partly from public calls for the harsher treatment of criminals. This paper reviews evidence from several studies of the impact of racial prejudice among whites on their desire that the criminal justice system treat suspects and criminals more harshly. Placing this discussion within conflict theory views of law and criminal justice in the United States, we argue that the influence of public punitiveness on crime policy is antidemocratic to the extent that public views stem from racial prejudice.

Introduction

Every democratic society must decide what balance to strike between the need to control crime and the need to protect citizens from mistakes and abuse of power by police and other government agents. In a classic article, Herbert L. Packer (1964) outlined two "models of the criminal process," that correspond to these needs, the crime control and due process models. The crime control model assumes that most suspects are guilty and that society's needs are best served by apprehending and processing them as efficiently as possible. In contrast, the due process model assumes that police and other government officials make honest errors and sometimes abuse their powers. The criminal justice system thus must protect suspects, defendants, and, more generally, the citizenry from governmental mistakes and abuse of power.

Since the 1970s the United States has moved dramatically from the due process emphasis favored by the Supreme Court under Chief Justice Earl

Warren to a crime control policy. Responding in part to growing public concern over crime and calls for the harsher punishment of criminals, federal, state, and local officials have adopted a "get tough" approach involving mandatory sentencing for drug and other offenses, longer prison terms, life imprisonment for repeat felony offenders, the growing use of the death penalty, limits on appeals of convictions in such crimes, greater numbers of police, "zero tolerance" of minor offenses such as disorderly conduct, and other measures. As a result, the number of state and federal prisoners and jail inmates grew more than fourfold since the 1970s to more than 1.9 million by 1999, and today the U.S. imprisonment rate is the highest in the Western industrial world. Much of the impact of this new crime control approach has been on racial and ethnic minorities; today about one-third of young black men are in prison, jail, or otherwise under correctional supervision (Mauer 1999).

Other works have examined the reasons for this crime control emphasis and its various effects (Beckett and Sasson 1999; Chambliss 1999; Mauer 1999). This article takes a step back and discusses a possible reason for the public's desire for harsh punishment that partly underlies this emphasis. This reason is racial prejudice. We first place the discussion within a larger theoretical debate on law and the criminal justice system and then review findings showing that racial prejudice motivates public preferences for a more punitive approach to the treatment of suspects and defendants. Although the theories we discuss apply to racial prejudice by whites against people of color generally, the research of which we are aware deals only with white prejudice toward blacks. Thus, the findings we review concern this type of prejudice only. Final remarks spell out areas for future research on racial prejudice, attitudes about punishment, and crime control policy.

Consensus, Conflict, and Criminal Justice

Two general views dominate theoretical treatments of law, crime, and criminal justice in U.S. society (Hopkins 1975). The first, the consensus view, reflects the Durkheimian sociological tradition stressing the need for social stability and the ways in which stability is created both by social institutions and by a societal consensus on values and norms of behavior (Collins 1994). In this view, law is an essential means through which modern societies maintain social order. As such, the implementation of law and operation of the criminal justice system benefit all segments of the public, not just those at the top of the socioeconomic system. Further, support for the criminal justice system is assumed to be reinforced by public consensus on norms for behavior and for the punishment of criminals.

The second, the conflict view, reflects the conflict tradition in sociology that derives from the work of Karl Marx, Friedrich Engels, and Max Weber. This tradition views the most fundamental process within a society as conflict between self-interested individuals and groups seeking to maximize their control over scarce, desirable resources at the expense of others (Collins 1994). When applied to law, crime, and criminal justice, the conflict view assumes that law is one of the many means through which the powerful in society dominate the powerless and maintain their position at the top of the social hierarchy (Lynch 1997; Turk 1969). Further, because the law is assumed to advantage some groups and disadvantage others, individuals and groups are hypothesized to disagree on legal norms for behavior and for the punishment of criminals.

The argument in this paper is that one of the motivations among whites for favoring harsh treatment of criminals is racial prejudice, and that this prejudice flows from conflict between whites and members of other races. But why should racial prejudice lead to more punitive attitudes? Reasons for this linkage flow from Weber's (Gerth and Mills, 1946) analysis of status group conflict and from modifications of Marx's theory of exploitation. For Weber, a status group is a group of people who are treated the same by others (in Weber's terms, share the same life fate) as a result of the prestige (honor) they are given by others. Weber emphasizes that the ranking of status groups is the result of inter-group conflict: high ranking (positively privileged) status groups attain their positions by usurpation, forcing other groups into lower ranks.

Positively privileged status groups claim prestige by asserting their superiority over other groups and develop ideologies claiming that members of other groups are deficient in socially relevant ways. This claim, in turn, forms the basis for social exclusion, a restriction of intimate social interaction to members of the status group, and economic and political exclusion, in an attempt to restrict access to the more desirable political and economic positions to status group members (Parkin 1979). These claims of superiority, then, can easily form the basis for prejudice; defined as "attributions (1) about groups or members of groups by virtue of their membership in the group, that are (2) disparaging and hostile, (3) false or at least without warrant, and (4) consistently made" (Sniderman, Piazza, and Harvey 1998:26–27), and thus the basis for discrimination. Noel's (1968) theory of ethnic stratification and contemporary Weberian theories of racial and ethnic stratification and their application to U.S. race relations include characterizations of race relations as involving both caste and class relations (van den Berghe 1967; Berreman 1960, 1972; Myrdal 1944; Willie 1979).

Theories rooted in Marx's theory of exploitation tend to locate the origins of contemporary racial stratification in the United States and other capitalist societies in capitalists' search for captive markets and cheap labor sources (Allen 1969; Blauner 1972; Bonacich 1972, 1980; Carmichael and Hamilton 1967; Cox 1948, 1964). This search leads capitalist states to seize and exploit colonies abroad, to import slaves and other sources of exploitable labor, and to dominate exploitable sources of domestic labor. While these efforts at exploitation have their origins in a search for profits, the fact that colonized peoples and domestically exploitable sources of labor are largely people of color facilitates the development of racial ideologies that justify this exploitation. Employers use these beliefs to foster racial conflict, thus dividing the working class, weakening workers' political and economic power, and enhancing profits (Key 1949; Reich 1977; Szymanski 1976).

For both Marxists and Weberians, the power of the state is a crucial instrument affecting the outcome of group conflict. Groups in conflict will try to control, or at least influence, how laws are created and the ways in which they are enforced. Thus both sets of theories would predict that in countries in which one racial group is dominant, legal structures will be used in a discriminatory way, as a means of oppressing subordinated groups (Hopkins 1975). These theories would also predict that the dominant group's desire to use the legal system oppressively would increase in situations in which their dominance is threatened.

Data and observations consistent with these predictions come from several sources. Jackson (1989) finds greater spending on policing in cities characterized by higher levels of racial economic inequality, larger minority populations, and inner-city riots. As Skogan (1995) states, "More is spent on policing in cities where white interests appear to be threatened." Liska, Lawrence, and Sanchirico (1982) find that the positive correlation between city expenditures on policing and the proportion of the city population that is black is higher in less segregated cities than in more segregated cities. This result suggests that whites are particularly likely to support large police expenditures when they do not feel protected by residential segregation. Finckenauer (1988) suggests that the large increase in public support for the death penalty after 1967 (Bohm 1991) was due, in part, to a fear of increasing black demands for civil rights and social justice. A number of authors (Paternoster 1984; Radelet and Vandiver 1986; Staples 1976) have observed that "white persons' support for punitive measures for criminals has increased in accordance with the enhanced visibility of black persons within crime contexts" (Aguirre and Baker, 1993:151).

Finally, motivated by disproportionately high rates of arrest and imprisonment among the poor and people of color, other tests of conflict theory predictions come from studies of race, class, and criminal justice outcomes. Although these studies are voluminous, they disagree over the extent to which the poor and people of color are disadvantaged in the criminal justice system (Mann 1993; Wilbanks 1987). A cautious conclusion is that race and class bias exists, especially for less serious offenses and for drug offenses, but that differences in offending rates account for the bulk of the race and class differences in arrest and imprisonment rates (Tonry 1994; Walker, Spohn, and DeLone 1996; Zatz 1987). Thus this literature on criminal justice outcomes provides some support for conflict theory, but support that is nonetheless limited.

Conflict Theory, Racial Prejudice, and Punitiveness

Most tests of conflict theory have focused on its assumptions about the operation of the criminal justice system, but this theory also has implications for public views on crime and the treatment of criminals. In contrast to consensus theory, it assumes that demographic subgroups disagree on norms of behavior and the punishment of criminals (Thomas, Cage, and Foster, 1976). It further would predict that those in the dominant group who are more oriented toward conflict—e.g., those who are more prejudiced against subordinate groups—would be more likely to want to see the legal system used to control these groups. This prediction yields the following hypothesis: among whites, higher levels of prejudice lead to a greater desire to see criminals punished harshly.

This hypothesis rests on two assumptions in addition to those of conflict theory: (1) negative racial attitudes are developed before people develop attitudes toward political issues such as appropriate levels of punishment; and (2) there is a widespread belief that most criminals come from minority backgrounds and hence that majority group interests are potentially threatened by minority criminal activity. Support for these assumptions comes respectively from Peffley and Hurwitz (1998) and from Doleschal (1979). As a result, and as many authors have argued (Borg, 1997; Hacker, 1992; LaFree, 1995; Skogan, 1995), crime in the United States has become a "code word" for race, fostered by media portrayals of violent criminals as largely black and by "the political rhetoric of politicians who often talk about crimes in racially coded language" (Peffley and Hurwitz, 1998:86; Edsall, and Edsall, 1992; Entman, 1992; Jamieson, 1992). As these authors suggest, a desire to punish criminals harshly can, for some whites, conceal a desire to maintain the favorable position of whites by punishing "dangerous" blacks, or all blacks as a group. Thus, in addition to the four reasons commonly considered legitimate reasons to punish criminals (retribution, deterrence, incapacitation, and rehabilitation), there would be a fifth, illegitimate reason: the desire to maintain group privilege and a rejection of non-group members.

A substantial literature tests conflict theory's assumption that racial and other demographic subgroups of the population should disagree on norms for behavior and for the punishment of criminals. Operationally, this literature addresses the extent of agreement in ratings of crime seriousness and preferences for the punishment of criminals. Several studies find considerable agreement on both sets of attitudes and interpret their findings as support for consensus theory (Blumstein and Cohen, 1980; Figlio, 1975; Rossi, Waite, Bose and Berk, 1974; Thomas, Cage and Foster, 1976). However, other studies suggest this interpretation may be premature. Racial and class differences exist in perceptions of bias in the criminal justice system (Hagan and Albonetti, 1982) and in opinions on the causes of crime, and on possible solutions to it (Browning and Cao, 1992). Differences also exist in support for the death penalty, with whites much more likely than blacks to favor capital punishment, even if differences don't exist for other types of sentence preferences (Barkan and Cohn, 1994).

Moreover, the studies finding consensus on crime seriousness and sentence preferences are open to challenge because people may hold similar opinions, but for different reasons. For example, many feminists and religious fundamentalists dislike pornography, but have different reasons for disliking it. Thus they have consensus on their overall aversion to pornography, but not on the reasons for their aversion. Hence the consensus is apparent rather than real. For consensus theory to be fully supported, agreement would have to exist on the reasons for opinions as well as on the opinions themselves.

Using this reasoning, Cohn, Barkan, and Halteman (1991) questioned the conclusions of consensus on punitiveness reached by many studies. They argued that the degree of consensus was apparent rather than real and that explanations rooted in conflict theory and in differing self-interests of whites and blacks could produce a superior explanation of apparent consensus. They suggested that it is in the self-interest of whites to be punitive for the reasons discussed above, while it is in the self-interest of African Americans to wish to see convicted criminals treated harshly because African Americans are disproportionately the victims of crimes. "Simply put, whites tend to be punitive because of racial prejudice, while blacks tend to be punitive because of fear of crime. This all 'works out' so that the two races hold similar views on punitiveness when these variables are not controlled. If this is true, then the widely reported racial consensus on punitiveness is apparent rather than real and reflects underlying conflicting interests" (Cohn, Barkan and Halteman, 1991:289).

Cohn, Barkan, and Halteman's (1991) analysis of data from the 1987 General Social Survey (GSS), a nationally representative sample of noninstitutionalized U.S. residents conducted regularly by the National Opinion Research Center, supported their hypothesis. In particular, they found that racial prejudice among whites predicted their support for harsher treatment of criminals by the courts. Other studies of GSS data using additional measures of punitiveness find further support for the racial prejudice-punitiveness hypothesis. Analyses of the 1984 and 1990 GSS, respectively by Aguirre and Baker (1993) and Barkan and Cohn (1994), showed a positive relationship among whites between racial prejudice toward blacks and support for the death penalty, as did a psychometric study of Los Angeles adults (Comrey and Newmeyer, 1965). Barkan and Cohn (1998), again analyzing data from the 1990 GSS, also showed that racial prejudice among whites predicted their support for the excessive use of force by police.

In an additional study, Hurwitz and Peffley (1998) and their colleagues interviewed by telephone a sample of whites to gauge their willingness to support random stops and searches by police of young men near a house where illegal drugs were being sold. In their interviews a number of experiments were conducted in which subsamples were read cases that were identical in most respects, but that differed in a few crucial ways. For example, one subsample was asked whether it was reasonable for the police to stop and search two young white men, both well-dressed and well-behaved, who were walking near the drug house. A second subsample was asked about police stopping and searching two young white men using foul language near the drug house. Two additional subsamples were asked, respectively, about two young black men who were well dressed and well behaved and two who were using foul language. (The study also included analogous experiments involving questions about the willingness of black and white women on welfare to find jobs and to have more children to get bigger welfare checks.) All subsamples were also asked to respond to items measuring racial stereotypes of blacks.

This methodological sophistication allowed Peffley and Hurwitz (1998) to present a nuanced view of the effects of prejudice. Comparisons of aggregate subsample scores on the reasonableness of police stops and searches enabled them to determine: (1) how much difference race makes; (2) how much difference demeanor makes; and (3) how much difference demeanor makes for each race. They were also able to compare how people at each level of racial stereotyping in each of the four subsamples answered the questions on reasonableness. They were then able to make comparisons within and between subsample to determine how racial stereotyping affects how much of a difference race, demeanor, and the interaction between race and demeanor make. All of these comparisons were made through the use of nonobtrusive measures (Webb, Campbell, Schwartz, and Sechrest, 1966). Since each respondent was read only one of the four cases, the respondent was not asked to compare whites with blacks, or well-dressed men with men using foul language. Thus the respondent was not induced to conceal any desire to see the police act in a discriminatory way.

Peffley and Hurwitz's (1998) results provide compelling support for the racial prejudice-punitiveness hypothesis. They found that their respondents were more likely to support the random stops and searches of young black men using foul language than of their young white male counterparts. They also found that racial stereotyping by respondents was related to their support for such stops and searches and concluded that "our results clearly demonstrate that racial stereotypes play a powerful role in shaping whites' political views of blacks in the highly charged" area of crime. More generally, their study showed that whites' attitudes toward blacks are linked to their attitudes toward issues such as crime and welfare that are not explicitly racial, and also toward the treatment of individual African Americans suspected of crime or on welfare.

However, two conditions also modified their findings. First, attitudes on policies were affected only by stereotypes that were conceptually relevant to the policy. For example, attitudes toward welfare were affected by beliefs that blacks are lazy, but not affected by beliefs that blacks are violent. Second, whites who held negative stereotypes of blacks responded exceptionally positively to an individual African American if the whites were presented with clear information that that person was not characterized by the negative stereotype; i.e., that the person is "an exception to the rule." Thus whites holding negative stereotypes were *less* likely to favor police stops and searches for well-dressed black men than for well-dressed white men.

Directions for Future Research

In summary, a range of studies indicates that racial prejudice is related to a desire by whites to see criminals treated punitively. This said, these studies also leave several areas unclear.

First, prejudice is only one of a number of variables that have been shown to influence punitive attitudes (Aguirre and Baker, 1993; Barkan and Cohn, 1994; Barkan and Cohn, 1998; Cohn, Barkan and Halteman, 1991; Langworthy and Whitehead, 1986; Peffley and Hurwitz, 1998; Stinchcombe et al., 1980; Young, 1991). While the studies cited above have shown that, among whites, prejudice against blacks does influence punitive attitudes, they have used statistical techniques that are not suitable for measuring the strength of this influence. Future research will need to measure punitiveness in a way that permits the use of OLS regression or a comparable technique.

Second, more effort needs to be expended to determine the conditions under which prejudice might be expected to influence punitiveness and when it might not. Several studies show that various circumstances affect how and when prejudicial attitudes are invoked. As just seen, negative stereotypes that are logically irrelevant to the issue at hand are not necessarily used in making judgments about the treatment of suspects and other racially coded issues (Peffley and Hurwitz, 1998). Further, if whites holding negative stereotypes are given information that a particular African American is "an exception to the rule," these whites are likely to respond very positively to the person.

Barkan and Cohn (1998) further argued that "prejudice should affect punitiveness more strongly under two conditions: (1) when the case against a suspect or defendant is relatively weak; and (2) when the offender's alleged wrongdoing is less serious." This argument was based on the "liberation hypothesis" advanced by Kalven and Zeisel (1966), who found that juries were more likely to let their beliefs and biases influence their decision-making when the evidence against defendants was weak. Barkan and Cohn's (1998) analysis of 1990 GSS on police use of excessive force supported their argument. As noted earlier, racial prejudice by whites predicted their support for police use of excessive force, i.e. against citizens described in GSS items as suspected of murder or as uttering profanities. But it did not predict their support for police use of reasonable force, i.e. against suspects described as attacking a police officer or attempting to escape from custody. Finally, both Myers (1990) and Olzak (1992) have found that whites are more likely to act on their prejudices in periods of economic stress.

Third, the nature of prejudice among whites needs to be more carefully differentiated between whites who hold a generalized antipathy toward blacks, and whites who are tolerant of blacks on some dimensions but intolerant on others, before the relationship of prejudice to punitiveness can be fully understood. As extreme, "Jim Crow" racial prejudice has declined (Bobo, Kluegel and Smith, 1997; Taylor, Sheatsley and Greeley, 1978), attitudes among many whites on racial matters have become multidimensional and "linked to larger political and ideological views on issues such as individual responsibility (and) the role of government" (Skogan 1995:70). Gaertner and Dovidio (1986) distinguish between dominative and aversive forms of racism. They argue that the form of racism among whites has largely changed from dominative racism, in which whites hold racially prejudiced attitudes and do not apply norms of equity to African Americans, to aversive racism, in which whites hold conflicting attitudes, combining racially prejudiced beliefs with beliefs in fairness and equity. It is among dominative racists that a categorical rejection of racial minorities across all dimensions of evaluation might be expected to apply, whereas among aversive racists, with their more nuanced and complex views, one might expect multidimensional structures of evaluation. If this is the case, it would be important to distinguish whites with multidimensional attitudinal structures from those who reject racial minorities on all dimensions.

Fourth, the effects of prejudice upon attitudes toward racially coded policies need to be more carefully determined. The welfare mother experiment included in the study of Peffley and Hurwitz (1998:72–79) described above raises the possibility that a policy's becoming racially coded might have little effect on aggregate public opinion toward the policy. In the welfare mother experiment, Peffley and Hurwitz find that whites who hold negative stereotypes of blacks tend to judge black welfare mothers more harshly than white welfare mothers, while those who hold positive stereotypes of blacks tend to do exactly the reverse. If this finding generalizes to policy preferences, then a policy's becoming racially coded might lead whites holding negative stereotypes of blacks to view the policy more unfavorably, and whites holding positive stereotypes to view the policy more favorably. The overall effect of the racial coding on aggregate white opinion might then be nil, depending on the distribution of negative and positive stereotypes among the white population and the strength of the biasing effects among each.

Fifth, the generality of the linkage between white prejudice against blacks and punitiveness needs to be tested by examining white prejudices toward other peoples of color. Finally, the sources of racial hostility need to be examined more carefully. The literature contains a significant debate between the proponents of the symbolic racism thesis (Kinder and Sears, 1981; Sears, Hensler and Speer, 1979; Sears et al., 1980; Tyler and Weber, 1982), which argues that racial hostility is the result of prejudices instilled in childhood, and proponents of the realistic group conflict position (Bobo 1983; Skogan 1995:70–71), which argues that much racial hostility is the result of contemporary conflicts between status groups for scarce resources.

Several points need to be made about this debate. First, Bobo does not contend that prejudice inculcated in childhood plays no role in racial hostility, but only that this role has been overstated. Second, the two positions both involve elements of group conflict. The Weberian and Marxian theories that we cited earlier all locate the origins of racial prejudice in group conflict for scarce resources. These conflicts lead to hostility and negative stereotyping, which are then passed down the generations. Thus, the differences between the symbolic racism and realistic group conflict theories are differences about whether the origin of racial hostility is to be found in present or past group conflicts.

Third, it is difficult for several reasons to establish empirically the extent to which each theory is able to account for contemporary racial hostility, at least when using the conventional measures of prejudice commonly used in contemporary surveys. To the extent that social structures are stable, previous patterns of group conflict will be reproduced in present generations. Further, as the Robbers Cave experiment (Sherif et al., 1961) shows, contemporary group conflicts may lead to hostility toward, and negative stereotyping of, opponents. Thus, the existence of negative stereotypes and hostility, both components of prejudice, cannot differentiate between the two theories. Bobo (1983:201) proposes a criterion to distinguish prejudices inculcated in childhood from hostilities generated by contemporary group conflicts, but his criterion would be useful only in cases in which the prejudices instilled in childhood are unidimensional.

Conclusion: Racial Prejudice and Crime Policy

The findings we have discussed on racial prejudice and punitiveness raise important questions about public opinion and criminal justice policy in a democratic society. In such a society, it is entirely appropriate and even necessary that public opinion influence policy decisions by public officials (Dahl, 1956). But this influence is not appropriate if the reasons for public opinion violate democratic principles. If public opinion is racially prejudiced, then it would be inappropriate in a democratic society for this opinion to affect public policy.

This is true for criminal justice policy no less than for any other policy. The public holds strong views about the causes of crime, the punishment of criminals, and other crime-related areas. They have legitimate reasons, including a fear of crime, a concern for public safety, and even a desire for retribution, within a democratic context for favoring harsh treatment of criminals. But to the extent that racial prejudice among whites also motivates their support for punitive treatment, it is inappropriate for their orientation to affect public policy on crime control. To the extent, then, that the crime control emphasis of the last few decades reflects racial prejudice, both among the public and among public officials themselves, this emphasis departs from democratic principles.

As the United States continues to debate crime, welfare, and other racially-coded problems and policies, public opinion will no doubt influence official decision-making. In a democracy, this is how it should be. Yet the growing literature on the role played by racial prejudice in public opinion on these issues suggests that this influence rests to some degree on antidemocratic sentiment. Although the last few decades are hardly the first period in which antidemocratic sentiments have held sway in U.S. politics and policies, the literature discussed in this paper underscores the need to pay continued attention to the impact of racial prejudice on public views on the issues of the day.

References

Aguirre, Adalberto and David V. Baker. (1993). Racial Prejudice and the Death Penalty: A Research Note. *Social Justice* 20:150–155.

Allen, Robert L. (1969). *Black Awakening in Capitalist America.* Garden City, NY: Anchor Books.

Barkan, Steven E. and Steven F. Cohn. (1994). Racial Prejudice and Support for the Death Penalty by Whites. *Journal of Research in Crime and Delinquency* 31:202–209.

Barkan, Steven E. and Steven F. Cohn. (1998). Racial Prejudice and Support by Whites for Police Use of Force: A Research Note. *Justice Quarterly* 15:743–753.

Beckett, Katherine and Theodore Sasson. (1999). *The Politics of Injustice: Crime and Punishment in America.* Thousand Oaks, CA: Pine Forge Press.

Berreman, Gerald D. (1960). Caste in India and the United States. *American Journal of Sociology* 66:120-127.

Berreman, Gerald D. (1972). Race, Caste and Other Invidious Distinctions, in Social Stratification. *Race* 13:385-414.

Blauner, Robert. (1972). *Racial Oppression in America.* New York: Harper and Row.

Blumstein, Alfred and Jacqueline Cohen. (1980). Sentencing of Convicted Offenders: An Analysis of the Public's View. *Law and Society Review* 14:223-261.

Bobo, Lawrence. (1983). Whites' Opposition to Busing: Symbolic Racism or Realistic Group Conflict? *Journal of Personality and Social Psychology* 40:414-431.

Bobo, Lawrence, James R. Kluegel, and Ryan A. Smith. (1997). Laissez-Faire Racism: The Crystallization of a Kinder, Gentler, Antiblack Ideology. In S. A. Tuch and J. K. Martin (Eds.), *Racial Attitudes in the 1990s: Continuity and Change* 15–44, Westport, CT: Praeger.

Bohm, Robert M. (1991). American Death Penalty Opinion, 1936–1986: A Critical Examination of the Gallup Polls. In R. M. Bohm (Ed.), *The Death Penalty in America: Current Research.* 113–145, Cincinnati: Anderson Publishing Co.

Bonacich, Edna. (1972). A Theory of Ethnic Antagonism: The Split-Labor Market. *American Sociological Review* 37:547–559.

Bonacich, Edna. (1980). Class Approaches to Ethnicity and Race. *Insurgent Sociologist* 10:9–23.

Borg, M.J. (1997). The Southern Subculture of Punitiveness: Regional Variation in Support for Capital Punishment. *Journal of Research in Crime and Delinquency* 34:25–45.

Browning, Sandra Lee and Liqun Cao. (1992). The Impact of Race on Criminal Justice Ideology. *Justice Quarterly* 9:685–701.

Carmichael, Stokley and Charles V. Hamilton. (1967). *Black Power.* New York: Vintage Books.

Chambliss, William J. (1999). *Power, Politics, and Crime.* Boulder: Westview Press.
Cohn, Steven F., Steven E. Barkan, and William A. Halteman. (1991). Punitive Attitudes Toward Criminals: Racial Consensus or Racial Conflict? *Social Problems* 38:287–296.
Collins, Randall. (1994). *Four Sociological Traditions.* New York: Oxford University Press.
Comrey, Andrew L. and John B. Newmeyer. (1965). Measurement of Radicalism-Conservatism. *Journal of Social Psychology* 67:357–369.
Cox, Oliver C. (1948). *Caste, Class and Race.* New York: Monthly Review Press.
Cox, Oliver C. (1964). *Capitalism as a System.* New York: Monthly Review Press.
Dahl, Robert A. (1956). *A Preface to Democratic Theory.* Chicago: University of Chicago Press.
Doleschal, Eugene. (1979). Crime: Some Popular Beliefs. *Crime and Delinquency* 25:1–8.
Edsall, Thomas B. and Mary D. Edsall. (1992). *Chain Reaction: The Impact of Race, Rights and Taxes on American Politics.* New York: W.W. Norton.
Entman, Robert. (1992). Blacks in the News: Television, Modern Racism, and Cultural Change. *Journalism Quarterly* 69:341–361.
Figlio, Robert M. (1975). The Seriousness of Offenses: An Evaluation by Offenders and Non-offenders. *Journal of Criminal Law and Criminology* 66:189–200.
Finckenauer, James D. (1988). Public Support for the Death Penalty: Retribution as Just Deserts or Retribution as Revenge? *Justice Quarterly* 5:81–100.
Gaertner, Samuel L. and John F. Dovidio. (1986). The Aversive Form of Racism. In J. F. Dovidio and S. L. Gaertner (Eds.), *Prejudice, Discrimination, and Racism,* 61–90 New York: Academic Press.
Gerth, Hans and C. Wright Mills. (1946). From Max Weber: Essays in Sociology. New York: Oxford University Press.
Hacker, Andrew. (1992). *Two Nations: Black and White, Separate, Hostile, Unequal.* New York: Scribner's.
Hagan, John and Celesta Albonetti. (1982). Race, Class, and the Perception of Criminal Injustice in America. *American Journal of Sociology* 88:329–355.
Hopkins, Andrew. (1975). On the Sociology of Criminal Law. *Social Problems* 22:608–619.
Hurwitz, Jon and Mark Peffley (eds.) (1998). *Perception and Prejudice: Race and Politics in the United States.* New Haven: Yale University Press.
Jackson, Pamela I., (1989). *Minority Group Threat, Crime, and Policing.* New York: Praeger.
Jamieson, Kathleen Hall. (1992). *Dirty Politics: Deception, Distraction, and Democracy.* New York: Oxford University Press.
Kalven, Harry and Hans Zeisel. (1966). *The American Jury.* Boston: Little, Brown and Co.
Key, V.O. 1949. *Southern Politics.* New York: Vintage Books.
Kinder, Donald and David O. Sears. (1981). Prejudice and Politics: Symbolic Racism Versus Racial Threats to the Good Life. *Journal of Personality and Social Psychology* 40:414–431.
LaFree, Gary. (1995). Race and Crime Trends in the United States, 1946–1990. In D. F. Hawking (Ed.), *Ethnicity, Race, and Crime: Perspectives Across Time and Place,* 169–193. Albany, NY: State University of New York Press.

Langworthy, Robert H. and John T. Whitehead. (1986). Liberalism and Fear as Explanations of Punitiveness. *Criminology* 24:575–591.

Liska, Allen E., Joseph J. Lawrence, and Andrew Sanchirico. (1982). Fear of Crime as a Social Fact. *Social Forces* 60:760–770.

Lynch, Michael J. (ed.). (1997). *Radical Criminology.* Brookfield, VT: Dartmouth Publishing Company.

Mann, Coramae Richey. (1993). *Unequal Justice: A Question of Color.* Bloomington: Indiana University Press.

Mauer, Marc. (1999). *Race to Incarcerate.* New York: New Press.

Myers, Martha A. (1990). Economic Threat and Racial Disparities in Incarceration: The Case of Postbellum Georgia. *Criminology* 28:627–656.

Myrdal, Gunnar. (1944). *An American Dilemma: The Negro Problem and Modern Democracy.* New York.

Noel, Donald L. (1968). A Theory of the Origin of Ethnic Stratification. *Social Problems* 16:157–172.

Olzak, Susan. (1992. *The Dynamics of Ethnic Competition and Conflict.* Stanford: Stanford University Press.

Packer, Herbert L. (1964). Two Models of the Criminal Process. *University of Pennsylvania Law Review* 113:1–68.

Parkin, Frank. (1979). *Marxism and Class theory: A Bourgeois Critique.* London: Tavistock.

Paternoster, Raymond. (1984). Prosecutorial Discretion in Requesting the Death Penalty: A Case of Victim-Based Racial Discrimination. *Law and Society Review* 18:437–478.

Peffley, Mark and Jon Hurwitz. (1998). Whites' Stereotypes of Blacks: Sources and Political Consequences In J. Hurwitz and M. Peffley (Eds.), *Perception and Prejudice: Race and Politics in the United States*, 58–99. New Haven: Yale University Press.

Radelet, Michael L. and M. Vandiver. (1986). Race and Capital Punishment: An Overview of the Issues. *Crime and Social Justice* 25:94–113.

Reich, Michael. (1977). The Economics of Racism. In D. M. Gordon (Ed.), *Problems in Political Economy: An Urban Perspective*, 183–188. Lexington, MA: D.C. Heath.

Rossi, Peter H., Emily Waite, Christine E. Bose, and Richard E. Berk. (1974). The Seriousness of Crime: Normative Structure and Individual Differences. *American Sociological Review* 39:224–237.

Sears, David O., Carl P. Hensler, and Leslie K. Speer. (1979). Whites' Opposition to 'Busing': Self-interest or Symbolic Politics? *American Political Science Review* 73:369–384.

Sears, David O., R.R. Lau, Tom R. Tyler, and H.M. Allen. (1980). Self-Interest or Symbolic Politics in Policy Attitudes and Presidential Voting. *American Political Science Review* 74:670–684.

Sherif, Muzafer, O.J. Harvey, B.J. White, W.R. Hood, and C.W. Sherif. (1961). *Intergroup Conflict and Cooperation: The Robbers Cave Experiment.* Norman, OK: Institute of Group Relations, University of Oklahoma.

Skogan, Wesley G. (1995). Crime and the Racial Fears of White Americans. *Annals of the American Academy of Political and Social Sciences* 539:59–71.

Sniderman, Paul M., Thomas Piazza, and Hosea Harvey. (1998). Prejudice and Politics: An Intellectual Biography of a Research Project. In J. Hurwitz and M. Peffley. (Eds.), *Perception and Prejudice: Race and Politics in the United States*, 17–34. New Haven: Yale University Press.

Staples, Robert. (1976). White Racism, Black Crime and American Justice: An Application of the Colonial Model to Explain Crime and Race. *Phylon* 7:14–22.

Stinchcombe, Arthur L., Rebecca Adams, Carol A. Heimer, Kim Lane Scheppele, Tom W. Smith, and D. Garth Taylor. (1980). *Crime and Punishment: Changing Attitudes in America.* San Francisco: Jossey-Bass.

Szymanski, Albert. (1976). Racial Discrimination and White Gain. *American Sociological Review* 41:403–414.

Taylor, D. Garth, Paul Sheatsley, and Andrew Greeley. (1978). Attitudes Toward Racial Integration. *Scientific American* 238:42–51.

Thomas, Charles W., Robin J. Cage, and Samuel C. Foster. (1976). Public Opinion on Criminal Law and Legal Sanctions: An Examination of Two Conceptual Models. *Journal of Criminal Law and Criminology* 67:110–116.

Tonry, Michael. (1994). *Malign Neglect: Race, Crime, and Punishment in America.* New York: Oxford University Press.

Turk, Austin T. (1969). *Criminality and Legal Order.* Chicago: Rand McNally.

Tyler, Tom R. and R. Weber. (1982). Support for the Death Penalty: Instrumental Response to Crime or Symbolic Attitude? *Law and Society Review* 17:21–45.

van den Berghe, Pierre. (1967). *Race and Racism: A Comparative Perspective.* New York: John Wiley and Sons.

Walker, Samuel, Cassia Spohn, and Miriam DeLone. (1996). *The Color of Justice: Race, Ethnicity, and Crime in America.* Belmont, CA: Wadsworth Publishing Company.

Webb, Eugene J., Donald T. Campbell, Richard D. Schwartz, and Lee Sechrest. (1966). *Unobstrusive Measures: Nonreactive Research in the Social Sciences.* Chicago: Rand McNally.

Wilbanks, William. (1987). *The Myth of a Racist Criminal Justice System.* Monterey: Brooks/Cole Publishing Company.

Willie, Charles V. (1979). *The Class and Caste Controversy.* Bayside, NY: General Hall.

Young, Robert L. (1991). Race, Conceptions of Crime and Justice, and Support for the Death Penalty. *Social Psychology Quarterly* 54:67–75.

Zatz, Marjorie S. (1987). The Changing Forms of Racial/Ethnic Biases in Sentencing. *Journal of Research in Crime and Delinquency* 24:69–92.

Section 2

Class and the Social Control of Law

"Defending the Poor: Commonsense 'Class'ism in the Adjudication of Criminal Cases"

Debra S. Emmelman,
Southern Connecticut State University

Abstract

By focusing on the conduct of one group of court-appointed attorneys, this chapter examines some important components in the defense lawyer's management of criminal cases on behalf of the poor. It is asserted that, because the judge and jury have ultimate control over case outcomes, defenders orient their behavior toward these court actors. Moreover, because the judge and jury are expected to employ "common sense" in their decision-making, defenders attempt to portray their clients in a manner consistent with commonsense standards. However, common sense is the cultural knowledge system of the status quo. Consequently, poor defendants frequently lack the requisite resources with which to be characterized as generally respectable and credible people. Thus, poor defendants fall victim to commonsense "class"ism in the adjudication of criminal cases. The chapter concludes by noting some evidence of commonsense sexism and racism in adjudication procedures as well.

Introduction

Contrary to popular opinion, most research today indicates that publicly provided defense attorneys accord their clients legally ethical representation.[1] Nevertheless, poor criminal defendants continue to endure higher conviction rates, higher rates of conviction for more serious crimes, and more severe sentences. Given this state of affairs, should we conclude that poor people are more likely to commit crime, as well as more serious crime, and that they are simply receiving their just desserts? Or might we conclude that something other than unethical defense procedures is unduly tipping the scales of justice against them? In this chapter, I show how poor defendants endure inequities in the adjudication of criminal cases *not* because their attorneys behave incompetently or because they are more criminally culpable than other defendants, but because litigation procedures involve commonsense "class"ism, or, unequal treatment on the basis of social class which derives from commonsense reasoning.

Methods

Between September of 1984 and September of 1988, field research was conducted on a private, nonprofit corporation of court-appointed defense attorneys. (Henceforth, this corporation will be referred to as "Defense Alliance" and its attorneys will be referred to as "defenders".) The corporation was located in a large, well-populated urban area on the west coast, and employed approximately fifteen attorneys at any given time. Approximately half of the attorneys were men and half were women. Their ages ranged from the early thirties to the early fifties; the average age was in the late thirties. With the exception of one African-American attorney, who worked at this office for only a brief time, all of the attorneys were white. All but one of the attorneys handled felony cases.

Data were initially collected through participant observation. For an average of about eight hours per week, I observed the defenders' behavior while serving as a student intern and law clerk. I was permitted to observe virtually every aspect of their behavior, including that which occurred in such behind-the-scenes places as the attorneys' offices, judges' chambers, and jail.

Throughout the observational phase of the study, field notes were recorded and then later analyzed through a grounded theory methodology (see Glaser and Strauss 1967; and Lester and Hadden 1980 for further details on the use of this methodology.) In order to clarify and refine these research findings, in-depth interviews were conducted toward the end of the study.

---

1. See for example, Emmelman 1993; 1996; Hermann et. al. 1977; McIntyre 1987; Wice 1985.

The interviews were designed to ascertain the manner in which defenders routinely defend criminal cases. They lasted between three and a half and four hours. All the attorneys who were currently employed by the corporation (five men and six women), as well as four ex-Defenders (three men and one woman) participated in the interviews. All the interviews were taped, transcribed and then later analyzed.

The Everyday Context of Criminal Defense: Court Actors' Roles and Expectations

Like the social world in general,[2] the criminal court system is the product of ongoing interaction among diverse social actors. It is only because defense attorneys, prosecutors, judges, juries, and numerous other court actors share certain understandings and behave in interrelated manners that the criminal court system is possible. Accordingly, defense attorneys perform their tasks in relation to the roles and expectations of others.

Although the District Attorney is ideally responsible for upholding the law and executing justice, defenders expect prosecutors to harbor an inordinate desire to convict defendants.[3] However, it is the judge and jury who are delegated the authority to draw conclusions regarding the success of the legal combatants. After receiving input from both attorneys, for example, the judge decides whether a defendant will be released on bail, whether a plea bargain will be accepted, whose argument regarding a motion is most convincing, and what sentence will be imposed. Similarly, the jury decides whether a defendant will be found guilty at the conclusion of a trial and, under certain circumstances, influences sentencing. For this reason, defenders find it especially useful to postulate the judge and jury's viewpoints toward cases when they evaluate them for viable defense strategies.[4]

Because they are the "house rules" by which all court actors are supposed to proceed, the defenders find it necessary to understand fully, apply and comply with established laws and legal procedures while defending clients.[5] However, this is not the only or perhaps even the most important type of understanding that defenders anticipate the judge and jury will employ. Instead,

2. Berger and Luckmann, 1967; Blumer, 1978; Cicourel, 1968; 1974; Garfinkel, 1967; Mehan and Wood, 1975.

3. See also, Frohmann, 1991; Stanko, 1981.

4. See also, Mather, 1979; Neubauer, 1974.

5. American Bar Association, 1986; Emmelman, 1993; 1996.

they expect the judge and jury to reason and reach conclusions on the basis of "common sense".

Webster (1976) defines common sense as "practical judgement or intelligence; ordinary good sense". Sociologically (as well as anthropologically), what is "practical", "intelligent", or "good sense" is *cultural.* For example, it makes "good sense" to us that if we want to survive in this society, we should find a job in order to make money. However, the very idea of "jobs" or "getting a job" is possible only within the context of relatively recent historical societies. A woman in a hunting and gathering society never fathomed the possibility of deciding whether she should become a "gatherer" in order to make a living and survive. It was simply understood that this was who she was born to be and that this was how she would contribute to survive in the group.

Consequently, common sense is better defined as the shared stock of knowledge in a society or the core understandings which most people in a specific cultural community hold in common.[6] It enables people within that community to interact meaningfully by providing them with a set of shared, taken-for-granted understandings which form the context for communication. It also prescribes what is *and is not* expected, normal and acceptable behavior in that cultural community. For example, in developed western societies, we know how to behave as well as how people *should* behave in a store, a library, and a hospital. Such understandings are not possible in societies where stores, libraries and hospitals do not exist and members of such societies do not know how to behave "appropriately" in such contexts. Yet common sense is not knowledge about which we typically think or talk. Instead, it is tacitly understood and taken-for-granted. In other words, it makes our everyday communication possible, but it is rarely acknowledged as anything worth talking about.

As Gusfield (1981) finds, common sense also entails a recognition of the conventional social hierarchy and structure of authority. In our developed, western society, for example, scientific spheres of activity are implicitly accorded more legitimacy than enterprises in such mystical domains as astrology.[7] We also have more respect for scientists than business people, and treat the latter with more deference than prostitutes. Yet it is important to realize that such collective sentiments are not culturally or historically invariant; scientists have been regarded as heretics, merchants have been despised, and prostitutes have had high status in other societies.[8] Consequently, *common*

---

6. Berger & Luckmann, 1967; Geertz, 1983; Mehan and Wood, 1975; Schutz, 1962.
7. See also, Weber, 1979.
8. See for examples, Reston, 1994; Sanger, 1974; Weber, 1958.

sense should be seen as the shared values, beliefs and norms of the status quo in particular societies.

Regardless of whether they themselves wholly embrace commonsense values and beliefs, defenders expect ruling authorities to do so: both judges and juries are beheld as middle class and thought to harbor a middle class value system.[9] In addition, because they consist of licensed drivers and registered voters drawn from a conservative surrounding community, juries are thought largely to exclude persons sympathetic to the disenfranchised or unorthodox. Similarly, judges are deemed extremely sensitive to public opinion and social proprieties because they are elected officials. Thus, judges and juries are generally regarded as social conformists who sustain conventional viewpoints, or the viewpoints of the status quo.

The defenders' expectations regarding the judge and jury's viewpoints are illustrated in the following comments:

> Nora: [The typical jury is] middle-class. Very different from our clients in lifestyle, experiences, with the justice system, experience with crimes—they've never been accused of crimes usually... The biggest problem I guess is that they're too far removed from our clients. I mean, our clients are not really judged by their peers, but another social strata up... [Judges are influenced by their] career. Desire for advancement. Judges have to be approved by the voters. And they really don't want to do anything that puts them in the public's eyes. They don't want to make waves, first of all. And secondly, they are concerned about their own advancement.
>
> Kathy: [She had been referring to the "right frame of reference" for juries.] [What is the "right frame of reference" for the jury?] I had a client—a cute little white kid who was 22, and he was charged with battery on his wife's lesbian lover. Well, now, all I had to do—there was a fight and he told the lesbian lover to get out of the house, and she basically told him to fuck off, and so he threw her out. And I think technically he was guilty of a battery. But all I had to do was give the jury something they could use to acquit him with, and they did... Now it's hard for a jury... If I can't put the act into some kind of frame of reference to make it acceptable. [Are they behaving on the basis of certain traditional values?] Right. [One is that a woman shouldn't have a lesbian lover?] Right.

---

9. See also, Wiseman, 1979.

> [From the researcher's field notes dated 1-7-85] I began the day with Karl...and two other law interns. He called the day "orientation day" and began by telling us about the organization of his daily calendar and case files. He had a total of three appearances today—two of which were scheduled at the same time in two different courts. He told us that judges were "prima donnas" [meaning that they are elitist and extremely sensitive to social proprieties] and that he would have to figure out a way not to upset the two judges.

Unfortunately, while the judge and jury are expected to maintain commonsense (or status quo) sentiments in their decision-making, the social conditions and types of relationships associated with poverty frequently preclude the ability of poor defendants to provide information that measures up to those standards. Thus, poor defendants are less able than others to be portrayed throughout litigation proceedings as generally respectable, trustworthy and credible individuals *regardless* of their actual moral propensities or their innocence or guilt of specific crimes. This is illustrated in the following comments made by defenders in response to the question "How do you think the typical indigent defendant tends to differ from other types of defendants?":

> Robert: Well, he is almost definitionally a member of the underclass. Which means that he is under or uneducated. Likely to be illiterate. He is typically inarticulate. He is often—usually a racial minority. All those things are important factors in how his case is gonna be heard and looked upon, and what the final determination is gonna be for his case. The fact that a defendant is inarticulate limits his ability to get on the witness stand and express himself to the jury. That goes hand in hand with his educational background. Members of the underclass [also] have—it is a subculture in which certain things are accepted or tolerated which may not be tolerated by jurors who come from more of a mainstream kind of background. Living together with girlfriends, children out of wedlock, situations like that which may not be as well-accepted by jurors. Those kinds of factors play heavily...And if you're able to present to the jury a defendant who is a working stiff, that makes him a much more loveable kind of person, a sympathetic kind of person, a person more like the jurors, and is a great advantage. And if the defendant is truly indigent, that's not something you can do for him. You can't present that.
>
> Ingmar: I think in general they have a lot more difficult cases to defend. I mean there's certain things you don't have. You don't have wonderful character witnesses for them because you can't bring in all

> these members of the business community, and politics, and "what have you" to come in and testify that this person's character is unimpeachable.

The defenders' expectations of how judges and juries make decisions influence virtually all aspects of their litigation practices; within legally prescribed guidelines, defenders fashion and execute bail pitches as well as plea bargaining, and trial and sentencing tactics oriented toward their tacit expectations of what judging authorities will find plausible and convincing. Described below is how inequities brought about by a defendant's social class and expressed through the cultural context of common sense influence bail, evidentiary and plea bargaining inquests.

Commonsense "Class"ism in Bail Review Hearings

A number of researchers[10] have found that a defendant's social class effects criminal case outcomes only indirectly; i.e., through the type of attorney procured, which then influences pre-trial release and the defendant's ability to assist with his or her defense. Although certainly a poor defendant's pretrial release is effected both by the timeliness in which they are assigned an attorney, and by their ability to post bail, this study indicates that at least some of this effect is the direct result of the defendant's social class. Specifically, circumstances reflecting the defendant's social class and expressed through the taken-for-granted cultural context of common sense shape the adjudicative procedures and outcomes of bail hearings.

The major issue in a bail review hearing is whether or not the defendant can be counted upon to show up at court hearings. Defenders attempt to demonstrate this by providing information to the judge that downplays the seriousness of the crime and/or signifies the defendant's investment in attendance at these hearings. Investment is thought to be documented through commonsense or culturally understood "ties" to the local area, such as permanent residency, employment, a supportive family, and/or other culturally valued assets located in the vicinity. However, because many poor defendants do not have a permanent residence, a job, stable family relationships, or other culturally valuable ties to the community (most of which can be seen to mirror as well as actually contribute to the defendant's poverty!), defenders are

10. See for example, Swigert and Farrell, 1977; Holmes, Daudistel and Farrell, 1987.

constrained in their ability to make viable bail pitches on their behalf and these clients are frequently deemed to be high risks for pre-trial release. Compare, for example, the different manners in which the same defender handled bail review hearings for two different defendants:

> [4/23/85] Karl asked [the defendant] how much bail he could afford. The defendant told Karl he could afford somewhere between $2,000 and $3,000 bail—$200–$300 actual amount paid. [In the Bail Review hearing,] Karl...told the judge that the defendant's father was in the courtroom in support of his son. He also emphasized the amount of time the defendant had spent in the area and stated that the defendant had only one count alleged against him. (In essence, it appeared Karl was emphasizing all the positives regarding a release on bail.) The judge reduced the bail to $1500 after having asked the DA if he had any objections. The DA said "No", but added that the defendant uses five or six other names.
>
> [4/19/85] Karl had only one bail review hearing which involved a man charged with burglary. The defendant had only been in the area about two weeks, had no job and no relatives in the area. (He was homeless and originally from another state.) Karl told him there was little hope he would be released from custody because of this. During the hearing, Karl did not make a bail pitch in this case. He simply removed the issue from the court calendar.

At an ideological level, people frequently insist that there is nothing wrong with being poor and that the poor are no more contemptuous than others. However, it is important to note here that the implicit message generated in bail review hearings and illustrated here is that because poor people do not possess many of the cultural or social assets associated with a higher social class, they do not have the integrity or moral fortitude to show up at court hearings. Thus, a character judgment is being made *not* on the basis of whether a person is *actually* trustworthy, but on the basis of commonsense understandings which recapitulate the defendant's social class.

Commonsense "Class"ism in Evidentiary Issues

For defenders, the most important consideration regarding whether a case can be won at trial is the strength of the evidence. They assess the strength of evidence by gauging whether judging authorities will find the prosecution more convincing than that presented by the defense.[11] Because judging authorities are expected to employ common sense in their decision-making, the strength of evidence can also be seen as determined on the basis of whether information presented at a trial will conform to the standards of the status quo. Due to factors associated with poverty, poor defendants encounter more disadvantages in this assessment activity. More precisely, poor defendants are likely to have weaker defense cases because circumstances produced by their social class, such as residency and employment patterns, social alliances, credentials, oral fluency, as well as physical appearance and comportment, shape the "facts" that are presented as evidence in the courtroom. Consider, for example, the following three incidents in which defenders considered taking certain cases to trial:

> Case #1: [An] investigator [working for Nora] asked me to analyze or map out a particular case for him from the available police and investigative reports that is getting ready to go to trial. It was regarding a young male (approximately 21 years of age) accused of stealing and pawning about $15,000 worth of gold jewelry from his parents' residence in [a wealthy community]. According to the police reports, the defendant broke into the home while his parents were on vacation (he was barred from the home and spending time in an out-of-state home for delinquent children) and had a party with about eight people—most of whom he was not acquainted with. The defendant is being charged with the theft because several people supplied the police with descriptions of a male which matched the defendant's description who sold the stolen jewelry at two pawn stores. The defendant, who insists he is innocent and has no previous record, has pointed out another person as the actual thief. He has provided a picture of the alleged thief and the two are amazingly similar in looks. [The investigator] also told me that Nora's defendant had a job (and therefore less reason to steal), and that during the time he was supposed to have been pawning the jewelry, the defendant was at work—where he is not permitted to leave the premises. The alleged thief, however, has no job and therefore more reason to have committed the theft. [The investigator] said he would keep me posted regarding this case. [The charges against the defendant were ultimately dropped.]

11. See Emmelman (1997) for more details on this process. See also, Mather, 1979; Neubauer, 1974.

In this example, we can see how the defendant's employment situation strengthened the evidence which could be presented on his behalf; not only could he claim he had a job (which presumably implied no motive to steal), but he was working at the time of the crime (an alibi), and his employer (a credible witness) was willing to testify on his behalf. Moreover, the prosecution case was weakened further because the defendant could point a finger at an unemployed person, who presumably had greater motive to lie. Yet it is important to note here that numerous studies show that employed persons, including those who are wealthy, commit the vast majority of theft and fraud, and frequently collude in doing so.[12] But because the defendant and his employer conformed to commonsense social standards (more so than an alternative suspect), his case was deemed convincing.

A similar scenario can be seen in the next example:

> Case #2: [The following case involved a possession of cocaine charge and was scheduled for trial.] According to Betty, the arresting police officer in this case, pulled the defendant over, along with several other males in a car, in an attempt to protect the defendant. [Betty stated that] the defendant was associated with the Navy and "looked the part", even though he was actually only a civilian employee of the Navy. On the other hand, the other males in the car were known by the police officer to take advantage of military personnel. According to the police officer, he was politely questioning the suspects outside of their car when he noticed that the defendant dropped about a gram of cocaine from his pocket. In contrast, the defendant [stated that] the officer, in fact, *ordered* the suspects out of the car. Betty and the investigator also discussed some trial tactics for this case. Betty said she hoped there were some Black jurists in the trial. The investigator agreed that would be a good idea: "You get some Black people on the jury and they'll know how Black people are treated by the police." (The defendant is Black.) Betty said that because the defendant was well-spoken and clearly not a criminal, that would be a plus for him, too.

In this instance, we can see not only that the defendant's employment status would necessarily enter into the evidence presented at a trial (i.e., by both

12. See Beirne and Messerschmidt (1995) and Reiman (1998) for good overviews of this issue.

his physical appearance and the police officer's need to establish his reason for detaining the defendant), but also that his level of literacy and consequent command of English indicated that he was "obviously" (based on common-sense sensibilities) not a criminal. This contrasts rather sharply with the following example.

> Case #3: After lunch, Karl had a case where a defendant (who was on probation for previous crimes) was charged with four drug crimes, including "possession for sale". [The defendant was a Black, medium-built, rather muscular male in his mid-twenties who wore his hair in short braids.] This was a preliminary hearing. According to the police report, the police spotted the defendant and noted that he was making slow and rigid movements and was expressionless. The police suspected he might be under the influence of PCP because the area was known for PCP usage. When approached [by the police], the defendant apparently acted confused, spoke slowly and deliberately, and smelled of an odor "which I generally associate with PCP usage" (i.e., ether). The police administered a [field test] and the defendant apparently didn't pass. They then arrested the defendant, patted him down for weapons, took him to the station for a blood test (he flunked again), and then noted that five PCP cigarettes had been dropped beside the defendant before he was actually given the blood test...Karl first told the defendant that he could get the charges reduced to one count of "under the influence of PCP", [with local jail time]. He noted that the defendant had a previous record [and] that the prosecution *did* have some proof problems; i.e., five PCP cigarettes are not enough for "possession for sale". The defendant asked about the chances of fighting the charges. Karl told him that he had a chance, but that the possession for sale is a big issue. The defendant was not going to win the case [altogether] because he had five "sherms" (PCP cigarettes) on him. The defendant stated that the police did not find the five sherms *on* him but beside him at the jail. He indicated that they had found only one sherm on him. Karl responded that although the police had already patted him down before the sherms were found beside him, they would just say that they had only done a weapons check—not a thorough one which would suggest that the sherms really were not on him. Karl also told him that the police *do* lie. He then told the defendant about other problems concerning a jury trial; there was a problem with status. The jury is usually composed of white, middle-class, aged people who are

> retired from the Navy or work in the aerodynamics field. He would be lucky if he got one or two Black people. He also said the police are expert witnesses who will be acting like "Mr. Nice Guy," not like they usually act out in the streets. The defendant would also have problems testifying in court because he would be in custody and have a bailiff breathing down his neck, not be free to roam around and let the jury know him during recesses. The jury will only see a rather formal and contrived performance of him during the trial. According to Karl, the cards were stacked against the defendant.

Like the second case, the defendant in the third example insinuated that the police fabricated evidence against him. Also like the second case, the defender in the above example acknowledged that police officers lie. Moreover, publicity throughout the mid and late 1990's concerning the behavior of law enforcement in the O.J. Simpson murder case and the F.B.I. crime lab makes it clear that forensic evidence is subject to error, if not outright falsehoods, and that there is no actual reason why attorneys should assume that this type of evidence is unimpeachable. Yet unlike the second defender, the third did not deem these potential evidentiary issues significant enough to consider taking the case to trial. Instead, he simply explained that he could not present convincing evidence of such indictments because the defendant's physical appearance and comportment would be no match to the police officer's, which would nicely conform to the jury's mainstream expectations. What the defender left unstated was that other factors related to a higher social class, such as a respectable career, public distinction, noteworthy credentials and/or reputable witnesses who could vouch for the defendant's behavior, would also make his case substantially more convincing.

Circumstances associated with defendants' social class influence the strength of their cases. Because poor defendants are less able to produce information consistent with commonsense (or status quo) standards of respectability and, consequently, plausibility, they are more likely to have weak defense cases. This occurs despite the fact that more "respectable" persons are frequently found to commit more costly and inhumane crimes. Thus, poor persons are more apt to be viewed as culpable on the basis of factors which may be completely unrelated to the commission of a specific crime.

Because indigent defendants are more likely to have weak defense cases, they are more likely to be convicted of crimes. This inequity may also result in a vicious cycle, because they are more apt to be convicted of crimes, they are more likely to acquire a criminal record. A prior record then adversely effects the strength of subsequent defense cases because it limits a defendant's ability to testify on his or her own behalf. As discussed in more detail below, prior convictions also lower the value of criminal cases for plea bargaining purposes. This ultimately means that poor defendants are more apt to acquire a lengthy and more serious prior record, and thereby receive more severe penalties.

Commonsense "Class"ism in Plea Bargaining

At the same time they are considering whether a case might be won at a trial, the defenders contemplate whether a defendant might be better off by plea bargaining. Their assessment of this issue is based on what they refer to as the "value" of a case.[13]

The value of a case is determined on the basis of three factors. These are 1) the seriousness of the crime(s) with which the defendant is charged (which means both how serious the charge itself is, as well as how serious or atypical the actual crime is), 2) the strength of the evidence (which means how strong or weak the evidence is on both sides of the issue), and 3) the defendant's background characteristics (which includes, but is not limited to, the defendant's prior criminal record). The value of a case increases the more the crime at issue is minor, the weaker the evidence is against the defendant, and the more reputable the defendant's background is. Defenders expect that cases deemed to have high value will result in considerable incentive (i.e., substantially reduced charges) from the prosecutor for defendants to plea bargain. The opposite is also true.

How defenders gauge the strength of evidence and the manner in which social class biases this process were described earlier. It was also noted above that because poor defendants are more apt to have weak defense cases, they are also more likely to have prior records. Not yet discussed (but perhaps rather obvious) is how social class shapes the value of criminal cases by shaping interpretations of the defendant's characteristics apart from a prior record. Quite simply, poor defendants are less able than others to exhibit behaviors consistent with judging authorities' expected appreciation of commonsense (or status quo) proprieties and respectability. Consequently, defenders are less able to portray these defendants during plea bargaining as generally respectable, trustworthy and

13. See also, Heumann, 1975; Mather, 1979; McDonald, 1985; Neubauer, 1974; and Rosett and Cressey, 1976.

moral people who have suffered temporary lapses and who therefore warrant greater consideration. This is illustrated in three defenders' comments regarding their attempts during plea bargaining to increase the value of their clients' cases:

> Mindy: I go to the dispo department, you wait your turn, you go in and talk to the D.A. and the judge at the same time. The D.A. makes you an offer, and I do different things. I usually "puff" (i.e., inflate the value of the case) if I want to settle the case, and I make the D.A. think his case is not as good as he thought. And sometimes they come down. Sometimes I'll do things like "Hey, my guy's got a great military record" or—sometimes I'll do my sentencing stuff—I'll say "Hey look at this medal of honor he has, look at this and that." Sometimes they'll buy into it and say "Yeah you're right. This isn't your average schlock."
>
> Steve:... Sometimes I might be able to get a little better deal on some type of charges than they originally offered. [An example of how you might do this?] Right now their offers on petty theft is $300 and ten days public service work. You have a client who has a clean record and he [stole] a shirt from Nordstroms. And you talk to your client and you find out he's got a job which requires a security clearance. You go to [the prosecutor] the first time and say "My client has a job which requires a security. Look at him, he's got a clean record. He admits he did it. It seems like he did it. But it's only a $20 shirt and it was an impulse type thing. Will you reduce it to a trespass?"
>
> [Interviewer: You said you know what a case is worth beforehand, then you go into the judge's chambers and talk to the D.A., and then the D.A. makes you an offer?] Kathy: Right. I go in and say "What's the offer on this case, Rick?" He tells me, and I usually respond "Geez Rick! You can give me something better than that!" And [then I] give the D.A. information about the client, information about the case—mitigating factors in essence. [For example?] The client has no record. The client is young. Actually—to be quite truthful—the client's white. [Actually?!] I do indeed. If I've got a young blonde kid out there, you think I'm not gonna tell the D.A. that I've got a young blonde kid out there? You better believe I do! [Wow!] I tell the D.A. "This kid's really middle-class." Or "This man's worked all his life and now after twenty years this whatever, this embezzlement happened", or y'know, "This woman was going through medical problems." Mitigating factors.

Because poor defendants are more likely to have prior records and because they are less likely to have jobs, educational credentials, acceptable networks of social support, and ultimately, promising futures (all of which can be seen as both a cause and a consequence of their poverty), their cases are likely to be worth less than those of other defendants for plea bargaining purposes. This means not only that they are more likely to be convicted of crimes, but also that they are prone to more serious convictions and, consequently, harsher sentences than other defendants.[14]

Conclusion: Commonsense "Class"ism *as well as* Racism and Sexism in the Adjudication of Criminal Cases

Not surprisingly, this study concludes that poor criminal suspects are more likely to be convicted of crimes, be convicted of more serious crimes and receive more severe sentences than other defendants. What may be surprising is the reason provided for such rates. It has been argued that these outcomes occur *not* because the poor are improperly represented by their attorneys or because the poor actually warrant such sanctions, but because circumstances associated with the defendants' social class enter into adjudication procedures and unduly tip the scales of justice against them. Specifically, because defenders are less able to portray their cases in a manner consistent with commonsense or (what is the same thing) status quo expectations, indigent defendants are more likely to be deemed noncredible and/or disreputable persons *regardless of* their actual moral proclivities or their actual innocence or guilt of specific crimes.

While commonsense reasoning in the adjudication of criminal cases can be seen to involve discrimination against the poor, it also appears to entail some sexism and racism. Regarding the first, the use of "common sense" in criminal court proceedings means that traditional or status quo standards pertaining to men and women underlie these proceedings and produce inequitable outcomes for men and women. Evidence for such a situation can be seen in Daly's (1987) findings regarding court officials' rationale for imposing different sentences on men and women and in Matoesian's (1995) study of the Kennedy Smith rape trial.

---

14. However, this does not necessarily mean that poor defendants are more likely to plea bargain. Instead, cases which have little or no value typically go to trial because such defendants have little or nothing to lose. Regardless, the outcome is the same.

According to Daly (1987), judges make distinctions not merely between familied and nonfamilied defendants, but between familied men and familied women. Defendants with families receive leniency when more severe penalties would result in suffering on part of innocent family members. Familied men, however, are treated more leniently when they are employed and supporting a family, and familied women are treated more leniently simply when they have children because the mother's childcare is deemed more important than the economic support they could provide. Herein we can see that the judges in this study made decisions on the basis of traditional (or commonsense) notions regarding men's and women's roles in our society, and thereby imposed inequitable sentences on them.

According to Matoesian (1995), defense attorneys in the Kennedy Smith rape trial attempted to impeach the victim (apparently successfully insofar as they won the case) by eliciting information that implied her behavior and background were inconsistent with the stereotype of male/female sexual relations. Like that employed by the judges in Daly's (1987) study, this image consisted of traditional (or commonsense) expectations regarding "appropriate" sexual conduct for men and women in our society. That prosecutors did not attempt to impeach the defendant with some type of similar tactic (i.e., by attempting to establish that his behavior was inconsistent with *some other* ideal of male/female sexual relations) suggests further that the trial stratagems of both types of attorneys were circumscribed by their shared expectations concerning the jury's traditional *or commonsense* understandings of "appropriate" sexual conduct for men and women.

Both types of the commonsense discrimination described above can be seen to effect some minority groups a great deal more than the dominant group due to a minority group's overrepresentation in poverty rates.[15] However, there are also indications in this study that minority groups encounter some discrimination beyond that based on class and gender. This is revealed in the foregoing analysis by four defenders' explicit references to race as an important variable in predicting adjudicative outcomes. The data suggests that racial and ethnic minorities encounter additional disadvantages in the adjudication of criminal cases due to cultural practices and experiences which distinguish them from the dominant white group, and which make it more difficult to portray their cases in a manner which complies with the cultural views of the status quo, or, common sense. This appears to occur in two major ways.

15. See Walker, Spohn and Delone (1996) for an overview of these rates in conjunction with related crime statistics.

First, some discrimination is associated with the use of categories which designate membership in particular racial or ethnic groups. While conceding that their use is sometimes beneficial, these categories nonetheless stereotype people and indicate that some are "different" from others. When people are perceived as "different", they are also regarded as somewhat unfamiliar and therefore seem a bit more fearsome and morally suspect than others. Such perceptions are perhaps most apparent in Kathy's contention that asserting a defendant is white during plea bargaining has a moderating influence; i.e., this characterization portrays the defendant as a more familiar and appealing person than other types to those in positions of authority.

Second, and perhaps most importantly, due to their different experiences of the social order, the dominant group cannot understand or appreciate fully situations of racial oppression in their own society. Enmeshed in their own largely segregated and relatively safe social worlds, for example, most whites in this country cannot actually fathom why contemporary minority groups proclaim discrimination, and find minority experiences of police exploitation especially difficult to believe. Thus, Karl and Betty, along with other defenders, acknowledge some complications in portraying the cases of their minority clients in a manner which is consistent, not simply with common sense, but with what is the same thing, the cultural understandings of the *white* status quo.

Overall then, the use of "common sense" in the adjudication of criminal cases does *not* imply that the legal system safeguards the *common* good. Instead, it means that the sensibilities of the powerful are sustained at the expense of less powerful groups.

References

American Bar Association. (1986). *Standards for Criminal Justice.* Second edition. Boston: Little, Brown and Company.

Beirne, P. and J. Messerschmidt. (1995). *Criminology,* Second edition. Orlando, FL: Harcourt Brace College Publishers.

Berger, P.L. and T. Luckmann. (1967). *The Social Construction of Reality.* New York: Doubleday & Co., Inc.

Blumer, H. (1978). "Society as Symbolic Interaction. Symbolic Interaction" in Jerome G. Manis and Bernard N. Meltzer, eds. Pps. 97–103. Boston: Allyn and Bacon, Inc.

Cicourel, A. (1968). *The Social Organization of Juvenile Justice.* New York: Crane, Russak & Company, Inc.

_______. (1974). *Cognitive Sociology.* New York: The Free Press.

Daly, K. (1987). "Structure and Practice of Familial-Based Justice in a Criminal Court," *Law and Society Review,* 21: 267.

Emmelman, D.S. (1993). "Organizational Conditions that Facilitate an Ethical Defense Posture Among Attorneys for the Poor: Observations of a Private Nonprofit Corporation," *Criminal Justice Review,* 18: 223.

_______. (1996). "Trial by Plea Bargain: Case Settlement as a Product of Recursive Decisionmaking." *Law and Society Review,* 30:2.

_______. (1997). "Gauging the Strength of Evidence Prior to Plea Bargaining: The Interpretive Procedures of Court-Appointed Defense Attorneys." *Law and Social Inquiry,* 22,4: 927–955.

Frohmann, L. (1991). "Discrediting Victims' Allegations of Sexual Assault: Prosecutorial Accounts of Case Rejections." *Social Problems,* 38: 2.

Garfinkel, H. (1967). *Studies in Ethnomethodology.* Englewood Cliffs: Prentice-Hall, Inc.

Geertz, C. (1983). *Local Knowledge: Further Essays in Interpretive Anthropology.* New York: Basic Books, Inc.

Glaser, B. and A. Strauss. (1967). *The Discovery of Grounded Theory.* Chicago: Aldine Publishing Co.

Gusfield, J.R. (1981). *The Culture of Public Problems.* Chicago: The University of Chicago Press.

Hermann, R., E. Single, and J. Boston. (1977). *Counsel for the Poor.* Lexington, Massachusetts: Lexington Books.

Holmes, M.D., H.C. Daudistel, and R.A. Farrell. (1987). "Determinants of Charge Reductions and Final Dispositions in Cases of Burglary and Robbery." *Journal of Research in Crime and Delinquency,* 24, 3, Aug., 233–254.

Heumann, M. (1975). "A Note on Plea Bargaining and Case Pressure." *Law and Society Review,* 9:515–528.

Lester, M. and S.C. Hadden. (1980). "Ethnomethodology and Grounded Theory Methodology: An Integration of Perspective and Method." *Urban Life,* 9, 1:3–33.

Manis, J.G. and B.N. Meltzer, eds. (1978). *Symbolic Interaction.* Boston: Allyn and Bacon, Inc.

Matoesian, G.M. (1995). "Language, Law, and Society: Policy Implications of the Kennedy Smith Rape Trial." *Law and Society Review,* 29:4

Mather, L.M. (1979). *Plea Bargaining or Trial?* Lexington, Mass.: Lexington Books.

McDonald, W.F. (1985). *Plea Bargaining: Critical Issues and Common Practices.* Washington, D.C.: U.S. Dept. of Justice.

McIntyre, L.J. (1987). *The Public Defender.* Chicago: The University of Chicago Press.

Mehan, H. and H. Wood. (1975). *The Reality of Ethnomethodology.* New York: John Wiley & Sons, Inc.

Neubauer, D.W. (1974). *Criminal Justice In Middle America.* Morristown, New Jersey: General Learning Press.

Reiman, J. (1998). *The Rich Get Richer and the Poor Get Prison.* Boston: Allyn & Bacon.

Reston, J., Jr. (1994). *Galileo.* New York: HarperPerennial.

Rosett, A. and D. Cressey. (1976). *Justice by Consent.* New York: J.B. Lippencott Company.

Sanger, W.W. (1974). *The History of Prostitution.* New York: AMS Press, Inc.

Schutz, A. (1962). *Collected Papers,* Volume I. Nigjoff: The Hague.

Stanko, E.A. (1981). "The Impact of Victim Assessment on Prosecutors' Screening Decisions: The Case of the New York County District Attorney's Office." *Law and Society Review,* 16:2.

Swigert, V.L. and R.A. Farrell. (1977). "Normal Homicides and the Law". *American Sociological Review,* 42, 1, Feb., 16–32.

Walker, S., C. Spohn and M. Delone. (1996). *The Color of Justice: Race, Ethnicity and Crime in America.* Boston: Wadsworth Publishing Co.

Weber, M. (1958). *The Protestant Ethic and the Spirit of Capitalism.* Introduction by Anthony Giddens. New York: Charles Scribner's Sons.

_______. (1979). *From Max Weber: Essays in Sociology.* Translated, edited and with an introduction by H.H. Gerth and C. Wright Mills. New York: Oxford University Press.

Webster's New Collegiate Dictionary. (1976). Springfield, MA: G. & C. Merriam Company.

Wice, P.B. (1985). *Chaos in the Courthouse.* New York: Praeger Publishers.

Wiseman, J.P. (1979). *Stations of the Lost.* Chicago: The University of Chicago Press.

"The Feminization of Poverty in Rural Kentucky: Creating Crime and Excessive Social Control"

Rebecca S. Katz,
Morehead State University

Amy Kelley,
Morehead State University

Introduction

A variety of research supports that gender discrimination, in the arrest, sentencing, and incarceration of women exists especially with regard to a women's class and race membership (Crawford, 2000; Spohn and Holleran, 2000; Casey and Wiatrowski, 1996). We posit that gender discrimination in the criminal justice system is the result of a multitude of factors including the backlash against feminism or the backlash against the gains of white middle class women (increasing economic, social and political gains), and the feminization of poverty, particularly among women of color. This paper argues that excessive punishment reflects new efforts by the established white male criminal justice system to socially control women, especially women of color.

Race, Class and the History of Women's Criminal Justice System Processing

Across time and space, the response of the criminal justice system to women has varied. Messerschmidt explains the over-incarceration of women in the early 20th century as resulting from the backlash against the suffrage movement. Specifically, he states that the "roaring twenties" brought new social and sexual freedom to women which was perceived by the existing status quo as threatening (Messerschmidt, 1986). For example, Messerschmidt describes most incarcerations of young women as due to minor rule violations of traditional gendered norms, like staying out too late. Additionally, other young women were incarcerated as the result of the parents' inability to socially control their daughters at home. Thus, historically women and girls appear to be incarcerated not for crimes, but for the violations of gendered norms. Criminal justice system leniency towards women may be attributed to specific historical-periods in which the private social control of women was increasing, thereby decreasing the need for public methods of social control (Faith, 1993, Chesney-Lind, 1997; Miller, 1998). Support exists for this tenet that the gender, race, and class of women and all institutional methods of social control must be examined to explain women's increased poverty, mental hospitalization and imprisonment (Bridges and Beretta, 1994). Similarly, when women's mental institutionalization decreases, incarceration rates of women increase significantly. Moreover, white women are more likely to be medically diagnosed while women of color are more likely to be criminalized (Bridges and Beretta, 1994).

Another example of this effort at social control is reflected in more recent research revealing that young women have typically been arrested at much greater numbers for status offenses than young males. These status offenses include liquor law violations, running away, curfew violations, and loitering. Unfortunately, little research discusses the differential incarceration rates of adult men and women (Chesney-Lind, 1989; 1996; Messerschmidt, 1986; Casey and Wiatrowski, 1996; Spohn and Holleran, 2000; Crawford, 2000). For example, Crawford recently discovered that black women were significantly more likely to receive harsher sentencing for contexts in which the black white ratio was high, and violent crime and drug arrests were high. Both Messerschmidt's 1986 work (see above) and Medna Chesney-Lind's ongoing work on the history of the social control of girls and women in the criminal and juvenile justice system also reveal gender discrimination in incarceration rates. Chesney-Lind found that in Chicago, one-half of all delinquent girls and only one-fifth of all delinquent boys were sent to reformatories between 1899–1909 (Chesney-Lind, 1989). Similarly, Milwaukee saw twice as many girls as boys committed to training schools. Also in Memphis, females were twice as likely to be sent to training schools as boys (Chesney-Lind, 1989). Many of the girls appearing before family courts were charged with immorality or waywardness. These girls were more severely punished than boys who had committed similar offenses. However, other work exists which contradicts this evidence.

Specifically, some work reveals that female defendants are treated with more leniency than male defendants with regard to both sentencing and imprisonment (Steffensmeier; Kramer; Streifel, 1993). This lenient treatment is explained as having occurred through judicial paternalism, familial justice and the rehabilitative value of the female defendant (Daly, 1987; Steffensmeier, 1980). However, Steffensmeir's early work fails to include adequate controls for either race or class, thus his conclusions regarding lenient treatment may only exist for middle class women, or specifically, middle class white women. Other more recent research across three cities finds than young unemployed Black or Hispanic males are treated more harshly than other gender and racial groups, including women. In such cases, women appear to be the recipients of judicial leniency. Yet other work reveals that such leniency depends upon the specific type of crime committed. Some work notes that men are convicted at higher rates than women for crimes such as robbery and burglary while women are convicted at higher rates for crimes such as forgery and larceny. However, we believe what is most important to note about much of this empirical work, other than Crawford's recent work and Spohn and Hollerman's work, is the absence of a focus on the interaction of the class or race of the female defendant. Along a similar vein, other recent work which attempts to analyze gender similarities and differences in offending rates across cities using arrest data, although analyzing the effects of economic deprivation, treats race only as a control variable (Steffensmeir and Haynie, 2000). Furthermore, no independent variables are included that take into account the differential ratio of male to female economic deprivation, or macro level measures of patriarchy. Also, any work that simply attempts to account for gender differences by using official data ultimately avoids the issue of the social control of women through the feminization of poverty and criminal justice sanctioning, both of which are tools of oppression in a white privileged patriarchal society. We believe that when such measures are taken into account that the evidence will reveal a clear gender disparity in criminal justice sanctioning with regard to women of color and particularly poor women of color.

Simon and Landis's 1991 review of the literature reveals the existence of some of this gender disparity. Their review of Nagel and Weitzman's 1971 study of data from all fifty states notes that the work was designed to examine the existence of chivalry or paternalism within the criminal justice system. Nagel and Weitzman found that women who committed stereotypical female crimes, that is nonviolent offenses, were more likely to be treated leniently than similar male offenders. Unfortunately, race or class in this early work was not taken into account. Secondly, Nagel and Weitzman found that women who committed crimes of violence, were more likely to be severely punished not only for committing violence, but for transgressing notions of appropriate gender behavior (Simon and Landis, 1991). Simon and Landis also reviewed Debra Anthony's 1979 study of Judges, Angela Musolino's 1988 study of judges, and Simon and Sharma's 1979 study of Washington D.C. circuit court sentencing processes. All three area studies revealed that paternalism in dealing with female defendants existed, however controls for the race or class of the women were omitted from the analyses. Simon and Landis also noted a number of other studies from the late 1970s and early 1980s revealing no gender effects in criminal justice system processing. However, again, race or class was not taken into account in these studies. Finally, Simon and Landis discuss Kruttschnitt's (1980–82) and Kruttchnitt's (1976) studies revealing that socio-economic class acts to protect women from severe court sanctions (Simon and Landis, 1991, p. 62). Specifically, women who were economically successful, women who were economically dependent, or women already subject to high levels of informal social control were least likely to receive severe court sanctions. Similarly, middle and upper class males were also least likely to receive severe court sanctions. Thus, more thorough analyses that include socio-economic differences clearly reveal the existence of a class bias in our criminal justice system.

However, Simon and Landis's own analysis of sentencing in New York and Pennsylvania over a five-year period from the early 1980s to the late 1980s remains incomplete. They concluded that gender disparity did not exist in either state except for one or two offense types in which females were treated more leniently. Unfortunately, Simon and Landis failed to take into account the race and class of either men or women in their examination of this data. Similar work which also omitted the race and the class of the women, supports the thesis that chivalry and male paternalism do not exist, at least with regard to charge reduction of female defendants (Bishop and Frazier,1984). Moreover, Martha Myers classic work also found no evidence of judicial paternalism towards female offenders (Myers, 1988). Other research also failed to account for gender, race or class but found that pretrial release and bond decisions were highly influenced by the defendants courtroom demeanor (Frazier, Bock, and Henretta, 1980). Again, the main problem with this body of work is that information with regard to the race, class and sometimes gender of the individuals involved was omitted or used only as a control variable.

More sophisticated research exists which clarifies some of these early contradictory findings. For example, more comprehensive macro level work, which includes the analysis of race, gender, and class, is quite revealing. Martha Myers found that black offenders were at a disadvantage in counties with large black populations and high levels of racial inequality (Myers, 1987). But Myers work, like the more recent and highly sophisticated research of Spohn and Holleran, only controlled for gender (Myers, 1987; Spohn and Holleran, 2000). Myers found that while white males were more likely to be imprisoned than females, women were given longer prison sentences than males (Myers, 1987). Myers discovered that white victims were more valued than black victims and that defendants who were black, female, unmarried, unemployed or poor were at a particular disadvantage. Moreover, Vishur's research more explicitly identifies the relationship between gender and race with regard to the chivalry hypothesis. Vishur found that chivalrous treatment of female offenders by police only occurred among those who displayed "appropriate gender behaviors" or "white middle class submissive behavior" (Vishur, 1983:23). Additionally, Spohn and colleagues discovered that women and men of color were more likely to be fully prosecuted than white female defendants (Spohn, Gruhl, and Welch, 1987). Although more recently Spohn and Holleran found that unemployed black and Hispanic men were more harshly sentenced, gender remained only a control variable. However, other empirical work illustrates that black women, poor women and those with previous sentences were more likely to be given severe sentences than other women (Kruttschnitt, 1980). Moreover, chivalrous treatment or paternalism is bestowed only upon certain women who conform to white middle class gendered norms (Nagel and Johnson, 1994). Clearly, our statistical analyses must examine women separately rather than treat gender as a mere control variable.

The bulk of the more sophisticated research reveals that poor women of color are treated more harshly in the criminal justice system while benevolent paternalism is reserved for white middle class and upper class women. Unfortunately, other shortcomings of this more complex work also exists. Primarily this research failed to take into account the effect of motherhood on criminal justice system processing. However, Kathleen Daly examined the effect of the presence of children in women's lives with regard to sentencing outcome. Daly argued that women with children were treated more leniently. Apparently actors within the criminal justice system used what she referred to as the familial based justice theory in order to avoid doing one of the following: 1) break up families because it would not be in the interest of the social order or 2) protect the innocent, in essence the family members, while punishing the guilty (Daly, 1987). Daly claims that familial based justice favors the woman because women are the ones responsible for the children and the home. Kathleen Daly states "...as long as women have primary responsibility for childcare and asymmetries remain in state supports for father and mother surrogates, we might expect that differences in the treatment of familied men and women will continue." While Daly's familial based justice model on the surface, appears to support the benevolent paternalism hypothesis, it only perpetuates the attitude that women were to conform to specific gender roles i.e., "good mothering" and were not to deviate from them in any way. Daly found some support for her model after querying court officials. Apparently, such leniency in sentencing revolved around the court's concern about locking up women who were singularly responsible for children (Daly, 1989 p.170).

However, there is increasing evidence that such official concern, if it once existed, has disappeared in the 1990s (Casey and Wiatrowski, 1996). As of 1991, 67% of women in state prisons had children under the age of eighteen and 72% of these women were living with their child before entering prison (Miller, 1998, p. 10). In 1994, 75% of the women in prison were the sole caretakers of their children prior to being incarcerated (Casey and Wiatrowski, 1996). Further, these women were much more likely than men to be incarcerated for non-serious or non-violent crimes. Also, black women were more likely to be incarcerated than both white women and black men, particularly for drug related crimes (Rush-Baskette, 1998; Casey and Wistrowski, 1996). Black women also represent a higher proportion of the prison population than do black men. In general, both white and nonwhite women are more likely to be incarcerated for nonviolent property offenses or drug offenses than white or nonwhite men (Bush-Baskette, 2000). Thus, the familial based model, if it once existed as described by Daly, may now only exist to make statements that women defendants' children must be protected from her; so let's lock her up, especially if she is poor.

The "feminization of poverty" and the "war on drugs" have disproportionately effected the imprisonment of poor women and women of color (Baskin and Sommers, 1998; Miller, 1998; Chesney-Lind, 1997; Faith, 1993; Hannon and DeFronzo, 1998). African-American women are more likely than white women to be convicted and to receive a longer prison sentence. Additionally, sentencing outcomes are less severe for white middle to upper class females, but such "benevolent paternalism" is absent for similarly classed women of color (Gilbert, 2001). Also African-American mothers are treated more harshly at sentencing than white mothers. These racial and gender disproportionalities in the criminal justice system in America have prevailed throughout history well into the present day (Gottfredson and Jarjoura, 1996; Shelden, 2001).

These differential sentencing practices with regard to specific racial and class membership are the result of a multitude of factors. We believe these factors include the personal prejudice of judges, larger macro level patriarchal forces that limit women's economic and political freedom, women's failure to conform to gendered norms, the feminization of poverty, and the backlash against some women's increasing economic, social and political power. Further, these processes are facilitated by recent changes in state sentencing statutes which legislate unfair treatment (Casey and Wiatrowski, 1996). For example, the "War on Drugs" mandates lengthy incarceration, particularly for "crack" related offenses, the drug of the poor, versus the cocaine-related offenses, the drug of the rich. Additionally, illicit drug economies have grown as the result of advanced capitalism (Baskin and Sommers, 1998; Pettiway, 1997). That is as major industrial employers abandoned the inner city for the suburbs or for more lucrative markets (cheap labor) abroad, fewer legitimate inner city jobs were available. Both critical theorists and qualitative researchers posit that such places become sites of extreme hopelessness and despair lending itself to the development of addiction or the pursuit of the American dream through illegitimate economies (Bohm, 1998; Anderson, 1997; Messner and Rosenfeld, 1994; Flavin, 1998). Furthermore, inner city poor women, who are disproportionately minority members, are being compelled to participate in the illicit drug economies as more and more inner city men are incarcerated as the result of the "war on drugs". (Baskin and Sommers, 1998; Mayer, 1996; Casey and Wiatrowski, 1996). Additionally, most of these women are also drug addicts themselves and sometimes are forced to engage in prostitution in order to support their addiction. In one study of three Pennsylvania counties, Rich, Metro and Southwest, researchers found that arrest, sentencing, and incarceration of women varied considerably by county and was predicted by increased rates of poverty. Women's arrests and convictions were lower in Rich County than in Metro and Southwest counties. Greater proportions of females in Metro and Southwest were charged with drug offenses. Clearly, more arrests for drug charges would act to increase the incarceration rate as the result of the new mandatory terms for drug sales or possession. These harsher guidelines restrict the judge's discretion but also force judges to provide determinate prison sentences in cases where drug or alcohol treatment or referral to the new drug courts may have been more efficacious and less costly (Johnson, Formichella, and Bowers, 1999).

The final problem with most of the research is that it has failed to explore these issues with regard to rural areas. Few criminologists explore rural crime and criminal justice and those who do appear to avoid discussions with regard to the increasing incarceration rates of women. Our goal is fill the gap in this area by exploring these issues in a primarily rural state. However, before review of our methodology, it is important to briefly identify some of the unique issues faced in rural parts of the country that we believe may contribute to the gender disparity in conviction rates.

Rural Criminal Justice and Rural Crime

Ralph Weisheit's research on marijuana production in rural Appalachia describes economic powerlessness as one of the primary motives for growing marijuana. Weisheit explains that rural, non-metropolitan poverty rates are generally higher than urban poverty rates, as is unemployment and the average mother's length of time on AFDC (more than six years) (Weisheit, Wells and Falcone, 1995). Drug cultivation appears to be a method of surviving economically in a place exploited by outsiders from the North. We believe that the exploitation of this area by northern industrialists also warrants the social control of locals through their criminalization or through the maintenance of poor wages, other types of worker exploitation and high levels of poverty. This exploitation of indigenous peoples is illustrated in ecological research revealing that waste dumps, landfills, smelters, factories, chemical plants and oil refineries are most likely to be located near the urban and rural poor, and communities of people of color (Bullard, 1994). This leaves those residents as the most likely to suffer from the effects of such toxins.

America's advanced form of industrial capitalism has led many corporations to move abroad and take advantage of the waning anti-imperialist movements in third world nations. In America, one result has been an increase in service sector employees. These workers are the lowest paid employees in our society. Many women in rural Kentucky counties are employed in part-time service sector work in which they have few benefits and are perhaps not even earning minimum wages. One method of insuring greater control of the rural population, in addition to poor wages, is to increase the passage of the laws favoring the wealthy and to provide more resources to law enforcement personnel to watch over the poor and working classes. A variety of studies have supported the idea that increased police presence or expenditures results in an increase in crime with few if any deterrent effects. Thus, increasing police presence simply results in more control of the workers who have been most recently laid off by the capitalists. Other classic research revealed that areas characterized by higher levels of inequality were more likely to have additional police and other law enforcement personnel, thus providing increased social control for the elites and the state.

The use of law enforcement and wage limits as methods of social control often coincide with the exploitation of the worker and his or her natural environment (Colvin, and Pauly, 1983; Manning, 1994; Mohiker, 1988). While many workers are underpaid for their labor, some geographic portions of the country more likely to suffer from environmental exploitation. These are typically areas populated by the urban and rural poor and people of color. For example, according to Weisheit et al., U.S. government estimates reveal that there are over sixteen-thousand active landfills containing hazardous wastes in rural areas which, according to the EPA, will eventually breach and penetrate the soil. Poor rural areas contain thousands of landfills and ground storage sites which are contaminated and leaking. Other social scientists refer to this process in which elite outsiders (in the case of Kentucky, wealthy capitalists from the North) exploit the geographic and cultural capital of indigenous peoples, as the process of "colonization". This also leads to the development of the false consciousness or what Patricia Hill Collins refers to as the "othering" of specific groups of people, like blacks and Native Americans. Historical criminological analysis also reveals a similar pattern with regard to the social control of ethnic minority groups. One of the first culprits in this colonizing process and the resultant pollution in rural Kentucky has been the coal mining industry. The coal industry has been one of the chief employers and exploiters of many Kentucky families for a number of generations. Thus, although coal mining violations have decreased since 1988, violations of performance standards, non-compliance with the law, cessation orders issued, and imminent harm cessation orders issued, still accounted for 4,364 violations of the federal law in 1993. Citizen complaints regarding coal mining activities in the state from 1982 through 1993 ranged from a high of approximately 1,400 in 1992, to a low of approximately 900 in 1988. A majority of these complaints originate in Eastern Kentucky. However, only about ten percent of complaints result in enforcement action. In addition to the coal mines' role in the production of environmental toxins, a variety of other industries are also responsible for the release of toxins into the water or air in Kentucky.

Although toxins released by industries in Kentucky declined from 1988 to 1992, there has been a steady increase since then. Kentucky was ranked fifteenth in the nation in the total amount of toxins released into the environment by industry in 1992. Likewise, across the nation, the EPA (Environmental Protection Agency) reported that criminal enforcement cases increased from 1994 to 1995 with 256 of an initial 562 cases being referred to the Department of Justice. In Kentucky the number of violations grew 183 percent from 1984 to 1993 as inspections of facilities increased by seventy-five percent during that time. Ten facilities in 1992 accounted for most of the toxins released into the state. One of these toxins, that has received substantial media attention, is lead. Monitoring of lead levels in children's blood between 1992 and 1994 reflected that lead levels were specifically linked to health problems. Most of the toxins were released into the air with some of these including sulfur dioxide from coal-fired electricity. Furthermore, in 1993, over three-thousand toxic spills were reported in the state of Kentucky. Interestingly, ten facilities were primarily responsible for generating approximately thirty-five percent of the total toxins released in 1992. Many of these chemicals have been determined to be carcinogenic. These toxins are produced by over three-thousand regulated air pollutant sources in Kentucky.

Readers may wonder why environmental pollution and the exploitation of coal and coal miners are important with regard to the identification of gender disparity in conviction. Many families have lost or suffered an incapacitated father (a primary wage earner in many Kentucky families) as the result of working in these mines. Consequently, mothers and wives are forced into the paid labor market out of necessity. These women are underemployed, exploited and underpaid. As this form of social control weakens, criminalization may be the result. This poverty is related to the early and continuing exploitation of Kentucky and its peoples, or what Patricia Hill Collins (1991) refers to as the colonization and othering of the locals, especially women. This colonization is evident when examining a 1983 study by the Appalachian Land Ownership Task Force which found that in eighty Appalachian counties across six states, only one percent of the local population controlled about fifty-three percent of the land surface. Further, of the twenty million acres of land and minerals owned by 30,000 people, fifty private owners and ten government agencies held forty-one percent of this land. Forty-six of the fifty private owners were corporations, most of them nationally known.

Finally, it is important to note that while there are more married couple households both white and black than there are single heads of households, there are also more female headed households in Kentucky than male headed among both blacks and whites. Moreover, Kentucky is predominately white with over 3 million white Americans and only 262 thousand black Americans. In terms of males and females in the labor force, 80,000 white males are in the paid civilian labor force compared to 65,000 white females. Conversely, there are more black females in the labor force than black males, 49,000 compared to 43,000. Additionally, there are over one million households on public assistance across the state. Thirty thousand white female heads of household are living under the poverty level compared to seven thousand white male heads of households. Additionally, almost ninety thousand white married couple households with children live under the poverty line. Among African Americans there are four thousand married couples living under the poverty line, while fourteen thousand African American single female heads of household live under the poverty line and one thousand African American male heads of household live under the poverty line. Clearly, a rural underclass exists among many family types across Kentucky with single female black and white households proportionately more likely to be living in poverty than single male heads of households.

Methods/Hypotheses

We anticipate that indicators of the feminization of poverty and capitalist exploitation of Kentucky counties will increase the likelihood that white and black women will be convicted across Kentucky counties. While we expect that capitalist exploitation will increase the likelihood of convictions for white and black men, we anticipate that the feminization of poverty will have no effect on the likelihood of white and black male convictions. Moreover, we expect that an increase in the black to white ratio of the population will positively affect the rate of black male and female convictions while having no effect on white convictions.

Dependent Variables

The Kentucky office for the administration of the courts provided conviction data on females and males across Kentucky counties for 1995. Conviction data was separated by race (black and white only) for which separate regression analyses were conducted. Across Kentucky counties, most convictions of females were of white females. One hundred and three Kentucky counties convicted no black females; however, fifty-nine Kentucky counties also convicted no white females. Across Kentucky counties one to one hundred and twelve white females were convicted in 1995. One to seventy-three black females were convicted across Kentucky counties in 1995. Unfortunately, nineteen percent of Kentucky counties convicted a person for whom neither gender nor race was recorded. Also, three percent of Kentucky counties had no information about the race of females who were convicted. Therefore, the analysis is restricted to counties where the race and gender of the convicted person is known.

Table 1. Dependent and Independent Variables

120 Kentucky Counties	
White Females Convicted 1995	**Frequencies**
5=Five or more convicted	16%
4=Four convicted	6%
3=Three convicted	2%
2=Two convicted	13%
1=One convicted	12%
0=None convicted	50%
Black Females Convicted 1995	
4=Seven to seventy-three convicted	6%
3=Three convicted	2%
2=two convicted	2%
1=one convicted	2%
0=None convicted	85%
Black Males Convicted 1995	
4=Thirty to forty-five convicted	5.8%
3=Seventeen to twenty-nine convicted	1.7%
2=Three to ten convicted	4.2%
1=One convicted	8.3%
0=None convicted	80%

White Males Convicted 1995	
4=Thirteen to one-hundred and fifty-three convicted	13.3%
3=Six to twelve convicted	14.2%
2=Two to five convicted	15.0%
1=One Convicted	19.2%
0=None Convicted	38.3%

Nineteen percent of Kentucky Counties did not record the race or gender of the convicted individual. Three percent of counties did not collect information on the race of the female.

Table 1 (continued). Coding for Independent Variables

Appalachian counties	Frequencies	
1=Appalachian county-Forty-nine counties are considered Appalachian counties.		
0=Non-applachian county		
Number of Police in each County 1990		
1=1–5	18.3%	
2=6–10	24.8%	
3=11–20	25.8%	
4=21–30	10%	
5=31–724	14.2%	
Tonnage of Coal Produced by County 1993		
	Recoded Values	**Frequencies**
0=0 tons	0	73%
1=1000–999,999 tons	1	10.8%
2=1 million to 9,999,999 million tons	1	10%
3=10 million to 34 million tons	1	5.8%
Toxic Air Emissions 1992		
	Recoded Values	**Frequencies**
0=0	0	45.8%
1=1,000–9,999	1	10%
2=10,000–99,999	1	15%
3=100,000–999,999	1	18%
4=1 million to 11 tons	1	6%

Table one illustrates the coding for both the dependent and independent variables. The number of white females convicted was coded from one to five. Counties having convicted five or more white females were coded as fives while one through four represented that specific number of convictions of white females. Fifty percent of the counties convicted no white females, twelve percent convicted one white female, thirteen percent convicted two, two percent convicted three, six percent convicted four white females and sixteen percent of the counties convicted five or more white females. Eighty-five percent of the counties convicted no black females, five percent convicted one, two percent convicted two, two percent convicted three and approximately six percent convicted seven or more black females. Counties were coded from zero to four with zero representing no convictions of black females, one representing one black female conviction, two representing two black females convicted, three, three black females convicted and four representing counties convicting from seven to seventy-three black females. We respectively compare white and black female convictions to white male convictions and black male convictions across Kentucky counties. Our hypotheses can only realistically be tested if we compare the macro level predictors of male versus female convictions between both blacks and whites. The 1995 convictions of white males across Kentucky counties range from none to one hundred and fifty-three. Moreover, thirty-eight percent of counties convicted no white males in 1995. Similar to the findings regarding the conviction of black females, eighty percent of Kentucky counties convicted no black males, while the remaining counties convicted one to forty-five black males. Convictions of white males were recoded such that counties convicting one male (nineteen percent of all counties) were coded as ones. Those counties convicting two to five white males were coded as twos. Convictions from six to twelve males were coded as threes and counties convicting thirteen to one hundred and fifty-three males were coded as fours. Kentucky counties convicted one to forty-five black males in 1995. However, eighty percent of Kentucky counties convicted no black males. Black male convictions were coded from zero to four. Zero indicates no black males were convicted, one represents one black male convicted, two represents three to ten black males convicted, three represents seventeen to twenty-nine black males convicted and four, thirty to forty-five black males convicted.

Independent Variables

Kentucky has one hundred and twenty counties, forty-nine of which have been federally designated as Appalachian counties. Most of these forty-nine counties are in the Eastern part of the state. Accounting for the Appalachian status of each of the counties is important as a variety of research points out that it is the Appalachian counties that are more rural and poor, as well as most likely to have been exploited by outside interests. Thus, including whether or not a Kentucky county is an Appalachian county is necessitated. Appalachian counties are coded as ones and all others were coded as zeros. It is also important to take into account available local law enforcement personnel within each county. The more police available in an area or the more available funds expended on increased police presence could artificially push up the crime rate. Thus, police within each county employed at the county and city level were taken into account in 1990. In 1990, forty percent of Kentucky counties contained ten or fewer local law enforcement officers, while twenty percent had between eleven and thirty officers. Only four counties contained one hundred or more police officers in 1990. Thus, coding for this indicator ranges from one to six, with one representing counties with one to five officers, two, representing counties with six to ten officers, three, indicating eleven to twenty officers, four, reflecting twenty-one to thirty officers, five, thirty-one to sixty officers and six, reflecting counties with sixty-one to seven hundred and sixty four officers.

In order to take into account both capitalist exploitation of the area and patriarchal methods of social control of women, we selected a variety of independent variables which reflect those processes. Three indicators represent the colonization of Kentucky and exploitation of Kentuckians or the purchase of land by northern interests to exploit the region's natural resources as well as its' people. These include the tons of coal produced by county in 1993, the industrial toxic air emissions by county in 1992, and industrial toxins released or transferred to waste water or streams in 1992. The first indicator of colonization or coal tons produced was gathered from the Kentucky Environmental Quality Commission which collects it's data from the Kentucky Geologic Survey. The geologic survey reviewed the top coal producing counties in Kentucky in 1993. This data was recoded such that the top tonnage produced by county from ten million to thirty-four million were coded as three's, one million to nine million were coded as two's, and one thousand to nine-hundred and ninety-nine thousand were coded as one's, and the remainder of counties were coded as zero's with no or minimal production of coal. This measure of toxic releases and transfers from reporting sources in 1992 was dichotomously coded such that nine thousand nine-hundred and ninety-nine pounds to eleven million pounds of air emissions was coded as one and the fifty-five counties without any toxic air emissions recorded were coded as zero's.

An additional measure reflects the top fifteen counties having companies that generate, release, distribute, recycle or recover the most toxic chemicals released into streams or municipal wastewater treatment plants in Kentucky. Each of the fifteen counties was coded with a one and all other counties were coded with a zero. We believe we have accounted for the pollution of the environment and thus, have tapped in to some extent the degree to which Kentucky county residents are exploited by major industries. But we still do not have a good indicator of the results of capitalism or economic inequality and direct physical harm done to Kentucky county residents. Therefore, we selected the number of occupational injuries, both fatal and non-fatal, from 1995 as an indicator of the manner by which industry exploitation immediately affects Kentucky county residents. We realize that not all of these injuries may be the result of safety violations or improper working conditions but we think it remains a viable indicator of the manner by which the working class and the working poor people are used to meet the needs of capitalists. Occupational injuries per county ranged from four to nine-thousand two hundred and ten. These values were recoded from one to six with higher numbers representing a higher incidence of occupational injuries. The family poverty rate and unemployment are viewed as indicators of the economic exploitation and "thingification" of indigenous peoples. These include the family poverty rate computed for each county in 1989 and the county unemployment rate as measured in 1991. The percentage of families within each county living under the poverty level is coded from one to five with higher numbers representing a higher incidence of family poverty. In 1989, forty percent of Kentucky counties contained twenty to forty-six percent of families who were living under the poverty guidelines. Another indicator of family poverty was utilized for the analysis; this is the number of families receiving public assistance in 1990. The final indicator of economic exploitation, is the county unemployment rate in 1991. This variable is coded from one to four with higher numbers indicating more unemployed county residents. In 1991, thirty-two percent of Kentucky counties had alarmingly excessive unemployment rates from ten percent to twenty-two percent.

To measure the patriarchal social control of women and the feminization of poverty we utilize several other indicators. Black female heads of household, and white female heads of household are respectively included in the analysis of black female and black male convictions, while white female heads of household is included in regressions of white female and white male convictions. The number of white female heads of household varied from 33 to 13,715. These were recoded from one to six with higher codes representing more single female heads of household. Black female heads of household ranged from none to 11, 093. These were recoded from 0 to 5 with higher codes indicating more single mothers. The number of females working part-time is another indicator of the feminization of poverty. These are respectively included in both regressions on white female and black female convictions. Females working part time ranged from 141 to 180,382 across Kentucky counties. These numbers were recoded from 1 to 7 with higher codes reflecting more part-time female employees. The number of black females over 16 working and the number of white females over 16 working for pay are also included in the analysis of black female convictions and white female convictions. The number of white females with jobs across Kentucky counties ranged from 351 to 125,878. These scores were recoded from 1 to 7, again with higher codes reflecting more females working for pay. Black females over 16 working for pay ranged from none to 23,551. These were recoded from 0 to 5 with higher codes reflecting more black females working. The number of households in each county receiving public assistance was also included in the analyses, ranging from 121 households to 19,488 households. These were recoded from 1 to 6, with higher codes reflecting more households receiving public assistance. One ratio of the total number of black individuals divided by the total number of whites within each county was also developed to be included as an independent variable in the convictions of both black females and black males. We also developed a second indicator of this attempt to measure the threat hypothesis by developing a second ratio of the total number of minority people (except those of unknown race or ethnicity) divided by the total number of whites. This data will be used separately in the models explaining black female convictions and black male convictions.

Results

First order correlation coefficients reflected that several indicators were multicolinear. Unemployment and family poverty were co-linear (r=.604). Therefore, only family poverty was used in the regression analyses. Secondly, white female heads of household was co-linear with the number of households receiving public assistance (r=. 757). Factor analysis revealed that both homes receiving public assistance and white female heads of household loaded onto one dimension (factor loading .937) and had consistent internal validity (alpha. 800). The index was the result of the summing of both recoded indicators resulting in scores from 2 to 11. These values were then recoded from one to ten with higher scores representing the increased feminization of poverty among white women. Finally, females working part time, white females working, black females working and female heads of household for both black women and white women were also multicolinear. Moreover, both black female heads of households and black females working part time were multicolinear with the black to white population ratio. Therefore, black female heads of households and black females working part time were omitted from the analysis. Similarly, females working part-time were also dropped from the analysis of white females convicted. Appalachian county designations were multicolinear with family poverty (r.=.721) thus only family poverty was included in the regression models. Occupational injuries per county in 1995 was multicolinear with the white female poverty index, the number of police in each county and the number of homes receiving public assistance. Therefore, separate models were analyzed by including occupational injuries in one model while omitting the number of police in each county and number of homes receiving public assistance. Conversely, separate models were analyzed by including the number of police in each county and the homes receiving public assistance while omitting occupational injuries and then reversing that process in the second model.

Regression Analyses

Table 2. Independent Variables

Toxic Releases or Transfers 1992

Coding	**Frequencies**
0=0	87.5%
1=1–8 Top fifteen counties	12.5%
originally coded from one to eight (see below)	

Number of Companies located in 15 Counties that are most likely to release chemicals into Municipal Waist Water or Streams

Jefferson County=8
Carroll=1
Boyd=4
Marshall=5
Madison=1
Scott=1
Hardin=1
Woodford=1
Logan=1
Hancock=1
Simpson=1
Greenup=1
Washington=1
Fayette=1

Number Occupational Injuries Fatal and Nonfatal by county 1995

1=4–49	12.5%
2=51–95	20.0%
3=101–193	23.7%
4=200–344	16.7%
5=434–692	13.3%
6=711–9210	12.5%

Percent of Families in Poverty by county 1989

1=5–10 Percent	9.2%
2=10.2–15 Percent	30.8%
3=15.5–20.00 percent	19.2%
4=20.2–29.7 percent	24.2%
5=30.5–46.8 percent	15.8%

White Female Heads of Household with Children

5=1096–13715	22.5%
4=481–1095	15.8%
3=303–480	15.0%
2=186–302	31.7%
1=33–185	15.0%

Black Female Heads of Household with Children

5=248–11,093	7.5%
4=74–247	19.2%
3=33–76	17.5%
2=7–32	18.3%
1=1–6	17.5%
0=0	

Households Receiving Public Assistance

6=1948–19,488	13.3%
5=966–1947	20.0%
4=776–965	18.3%
3=574–775	13.3%
2=291–573	23.3%
1=121–290	11.7%

White Female Poverty Scale

(Combination of Homes on Public Assistance & Female Heads of Household)

10=11
9=10
8=9
7=8
6=7
5=6
4=5
3=4
2=3
1=2

Black to White Ratio

(Total Blacks in each County divided by Total Whites)

.00 to .34	In 25% of Kentucky counties this ratio is zero. In 12.5% of Kentucky counties the ratio is from .10 to .34.

Table 2. Regression Models for Male/Female Convictions Across Kentucky Counties

Independent Variable	White Females Convicted	Black Females Convicted	White Males Convicted	Black Males Convicted
Model One				
White Female Poverty Scale	.377**		.328*	
Toxic Air Pollution			.209*	
Blacks/white Ratio		.346**		.524**
Model One				
Homes on Public Aid For Blacks				.274*
Families Living under Poverty 1989			-.202+	
Model Two				
Occupational Injuries			.397**	.200**
Adjusted R Squared	.164**	.212*	.190**	.380**
Constant	.506	-.177	.744	-8.689

+=p=.06–.10
*=p=.002–.05
**=p=.000–.001

Table 2 illustrates the results of the regression of on each of the four models of white females convicted, black females convicted, white males convicted, and black males convicted across Kentucky counties. Only standardized and significant effects are illustrated in the table. In the model for white females, about sixteen percent of the variance is explained and only one indicator approaches significance. The feminization of poverty increased the likelihood that white women will be convicted (p=<.000). Including occupational injuries in the second model increased the explained variance to thirty-one percent and led the black and white population ratio to approach significance (p=<.102) (not shown in table). Using the initial model (excluding occupational injuries) for white males convicted across Kentucky counties, two of the indicators were significant predictors. The toxic air emissions released by Kentucky industries significantly increased the likelihood that white males would be convicted (p=<.036). The white feminization of poverty index also predicted higher white male incarceration rates (p=<022). Finally, the percentage of families living under the poverty line approached significance (p=<.087) but decreased the likelihood that white males would be convicted. The second model, which included occupational injuries (not shown), increased the explained variance to thirty-three percent and decreased the effect of toxic air emissions while the effect of occupational injuries significantly increased white male incarcerations (p=<.000). Both of these models clearly support and contradict the primary hypotheses. Although contrary to expectations, the feminization of poverty increased both white male and female incarceration rates.

The initial model (without occupational injuries) used to explain black female convictions was poor and contained only one effect that approached significance (not in table). The black/white ratio slightly increased black female convictions (p=<.100). However, the second model including occupational injuries, was an improved model that explained twenty-one percent of the variance in black female convictions across Kentucky counties. Consistent with our predictions, the presence of greater numbers of blacks relative to whites across Kentucky counties significantly increased black female conviction rates (p=<.000). Similarly, in the initial model used to explain black males convicted the black/white ratio significantly increased the likelihood that black males would be incarcerated (p=<.000). In this model, approximately twenty-one percent of the variance was explained in predicting county level convictions of black males (p=<.000). Also, the number of families receiving welfare assistance also significantly increased male conviction rates (p=<.027). Finally, families living under poverty decreased black male conviction rates but only approached significance (p=<.085). In the second model for black males, two indicators significantly increased black male conviction rates. These included occupational injuries (p=<.032) (see Table 2) and the black to white population ratio (p=<.000). In this model, thirty-eight percent of the variance was explained.

Discussion

This research supports empirical work which separates the study of criminal justice system processes by the race, gender and class of those individuals subjected to this type of social control. Clearly, both white and black males are more subjected to criminal justice system control as the result of capitalist exploitation and the subsequent poverty that ensues. However, among both black males and females, the threat hypothesis also operates by increasing their conviction rates as they become a larger percentage of the population relative to whites. Finally, among white women, being poor translates into a greater likelihood of conviction. We argue that the impact that the system has on poor women and minorities clearly violates the 8th amendment to the constitution and our equal protection laws. Thus, both policy makers and the public must be made aware of the disparate impact with which the criminal justice exerts on both poor women and minority populations. Such awareness should lead to the creation of an equitable system of justice, such as restorative justice and social policies that prevent poverty and the capitalist exploitation of workers.

References

Appalachian Land Ownership Task Force. (1983). *Who Owns Appalachia? Land Ownership and its Impact. Kentucky:*The University Press.

Anderson, E. (1997). "Violence and the Inner-City Street Code." *Violence and Childhood in the Inner City*. McCord, J. (Ed). Cambridge:University Press.

Baskin, Deborah R., and Sommers, Ira B. (1998). *Casualties of Community Disorder: Women's Careers in Violent Crime (Crime and Society Series).* Westview Press

Bishop, D.H., & Frazier, C. (1984). The Effects of Gender on Charge Reduction. *The Sociological Quarterly*, 25, 385–396.

Black, Donald. (1976). *The Behavior of Law.* New York: Academic Press

Bridges, George S. and Beretta, Gina. (1994). Gender, Race, and Social Control: Toward an Understanding of Sex Disparities in Imprisonment. In George S. Bridges and Martha A. Myers (Eds.), *Inequalitiy, Crime, and Social Control.* Chapter 10.

Bullard, R.D. (Ed). (1994). *Unequal Protection-Environmental Justice and Communities of Color.* San Francisco: Sierra Club Books.

Casey, K. A. & Wiatrowski, D. M. (1996). Women Offenders and Three Strikes and You're Out. In Schichor, D. & Sechrest, D.K (Eds.) *Three Strikes and You're Out Vengeance as Public Policy.* Sage Publications.

Chesney-Lind, M. (1997). The Female Offender Girls, Women and Crime. *Women and the Criminal Justice System.* Sage Publications.

Chesney-Lind, M. (1989). Girls' Crime and Woman's Place: Toward a Feminist Model of Female Delinquency. *Crime and Delinquency*, 35:1, 5–29.

Cole, L.A., Pauley, P., Richards, S., & Nye, P. (1995). Kentucky Environmental Quality Commission. *State of Kentucky's Environment: 1994 Status Report*

Collins, P.H. (1991). *Black Feminist Thought: Knowledge, Consciousness, and the Politics of Empowerment.* New York: Routledge.

Colvin, M. & Pauly, J. (1983). A Critique of Criminology: Toward an Integrated Structural-Marxist Theory of Delinquency Production. *American Journal of Sociology*, 89, 513–531.

Crawford, C. (2000). Gender, Race, and Habitual Offender Sentencing in Florida. *Criminology*, 38:1, 263–280.

Daly, K. (1987). Discrimination in the Criminal Courts: Family, Gender, and the Problem of Equal Treatment *Social Forces*, 66:1, 152–175

Daly, K. (1989). Neither Conflict Nor Labeling Nor Paternalism Will Suffice: Intersections of Race, Ethnicity, Gender, and Family in Criminal Court Decisions. *Crime and Delinquency*, 35:1, 136–168

Faith, Karlene. (1993). *Unruly Women: The Politics of Confinement and Resistance.* Press Gang Publishers

Flavin, J. (1998). Razing the Wall: A Feminist Critique of Sentencing Theory, Research and Policy. *Cutting the Edge, Current Perspectives in Radical/Critical Criminology and Criminal Justice*, Ross, J.I. (Ed.).

Frazier, C.E., Bock, E., Wilbur, H., and Henretta, John C. Pretrial release and bail decisions. *Criminology*, 18, 162–181.

Gottfredson, S.D & Jarjoura, G.R. (1996). Race, Gender, and Guidelines-Based Decision Making. *Journal of Research in Crime and Delinquency*, 33:1, 49–69.

Hannon, L. & DeFronzo. (1998). The Truly Disadvantaged, Public Assistance and Crime. *Social Problems*, 45:3, 383–392.

Johnson, D. G., Formichella, C. M., & Bowers, D. A. (1999). Do Drug Courts Work? An Outcome Evaluation of a Promising Program. *Journal of Applied Sociology*, 15:1, 44–62.

Kruttschnitt, Candace. (1980–81). Social Status and Sentences of Female Offenders. *Law and Society Review* 15:2:246–2265.

Maher, Lisa, and Daly, Kathleen. (1996). Women in the Street-Level Drug Economy: Continuity or Change? *Criminology* 34:465–491.

Manning, P.K. (1994). The police: Symbolic capital, class, and control. In Bridges, G.S. and Meyers, M. (Eds.), *Inequality, Crime and Social Control.* Crime and Society Series. Westview Press.

Messerschmidt, James. (1986). Capitalism, Patriarchy and Crime: Toward a Socialist Feminist Criminology. Rowman and Littlefield.

Messner, S. F. & Rosenfeld, R. (1994). *Crime and the American dream.* Wadsworth Publishing.

Miller S. (Ed.) (1998). *Crime Control and Women: Feminist Implications for Criminal Justice Policy.* Sage Publications.

Mokhiber, Russell. (1988). *Corporate Crime and Violence-Big Business Power and the Abuse of the Public Trust.* California: Sierra Club Books.

Myers, M.A. (1987). Economic Inequality and Discrimination in Sentencing. *Social Forces*, 65, 746–766.

Myers, M. A. (1988). Social Background and the Sentencing Behavior of Judges. *Criminology*, 26, 649–675.

Nagel, I. H & Johnson, B. L. (1994). The Role of Gender in a Structured Sentencing System: Equal Treatment, Policy Choices, and the Sentencing of Female Offenders Under the United States Sentencing Guidelines. *Journal of Criminal Law and Criminology*, 85:1, 181–221.

Nagel, S.S., and Weitzman, L.J. (1971). *Women as Litigants.* Hastings Law Journal 23:1:171–198.

Pettiway, Leon E. (1997). *Workin' It: Women Living Through Drugs and Crime.* Temple University Press.

Rush-Baskette, S. R. (1998). The War on Drugs as a War Against Black Women. In Miller, S. (Ed.), *Crime Control and Women: Feminist Implications for Criminal Justice Policy.* Sage Publications.

Simon, R. J. & Landis, J. (1991). *The Crimes Women Commit, The Punishments They Receive.* Lexington Books.

Spohn, C., Gruhl, J. & Welch, S. (1987). The Impact of the Ethnicity and Gender of Defendants on the Decision to Reject or Dismiss Felony Charges. *Criminology*, 25, 175–190.

Spohn, C. & Holleran, D. (2000). The Imprisonment Penalty Paid by Young, Unemployed Black and Hispanic Male Offenders. *Criminology*, 38:1, 281–306.

Steffensmeier, D. (1980). Assessing the Impact of the Women's Movement on Sex-Based Differences in the Handling of Adult Criminal Defendants. *Crime and Delinquency*, 23, 344–356.

Steffensmeir, D., Kramer, J. & Streifel, C. (1993). Gender and Imprisonment Decisions. *Criminology,* 31:3, 411–446.

Steffensmeir, D. & Haynie, D. (2000). Gender, Structural Disadvantage, and Urban Crime Do Macrosocial Variables Also Explain Female Offending Rates? *Criminology*, 38:2, 403–438.

Visher, C. (1980). Gender, Police Arrest Decisions and Notions of Chivalry. *Criminology*, 21, 5–28.

"Black's Theory of Law and Homicide Clearance Rates: Modeling the Use of Law in the Context of Urban Areas"[1]

Karen F. Parker, Ph.D.,
University of Florida

Marian J. Borg, Ph.D.,
University of Florida

Introduction

Although national expenditures toward crime-fighting have increased more than 150 percent over the last two decades (Chambliss 1994), the ability of police to clear crimes has not improved significantly. In 1997, the clearance rate for all index crimes was approximately 20 percent. And while clearance rates tend to be higher for more serious offenses, many violent crimes remain unsolved. Nationally in 1996, the police failed to clear about one-third of all homicide cases, and in some locations the failure rate was as high as 45% (FBI 1997:205–206). Moreover, FBI's UCR sources document the steady decline in clearance rates for homicide since 1976, while also reporting that homicide offending increased dramatically throughout the 1980s and into the early 1990s.

At the same time police officials were confronting a growth in crime rates and unsolved cases, urban residents faced heightened levels of disadvantage. The economic transformation that began in the 1970s, accelerated in the 1980s, marking the removal of manufacturing jobs out of cities. This only contributed to even higher rates of joblessness, poverty and racial residential segregation in urban areas (Massey and Eggers 1990; Wilson 1987; 1996; Kasarda 1989). This transformation created a highly polarized labor market structure, in that low-skilled workers were not among those employed by the expanding service sector, and led to inequalities within the urban environment. Researchers have linked these economic conditions to the social environment—deteriorated houses, vacant units, family disruption (Anderson 1990; Wacquant & Wilson

1. Contributions of the authors are equal in the research endeavor.

1989; Sampson and Wilson 1995; Wilson 1996)—and the increase in crime rates (Jacobs and Wood 1999; Krivo and Peterson 2000; Parker and McCall 1997; 1999; Peterson and Krivo 1993; Sampson 1987).

In this chapter, we seek to explore the relationship between homicide clearance rates and the social and economic context of urban areas.[2] Despite evidence of a widespread decline in clearance rates for many crimes in urban areas, researchers have yet to examine how the ability of police to clear crime is influenced by the structural characteristics of the location where it occurs. This void is especially noteworthy in light of scholarship that underscores an ecological approach to crime rates. Many studies have argued that the linkage between urban disadvantage and crime rates is due to the lack of social, economic and institutional resources to effectively prevent and fight crime, either informally through family, church and neighborhood efforts, or formally, through police activity (Shaw and McKay 1942; Kornhauser 1978; Bursik 1988; Sampson and Groves 1989; Messner and Sampson 1991). Yet, while these studies emphasize social control mechanisms, empirical analyses that measure social control have not been plentiful.[3]

We believe Donald Black's (1976) theory of law provides an important avenue to investigating clearance rates in urban areas for two reasons. First, to the extent that clearance rates are a measure of formal social control, examining these rates in the context of urban areas contributes to our understanding of the underlying processes that influence criminal activity (Krivo and Peterson 1996:642). That is, by identifying factors associated with higher clearance rates, this research may offer suggestions that enhance the ability of police to clear cases and that leads to a reduction in the overall level of crime. Moreover, noting the lack of attention to the impact of community composition on the effectiveness of *formal* social control, we argue Black's theory provides a framework to assess how urban areas mobilize the law in response to conflict.

---

2. This research is based arguments made in our *Law and Society Review* manuscript titled, "Applying Black's Theory to the Study of Homicide Clearance Rates" (Borg and Parker 2001). We direct the reader to that article for more detailed information on our conceptual and empirical work.

3. The exceptions are those recent studies examining the effects of informal social control on the relationship between community conditions and crime. Using measures such as the willingness of residents to watch over one another's property to indicate informal social control, or "collective efficacy," Sampson, Raudenbush and Earls (1997; 1998) found empirical support for the mediating relationship between neighborhood characteristics, levels of collective efficacy, and crime rates.

Second, Black argues his theory of law is applicable at multiple (including individual and structural) levels. While evaluations of Black's theory at the individual level are numerous (Gottfredson and Hindelang 1979; Braithwaite and Biles 1980; Myers 1980; Kruttschnitt 1980–81; Smith 1987; Massey and Myers 1989; Doyle and Luckenbill 1991), the utility of this theory for explaining macro-sociological processes, as reflected in clearance rates, remains an open question. Macro-level investigations are rare in the sociological literature (for exceptions, see Borg and Parker forthcoming; Lessan and Sheley 1992). Given that Black argues that his perspective is applicable to groups, neighborhoods, and societies as well (for a review of the empirical research, see Doyle and Luckenbill 1991; Lessan and Sheley 1992), our current investigation contributes to the existing empirical work based on Black's theory, particularly at the macro-level. Our main question is: What is the unique contribution of Black's theory of law to explaining the mobilization of law in the urban context?

Are Clearance Rates a Measure of Law?

Black (1976:2) defines law as "governmental social control... the normative life of a state and its citizens, such as legislation, litigation, and adjudication." Activities that involve mobilizing the criminal or civil justice system, including reporting a crime to the police, investigating an offense, collecting evidence, or making an arrest, are all empirical examples of law. Insofar as clearance statistics are a cumulative outcome of each of these stages, we argue clearance rates provide an aggregate-level measure of law in accord with Black's definition.

Specifically, we offer two distinct ways clearance rates can be understood as a structural indicator of the mobilization of law. First, the likelihood of clearing any specific crime is partially a function of the criminal justice resources expended toward its investigation. Most directly, this involves police activities such as collecting and preserving evidence, interrogating suspects, interviewing witnesses, and pursuing leads. Existing research finds that these activities vary greatly, suggesting that the allocation of such resources is not consistent across cases, even by offense type (Cooney 1994; LaFree 1989).

Second, in conducting investigations, police are heavily dependent on the willingness of victims, witnesses, and area residents to provide information regarding a case, particularly the offender's identity. Here again, research suggests that such willingness is far from a fixed commodity, but instead seems to be influenced by two important social dynamics—1) the state of relations between police and community residents and 2) the nature of the relationship between the victims, offenders and witnesses of crime. For example, descriptive studies suggest that members of lower status groups view the police, and the criminal justice system in general, with distrust and disdain and are therefore reluctant to become involved in any official investigations (Cooney 1994, 1997; Canada 1995; Marshall and Wheeler 1996). In regard to relations among parties to a crime, Cooney (1994) finds that witnesses are more likely to come forward to support their intimates rather than strangers. Hence, to the extent that clearance rates reflect the variable involvement of both citizens and police in the process of collecting evidence that culminates in an arrest, they are consistent with Black's conceptualization of law.

Moreover, Black generally argues that the variation in clearance rates has a social basis (see also Black 1970) and clearance statistics offer useful information about mobilizing the law in urban areas. To address this variation, Black proposes that law increases or decreases in response to five aspects of social life: stratification, morphology, culture, organization and social control. Next we offer a brief description of each of these elements and delineate our attempt to empirically measure these constructs at the aggregate level, followed by our specific hypotheses to be tested later in this chapter.

Theoretical Model and Hypotheses

Stratification

Black defines stratification as the vertical aspect of social life, including "any uneven distribution of the material conditions of existence" (1976:11). According to Black, one way to assess stratification is in terms of "the vertical distance between the people of a social setting. This is measured by the difference in wealth, on the average, between each person or group and every other" (Black 1976:13). Arguing that stratification varies historically, cross-culturally and across groups within the same society, Black hypothesizes that law varies directly with stratification, whereby increasing levels of inequality lead to a greater quantity of law:

> As traditional modes of production and distribution disappear, inequality proliferates across the world and law increases in every way. Legislation increases, as do policing and inspection, litigation, damages and punishment....the same applies across settings of every kind, even within a single community. There is less law among neighbors, colleagues, friends-less wherever people are more equal (Black 1976:14–15).

At the aggregate level, Black's argument suggests that communities with greater inequality will tend to have more law compared to their more egalitarian counterparts. Similarly Horwitz (1990:146–149) argues that authoritative forms of social control, like the law, develop in settings marked by increasing social distance. Here social distance evolves from a variety of sources, including stratification, heterogeneity, mobility and urbanization, and it encourages governmental social control. In this way, stratification is a structural condition that should impact *formal* control mechanisms, like the law. Basically, Black's arguments suggest that as stratification expands, formal social control systems will actually grow.

Considering Black's propositions regarding stratification in light of recent literature that depicts the vast racial disparities and disadvantages in urban areas, we conceptualize stratification with three indicators of racial inequality in socioeconomic statuses: racial differences in educational attainment, unemployment rates, and median family income levels. Black's theory clearly indicates that stratification is more likely to be found between certain race and ethnic groups (see discussion in *The Behavior of Law*, Chapter 2). In addition, we extend our measure of stratification to also include an indicator of racial residential segregation. Racial segregation has been used in previous research to reflect the residential isolation and separation between blacks and whites in urban areas and thus marks a specific form of social disadvantage (see for instance Massey and Denton 1988; Massey and Eggers 1990; Messner and Golden, 1992). With these four measures of stratification in mind, we expect that clearance rates will be highest in cities with the highest levels of inequality and the highest levels of racial segregation:

> H_1: As stratification income increase, clearance rates will increase.

Morphology

Black's second proposition refers to the relationship between "morphology" and the mobilization of law. According to Black, morphology is the "horizontal aspect of social life, the distribution of people in relation to one another, including their division of labor, networks of interaction, intimacy, and integration" (1976:37). We focus on the last dimension of morphology identified by Black, integration, or the extent to which people participate in social life. Among other indicators, Black suggests that law increases with participation in social institutions:

> An offense between two employed men is more likely to result in legal action than an offense between two who are unemployed... one between two residents more than one between two transients. If a va-

> grant victimizes another vagrant, for instance, the police are less likely to hear about it. If they are summoned, they are less likely to make an arrest, and if they do, a prosecutor, judge or jury is less likely to be severe. An offense between marginal people is less serious than an offense between people more integrated in social life (1976:49).

In this chapter, we operationalize morphology at the aggregate level in terms of the extent to which a city's residents participate in three important aspects of social life: marriage, employment, and community stability. Specifically, we offer aggregate measures of divorce, joblessness and residential mobility in urban areas. In this way, Black's conceptual arguments mirror other structural research that links family disruption, joblessness, and residential mobility to crime rates (Sampson 1987; Wilson 1987; Shihadeh and Steffensmeier 1994; Krivo and Peterson 1996). Bursik and Grasmick (1993) suggest that without the strong stake in community life that marriage, employment, and long-term residence encourage, individuals may be less inclined to protect one another's property, involve themselves in community crime-fighting efforts, or to cooperate with the police in reacting to criminal incidents. To the extent that we can offer these measures as indicative of integration and a community's effort to mobilizing the law, Black postulates that social integration will be associated with lower levels of law. Our second hypothesis states:

> H_2: As morphology decreases, clearance rates will increase.

Culture

Culture is the third aspect of social life hypothesized by Black to affect the quantity of law. Black (1976:61–63) defines culture as the "symbolic aspect of social life" as manifested through language, concepts, religions, values and customs, food, clothing and the like. He argues that variations in the *quantity* of culture affect the behavior of law: individuals and settings with more culture will tend to have greater levels of law. Black suggests education and literacy as measures of the quantity of culture. Moreover, educated individuals are more likely to use the legal system in response to conflicts, and they are more likely to be successful when they do (1976:64; see also Horwitz 1990:159). Beyond the individual, communities and neighborhoods also vary in the quantity of culture and the corresponding quantity of law that characterizes them:

> The quantity of culture varies across a single society as well. Some regions may have more than others, for instance with coastal regions

> typically having more culture than interior regions, urban areas more than rural.... Some communities have more than others, some neighborhoods, occupations, organizations or families have more than others.... [W]herever symbolic life is most advanced, so is law (Black 1976:64).

Insofar as culture is one measure of social status, these propositions are consistent with Cooney (1994), who argues that criminal cases involving victims of higher status typically generate more evidence and a greater willingness on the part of witnesses to come forward and assist in police investigations (see also Simon 1991:147). In terms of clearance rates, then, these arguments suggest that homicides occurring in areas with more status—i.e., more culture—are more likely to be resolved by the police compared to those occurring in lower status areas.

Available measures of culture at the aggregate level are rather limited, and hence our analysis in this aspect is perhaps best viewed as preliminary and suggestive (we return to this point later in this chapter). Based on Black's theoretical arguments, we use an aggregate level measure of education to differentiate the variation in culture across cities. We hypothesize that clearance rates will be highest in cities with the highest percentage of high school graduates:

> H_3: As culture increases, clearance rates will increase.

Organization

Fourth, Black refers to the relationship between organization and law. "Organization is the corporate aspect of social life, the capacity for collective action" (Black 1976:85). Among other indicators, Black suggests the presence and number of administrative officials, the number of voluntary associations or memberships, the degree of centralization of a government, and the number of organizations per capita as alternative measures of organization. According to Black, organization shares a direct relationship with law: the more organization, or the greater the capacity for collective action, the greater the quantity of law:

> Law varies directly with private as well as public organization, and with informal as well as formal organization. It varies with the number of groups and with the internal structure of groups.... At one extreme is a simple society, such as a tribe of hunters or herdsmen, with little organizational life at all, private or public. Compared to a modern society, people of this kind are groupless. They have no economic

> organizations, no interest groups or other voluntary associations, no service establishments such as hospitals or schools.... People of this kind have little or no law either (Black 1976:91).

At the aggregate level, Black's argument suggests that cities with greater collective capacity will have more law-and by extension, higher clearance rates. Local agencies such as churches, schools and recreational organizations, provide a connection between community residents and police that fosters cooperation and trust, and in turn, should increase police ability to solve the crimes that occur there (Krivo and Peterson 1996:642; Rose and Clear 1998:445). Along these lines, Bursik and Grasmick (1993) use the term "public controls" to refer to networks between a community and outside agencies, including those operated by the criminal justice system. These networks are vital for the health of a community to the extent that they play a role in determining a community's access to public goods and services. Implicit in this argument is the idea that more organized communities will be in a better position to lobby for and receive higher levels of police resources. Hence, both by fostering better relations between police and community residents and by increasing access to economic resources, strong local organizations should increase the capacity of the police to investigate crime. Higher clearance rates should be an outcome.

To account for these arguments, we operationalize organization at the city-level in two ways: expenditures toward public goods and services and the percentage of vacant housing units in a given area. First, we use a city's general expenditures directed toward education and public welfare as indicative of an area's collective capacity. As Black suggests, the number of administrative positions, service establishments, and organizations in general measure a group's level of organization. General expenditures suggest the level of support for these organizations, and hence should differentiate the level of collective capacity among cities.

Our second measure of organization is the percentage of vacant housing units within a city. Although an indirect indicator of organization, the extent that abandoned buildings and vehicles, vacant lots, graffiti, and the like are signs of neighborhood decay and often encourage and facilitate criminal activity, removing them is typically a high priority for community residents (see for example Hartnett and Skogan 1999:6). Clean-up efforts depend on the cooperation of municipal agencies (Hartnett and Skogan 1999:10), reflecting its organizational capacity, and thus the extent to which residents can protect their communities from these signs of incivility may be an outcome of the degree to which their communities are sufficiently organized to demand and receive service. Hence we use the percent of vacant housing units in a city as a measure of its ability to organize in order to achieve a collective goal. The lower the percentage of abandoned units, the more organized the community and hence, as Black hypothesizes, the greater the quantity of law.

> H_4: As organization increases in urban cities, clearance rates will increase.

Alternative to Social Control

Black's fifth and final proposition refers to the relationship between social control and the law. For Black, "social control is the normative aspect of life... it defines and responds to deviant behavior..." (1976:105). In his theory, Black distinguishes between formal or governmental social control (i.e., law) and informal or non-governmental social control, and he hypothesizes an inverse relationship between the two. That is, law grows "as every other kind of social control dies away—not only in the family, but in the village, church, workplace, and neighborhood" (Black 1976:109). Important in Black's conception of social control is the idea that any response to deviance, even one considered criminal, is a form of informal social control.

At the aggregate level, Black's argument suggests that declining levels of informal social control will be associated with increasing levels of formal social control (i.e., law). Similar to Lessan and Sheley's (1992) macro-level analysis of Black's theory, we use the rate of homicide to indicate a lack of informal social control. However, in contrast to Lessan and Sheley's interpretation of homicide rates, we conceptualize homicide as an indicator of the *presence*, rather than the absence, of informal social control. We argue that this is more consistent with Black's overall theoretical argument. Recall that Black suggests, as a measure of informal social control, homicide rates should vary *inversely* with formal social control (law). Thus, we would expect:

> H_5: As homicide rates decrease across cities (indicating decreasing levels of informal social control), clearance rates will increase.

Data and Methodology

Cities with a population of 100,000 or more residents in 1990 is the unit of analysis in this chapter. We limit our dependent variable to homicide clearance rates because homicide statistics are generally considered more accurate than any other crime statistics collected by the FBI. That is, due to their seriousness, homicides are more likely than other crimes to be reported to the police and also more likely to be officially recorded by law enforcement (Shihadeh and Flynn 1996:1334).

Dependent Variable

Because homicide clearance data at the city-level are not typically reported in FBI publications, these data were obtained by special request. Clearance rates refer to the proportion of reported crimes that result in the arrest of one or more offenders. We calculated the homicide clearance rate for each city as the number of homicides cleared by an arrest divided by the total number of homicides known to the police. Following acceptable procedure for structural-level analysis, each city's 1990 clearance rate is calculated as its average rate over a three-year period (1989–1991). This procedure helps minimize the impact of year-to-year fluctuations in the data and increases the reliability of city-level estimates (Messner and Golden 1992; Parker and McCall 1997, 1999).[4]

Independent Variables

The data for operationalizing our measures of stratification, morphology, culture, organization and other social control were obtained from the US Bureau of the Census 1990 Population Characteristics, the City and County Data Book (1994), and the FBI's Uniform Crime Report. Measures from the U.S. Census population database include: racial residential segregation, three measures of racial inequality (education, income, and unemployment), percent of unemployed persons, percent divorced, residential mobility, percent of persons with a high school degree or higher, and population size. Measures from the City and County Data Book include: percent of a city's expenditures toward education, public welfare, and its police force during 1900–1991 and the percent of vacant housing units. Finally, UCR data were used to calculate an average homicide rate for each city (1989–1991). The operational computations of these measures are provided below.

First, our stratification variable is based on four measures: racial residential segregation, the ratio of white to black educational attainment for individuals aged 25 and older, the ratio of white household income to black household income, and the ratio of the white unemployment rate to the black

---

4. In some instances, information on the number of homicide cases cleared by arrest was missing for one or more of the three years (1989–1991) of interest in this study. As a precautionary measure, two different sets of regression models were analyzed and no differences in the parameter estimates were found. Hence, we included all cities with at least one year of clearance data.

unemployment rate. The three ratio measures are typically offered as indicators of racial inequality and indicate the overall extent of racial disparity and stratification in income, education, and employment opportunities among blacks and whites in American cities (e.g., Messner and Golden 1992; Parker and McCall 1999). Racial residential segregation is measured using the index of dissimilarity. This index is an indicator of unevenness in the distribution between black and white racial groups across census tracts within a city (Massey and Denton 1988; Peterson and Krivo 1993; Parker and McCall 1999) and is one of the most commonly used measures of segregation in aggregate level analyses (see Shihadeh and Maume 1997).

Next, we use three measures of morphology to indicate participation in family, work, and community: the percent of divorced persons, the percent unemployed, and residential mobility. The percent divorced measure is computed by dividing the number of divorced individuals by the total number of persons 18 years and older. The unemployment measure is calculated by dividing the number of persons not employed by the total number of persons aged 16 years and older (excluding those persons currently in the armed forces). Residential mobility is the percent of individuals who have moved within a city area during the last five years (i.e., since 1985).

Third, we operationalize culture in terms of the educational attainment of the population within each city. This variable is calculated by dividing the number of persons with a high school diploma or more by the total number of persons 25 years and older.

Next, we use three measures to operationalize the concept of organization: the percent of a city's expenditures for education and for public welfare, and the percent of vacant housing units within a given city area. The two expenditure measures reflect the proportion of funds allocated by each city toward education and public welfare during the 1990–1991 budget year. The variable indicating vacant housing units is computed by dividing the number of housing units identified as vacant by the total number of housing units in an area.

Fifth, our measure of alternative social control is calculated from UCR homicide data. The homicide rate for each city is based on three years of homicide data, 1989–1991, and is computed by dividing the total number of homicides by the total number of persons in the population and then multiplying the result by 100,000.[5]

---

5. As with the clearance rate, although to a lesser extent, missing data were present in the UCR homicide counts. In our analysis, the models include all cities with at least one year of homicide data.

Finally, we include two control variables in the regression model: population size and the percent of city expenditures to police. Population size is measured by the total number of residents living in each city in 1990 and is usually included in aggregate models evaluating criminal justice processes. The percent of police expenditures measures the proportion of a city's budget allocated for its police force during the 1990–1991 year. Including this variable is important since cities that devote more resources towards law enforcement personnel might be expected to have greater success in clearing homicide cases. We control for this measure to evaluate whether the social variables in Black's theory will have a significant impact on clearance rates even after accounting for differences in each city's police expenditures.

Methodological Issues

A few comments concerning the particulars of our data and methodological issues are warranted before presenting the results of our multiple regression analyses. First, based on preliminary analysis, two variables were transformed into their natural logarithmic equivalent in order to reduce the skewness of these measures in our OLS models: population size and the UCR homicide rate. Second, in terms of the potential for collinearity and partialling among the regressors, researchers have long acknowledged that these issues plague studies of aggregate level homicide. Because some researchers propose principal components analysis helps reduce the regressor space and the likelihood of inefficient parameter estimates (see Land, McCall and Cohen 1990 for a detailed description), we employ this statistical technique in our study. As a result, one dimensional composite was generated. This composite includes the three racial inequality measures—the ratio of white to black median family income, the ratio of white to black educational attainment, and the ratio of black unemployment to white unemployment rates—in addition to the racial residential segregation measure (see Messner and Golden 1992; Parker and McCall 1999). We refer to this dimension as the stratification/racial segregation index, as it reflects Black's concept of stratification or inequalities in wealth across cities. A summary of our measures and univariate statistics are displayed in Table 1.[6]

---

6. Our examination of the bivariate correlation matrices is not the only test that has led us to conclude that multicollinearity is not problematic in this study. As an additional test, we examined the VIF (variance inflation factors) for all the covariates included in the analysis. Based on Fisher and Mason's discussion of VIF, the value of 4 is the acceptable cutoff point (Fisher and Mason 1981). The largest VIF in our models is 2.215, which falls well below the acceptable value of 4. Overall, based on our robust statistical diagnostics,

Results and Discussion

The discussion of our results will take two forms. First, we will provide the findings for each of our hypotheses. This discussion will focus on the results presented in the final model in Table 2 (Model 6). Second, in our effort to assess the unique contributions of each of Black's aspects of social life on clearance rates, we estimated a series of nested models and calculate the change in the R squared and F statistics across each of the models presented in Table 2 (Models 1 through 6). A discussion of these results will follow our hypotheses tests.

Table 1. Means of Dependent and Predictor Variables for Homicide Clearance Rate Model, 1990

Variables	Mean (Standard Deviations)
Homicide Clearance Rate	.7487 (.2108)
Stratification	
• Ratio of white to black median family income	1.666 (.3951)
• Ratio of white to black median educational attainment	1.039 (.0822)
• Ratio of white unemployment rate to black unemployment rate	2.357 (.8108)
• Racial Residential Segregation	.5106 (.1819)
Morphology	
• Percentage Divorced Persons	10.240 (1.849)
• Percent Unemployed Persons	7.334 (2.596)
• Residential Mobility within 5 years	56.497 (6.280)
Culture	
• Percentage of Persons with High School Degree	75.177 (8.833)
Organization	
• Percentage of City's Expenditure toward Education	7.844 (16.637)
• Percent of City's Expenditure toward Public Welfare	1.334 (2.999)
• Percentage of Vacant Housing Units	8.434 (3.304)
Alternative Social Control	
• UCR Homicide Rate	15.817 (13.709)
Control Measures	

we feel confident in the stability of the regression coefficients, standard errors, and test statistics presented here (see Belsely, Kuh, and Welsch 1980 for details).

• Population Size (log)	12.351 (.7633)
• Percentage of City's Expenditure toward Police Force	14.098 (5.824)
N	157

Stratification

Our first hypothesis predicts that stratification and law will vary together: cities with greater levels of inequality, indicated by higher scores on the racial stratification and segregation index, will have higher clearance rates. Our analysis supports this hypothesis. The results suggest that police are more likely to solve homicide cases in cities that have greater disparities in unemployment, educational attainment and income between white and black residents, and where racial residential segregation is more pronounced. This is consistent with Black's hypothesis that settings characterized by greater inequality will tend to have more governmental social control.

Morphology

Our second hypothesis predicts a direct relationship between morphology, or participation in social life, and clearance rates. Specifically, we expect that cities marked by lower rates of divorce, unemployment, and mobility will have higher clearance rates for homicide. Of the three measures of morphology offered in our model, only one shares a significant relationship with clearance rates—residential mobility. This finding suggests that for cities with higher levels of stability among its population, the ability of the police to make arrests in homicide cases is significantly enhanced. This finding may reflect the greater willingness of long-time residents to become involved in police investigations. In addition, it may also imply something about the types of homicide cases more likely to occur in areas with more or less transient populations. If cities with more stable populations tend to experience a greater proportion of non-stranger homicides, for example, then their clearance rates may be higher insofar as offenders in such cases are easier to identify and apprehend. In contrast, stranger homicides may be more common in cities with more transient populations, and furthermore, the offenders' identity less well-known in the community. Here police might experience greater difficulty when conducting investigations and arresting offenders. If this occurs, lower clearance rates would result. In terms of the other measures of morphology, the level of divorce and unemployment do not seem to make a significant difference in the use of the law in urban areas. This finding is contrary to Black's argument that groups with more integrated members—as measured through participation in marriage and the workforce—will be more likely to mobilize the police compared to groups with less integrated members.[7]

Culture

Hypothesis three predicts a direct relationship between culture and the mobilization of law: as culture (the proportion of city residents with at least a high school degree) increases, clearance rates for homicide will also increase. Our data support this relationship. In fact, the education variable is the strongest predictor in the homicide clearance model (model 6), when compared to the contribution of Black's other indicators of social life. Consistent with Black's argument, the mobilization of law increases as the cultural status of a group increases. The pattern may reflect a greater willingness on the part of more educated individuals to involve themselves in police investigations as witnesses, and also greater attention on the part of law enforcement to investigate homicides that occur in cities with a greater proportion of more educated residents. Insofar as education is one measure of social status, this is consistent with arguments in the literature that the quantity and quality of evidence collected in legal cases increases with the status of victims, that individuals with higher social status are more likely to mobilize the law in response to conflict, and that witnesses are more likely to come forward to support victims of higher status (Cooney 1994; Black 1980). Thus, our research provides macro-level support for this claim.

Organization

The hypothesis concerning organization predicts a relationship between the organizational capacity of cities and the homicide clearance rates, where cities with greater organizational capacity will have higher clearance rates. Of the three measures of organizational capacity—expenditures toward education, public welfare and percentage of vacant housing units, only the education expenditure measure shares a significant relationship with clearance rates. That is, cities that devote a greater proportion of their budgets to education tend to have higher clearance rates for homicide.

These mixed results are not unexpected, particularly given the difficulty in operationalizing organizational capacity at the city-level. Given the impor-

---

7. Similarly, Doyle and Luckenbill (1991) also failed to find a relationship between an individuals' marital or employment status and their likelihood of contacting the police regarding a community problem. Myers' (1980) structural-level analysis of Black's theory failed to support the proposed relationship between morphology and governmental social control, although her model used different measures of morphology.

Table 2. Unstandardized (and Standardized) Nested Regression Coefficients for Black's Theory on Homicide Clearance Rates

	Model 1	Model 2	Model 3	Model 4	Model 5	Model 6
Stratification						
Racial Stratification/ Segregation Index	—	.0275** (.139)	.0245* (.124)	.0153 (.077)	.0258* (.127)	.0364** (.175)
Morphology						
Percent Divorced Persons	—	—	.0041 (.037)	-.0005 (-.041)	.0015 (.014)	.0044 (.039)
Percent Unemployed Persons	—	—	-.0161*** (-.210)	-.0009 (-.127)	.0021 (.026)	.0077 (.094)
Residential Mobility	—	—	-.0038* (-.119)	-.0054** (-.168)	-.0052** (-.158)	-.0046* (-.133)
Culture						
Percent Person w/ HS Degree	—	—	—	.0096*** (.426)	.0113*** (.486)	.0088*** (.370)
Organization						
Percentage of City's Expenditures Toward Education	—	—	—	—	.0027** (.209)	.0024** (.188)
Percentage of City's Expenditures Toward Pubic Welfare	—	—	—	—	-.0003 (-.044)	-.0029 (.040)
Percentage of Vacant Housing Units	—	—	—	—	-.0044 (-.070)	-.0012 (.019)
Alternative to Social Control						
UCR Homicide Rate 1990	—	—	—	—	—	-.0048*** (-.313)

Table 2 (continued).

Control Measures						
Population Size (log)	-.0671***	-.0759***	-.0704***	-.0505***	-.0429**	-.0028
	(-.226)	(-.277)	(-.257)	(-.184)	(-.156)	(-.101)
Percentage of City's Expenditures Toward Police Force	.0018	-.0021	-.0023	-.0007	.0039	.0037
	(-.050)	(-.057)	(-.063)	(-.020)	(.109)	(.101)
R^2	.051	.089	.122	.241	.267	.314
F CHANGE	5.080	5.441***	3.834***	7.422***	5.418***	6.024***

* $p < .10$ ** $p < .05$ *** $p < .01$

tance of organizational capacity to Black's theoretical perspective and other frameworks, such as social disorganization theory, future analyses should consider alternative measures. Possible indicators might include, but not be limited to: the presence of community policing programs; programs that offer services to community members, such as shelters for women and children; the existence of agencies that combine police officers and public community members; and other community institutions, such as the church, or the extent of residents' involvement in local politics.

Alternative Social Control

The fifth hypothesis predicts an inverse relationship between law and alternative social control. As predicted, cities with lower homicide rates tend to have higher homicide clearance rates. This relationship is one of the two strongest in the model and is significant even after controlling for the other aspects of social life offered by Black. This supports Black's argument that confrontational forms of conflict management will be found more often in settings where law is unavailable or less often invoked to manage conflict.

In sum, we find empirical support for each of our aggregate level indicators of Black's theory on the mobilization of law (clearance rates) in urban areas. That is, our results reveal empirical support for all five aspects of Black's theory in the expected direction. Interestingly, Black's aspects of culture and alternatives to social control offer considerable insight into the mobilization of the law in the urban context, relative to the other dimensions. Given this, we now turn to our discussion of the nested models for a closer look at the unique influences of each of these constructs in our models.

Also displayed in Table 2 are the results of our nested models. The nested models allow us to determine the relative contribution of each aspect of social life on homicide clearance rates as each theoretical construct is successively entered into the model one at a time (see Models 1 through 6). Specifically, these analyses permit us to assess the influence of each of Black's aspects of social life on homicide clearance rates by providing information on any changes in the direction and magnitude of the regression coefficient estimates. If the change in the R squared statistic is large and the F score is statistically significant, evidence is provided that the added construct is a good predictor of our dependent variable and thus significantly improves the overall fit of our model.

The results of these tests reveal that each aspect of Black's theory contributes significantly to our understanding of homicide clearance rates and, as such, the overall fit of our model is improved by our effort to include all aspects of social life proposed by Black's theory. That is, we find that the change in the R squared statistic and F score to be statistically significant across the models (see Models 1 through 6). Moreover, the greatest change in the R squared statistic takes place between models 3 and 4 due to the inclusion of culture (R2 change from .122 to .241, difference of .119). In fact, the fit of the model doubles when our measure of culture (high school educational attainment) is added to the model. Given these findings, we offer some concluding remarks about the potential contributions of Black's theory to future studies of crime, law and social control at the macro level.

Implications of Black's Theory at Aggregate Level

In this chapter we have assessed the utility of Black's theory of law to explain the variation in homicide clearance rates for urban areas. The empirical results suggest support for the argument that the variation in aspects of social life in urban areas—economic conditions, racial disparities and isolation, cultural and organizational factors—influence the likelihood of police to clear homicide cases at the aggregate (city) level. Insofar as clearance rates have not been empirically examined in this way, our analysis raises some important issues for the application of Black's theory in further investigation at the macro level.

First, by incorporating Black's theory into the study of the use of law within an urban context, we demonstrate the importance of studying formal and informal processes of social control as both levels are affected by structural characteristics (like inequality, segregation, mobility and collective capacity) of urban areas. Importantly, our results indicate that these structural factors may not influence formal social control mechanisms in the same manner as informal social control. For instance, previous empirical studies indicate that high levels of inequality impede informal social control within urban areas and thereby lead to higher rates of crime, including homicide. Our current analysis indicates that when homicides do occur, their likelihood of being cleared is greater in more stratified urban locations. Moreover, not only do these patterns suggest a distinct relationship between urban disadvantage and informal and formal social control, but, the results also suggest important *indirect* effects between structural factors and social control processes. For example, the impact of racial inequality on homicide clearance rates may be mediated by family disruption, the organizational capacity of the urban area or perhaps be a consequence of resources in the police department. Future analyses that attempt to model both the direct and indirect links between structural conditions and informal and formal processes of social control will contribute to our understanding of these complex relationships.

Second, by conceptualizing culture as a mechanism of social control, Black's theory gives researchers a new avenue to incorporate culture into the study of crime and violence at the aggregate level. Discussions that focus primarily on cultural versus structural arguments of crime have long been offered in the literature (Gastil 1971; Hackney 1969; Loftin and Hill 1974; McCall et al. 1992; Messner 1983a, 1983b; Smith and Parker 1980) and the conceptual linkage between culture, region (particularly Southern region) and violent attitudes has been extensively debated (Dixon and Lizotte 1987, 1989; Ellison and McCall 1989). Some researchers have argued (and found empirical support for the claim) that structural explanations are a viable and important alternative to explaining violence as culturally influenced (see Loftin and Hill 1974). Black's propositions that law increases with greater culture offer researchers an avenue to incorporate cultural indicators within existing structural explanations, through both direct and indirect linkages, and extends the discussion about the relationship between culture and violence beyond the current focus on region (Southern region). Greater attention should be given to measuring culture at the structural level in accordance with Black's theory. For example, efforts to model Black's discussion of cultural distance and conventionality as two dimensions of culture might be particularly useful in future studies of crime and social control at the macro level (Black 1976, 1980; Borg 1998).

Our analysis also suggests the importance of examining variation in homicide clearance rates disaggregated by the status of victims and offenders and by the type of the relationship between parties. As noted earlier, Black's theory gives every reason to expect that clearance rates for different types of homicide will vary according to such factors. To the extent that victims and offenders of different economic, cultural, and social status will attract different levels of official police investigation and a variable number of witnesses willing to assist with investigations (Cooney 1994), we should expect differences in clearance rates depending on the status of victims and offenders. In addition, the context leading to homicide may also influence its likelihood of being cleared. Stranger homicides, for example, may be more difficult to resolve compared to those involving intimates or acquaintances. Analyzing disaggregated clearance data may provide further insights into the relationships between the mobilization of law and each of the five aspects of social life identified in Black's theory. For example, many studies suggest that differences in crime rates by racial groups are due to the social and ecological structure in which these groups find themselves. Whites and blacks reside in urban communities that are ecologically and economically very different, and therefore, face different social and economic realities (e.g., Wilson 1987; Sampson and

Wilson 1995). Research on the racial variations in lethal violence reveals that structural conditions are pivotal to understanding the unique, violent offending patterns for various racial groups (Messner and Golden 1992; Sampson and Wilson 1995; Krivo and Peterson 1996, 2000; Shihadeh and Flynn 1996; Parker and McCall 1997, 1999). In similar fashion, an examination of the impact of these structural conditions on homicide clearance rates disaggregated by race may contribute significantly to our understanding of urban areas, particularly racial differences in the mobilization of law.

On a final note we acknowledge some of the limitations that hinder our macro-level application of Black's theory. While we find support for our hypotheses, particularly with regard to stratification, culture and alternative social control, the results with regard to integration (morphology) and organizational capacity were less consistent. Previous studies, as well as our own, recognize the difficulty in operationalizing some of the concepts in Black's theory, particularly at the aggregate level. Indeed, some of the inconsistent findings in our own analysis may be a consequence of the measures used, rather than evidence of the theory's lack of validity. On the other hand, mixed results may also indicate the need for greater specification of Black's propositions. It is certainly possible that the multiple dimensions of each concept identified in his theory are not all relevant to every process of law, at every stage, or at every level of aggregation (see Greenberg 1983:357–358). Applying Black's framework at a different level of aggregation is required to fully address this issue and thus encouraged in this regard.

References

Anderson, Elijah. (1990). *Streetwise: Race, Class, and Change in an Urban Community.* Chicago: The University of Chicago Press.

Black, Donald. 1970. Production of crime rates. *American Sociological Review* 35:733–748.

_______. (1976). *The Behavior of Law.* Orlando: Academic Press, Inc.

_______. (1980). *The Manners and Customs of the Police.* New York: Academic Press.

Belsely, David A., Edwin Kuh, and Roy E. Welsch. (1980). *Regression Diagnostics: Identifying Influential Data and Sources of Collinearity.* New York: John Wiley & Sons.

Braithwaite, John and David Biles. (1980). "Empirical Verification and Black's The Behavior of Law." *American Sociological Review* 45:334–338.

Borg, Marian J. (1998). Vicarious Homicide Victimization and Support for Capital Punishment: A Test of Black's Theory of Law *Criminology* 36:537–568.

Borg, Marian J. and Karen F. Parker. (2001). Applying Black's Theory to the Study of Homicide Clearance Rates. *Law and Society Review* 35(2): 435–466.

Bursik, Robert J. (1988). Social disorganization and theories of crime and delinquency: Problems and Prospect. *Criminology* 26:519–551.

Bursik, Robert J. and Harold G. Grasmick. (1993). *Neighborhoods and Crime: The Dimensions of Effective Community Control.* New York: Lexington Books.

Canada, Geoffrey. (1995). *Fist Stick Knife Gun: A Personal History of Violence in America.* Boston: Beacon Press.

Chambliss, William J. (1994). "Policing the ghetto underclass: The politics of law and Law enforcement." *Social Problems* 41:177–194.

Cooney, Mark. (1994). Evidence as partisanship. *Law and Society Review* 28:833–858. (1997). The decline of elite homicide. *Criminology* 35: 381–407.

Dixon, Jo and Alan J. Lizotte. (1987). Gun Ownership and the "Southern Subculture of Violence" *American Journal of Sociology* 93(2):383–405.

_______. (1989). The Burden of Proof: Southern Subculture of Violence Explanations of Gun Ownership and Homicide. *American Journal of Sociology* 95:182–186.

Doyle, Daniel P. and David F. Luckenbill. (1991). Mobilizing law in response to Collective problems: A test of Black's theory of law. *Law and Society Review* 25: 103–115.

Greenberg, David F. (1983). Donald Black's sociology of law: A critique. *Law & Society Review* 17:337–367.

Ellison, Christopher G., and Patricia L. McCall. (1989). Region and Violent Attitudes Reconsidered: Comment on Dixon and Lizotte. *American Journal of Sociology* 95:174–178.

Federal Bureau of Investigation. (1997). Crime in the United States, 1996. Washington: U.S. Government Printing Office.

Fisher, J.C., and R.L. Mason. (1981). The Analysis of Multicollinear Data in Criminology. In J. A. Fox (Ed.), *Methods in Quantitative Criminology*, 99–125. New York: Academic Press.

Gastil, Raymond D. (1971). Homicide and a Regional Culture of Violence. *American Sociological Review* 36:412–427.

Gottfredson, Michael and Michael Hindelang. (1979). A Study of the *Behavior of Law. American Sociological Review* 44:3–18.

Hackney, Sheldon. (1969). Southern Violence. *American Historical Review* 74:906–25.

Hartnett, Susan M. and Wesley G. Skogan. (1999). Community Policing: Chicago's experience. *National Institute of Justice Journal* April 1999:2–11.

Horwitz, Allan. (1990). *The Logic of Social Control.* New York: Plenum Press.

Jacobs, David and Katherine Wood. (1999). Interracial Conflict and Interracial Homicide: Do Political and Economic Rivalries Explain White Killings of Blacks or Blacks Killings of White? *American Journal of Sociology* 105: 157–190.

Kasarda, John. D. (1989). Urban Industrial Transition and the Underclass. *The Annals of the American Academy of Political and Social Sciences* 501:26–47.

Kornhauser, Ruth. (1978). *Social Sources of Delinquency: An Appraisal of Analytic Models.* Chicago, Illinois: University of Chicago Press

Krivo, Lauren J. and Ruth D. Peterson. (1996). Extremely Disadvantaged Neighborhoods and Urban Crime. *Social Forces* 75:619–650.

_______. (2000). The Structure Context of Homicide: Accounting for Racial Differences in Process. *American Sociological Review* 65 (4): 547–559.

Kruttschnitt, Candace. (1980–81). Social Status and Sentences of Female Offenders." *Law And Society Review* 2:247–265.

LaFree, Gary D. (1989). *Rape and Criminal Justice: The Social Construction of Sexual Assault.* Belmont, CA: Wadsworth.

Land, Kenneth C., Patricia L. McCall, and Larry E. Cohen. (1990). Structural Covariates Of Homicide Rates: Are There Any Invariances Across Time and Social Space? *American Journal of Sociology* 95:922–963.

Lessan, Gloria T. and Joseph F. Sheley. (1992). Does Law Behave? A Macrolevel Test of Black's Propositions on Change in Law. *Social Forces* 70:655–678.

Loftin, Colin, and Robert H. Hill. (1974). Regional culture and homicide: An examination of the Gastil-Hackney thesis. *American Sociological Review* 39:714–24.

McCall, Patricia L., Kenneth C. Land, and Lawrence E. Cohen. (1992). Violent Criminal Behavior: Is There a General and Continuing Influence of the South? *Social Science Research* 21:286–310.

Marshall, Joseph, Jr. and Lonnie Wheeler. (1996). *Street Soldier: One Man's Struggle to Change a Generation-One Life at a Time.* New York: Delacourte.

Massey, Douglas and Nancy A. Denton. (1988). Suburbanization and Segregation in U.S. Metropolitan Areas. *American Journal of Sociology* 94:592–626.

Massey, Douglas and Mitchell L. Eggers. (1990). The Ecology of Inequality: Minorities And the Concentration of Poverty, 1970–1980. *American Journal of Sociology* 95:1153–1188.

Massey, James L. and Martha A. Myers. (1989). Patterns of repressive social control in post-reconstruction Georgia, 1882–1935. *Social Forces* 68:458–488.

Messner, Steven F. (1983a). Regional and Racial Effects on the Urban Homicide Rates: The Subculture of Violence Revisited. *American Journal of Sociology* 88(5):997–1007.

_______. (1983b). Regional Differences in the Economic Correlates of the Urban Homicide Rate: Some Evidence on the Importance of Cultural Context. *Criminology* 21:477–488.

Messner, Steven F. and Reid M. Golden. (1992). Racial Inequality and Racially Disaggregated Homicide Rates: An Assessment of Alternative Theoretical Explanations. *Criminology* 30:421–447.

Messner, Steven F., and Robert J. Sampson. (1991). The sex ratio, family disruption, and rates of violent crime: The paradox of demographic structure. *Social Forces* 69:693–714.

Myers, Martha A. (1980). Predicting the Behavior of Law: a Test ofTtwo Models. *Law And Society Review* 14: 835–857.

Parker, Karen F. and Patricia L. McCall. (1997). Adding another piece to the inequality-homicide puzzle: The impact of structural inequality on racially disaggregated homicide rates. *Homicide Studies: An Interdisciplinary and International Journal* 1:35–60.

_______. (1999). Structural Conditions and Racial Homicide Patterns: A Look at the Multiple Disadvantages in Urban Areas. *Criminology* 37:447–473.

Peterson, Ruth D. and Lauren J. Krivo. (1993). Racial Segregation and Black Urban Homicide. Social Forces 71:1001–1026.

Rose, Dina R. and Todd R. Clear. (1998). Incarceration, Social Capital and Crime: Implications for Social Disorganization Theory. *Criminology* 36:441–479.

Sampson, Robert J. (1987). Urban Black Violence: The Effect of Male Joblessness and Family Disruption. *American Journal of Sociology* 93:348–382.

Sampson, Robert J. and W. Byron Groves. (1989). Community Structure and Crime: Testing Social Disorganization Theory. *American Journal of Sociology* 94:774–802.

Sampson, Robert J. and William Julius Wilson. (1995). Race, Crime and Urban Inequality. In *Crime and Inequality*, edited by John Hagan and Ruth D. Peterson. Palo Alto, Calif: Stanford University Press.

Sampson, Robert J., Stephen W. Raudenbush, and Felton Earls. (1997). Neighborhoods and Violent Crime: A Multi-level Study of Collective Efficacy. *Science* 227:2–25.

Shaw, Clifford, and Henry McKay. (1942). *Juvenile Delinquency and Urban Areas.* University of Chicago Press: Chicago.

Shihadeh, Edward S. and Nicole Flynn. (1996). Segregation and crime: The effect of Black social isolation on the rates of black urban violence. *Social Forces* 74:1325–1352.

Shihadeh, Edward S. and Michael O. Maume. (1997). Segregation and crime: The Relationship between black centralization and urban black homicide. *Homicide Studies: An Interdisciplinary and International Journal* 1:254–280.

Shihadeh, Edward S. and Darrell J. Steffensmeier. (1994). Economic inequality, family disruption and urban black violence: Cities as units of stratification and social control. *Social Forces* 73:729–751.

Simon, David. (1991). *Homicide: A Year on the Killing Streets.* Boston: Houghton Mifflin.

Smith, Douglas A. (1987). Police Response to Interpersonal Violence: Defining the Parameters of Legal Control. *Social Forces* 65:767–782.

Smith, M. Dwayne and Robert Nash Parker. (1980.) Type of Homicide and Variation in Regional Rates. *Social Forces* 59:136–147.

Wacquant, L., and William J. Wilson. (1989). The Cost of Racial and Class Exclusion in the Inner City. *Annals of the American Academy of Political and Social Science* 501:8–25.

Wilson, William Julius. (1987). *The Truly Disadvantaged: The Inner City, the Underclass, and Public Policy.* Chicago: The University of Chicago Press.

_______. (1996). *When Work Disappears: The World of the New Urban Poor.* NewYork: Alfred A. Knopf.

Section 3

Gender, Sexuality and the Law

"The Violence of Gender, the Gender of Violence: Law, Gender and Violence"

Lisa A. Crooms,
Howard University School of Law

Introduction

The law defines narrowly the space where gender and violence collide. There, sex and gender are synonyms, and legal sex/gender is presumptively both heterosexual and about women. Consequently, important differences between sex and gender are obliterated, the legal identity of all but heterosexuals is erased, and the various ways that men are gendered are obscured. This is the background against which the law defines gender-based violence as violence against women in general and male violence against women in heterosexual contexts in particular.[1]

This essay offers an alternative framework in which to analyze sex, gender and violence beyond the law's current discourse and its "gender-based violence = male violence against women in heterosexual contexts" formulation. Rather than see gender-based violence as only involving presumptively female victims, this alternative analysis begins with the idea that virtually all violence is gendered. Under this analysis, focusing solely on the victim's gender is no

---

1. These heterosexual contexts are either acts, in the case of rape and other sexual assault, or relationships, in the case of domestic violence and sexual assault between men and women as spouses or intimates, as well as that violence facilitated by these heterosexual relations, e.g. incest.

longer warranted; attention must also be paid to the relationship between the perpetrator's gender and the violence. This alternative analysis is not meant to deny the reality of either the violence suffered by many women at the hands of men or the predominance of men as perpetrators of violence. [2] Rather, it is designed to make explicit the connections between violence, which is largely a young male phenomenon, and destructive ideas about masculinity that terrorize entire communities. This essay proposes that we look anew at the relationship between gender and violence because violence may most productively be analyzed in terms of gender beyond the law's current focus on women as victims.

The remainder of this essay is organized as follows. Part I uses U.S. Supreme Court opinions to demonstrate how the law not only defines sex as gender and vice versa, but also conceptualizes its sex/gender as primarily a condition for women in heterosexual contexts. Part II turns specifically to the legal conceptualization of gender-based violence as male violence against women in heterosexual contexts and explores some of the limitations of this legal conceptualization. Part III introduces Black Feminist Thought and Critical Race Feminism, central to which are the ideas of intersectional identities and interlocking oppressions that operate in an overarching "matrix of domination." This section concludes with an alternative analytical framework for gender-based violence in which the perpetrator's gender is relevant. This analytical shift represents Black Feminist Thought and Critical Race Feminism as praxes that seek to interrogate fully the relationship between identity, op-

---

2. While a full discussion of the debate about sex and gender as matters of "nature," "nurture," or both is beyond the scope of this essay, it is important to note that the debate is hampered by the tendency of many feminists and others to avoid considering fully the biology that might be at work in gender because of concerns about biological determinism. As Carol Smart notes in FEMINISM AND THE POWER OF LAW, the desire of some feminists to avoid seeing any biology in gender for women while casting men as biologically-driven oppressors is problematic. This is clearly a double standard that does very little to further our understanding of the relationship between biology, on the one hand, and social constructions and conventions, on the other hand. Research exploring the prevalence of male aggression and violence, as well as female subordination and relative submissiveness, across both societies and species suggests that it may be more fruitful to abandon the "nature/nurture" dichotomy and to adopt an analysis that sees both nature and nurture as legitimate factors in the ways that sex and gender are both experienced and produced on continuums similar to the lesbian continuum discussed by Adrienne Rich in her essay *Compulsory Heterosexuality and Lesbian Existence* included in BLOOD, BREAD AND POETRY: SELECTED PROSE, 1979–1985 (1986). *See also* MICHAEL P. GHIGLIERI, THE DARK SIDE OF MAN: TRACING THE ORIGINS OF MALE VIOLENCE (2000) and RICHARD WRANGHAM & DALE PETERSON, DEMONIC MALES: APES AND THE ORIGINS OF HUMAN VIOLENCE (1996).

pression, and violence in light of the intra- and inter-gender hierarchies under which multiple masculinities and femininities co-exist.[3] Finally, Part IV uses two stories of gender-based violence to illustrate not only the limits of the current legal definition of gender-based violence, but also the possibilities of the alternative analytical framework proposed in Part III.

Sex, Gender and Law

For almost 25 years, the U.S. Supreme Court has been crafting a constitutional jurisprudence of sex and gender, central to which is the eliding of these two related, but distinguishable, concepts.[4] The Court's refusal to recognize constitutionally protected individual rights in contexts outside of heterosexuality further limits sex/gender, so that, as a legal matter, sex/gender is presumptively heterosexual. For example, while constitutional privacy is broad enough to include the rights of heterosexual couples and women in matters related to reproduction, it has been construed to exclude homosexual acts between consenting adults.[5] An additional, but entirely understandable, limitation concerns the specificity of the law's sex/gender, which casts it as primarily a matter for women oppressed by men, both institutionally and individually.[6] In many situations, patriarchy, male supremacy and, in the most

---

3. According to Michael S. Kimmel, "[t]he difference between male and female sexuality reproduces men's power over women, *and, simultaneously*, the power of some men over other men, especially of the dominant, hegemonic form of manhood—white, straight, middle-class—over marginalized masculinities." Michael S. Kimmel, *Clarence, William, Iron Mike, Tailhook, Senator Packwood, Spur Posse, Magic... and Us in* TRANSFORMING A RAPE CULTURE 119, 123 (1993).

4. *See e.g. G.E. v. Gilbert*, 429 U.S. 125 (1976), *Personnel Administrator of Massachusetts v. Feeney*, 442 U.S. 256 (1979), *Harris v. Forklift Systems Inc.*, 510 U.S. 17 (1993) (addressing legal sex/gender in the context of employment discrimination); *Mississippi University for Women v. Hogan*, 458 U.S. 718 (1982) and *U.S. v. Virginia*, 518 U.S. 515 (1996) (doing the same in the context of public education); *Califano v. Westcott*, 443 U.S. 76 (1979) and *Heckler v. Matthews* 465 U.S. 728 (1984) (same in the context of government benefits); *Michael M. v. Superior Court of Sonoma County*, 450 U.S. 464 (1981) (criminal law, statutory rape, and sex/gender under the Fourteenth Amendment's Equal Protection Clause).

5. *Compare Bowers v. Hardwick with Griswold v. Connecticut* and *Eisenstadt v, Baird. See also*, Robert S. Chang & Jerome McCristal Culp, Jr., *Nothing and Everything: Race,* Roemer, *and Gay, Lesbian and Bisexual Rights*, 6 WM. & MARY BILL OF RTS. J. 229 (1997) (describing the Supreme Court's opinion in Roemer v. Evans as recognizing individual rights despite, not because of, orientation.

6. This limitation is due, in large part, to the historical specificity of women's subordination and the role that the law plays in facilitating that subordination. For example, in

extreme cases, misogyny operate to construct male domination and female subordination as natural and, consequently, beyond legal redress. The Court's attempt to remedy the legally cognizable injuries resulting from this triumvirate of women's oppression are careful not to disturb the largely artificial line between public and private that marks the boundaries within which the law may properly operate and beyond which the law may not reach. These remedial efforts are further limited by the formal equality and sex- and gender-neutrality currently in fashion, which allow both men and women to pursue claims of sex/gender discrimination under laws commonly understood to protect women's rights.[7] Sex- and gender-neutral language, however, is interpreted in sex- and gender-specific ways that render sex/gender a woman's issue with which the vast majority of men rarely have to be directly concerned. While the messages are mixed, it is clear that what is largely absent from this legal discourse is an explicit analysis of the various ways in which men are gendered, the intra-gender hierarchy of masculinities, and how these two things are manifested in the law.

In the 1996 case of *Oncale v. Sundowner Offshore Services, Incorporated*, the Court concluded that same-sex sexual harassment was actionable under Title VII of the Civil Rights Act of 1964 provided that the claimant could show that not only was he harassed because he was a man, but also no women were or would have been treated in the same way. In reaching its conclusion, the

---

Orr v. Orr, 440 U.S. 268 (1979), the Court concludes that the sex-specific language of the challenged statute violated the Equal Protection Clause of the 14th Amendment because it not only relied on the gender-based roles of husbands and wives, but also rested on a presumption of female dependence. The Court went on to state that it "would initially approach the 'compensation' rationale [offered by the State] by asking whether women had in fact been significantly discriminated against in the sphere to which the statute applies a sex-based classification, leaving the sexes 'not similarly situated with respect to opportunities in that sphere'." It must be noted, however, that the likelihood that the law will assign legal liability for women's injuries resulting from even its limited sex/gender oppression is linked to how the causal chain between act and injury is constructed. *See e.g. infra.* discussion of *Personnel Administrator of Massachusetts v. Feeney.*

7. Beginning in the 1980s, the Court's anti-discrimination cases have embraced neutrality and eschewed the idea of group rights and "protected classifications." For example, Title VII of the Civil Rights Act of 1964 prohibits discrimination in employment based on, *inter alia*, sex. While many of the Court's Title VII cases have focused on the statute as a remedy for the employment discrimination suffered by women, as a class, the law has been interpreted so that it is consistent with formal equality and sex/gender-neutral so that it "protects men as well as women." *Oncale v. Sundowner Offshore Services, Incorporated*, 523 U.S. 75 (1998) *citing Newport News Shipbuilding & Dry Dock Co. v. EEOC*, 462 U.S. 669, 682 (1983).

Court interpreted Title VII as both sex/gender-neutral and sex/gender-specific, i.e. sexual harassment in employment can be experienced by both women and men, but it must be experienced specifically because of the claimant's sex/gender.

The Court's interpretation of Title VII, however, is both neutral and specific in another way. In reversing the lower court's interpretation of Title VII as excluding same-sex sexual harassment, the Court provides no guidance to help the lower court overcome the limited understanding of sexual harassment on which its reversed decision was based. The full implications of this failure on the part of the Court may best be appreciated in terms of the legal precedent of sexuality and sex/gender. Title VII's same-sex sexual harassment is heterosexual by default because Title VII's sex does not provide rights to sexual minorities on the basis of sexuality and sexual orientation. Title VII's prototypical sexual harassment victim is a heterosexual woman harassed by a heterosexual man. As such, victimization is primarily cast as a matter of femaleness because sex/gender is thought to be about women and data overwhelmingly show that women are harassed by men.

While Oncale's heterosexuality was not an issue, his legal credibility as a victim of sexual harassment would seem to turn on his ability to approximate the position of the law's presumptively female victim of sexual harassment. The law's gender narrowness would cast Oncale as a female surrogate in a case of heterosexual sexual harassment who was harassed because of his sex, i.e. male. By focusing on Oncale's sex-specific vulnerability to this sexual harassment, the law misses the larger context of the intragender hierarchy of masculinities in Oncale's workplace under which Oncale was both deemed the most devalued man and sexually harassed because of his status. This hierarchy also allowed Oncale's harassers to define their masculinity in terms of their ability to harass Oncale without compromising their legal heterosexuality by engaging in homoerotic acts.[8] In addition, understanding Oncale's harassment as a function of contested masculinities avoids making victimization turn on femaleness by seeing the gender at work in the production of masculinities under which Oncale could be (indeed, had to be) harassed. Unfortunately, this type of analysis is unlikely to feature in those cases which cite *Oncale* as precedent. It is more likely that the credibility of male victims of same-sex sex-

8. Oncale was restrained by two co-workers while his supervisor "placed his penis on Oncale's neck, on one occasion, and on Oncale's arm, on another occasion." Oncale was also threatened with rape by the same two co-workers and had a bar of soap pushed into his anus by his supervisor as he was restrained by one co-worker in the shower. *Oncale v. Sundowner Offshore Services, Inc.*, 83 F.3d 118, 118–119 (1996).

ual harassment will be contingent on their status as female surrogates in what would otherwise be heterosexual harassment by men.

Personnel Administrator of Massachusetts v. Feeney (442 U.S. 256 (1979)) demonstrates the limits of the Court's sex/gender in a context where it failed to analyze explicitly the connections between maleness, the military and the law on which the plaintiff's claim turned. Helen Feeney used the Fourteenth Amendment's Equal Protection Clause to challenge the constitutionality of Massachusetts' sex-neutral veterans' preference law. The Court deemed the statute constitutional because it extended a preference to veterans because they were veterans rather than because the class of veterans was overwhelmingly male. Because Helen Feeney proffered no direct evidence of intentional sex/gender discrimination by Massachusetts, the Court denied her relief. If the case involved sex/gender discrimination, according to the Court, then it was that of the federal government which enjoys considerable discretion to act in matters related to raising armies, conducting wars and defending "national security." According to the Court, Helen Feeney could not hold Massachusetts liable for the admittedly discriminatory policies of the Federal government.

In dispensing with Feeney's legal claim, the Court defines the gendered nature of the military—the overall context in which the preference operates—as legally irrelevant. Indeed, the Court rejects the idea that the "veterans' preference is 'inherently non-neutral' or 'gender-based'." While it recognizes the culpability of the federal government in "prevent[ing] all but a handful of women from becoming veterans," it focuses on intentional discrimination (or the lack thereof), which shields the State from liability for using a preference that is integrally linked to "historical[ly] gender-based federal military personnel practices..." In this way, the Court not only leaves Helen Feeney and other women without a legal remedy, but also fails to address the maleness on which the military relies as a legal matter of sex/gender.

Sex/Gender, Violence and Law

The Court's missteps in its construction of sex/gender and its accompanying analysis have particular implications for the legal treatment of violence as a function of gender. First, eliding sex and gender to produce sex/gender and limiting legally legitimate sex/gender to heterosexuality means that gender-based violence is most commonly understood in terms of male violence against women victims in heterosexual contexts. Moreover, because this jurisprudence is largely remedial and attached to real issues of historical and contemporary male domination and female subordination, when violence is analyzed as a legal matter, sex/gender neutral language tends to be interpreted in sex/gender-specific ways so that the credibility of male victims of gender-based violence may be compromised by the mutual exclusivity of maleness and victimization, which is presumed to be female.

To explore this more fully, consider the Violence Against Women Act of 1994 (VAWA) and the recent Supreme Court case of *Morrison v. U.S.* in which VAWA's constitutionality was challenged. As enacted by Congress, VAWA provided a civil rights remedy to those victims of crimes of violence motivated by gender, which it defined as "crime[s] of violence committed because of gender or on the basis of gender, and due, at least in part, to an animus based on the victim's gender."[9] While the Act's definition of crimes of violence motivated by gender is sex- and gender-neutral, VAWA's title, as well as the congressional record on which the Act is based, are sex- and gender-specific. That is, crimes of violence motivated by gender are those crimes of violence committed by perpetrators who are men against victims who are women in explicitly heterosexual contexts. To see this result as perfectly understandable, one need only look to the history which laws such as VAWA are intended to respond. Here, women have been subordinated by male domination operating at both an individual and an institutional level which, for the majority of the time, has been constructed as the result of largely extra-legal conduct protected by privacy, family and patriarchal prerogatives.[10]

During its 1999–2000 term, the Supreme Court considered the constitutionality of VAWA in light of Congress' power both "to regulate [c]ommerce... among the several states"[11] and "to enforce, by appropriate legislation, the provisions of [the Fourteenth Amendment]."[12] While the constitutional issues raised in Morrison's case did not turn on the specific facts of Christy Brzonkala's substantive claim, it is important to note that she was allegedly raped by two football players, only one of whom was mildly disciplined because of, *inter alia*, notice issues rather than issues of Brzonkala's credibility. Virginia Polytechnic Institute's mishandling of Brzonkala's rape as a student disciplinary matter led her to pursue a civil rights claim under VAWA, which had been

---

9. VAWA 42 USC §13981, Chapter 136. Violent Crime Control and Law Enforcement; Violence against Women; Civil Rights for Women (1994).

10. *See also United Nations Declaration on Violence Against Women* (using a similar approach to remedy women's injuries at the hands of male perpetrators based on the reality that men and the law have conspired to place many of these injuries beyond the proper reach of the law).

11. U.S. Const., Art. I, §8.

12. U.S. Const., Amend. XIV, §5.

passed about two weeks before Brzonkala was raped.[13] The Court concluded that VAWA's civil rights remedy could not properly be viewed as an appropriate exercise of congressional power. Consequently, the Court struck down VAWA's civil rights remedy as unconstitutional.

In his dissenting opinion, Justice Souter provides an example of the Court's production of sex/gender as a matter primarily concerned with women vis-à-vis men and heterosexuality. As noted by Souter, "while [VAWA's] civil rights remedy limits its scope to 'crimes of violence motivated by gender'...the meaning of 'motivated by gender' has not been elucidated by lower courts, much less by this one." [14] Souter, however, opts for a definition of "motivated by gender," central to which is "the problem of violence against women." Construed in this way, Souter sees VAWA as an appropriate exercise of Congressional power supported by ample evidence of the impact and the prevalence of male violence against women in heterosexual contexts. This violence is gender-based because of the perpetrator's animus towards the victim's female sex/gender.

This definition, however, leaves no room to consider the relationship between the perpetrator's gender and the violence, because this relationship is omitted from the legal analysis. Consequently, little serious thought is given to the connection between violence and the production of masculinities. Here, not all men are constructed as equal and this becomes the source of the gender-based oppression that too often manifests itself in the flashes of violence between men that are rarely seen as matters of gender.

Using Black Feminist Thought/Critical Race Feminism to Construct a New Analytical Paradigm

The remainder of this essay makes the case for expanding gender-based violence to include not only the relationship between the violence and the perpetrator's gender, but also violence involving male victims. In this analysis, the presence or absence of gender-based violence no longer turns on the presumed femaleness of the victim. Rather, gender becomes the central aperture through which all violence is seen, the genders of both the victim and the perpetrator are relevant, and violence beyond heterosexual contexts is included on its own terms. In other words, this alternative analysis begins from a point of inclusion rather than exclusion, which is a central principle on which both Black Feminist Thought (BFT) and Critical Race Feminism (CRF) are based.

---

13. *See generally,* Patrick Tracey, *Christy's Crusade,* MS. 53 (Apr./May 2000).
14. *U.S. v. Morrison,* 120 S.Ct. 1740, 1760 (fn. 2) [Souter, dissenting].

BFT is an ideological stance that simultaneously intervenes in two discourses of identity and oppression. One the one hand, it challenges mainstream feminism's tendency to de-emphasize differences among women and to ignore the sites of power from which some women either can or do oppress other women and some men. On the other hand, BFT challenges the men in communities of color who see their racial and ethnic struggle in terms of the white supremacist patriarchy which continues to deny them the manhood their "colored" patriarchies should guarantee. Chief among the things they are denied is their right to exercise patriarchal prerogatives and privileges vis-à-vis women of color without fear of the government intrusion with which many communities of color must constantly and disproportionately contend. In this way, BFT gives voice to the experiences and epistemologies of black women in contexts where both are often either ignored or cast as something beyond the proper bounds of sex, gender or race.

One of BFT's central principles is that identity is intersectional. That is, BFT's identity forms at the interstices of multiple axes, rather than along a series of severable and parallel single axes. For example, BFT rejects the idea identity as either sex/gender or race and replaces it with an identity that is both sex or gender and race [and class and ethnicity and sexual orientation/sexuality, etc.].

BFT's other central principle is that oppressions operate in an interlocking fashion as part of "the matrix of domination." This matrix recasts oppression's fundamental issue as "the social relations of domination regardless of either the identity of the individuals involved or the specific systems of oppression that drive the particular domination in question."[15] Although the real and substantive differences between the ways oppressions are experienced are not denied, these differences "become less important, and the overarching objective is understanding the commonalities of oppressive relations between 'groups [that] possess varying amounts of penalty and privilege in one historically created system.'"[16] In this way, neither patriarchy nor white supremacy, for example,

15. Lisa A. Crooms, *Indivisible Rights and Intersectional Identities or, "What Do Women's Human Rights Have To Do With the Race Convention?"*, HOWARD L.J. 619, 622 (1997).

16. *Id. quoting* Patricia Hill Collins, *Black Feminist Thought: Knowledge, Consciousness and the Politics of Empowerment* 225–26 (1990). *supra* note—at 225–26. This approach "should not be understood to deny that there are substantively different types of oppressions. For example, the violence of racist hate crimes committed by white supremacy is quite different from manifestations of the ableism with which the physically disabled must contend." Crooms, *supra* note 15—at 622.

can be analyzed independently, but must, instead, be viewed as working in concert in one multi-layered and historically-created system of oppression.

CRF represents the marriage of BFT principles with legal analysis and theory.[17] Like BFT, CRF intervenes in discourses in which race is normatively gendered male and gender is normatively sexed female and raced white. Both BFT and CRF embrace the complexities of identity and oppression, which can make oppressor and oppressed highly situational statuses. They challenge us to interrogate and to revise the assumptions on which our understanding of identity and oppression is based. They also implicitly call on us to move beyond focusing on gender as a matter of the multiplicity of women, which many of its adherents have explored and to consider, at the very least, the multiplicity of men as well.

A rigorous application of BFT and CRF principles allows us to see gender more completely, i.e. as a matter of both inter- and intra-gender hierarchies. Using BFT and CRF in this way reveals gender not to be an issue solely for women. Adhering to BFT and CRF principles compels us to include men in our gender analysis and theory because they are gendered in ways that are highly problematic and destructive for both themselves and their communities. The intersectional identity paradigm, the "both/and conceptual stance" and the "matrix of domination" also mean that being a victim of gender-based violence can no longer be the exclusive province of women. Rather, some men, particularly young black and Latino men, are victims of violence that is gendered to its core. Consequently, CRF and BFT implore us to explore the relationship between gender and violence beyond oppressive male perpetrators, oppressed female victims and heterosexuality. They push us to consider gender-based violence in terms of not only the gender of the victim, but also that of the perpetrator.

This shift should yield the following results. As an initial matter, it should facilitate a more complete understanding of the relationship between gender and violence that is contingent on neither the victim's gender nor presumed heterosexuality. This, in turn, should allow us to see the gender in virtually all violence, without fear that doing so will mean gains for men at the expense

---

17. Critical Race Feminism, as a legal theoretical stance, not only has roots in the oppositional discourses of Critical Legal Studies, Critical Race Theory and Feminist Legal Theory, but also represents an analysis that is, itself, oppositional within these discourses. Its method includes multiple consciousness and a bottom-based focus, which illuminates the position of the ignored and disempowered to challenge the biases and privileges left unaddressed by Critical Legal Studies, Critical Race Theory and Feminist Legal Theory. *See generally* CRITICAL RACE FEMINISM: A READER (Adrien K. Wing, ed., 1997).

of women in the law's zero-sum game of sex, gender and violence. Rather, focusing more intently on the gender in virtually all violence should mean that gender-based violence against women is no longer relegated to the margins of the violence discourse. This should create a sounder basis for both analytical and remedial purposes. This should also allow us to assess better the efficacy of and justice in not just those measures designed to protect women from men, but also current "Law and Order" initiatives which include mandatory minimum sentences, the growing prison-industrial-complex, and the brutal shows of police force crucial to "zero tolerance" campaigns. We can develop a gender critique of the criminalization of young black and Latino men that fuels lawmakers' efforts to fight crime, particularly the "War on Drugs."

In addition, using gender this way requires us to revisit the basic premises on which the law's treatment of sex, gender and violence is based, of which VAWA is just one example. It would allow us to confront John Oncale's sexual harassment not as a matter of sex/gender-neutrality and -specificity, but rather as a matter of Oncale's devalued position in a workplace ordered around an intra-gender hierarchy of masculinities. It would permit Helen Feeney's claim to be assessed explicitly in terms that make legally relevant both the military's gender (male) and the impact of this gendering on both men and women.

Seeing The Gender in Violence: Two Stories

Story I—The Murder of Grace Edwards

Everybody called her mom. No one would intentionally hurt her. Grace Josephine Edwards was a fixture in her neighborhood, east of the Anacostia River, beyond the Washington, D.C. featured on the maps tourists eagerly clutch as they make their way from the Washington Monument through Dupont Circle to Georgetown. In Ms. Edwards' neighborhood, the sounds of gunshots mix with the cursing and posturing of young black men trying both to keep it real and to watch their backs which, under some circumstances, is virtually impossible to do successfully.

A 76-year-old stroke survivor, Edwards was out at 6:30 a.m. for her early morning walk. She thought the morning was the safest time of day. On this morning, however, the 5100 block of 10th Place, S.E. was far from safe. Thirty minutes earlier, Nakia Roy spotted his girlfriend, Nacheta Harris, on the back of Edward Settles' motorcycle. This sighting started a chain of events that both included an exchange of gunfire and Roy's punching Harris in the face and culminated in Edward's death. These events were chronicled in newspaper articles with titles like, *Another Grandmother Gone*, by journalists who cited Edward's death as evidence of changes in the rules of engagement. Elders were no longer off-limits in the violence of the streets.

These rules are the subject of Elijah Anderson's ethnography, *Code of the Street: Decency, Violence and the Moral Life of the Inner City.* Although Anderson studied Philadelphia's Germantown Avenue, much of what he describes is universal for those in "the depths of the inner city—the so-called hyperghetto—[where] people.... are very much socially isolated from mainstream America."[18] According to Anderson,

> ...street culture has evolved a "code of the street," which amounts to a set of informal rules governing interpersonal public behavior, particularly violence. The rules prescribe both proper comportment and the proper way to respond, if challenged. They regulate the use of violence and so supply a rationale allowing those who are inclined to aggression to precipitate violent encounters in an approved way.[19]

"At the heart of the code," Anderson continues, "is the issue of respect."[20] Indeed, "[t]he rules of the code...provide a framework for negotiating respect."[21] While one who is sufficiently respected enjoys a certain amount of personal security, "in the troublesome public environment of the inner city, as people increasingly feel buffeted by forces beyond their control, what one deserves in the way of respect becomes ever more problematic and uncertain." [22] As Anderson sees it, "[t]he inclination to violence [among many poor inner city residents] springs from the circumstances of life among the ghetto poor—the lack of jobs that pay a living wage, limited basic public services...the stigma

---

18. Anderson at 26. Anderson, however, may have underestimated the reach of "the code." Indeed, the alleged criminal exploits and general thuggery of multi-million dollar businessmen Suge Knight and Sean "Puffy" Combs, as well as the tragic assassinations of the Notorious B.I.G. and Tupac Shakur are evidence that "the code" is no longer limited to those who Anderson describes as being socially isolated from mainstream America. *See e.g.* Steven Daly, *The Player King*, VANITY FAIR 130 (AUG. 2000) (describing Combs as both a "talent spotter with street cred whose Bad Boy label and underworld connections drew him into a gang war that may have killed Tupac...and Biggie..." and an "East Hampton music-mogul friend of Donald Trump, Ronald Perelman and Martha Stewart").

19. ANDERSON at 33.

20. *Id.*

21. *Id.*

22. *Id.*

of race, the fallout from rampant drug use and drug trafficking,..."[23] This is a world marred by a "profound sense of alienation from mainstream society and its institutions felt by many poor inner city black people, particularly the young."[24]

To see the gender at work here, one need only recognize that "many of the concerns of...young men relating to respect and identity have come to be expressed in the concept of manhood," i.e. "assuming the prerogatives of men with respect to strangers, other men and women—being distinguished as a man."[25] Anderson identifies "an existential link between the idea of manhood and one's self-esteem" so that "for many inner city youths, manhood and respect are two sides of the same coin; physical and psychological well-being are inseparable and both require a sense of control, of being in charge."[26] For those whose manhood is tested, "one of the most effective ways of gaining respect is to manifest nerve."[27] While nerve is shown "by taking another person's possessions, messing with someone's woman, throwing the first punch, 'getting in someone's face,' or pulling a trigger,... [t]rue nerve expresses a lack of fear of death."[28] Many of Anderson's interviewees, "fe[lt] that it [was] acceptable to risk dying over issues of respect. In fact, among the hard-core street-oriented, the clear risk of violent death may be preferable to being dissed."[29]

One of the code's primary functions is to order proper relations under the intra-gender hierarchy of masculinities at work in communities such as the 5100 block of 10th Place, S.E. and Germantown Avenue in Philadelphia. Here, definitive manhood is that which the most respected command and to which all aspire. This manhood is rare, remains out of reach for most men, and is the manhood beneath which all others fall within this community's hierarchy of masculinities. It is also the manhood for which groups of rival men contend in skirmishes that often temporarily reorder the hierarchy until another challenge is launched.

The code, however, operates in other ways that demonstrate its connection with the mainstream. First, the code can be seen as a ghetto adaptation of the rules according to which masculinities operate in mainstream society. The cen-

---

23. *Id.*

24. *Id.*

25. Anderson at 91.

26. *Id.*

27. *Id. See also* Geoffrey Canada, Fist, Stick, Knife, Gun, (1996) (describing "heart" in terms similar to those used by Anderson to talk about nerve).

28. Anderson at 92.

29. *Id.*

trality of respect to mainstream ideas about masculinity is integrally linked to wealth and the conspicuous consumerism associated with unquestionably powerful men.[30] This consumerism features prominently in "the code of the street" and its obsession with expensive designer wares that only drug dealing and hustling can buy. Second, the code has also been mainstreamed through the black cultural production, which has been embraced by young people across races, ethnicities and classes. While those who literally live and die by the code are, indeed isolated and alienated as subjects, they have been woven into the cultural fabric of the mainstream as objects.

What Anderson's study and analysis make clear is that gender is central to understanding the violence that ended Grace Edwards' life. Although her death involved a male perpetrator, female victims, murder and domestic violence, male gender-based violence against women is only part of the story's sub-plot. Consequently, we cannot call either Roy's violence against Harris the proximate cause of Edwards' murder or Edwards a victim of a man's violence against a woman in a heterosexual context.

Gender, however, is clearly at work in the violence that claimed Edwards' life. This gender is a function of respect, being dissed and seeking vengeance in the name of masculinity and in accordance with the rules of "the code." Roy and Settles understood the code because it both defined and threatened their status within the intragender hierarchy of masculinities operating in the 5100 block of 10th Place, S.E. Settles asserted his status through his nerve, i.e. riding in broad daylight with Harris, Roy's girlfriend, on the back of his motorcycle. The damage Settles did to Roy's status was ameliorated by not only his willingness to handle his business, i.e. discipline Harris, but also his nerve, i.e. pulling a trigger. Edwards died as an innocent victim caught in the crossfire of a dispute, which, according to the code, tested Roy's manhood and warranted a violent resolution.

Seeing Grace Edwards' murder as the result of gender-based violence reveals the limitations of measures such as VAWA either to understanding gender-based violence or to crafting solutions to address this type of violence. The

---

30. In a recent interview published in Ms. magazine, Susan Faludi talks about the masculinity-related anxiety felt by the mostly white men featured in her book, STIFFED: THE BETRAYAL OF THE AMERICAN MAN, in terms of "fear of losing face" and respect. Faludi also notes the problems with questioning manhood as disempowering because "to say out loud, 'There are no reins in my hand' is a great humiliation." Faludi concludes that "[m]asculinity seems to be a very insecure suit of clothes that can be ripped away at any moment... Everything seems to revolve around whether you are man enough." Gloria Jacobs, *The Male Box,* MS. 63, 68–69 (Apr./May 2000).

larger context of poverty, alienation and hypermasculinity in the inner-city makes it clear that tougher sentencing, more prisons and more extreme shows of police force are neither just nor likely to reduce the type of violence that ended Edwards' life. Any solutions must begin with an acknowledgement that complete disregard for the sanctity of human life is the lesson Roy and Settles learned well from a country that continues to treat them and those who look most like them as inherently dangerous and ultimately disposable. In many respects, the gender-based violence that killed Grace Edwards is a by-product of the criminalization and devaluation of communities of color, which help to justify "the ritual sacrifice of [their] constitutional rights". [31]

Story II—Sexual Assaults in Central Park and the National Puerto Rican Day Parade

Throngs of people celebrated in the streets during New York's annual National Puerto Rican Day Parade. The City displayed its diversity as all kinds of people joined the revelry. The seemingly intractable divisions of race, ethnicity and class for which New York has become a metaphor were temporarily erased. But the day turned ugly when a group of young men decided to grope, strip and, in some cases, sexually assault almost 60 women at the south end of Central Park—apparently undeterred by the presence of either video cameras or the police. In the weeks that followed, the details were filled in and 28 men were indicted because they chose to commit very public acts of sexual violence against unsuspecting women.

According to published accounts, the most serious attacks occurred in Central Park South where

> self-appointed 'scouts'...signal[led] to the larger group when they spotted women who fit their calculus of sexual appeal..."Yo, yo here comes a good one!," they would call out as unsuspecting women approached. Several older women got through. For the young and attractive, nearby fences helped form a natural chute into which they were steered. There was yelling of "Get 'em, get'em," and chants of "Go, go, go," and misogynistic curses and more young men joined the mob...and some of these men began to tear at shirts, to pull on bras, to tug on shorts. [32]

---

31. Katheryn Russell, *What Did I Do to Be So Black and Blue? in* Police Brutality (Jill Nelson, ed. 2000).

32. David Barstow & C.J. Chivers, *A Volatile Mixture Exploded into Rampage in Central Park*, N.Y. Times, June 17, 2000 at 1.

These published accounts also noted that members of the New York Police Department, neither protected the women from attack nor appeared concerned about "the rampant use of marijuana and alcohol." [33] It was hard to believe that it happened in New York, "...a city where the tiniest crimes have long been vigorously pursued....in the environs of an event...patrolled by four thousand officers."[34]

Almost immediately following the melee, questions were raised about the reported police inaction. Some claimed that the attacks were not treated seriously because of police and societal attitudes about gender-based male violence against women.[35] For this group, the presence of female victims, male perpetrators and sexual violence virtually guaranteed that the attacks would be ignored. Others tried to understand the police's failure to act in light of the reported belief that department higher-ups did not want to see "any confrontations between a largely white police force and Hispanic paradegoers."[36] For this group, the presence of ostensibly Puerto Rican men at a Puerto Rican parade patrolled by the NYPD virtually guaranteed that major transgressions would be ignored as the police attempted to curry favor with a community which, under normal circumstances, is terrorized by the NYPD's institutionalized brutality and violence.

While the answer to the question of what happened on that hot Sunday in New York is most probably a combination of misogyny and police inaction, this does not mean that gender is relevant to the former and not to the latter. Employing a rigorous gender analysis facilitates a more complete understanding of the ways that gender and violence work in tandem. Gender's role in the sexual attacks, as well as the police inaction, is best assessed within a context featuring the production of masculinities, particularly within Puerto Rican communities, and the intra-gender contests between men of color, on the one hand, and the NYPD, on the other hand. Rafael Ramírez's, *What It Means to Be a Man: Reflections on Puerto Rican Masculinity* provides important insights into both.

According to Ramírez, "[s]exuality, competition and power are elements that constitute the masculine ideologies...in all the societies through time and space in which...men have imposed [their] hegemony."[37] Among Puerto Ri-

---

33. Kevin Flynn, *Lower Morale, Yes. But Apathy?; Police Say They Are As Diligent As Ever, and the Numbers Agree*, N.Y. Times, June 28, 2000 at 25.

34. *Id.*

35. C.J. Chivers, *Suspension Cites Lax Response to Groping*, N.Y. Times, June 27, 2000 at B1.

36. *Id.*

37. Ramírez at 42.

cans, a man is constructed as "an essential sexual being" who "should enjoy his sexuality, declare it, boast about it, feel proud about it, and, above all, show it." [38] These same communities construct women as "objects of pleasure, so long as men abide by the taboo of incest and give the respect that is expected toward those women who are part of the family."[39] A real Puerto Rican man "pursues, punishes, repudiates, or devalues those women who reject him or pay no attention to his demands."[40] Indeed, "[s]exual harassment and violence against women are evidence of this orientation toward conquest and the use of sexuality in its aggressive articulation of power with pleasure."[41] Conquest "is also influenced by class and color differences and the relative power or influence that a man might have or believe he can have over a woman, or the relative equality that allows him to make the initial move."[42] The rules of engagement prohibit a Puerto Rican man from "try[ing] to seduce or conquer a woman who is socially or economically superior to him, unless the encounter occurs in a neutral environment, where class, power, or privilege differences are not involved or are minimized, or unless she sends signals that she is willing."[43]

The masculinity which most Puerto Rican men produce requires "real" men to "approach others by showing that [they] handle [them]selves with authority and are invulnerable and respectable, which are demonstrations of power that [their] masculinity bestows on [them]."[44] For these men, "to be a man whom others respect and to be respected is [one] of the basic demands of... masculinity."[45]

Being a man also means "always... be[ing] on guard so as not to lose [their] masculinity or have it questioned."[46] To this end, "men... compete among [them]selves to validate [their] constantly threatened masculinity."[47] Ramírez calls this dance the "constant competition and validation of masculinity" in which all non-marginalized Puerto Rican men participate."[48] This competition is "basically influenced by mechanisms of power; on oc-

---

38. *Id.* at 44–45.
39. *Id.* at 45.
40. *Id.* at 46.
41. *Id.*
42. *Id.*
43. *Id.*
44. *Id.* at 63.
45. *Id.* at 66.
46. *Id.* at 64.
47. *Id.*
48. *Id.*

casion power and respect become synonymous."[49] According to Ramírez, these public contests are particularly important for the production of Puerto Rican masculinities because their "ethnology stresses the importance of respect in enculturation."[50] Like the black communities studied by Elijah Anderson, Ramírez's Puerto Rican communities define respect as "the appropriate comportment in social encounters, in both the manner of behaving and the reaction to how others behave."[51] Like Anderson's code, this respect, is central to the structure of the intragender hierarchy of Puerto Rican masculinities, particularly in terms of who commands it, who threatens it, and who lacks it.

Finally, Ramírez considers the connection between masculinity and the police. To make his point, he recounts the story of "the notorious case of Cerro Maravilla, in which two young men who were *independentistas* were murdered by the police in 1978" and eyewitness testimony "of one of the policemen urinating on one of the cadavers after killing the young man." For Ramírez, this act was "[u]ndoubtedly...a demonstration of his power and his intent to devalue the defeated."[52] It is important to our analysis of gender and violence that this demonstration of power was by a member of a "police force...whose weapons and representation of the authority of the state allow law enforcement officers to be considered an occupation of power," i.e. masculinity.[53]

In New York, where the attacks took place, relations between the police and black and Latino communities are part of a history in which these communities were understood to be properly controlled by the police.[54] These police officers act according to a code that both encourages brutality and rallies behind violent cops who brutalize individuals with impunity. In addition, police discretion usually means that young blacks and Latinos are more likely to be diverted into the criminal justice system than their white counterparts, who

---

49. *Id.* at 66.
50. *Id.*
51. *Id.*
52. *Id.* at 58.
53. *Id.* at 63.
54. Derrick Bell describes this in terms of "*de facto* authorization" of police control over Black and Latino communities. Derrick Bell, *Police Brutality Portent of Disaster and Discomforting in* POLICE BRUTALITY 88, 92 (Jill Nelson, ed. 2000). *See also* Robin D.G. Kelley, *"Slangin' Rocks...Palestinian Style": Dispatches from the Occupied Zones of North America in* POLICE BRUTALITY (Jill Nelson, ed. 2000) (recounting the history of police brutality as carried out by both public and private actors against Black communities); KRS-One, *Sound of Da Police on* RETURN OF THE BOOM BAP (1993).

are more likely to be taken home to be disciplined by their parents.[55] For example, a recent study notes that "minority youths were disadvantaged at every stage of processing through the justice system. They were more likely to be arrested, charged, detained before trial, transferred to the adult system and incarcerated than were white youths, even for similar offenses."[56] Moreover, the predominant racial and ethnic makeup of the police department (primarily Irish- and Italian-American), means that race and ethnicity are central parts of the intragender hierarchy of masculinities under which relations between the police and the policed are formed.[57] Add to this Mayor Rudy Giuliani's "zero-tolerance" crusade, under which New York City has become a focal point for state violence in the form of police brutality against young black and brown men which much too often turns fatal.[58] This, oddly enough, is the New York City in which the NYPD allowed young black and brown men to attack scores of women on an oppressively hot Sunday afternoon.

Using Ramírez's work to analyze the events at the Puerto Rican Day Parade, it becomes apparent that his ideologies of masculinities help to understand not only the sexual attacks but also the apparent incongruity between the police inaction on that Sunday and the police terrorism with which these communities must contend virtually everyday. What follows is not meant to suggest that the Puerto Rican masculinities which both Ramírez describes and the events in New York illustrate are embraced by all Puerto Rican men. Rather, it merely recognizes the central role of those masculinities in the sexual attacks in New York's Central Park. This position is consistent with that taken by the more progressive members of New York's Puerto Rican community who see the attacks as a function of a "consciousness that 'being a man' is.... about dominating women.... [and not] about serving and protecting the community."[59]

---

55. *E.g.* Lieutenant Arthur Doyle (Retired), *From the Inside Looking Out: Twenty-nine Years in the New York Police Department in* POLICE BRUTALITY 171, 175 (Jill Nelson, ed. 2000).

56. Kristin Choo, *Minor Hardships*, ABA JOURNAL 20 (Sept. 2000).

57. *E.g.* Ishmael Reed, *Another Day at the Front: Encounters with the Fuzz on the American Battlefront in* POLICE BRUTALITY 189, 193 (Jill Nelson, ed. 2000). This is the case regardless of the actual race or ethnicity of the officers involved. Black and Latino officers are often involved in incidents of brutality in Black and Latino communities. These officers can be seen as acting in the interests of those the police protect who, under most circumstances, are neither Black nor Latino. *See also* KRS-One, *Black Cop on* RETURN OF THE BOOM BAP (1993).

58. *E.g.* Ron Daniels, *The Crisis of Police Brutality and Misconduct in America: The Causes and the Cure in* POLICE BRUTALITY 240, 243 (Jill Nelson, ed. 2000).

59. Statement of the National Congress for Puerto Rican Rights (June 2000).

Returning to Ramírez's analysis, first, the connection between Puerto Rican manhood and sexuality, as well as the importance of both conquest and control to that masculinity, as produced, played a key role in creating the conditions that gave rise to the attacks. The victims were seen as fair game because they were not perceived as women these men were bound to respect. The violence was the manifestation of masculine ideologies that encourage pursuit and, in some cases, conquest by violence of those women who dare either to rebuff their pursuers or to be caught unaware in unprotected space. Central Park South was the neutral ground on which all divisions of class, color, race and ethnicity were leveled, paving the way for this group of men to attack almost 60 women with impunity. This was clearly a case of gender-based violence, as a matter of both male violence against women in heterosexual contexts as well as the relationship between the violence and the gender of both the perpetrator and the victim.

Second, the masculinities produced in the attacks in Central Park almost demanded that those attacks take place in front of the police who, under most circumstances, have no regard for the respect to which these men believe they are entitled. Considered in the larger context of well-documented police brutality and terrorism against communities of color, the sexual attacks become an assertion of manhood in the face of the male institution that is often responsible for maintaining intra-gender hierarchies under which most Puerto Rican men occupy positions that lack value and respect. Because the police department, like the military, is an institution of masculine authority and power, choosing to attack women in full view of members of the NYPD was clearly a bold exercise of warped and misguided masculinities under which the women became the objects on and through which these masculinities were produced. The limited effectiveness of this exercise of masculine power is clarified by the context of police brutality and terrorism that mark everyday lives in communities of color. The police chose not to act because they had the power to do so. This choice made that Sunday an extraordinary day.

That extraordinariness, however, was short lived as investigations proceeded, arrests were made and indictments were handed down. This is where the trope on which justifications for the "gender-based violence = male violence against women" begins to falter and is replaced by the trope in which the criminal justice system is hostile toward communities of color, displaying a particular vengeance for young black and Latino men. As the National Congress for Puerto Rican Rights notes, "[g]iven the NYPD's history of racial profiling and indiscriminate 'sweeps' of young men of color, we should remain vigilant against innocent men being railroaded in this case and against the Mayor using this to justify increased police harassment of young men of color."[60] This reality of racially disparate treatment of people of color by law enforcement officials means that measures such as VAWA may become part of the criminal justice system's arsenal to be selectively deployed in ways that ultimately protect the interests of those who are white, male, heterosexual and middle-class. This approach evidences the inherent contradictions in "calls for increased policing, police presence and enhanced criminal penalties as a solution" for the poverty and violence with which many communities of color must contend.[61] As Stanley Crouch observes, this contradiction is the result of experiences with racist police and policing, on the one hand, and fears that "children, male and female, might become gunshot victims of gang violence, intentionally or accidentally." [62] Crouch continues, "no one hates violent black youth criminals more than black youth, because these knuckleheads are the people who might attack or kill a kid for something as trivial as 'eye fornication'—looking at them in a way that they don't like."[63] History, however, tells us that more laws and stiffer penalties are likely to increase the numbers of people of color who are both victimized by racial profiling and police violence and feed the burgeoning prison-industrial-complex. Less likely, however, is that these measures will pierce the veil of privilege that protects those whose maleness and/or whiteness and/or heterosexuality and/or socio-economic class shields them from being held responsible for their violence, regardless of the sex or gender of their victims. "While the NYPD must be held accountable for the inaction of officers...we must simultaneously continue to challenge the further criminalization of our communities as an easy solution to violence."[64]

Conclusion

What the foregoing should make clear is that we must change the ways in which we understand the relationship between gender and violence. While defining gender-based violence as male violence against women in heterosexual

60. *Id.*

61. The Audre Lorde Project, *Statement on Central Part and 116th Street Festival Attacks* (June 2000).

62. Stanley Crouch, *What's New? The Truth, As Usual in* POLICE BRUTALITY 165 (Jill Nelson, ed. 2000).

63. *Id.*

64. The Audre Lorde Project, *Statement on Central Park and 116th Street Festival Attacks* (June 2000).

contexts has yielded good results for some women, it has done so by recounting a partial understanding of the criminal justice system under which more laws and stiffer penalties are seen as necessary to demonstrate society's taking that violence seriously. The alternative analysis offered in this essay is intended to address not only this male violence against women, but also all other violence which can be viewed as being connected to the gender of either the perpetrator or the victim. In this way, it changes the violence discourse by making gender central to, rather than marginal in, the law's understanding of violence.

The analytical shift advanced in this essay should allow us to illuminate the workings of gender in contexts beyond what is currently understood to be gendered. Only if we begin to see gender and victimization as something with which both women and men must contend, will we be able to move toward real solutions to the dangerous and problematic ways in which gender is produced and maintained. If, however, we fail to make this shift, then we will continue to marginalize women and gender in the discourse of violence, as well as to encourage lawmakers to incarcerate disproportionate numbers of blacks and Latinos based on ideas about the inherent criminality and culpability of black and brown people. We can ill afford to concede the terrain on which the law defines gender and violence to those who would have us either ignore or misconstrue the injuries suffered by all who have to contend with the gender of violence and the violence of gender. Expanding the analysis of gender-based violence beyond its current limitations may be the most productive way to overcome the intensely polarized identity politics that characterize the space in which identity and oppression are both produced and contested.

References

Anderson, Elijah. (1999). *Code of the Street: Decency, Violence, and the Moral Life of the Inner City.* New York: W.W. Norton & Company.

Audre Lorde Project. (2000). Statement on the Central Park and 116th Street Festival Attacks. June.

Barstow, David and C.J. Chivers. (2000). A Volatile Mixture Exploded into Rampage in Central Park. *New York Times.* June 17. 1.

Bell, Derrick. (2000). Police Brutality Portent of Disaster and Discomforting. In Jill Nelson (Ed.) *Police Brutality: An Anthology.* (New York: W.W. Norton & Co. 88–101.

Canada, Geoffrey. (1996). *Fist, Stick, Knife, Gun: a Personal History of Violence in America.* New York: Beacon Press.

Chang, Robert and Jerome McCristal Culp, Jr. (1997). Nothing and Everything: Race, Roemer, and Gay, Lesbian and Bisexual Rights. In *William and Mary Bill of Rights Review.* 6:229.

Chivers, C.J. (2000). Suspension Cites Lax Response to Groping. *New York Times.* June 27. B1.

Choo, Kristin. (2000). Minor Hardships. *ABA Journal.* 20. September.

Collins, Patricia Hill. (1990). *Black Feminist Thought: Knowledge, Consciousness and the Politics of Empowerment.* New York: Routledge.

Crooms, Lisa A. (1997). Indivisible Rights and Intersectional Identities or, 'What Do Women's Human Rights Have To Do With the Race Convention?' *Howard Law Journal.* 40:619.

Crouch, Stanley. (2000). What's New? The Truth As Usual. In Jill Nelson, (Ed.) *Police Brutality: An Anthology.* New York: W.W. Norton & Co. 157–170.

Daly, Steven. (2000). The Player King. *Vanity Fair.* 130. August.

Daniels, Ron. (2000). The Crisis of Police Brutality and Misconduct in America: The Causes and the Cure. In Jill Nelson, (Ed.) *Police Brutality: An Anthology* New York: W.W. Norton & Co. 240–260.

Doyle, Arthur. (2000). From the Inside Looking Out: Twenty-nine Years in the New York Police Department. In Jill Nelson, (Ed.) *Police Brutality.* New York: W.W. Norton & Co. 171–188.

Flynn, Kevin. (2000). Lower Morale, Yes. But Apathy?; Police Say They Are As Diligent As Ever, and the Numbers Agree. *New York Times.* June 28. 25.

Ghiglieri, Michael P. (2000). *The Dark Side of Man: Tracing the Origins of Male Violence.* Cambridge, Mass: Perseus Books.

Jacobs, Gloria. (2000). The Male Box. *Ms.* 63. April/May.

Kelley, Robin D.G. (2000). 'Slangin' Rocks...Palestinian Style': Dispatches from the Occupied Zones of North America. In Jill Nelson, (Ed.) *Police Brutality.* New York: W.W. Norton & Co. 21–59.

Kimmel, Michael S. (1993). Clarence, William, Iron Mike, Tailhook, Senator Packwood, Spur Posse, Magic...and Us. In Emilie Buchwald, (et al. Eds.) *Transforming a Rape Culture.* Minneapolis: Milkweed Editions 119–138.

KRS-One. (1993). "Black Cop." Zomba Enterprises Inc./BDP Music. New York.

_______. (1993). "Sound of Da Police." Zomba Enterprises Inc./BDP Music. New York.

National Congress for Puerto Rican Rights. (2000). Statement. June.

Ramírez, Rafael. (1999). *What It Means to Be a Man: Reflections on Puerto Rican Masculinity.* New Brunswick: Rutgers University Press.

Reed, Ishmael. (2000). Another Day at the Front: Encounters with the Fuzz on the American Battlefront. In Jill Nelson, (Ed.). *Police Brutality: An Anthology.* New York: W.W. Norton & Co. 189–205.

Rich, Adrienne. (1985). Compulsory Heterosexuality and Lesbian Existence. In *Blood, Bread and Poetry: Selected Prose, 1979–1985.* New York: W.W. Norton & Co.

Russell, Katheryn. (2000). What Did I Do to Be So Black and Blue? In Jill Nelson, (Ed.) *Police Brutality: An Anthology.* New York: W.W. Norton & Co. 135–148.

Smart, Carol. (1989). *Feminism and the Power of Law.* New York: Routledge.

Tracey, Patrick. (2000). Christy Crusade. *Ms.* 53. April/May.

Wing, Adrien K. (1997). Introduction. In *Critical Race Feminism: An Anthology.* New York: New York University Press. 1–6.

Wrangham, Richard and Dale Peterson. (1996). *Demonic Males: Apes and the Origins of Human Violence.* New York: Houghton Mifflin.

Cases

Bowers v. Hardwick, 478 U.S. 186 (1986)
Califano v. Westcott, 443 U.S. 76 (1979)
Eisenstadt V. Baird, 405 U.S. 438 (1972)
G.E. v. Gilbert, 429 U.S. 125 (1976)
Griswold v. Connecticut, 381 U.S. 479 (1965)
Harris v. Forklift Systems Inc., 510 U.S. 17 (1993)
Michael M. v. Superior Court of Sonoma County, 450 U.S. 464 (1981)
Mississippi University for Women v. Hogan, 458 U.S. 718 (1982)
Oncale v. Sundowner Offshore Services, Inc., 523 U.S. 75 (1998)
Orr v. Orr, 440 U.S. 268 (1979)
Personnel Administrator of Massachusetts v. Feeney, 442 U.S. 256 (1979)
Morrison v. U.S., 120 S. Ct. 1740 (2000)

Constitutions, Statutes and Declarations

U.S. Constitution, Art. I, §8.
______________. Amend. XIV, §5.
Violent Crime Control and Law Enforcement; Violence Against Women; Civil Rights for Women, 42 U.S.C. §13981 (1994).
Declaration on the Elimination of Violence Against Women, G.A. Res. 48/104, U.N. GAOP, 48 Sess., Supp. No. 49, at 217, U.N. Doc. A/48/49 (1993).

"Explaining the Gentleness of Women: Control, Power, or 'Just Folks'"

Kathleen Gale,
Elmira College

Abstract

This chapter reviews various measures of violence by gender and considers a number of explanations of the differences. Using women's narratives from a series of in depth interviews, I investigate several theories of differences in criminal violence by men and women. The women who tell their stories also theorize about the nature and causes of the violence they have done or have suffered. In the first autobiography Mary Smith defines her own feelings and desire to be violent as "deviant." She seeks medical treatment and treats her own violent impulse. She chooses "self-control," even though her story shows a chaotic family life and shallow bonding with parents although not with siblings. The stories of Katy and Vera tell of the reverberating impact of woman abuse and child abuse. The criminal justice system, child protective services and the shelter systems of two states increase the harms done in the family. In their cases patriarchy, an intact family with the father present, did not reduce their "crime" as measured officially. The governmental systems did not work, rather, patriarchy operated through the last resort of violence from the father/husband, and the family interaction process ensured the perpetuation of violence into the next generation.

Introduction

Among several explanations for the gender difference in violent crime in the United States, one has persisted despite a lack of evidence. This is the theory that the gender gap is narrowing and that we are developing a 'new female criminal.' We have seen this figure fade in and out of public and scientific images of women and crime for the last twenty-five years. While feminist and critical criminologists argue that there is little evidence to support this image, we can still find this new "liberated" crook in our undergraduate texts of criminology and juvenile delinquency. I will argue that the picture of gender and crime presented by the convergence hypothesis is simplistic and evades questions of how women and girls are the same as men and boys, and how they are different.

We have several theories that explain gender differences in crime, but few that investigate peaceable cooperative behavior on the part of girls and women. This paper hopes to shift our focus from explaining gender difference in harm to gender difference in gentleness or resisting doing harm. Control theories were attractive to this project because they assume human behavior to be a consequence of internalized and externalized controls.

The Differences in Violent Offending by Gender

The observation that the gender gap in crime was narrowing (the convergence hypothesis) was first suggested by Adler and Simon in the 1970s (Adler, 1975, 1981, Adler and Simon, 1979.) Their data were arrests as counted in the Uniform Crime Reports, and were compared with similar data from other nations. These criminologists suggested that women's liberation accounted for the apparently rapidly rising rates of violence by women found between the 1960s and 1970s. They explained that the liberation of women from oppression and their new roles in the work world had given rise to a "new female criminal" and she was "liberated." This was one criminological hypothesis that made national headlines, and prompted sociologists and criminologists to question its validity (Chesney Lind, 1986; Daly and Cheney Lind 1988; Erez, 1988; Naffine, 1985; Naffine and Gale, 1989; Steffensmeier, 1980). Steffensmeier (1980) reviewed rates of offenses between 1965 and 1977. He found that the feminization of poverty explained the higher rates of property offending by women in the 1970s. Laidler advanced this interpretation of national data in the 1970s and Chesney Lind regarded changes in arrest rates of women and girls in the 1990s. They suggest that that the violence involved in the lives of marginalized women, as told in their accounts of their own lives, explains the rising rate of arrests of women for violent crimes from 1989 to 1997 (Chesney Lind, 1997).

Chesney Lind (1997; Chesney-Lind and Shelden, 1998) has commented extensively upon the resurgence of the liberation hypothesis. She finds that 1995 quantitative data about girls in gangs, as well as the interpretation of the national Uniform Crime Reports (UCR) rates of arrest for girls in 1995, do not provide support for the rise of a "new" violent female offender. Images of gangs are a code symbol for race in mass culture and therefore, in the 1990s, "the hype surrounding the issue has more to do with racism than with crime" (1997: 46).

Differences in national samples vary depending on the measurement taken. In the UCR arrests for all crimes in 1997 the male/female ratio was 3.5:1, in arrests for violent crimes it was 5:1 (Siegel, 2000: 69). Victims of violent crimes reported that the gender of their assailant was male in four out of five crimes. Among juveniles, reported in Chesney Lind (1997: 8), "there are considerable gender differences in official delinquency," the male to female ratio in all arrests of persons under 18 was 3:1, while the ratio for violent crime arrests was about 6:1.

Chesney Lind found a substantial increase in the rate of arrests of girls for violent assaults and other assaults, between 1970 and 1995 (Chesney-Lind, 1997: 11). "The arrest rates of girls for aggravated assaults increased by 188 percent between 1970 and 1980 and by 112 percent between 1980 and 1995," that constituted a 364 percent increase between 1970 and 1995. Subsequently, in the period 1994 through 1998, male arrests rose two percent while female arrests rose twelve per cent. In that time period "violent crime arrests showed a 53 percent increase for females and a 2 percent decrease for males (Uniform Crime Reports, 1999). Chesney Lind offers several explanations for the increasing arrest rates of girls: girls might be more involved in gang violence; they might be subject to more police attention in public places; Girls might be more frequently arrested in domestic violence situations when the police are called; or girls and boys might be more subject to arrest for violence towards parents, where previously this had been informally processed. Finally, this dramatic increase in youth arrests is undoubtedly the consequence of "poverty, violence at home, lack of hope, poorer occupational and educational opportunities," easy access to sophisticated weapons and a norm of carrying a weapon for self protection and/or reputation. (Chesney Lind 1997:11–12).

Turning to the self-report data from the national youth survey, Delbert Elliot (1994) and others have shown that the gender and race gap in self-reports of serious violent offenses is more narrow. Feminists respond that women and girls often exaggerate violence in their accounts of themselves, since it violates their socialization, while men and boys underreport violence. Overall this longitudinal national probability sample shows higher rates of youthful violence than are found in other national measures. Regarding desistance, or aging out of crime, Elliot (1994) concluded that white males had mostly desisted by the time they were in their twenties while black males had not. Elliot cautioned that this pattern of permanent adolescence for black males was a consequence of extreme disadvantage in urban ghettos.

Commenting upon explanations of the increase in youth violence revealed in official measures, Chesney Lind and Sheldon (1998) argue with another author that we explain girls' desistance because they are "over controlled," implying weak. On the other hand when women and girls do offend, we think they offend because they are vicious. Boys' increase in violence is to be expected. In this way "the construction of an artificial femininity lays the foundation for the demonization of young girls of color" (1998: 56). The interpretation of girls' violence in the media, and in much contemporary criminology, is that a 90s version of a "new breed" of violent women is being created. They are young women of color without an adequate home. There was lack of nurture and lack of discipline and supervision (low control) in the teen years. Also during this time, they experience low self-control and fail to desist from violence.

This popular gloss on girls in gangs is also found in the power and control model, suggested by Hagan, Simpson and Gillis (1985). The authors suggest that girls and women commit fewer offenses because they are controlled by "patriarchy" in their families. The power and control model supposes that an increase in girls' criminality is a result of an increase in single parent mother headed families as well as an increase in absent parent families. Extending this idea of patriarchy as control, the authors explain the low rate of adult female offending, and victimization. A combination of economic dependence on husbands, and power and control in homes, as well as fear of crime outside, keeps women isolated. Therefore, they are less likely to be victimized on the street than men, especially boys and young men. It appears to me that patriarchy, power and control within homes has led to the apparent and real increase in girls' and women's offenses found in official arrest statistics.

The demonization of girls and the power and control model can be seen as a new version of the hypothesis that women's liberation will lead to an increase in crime and the consequent narrowing of the gender gap. Siegel (2000:78), finds that it is too early to discard the idea of a new female criminal since rates of arrests of female offenders have continued to rise faster than those of males. This is surprising since numerous studies (Steffensmeier 1980; Naffine and Gale 1986; Chesney Lind and Daly, 1988 for example,) have disproved this hypothesis. Looking at the various measures of crime available, it appears that the difference between women and men and girls and boys is far less than appears on the surface. Furthermore, the increases in violent victimization of girls and women, as well as their increased economic marginalization, can adequately explain increases in female offenses.

Measures of crime by gender, race and age are complex, reconstructed accounts of events. Not that violence is a figment of our imagination, injuries do occur. In our interactions with others we reconstruct gender, race and crime. On the basis of these processes a violent act, "rape" for example, may mean rape for researcher (Koss, Gidycz and Wishiewski, 1987) but not the "victim" or the "offender." One consequence of "mandatory arrest" policies on some jurisdictions has been that police arrest both parties, showing by this action that each are equally culpable. Such arrests will increase the number of arrests counted for female offenders, whether or not they were responsible for the harm done. On the other hand, a violent crime can be 'uncriminalized' even before it is told to another. Men who are assaulted would prefer not to have the stigma of "victim" (which negates hegemonic masculinity) so they minimize their injury and would prefer to stay silent. Then in the case of the rape, or the aggravated assault, there is no official notice of the event. The National Crime Victimization Survey (NCVS) believes that men tend to under report victimization in personal crimes for this reason.

Ultimately, we constitute crimes of violence and gender. We construe them and construct them in social situations. This symbolic interactionist or ethnomethodological approach is consistent with the analysis of ethnographies and biographies. These studies shed new light on how statistics are created, and perhaps on whether or not our theories of crime apply to the actual situations in which gendered people find themselves. Simpson and Elis (1995:50–51) suggest, for example, that women accomplish femininity by "not doing crime or through crime in scripted ways." In doing this they enact gender in ways both women and men in their audiences conceive to be "natural." What is "natural" to men and women will depend upon the standpoint of the man or woman in a cultural and structured context.

In ethnographic studies gender is "more than a role or an individual characteristic: it is a mechanism whereby situated social action contributes to the reproduction of social structure" (West and Fenstermaker 1995:21, quoted in Miller 1998:38). Such actions are the "interactional scaffolding of social structure" wrote West and Zimmerman (1987), in a perspective consistent with that of Messerschmidt (1986). Thus crime may be a way of constructing masculinity, but will fail in presenting a feminine impression, for it is not normative for girls and women (Braithwaite and Daly 1994:190).

Miller (1998) uses an ethnographic approach to examine the interaction patterns of male and female robbers. She found that women's robbery "took place within the same structural and cultural underpinnings as men." However, the interactions during the crime are highly gendered. Men primarily robbed men, while women robbed women. Men used confrontation and threatening with a gun to the face or head of the male victim. Sometimes the robbery would be completed with gratuitous extra violence. In this way men told of accomplishing masculinity in doing robbery. A man who robbed a woman was unlikely to use the same actions/words. He characterized her as "frightened" and willing to "give it up" or "up it up" without force. Women robbers tended to rob women and used knives only when their victim "forced" them to by non-compliance. Miller found that women chose women victims pragmatically and concludes that there is a "clear gender hierarchy on the streets."

Like Campbell (1991) and Chesney Lind (1997:98), Miller suggests that we should ask "what protective factors keep the majority of women living in underclass settings from adopting violence as a culturally legitimate response." Women's desistance from crime is central to a full understanding of it. Why do fewer women resort to violence?

The Ethnographies

Perhaps control, self-control and patriarchy, as theories, will answer these questions in the examination of two narrative biographies of women who desisted. In rereading these women's stories I hypothesized that control and self-control, as well as aspects of power and control theory might explain the peacemaking choices that these women made in the face of violence in their lives. The stories were told to me as part of a project to write a book about contradictions in gender scripts. We interviewed several times for several hours. Usually I taped the interviews and then transcribed them. I then wrote the woman's story and placed it within a feminist sociological and political context. Then the storyteller and I met to revise and add to her story in the light of its place in the project. The methodology is collaborative, and the sample is a snowball sample with a twist. The original respondent's involvement in the project encouraged me to continue and find more women. Mary Smith, Katy and Vera were three women whom I interviewed in 1997, 1998, and 1999 respectively. My "subjects" are my colleagues in telling their own stories.

Mary Smith's Story

Mary Smith was aware that as a woman, her "rage and violence" were deviations from her script. She experienced "road rage" at men. She "didn't want to kill them" so she was "diagnosed" as suffering from "explosive personality disorder." She made a choice not to give in to her "poor self-control" which was a result of her childhood growing up in a small town, "red neck" bar. Her view of "normal behavior" informed this choice.

When interviewed Mary Smith was 56 years old and an elementary school teacher and published fiction writer. She described her relationship with her sisters as close. Her mother left her father.

Interviewer: Why did she do that?
Mary: I have to assume she was sick and tired of being beaten up all the time...In my father's family his brother was a cop. In his family all the guys beat up their wives...She must have been sighting it up quite a while. [Leaving my father]. It went off like clockwork and nobody knew where we were for three weeks.
Interviewer: What was their relationship like?
Mary: He was pretty rugged on Mom. He was least rugged on me, but that changed over time. I learned how to hate men, hate boys, hate anything male. [Not because of him but because my mother] never really had anything good to say about him until years later when she was in her fifties, and had been married five times, including him. She said, "maybe I should have stuck to your father after all." Course if she had she'd be dead. 'Cos he tried to kill her. He was picking her up and throwing her off the porch upstairs. Renee, my older sister said, "Dad what are you doing?" He said, "I'm throwing your Mother off the porch." She said, "Please don't do that." He put her down.

Mary presented herself as an independent successful woman.

Mary: Whatever we got we earned and nobody gave it to us. It made me strong. I have a house, a college education, acres of land, all mine. I earned it. I'm by myself. I have nobody.
Interviewer: What was the effect of your parent's relationship on your brothers and sisters?
Mary: We're all screwed up. One of the things we're all concerned about is going to the grocery store and not having enough money. We were always told how terrible poor we were. If there's a driver out there that makes us angry we will get out of the car and attack. It's explosive personality disorder. I could fly into such a rage that I'd kill the person. That's why I'm on Prozac, to taper the rage in me.
Interviewer: Did you have medication when you were younger?
Mary: No, when I seriously started considering murder—murdering someone who was hurting me. It wasn't normal, jumping out of a car, running off all men, getting them to move on. I'd get out of the car and meet him.
Interviewer: Did you punch him?

> **Mary:** I was willing. He flipped the bird at me. Anytime anybody hurts me, if I have a chance to kill them I will—if that's what it takes. Mostly it was men in cars. I would go after them. Normally their wives would call them back. When I was younger I used to slap 'em. Later on I'd get into a pretty screaming match with them. If it went on I'd hit them with intent to maim. The diagnosis was a defensive measure. It was foolish and dangerous. Now I'm older I feel more comfortable with men and boys. Boys don't scare me when they do that juvenile macho stuff in high school, throwing their weight around pretty well until they're out of college.
> **Interviewer:** What about the men you know now?
> **Mary:** Most men I know...are gentle and caring. They are normal, just folks.

She preferred to self-label as "sick" and takes medication, rather than to continue with a pattern of violent confrontation. Perhaps this scripted response to a woman's impulse to be violent occurs frequently. If so, it may account for a part of the gender gap in violent criminality. Self-control, theory does not fit well. Mary Smith's story shows inadequate parenting and a chaotic childhood that was violent and disrupted. This did result in an impulse to be violent that Mary Smith chose not to follow. Although before she decided to label herself "sick" she did get into confrontations which were sometime violent. She was shocked at the intensity of her feelings. It was her view of what was "normal" behavior that led her to do this. But it appears that her view of "normal" and "abnormal" is not "masculine" or "feminine", it is "just folks." The boys who "do gender" by macho acts are equally "abnormal" but they don't frighten her. Mary's humanistic view of being a person influenced her to desist from violent and aggressive behaviors. She wanted to be "normal," "just folks."

Katy and Vera

The gender script of a women: to "mother" and love her children and her husband, keep her motivated to act according to a pretense of a loving family and to keep the secrets of violence and abuse. The script of being a loving mother is not only externally constrained in our culture, it is also internally accepted and makes sense of a woman's actions whether licit or illicit. The patriarchal state has a vested interest in the scripted love of mothers, and therefore is loath to break up parental bonds and to interfere with the 'natural rights' of the biological mother and father. These rights appear to coincide with the "best interests of the child." The child's best interest is assumed by the

State to be in an intact family, with two loving parents. Each member of the family is highly motivated by their disparate gender roles to maintain the illusion of this loving family. Any investigation of child abuse will actually break that intact family apart.

Katy's story shows how patriarchy persists, as does domestic violence, despite Katy's divorce of her extremely violent second husband. Katy spoke with me with Vera, her daughter. They told their story as they were sewing clothes for the baby Vera expected who would be Vera's third child, and Katy's fourth grandchild.

Katy grew up in a western state. Sometimes her mother was frightening and she hid from her.

> **Katy:** My mother had a gun and was threatening to shoot my brother and I. We hid in my brother's room. I was about twelve.
> **Interviewer:** Why did she do that?
> **Katy:** She was crazy because my dad had left. She was trying to get him to come back. We thought she was crazy but it turned out to be the medication the doctor had put her on for depression. My father left because he was seeing another woman. She got my brother's gun out. He was thirteen or fourteen.
> **Interviewer:** How was it that your brother had a gun so young?
> **Vera:** They were a farm family.
> **Katy:** We all had guns. I had a gun, and bows and arrows. We used to hunt. Then everybody wasn't shooting everybody else.

Katy described how she met and married her first husband. She left Rod because he was involved with drugs and promiscuous sex.

> **Katy:** Vera was only one year old. I went to work at the plastics factory, that's where I met Julio.
> **Interviewer:** When did you get married?
> **Katy:** Right after we moved to M______ State, he wouldn't let me go anywhere or see anyone. He would throw me around, and when we went to the hospital he would have a story. One time he said a set of golf clubs fell on my head. We went to the hospital twice. The second time he told the doctor I fell down the steps. That time I injured my back. I remember a lot of it. Julio began to beat me up in front of Vera, and he also forced Vera to eat food. Even if she gagged she had to eat the vomit. He also developed a torture of Vera, as discipline called *standing on the wall.* What would happen is that Vera, at age

> two, would have to stand with her feet back from the wall leaning forward with her hands propping her against the wall.
> **Vera:** I was not allowed to move, and then he would come along and take a stick and beat me in the back of my legs so I would fall down.
> **Katy:** She had bruises all over her. My mother came to visit. While Julio and I were at work she took Vera to the police and showed them the bruises. The police sent my mother back to C_____ and said, 'we'll take care of it.' My mom went home and the police came and arrested Julio and me at the factory.

We both went to jail. They said I was responsible because I didn't do anything to stop it. Julio's brother came and bailed him out. It was two weeks before I could get out of jail. Vera was sent to a foster home.

Julio told the police that my mother had done it, because he knew that she was taken to the mental hospital when she threatened us with a gun. His excuse was that my mother had done it and then taken Vera to the police. But the doctor said the bruises were old. Vera had a woman attorney who kept on trying to get Julio jailed for child abuse. But they never got him.

Katy stayed in jail for two or three weeks, but Vera was in the foster home for four to six months. While in jail, Katy cleaned the entire woman's part of the jail, and began the anorexia, which has plagued her since. At the time she was just nineteen.

> **Katy:** When I was in jail I asked to see Vera. The visit had to be supervised since I had been accused of child abuse. They brought her to me. She clung to me and was crying. She had cigarette burns on her arms, and the foster father had cut off all her hair. I pointed out the cigarette burns to the social worker supervising the visitation and said to her, "you can't send her back there," the social worker said "it's a good home." She has to go back there." I was powerless. The abuse in the foster family continued until Katy got out of jail and the family was reunited with Julio.

Child protective services law in various states holds both parents jointly responsible for the violence of one of them. If a parent does not report abuses perpetrated on the child by the other parent or partner then she is "abusive." In addition, by 1987, in the state of New York, if a woman allows her husband to beat her up or abuse her in front of children she is "abusive," if she does not stop this abuse. Ironically, if she reports abusive behavior of children or herself in New York, then the abuser can still evade conviction. His attorney can argue that the mother hot-lined the abused as a tactic in divorce. Ultimately the mother/wife could be blamed for "using" the children as part of the battle for divorce. The husband/father meanwhile would escape responsibility and maintain his power.

In M______ Katy did not report Julio's child abuse on Vera. Julio got away with the abuse, and continued the behavior. After one year the abuse charges against Katy were dropped and Julio was found not guilty. In court an attorney who saw her for only one hour before her court appearance represented Katy. Katy continued her story:

> **Katy:** We got married in 1975. We moved to a new plastic factory. He was always on the run from consequences. The first time I went to a home for battered women Charlie [Julio and Katy's baby] was really small. I went to one in the city. I'd only been there for about an hour or two when the counselor came in with Julio. "He misses you so much" she said, "he wants you to come home." I had to go home with him. When I was home, after I stopped working, he used to call me every half-hour and say, "how far are you on my list?" I don't know how he found me at the city shelter. The counselor said, "He's willing to come in for counseling, we just think you should go home with him." We built this beautiful house and Vera has scars to prove it. He forced her hand into a pipe to get the concrete out.
> **Vera:** I remember brushing my teeth with Ajax and dish soap. I got threatened with the wire brush too.
> **Interviewer:** (Speaking to Katy) what happened if you tried to stop him?
> **Katy:** If I tried to stop him I'd get knocked out cold.
> **Vera:** He'd grab you by the throat.
> **Katy:** He didn't do it for every little thing. In 1972 I know he wrapped coat hangers around my neck. He knocked me out three times.
> **Vera:** That time I thought for sure she was dead. He used to kick me in the stomach when he made me *stand against the wall.*
> **Katy:** And he would say if you ever tell anybody I'm going to kill you both.
> **Vera:** In that house we built I had a beautiful pink bedroom.
> **Katy:** After Charlie was born I went back to work in the factory.
> **Vera:** I would have to stay home and take care of Charlie. I was about eight at the time. He was about one year old. One time Charlie's eardrum burst. Another time he came in my room about one o'clock in the morning to get a sucker that was on the bureau. The television I had up there fell off. It still has a dent in it. I was beat up for that,

then told to *stand up against the wall.* I hated weekends. I wanted to stay in school forever.
Katy: The next time I tried to get away I went to shelter in T______ City. John and Toni, a husband and wife who were co-workers helped me. I managed real estate for them.
Vera: I was eleven that time.
Katy: We went to another shelter and were there almost a month. The first time, when Charlie was one year old, the shelter manager tells him we were there and he comes to the Shelter and picks us up. [Katy and the kids] Then he drives around the corner from the shelter, stands the truck on the side of the road and beats me in front of the two kids. Kill or be killed was the only choice left. I thought about it, but never did work it out because of the kids. [If she killed her abuser she would go into prison and the kids would go into foster homes.]
Interviewer: What happened then?
Katy: I got pregnant again, and he got a job offer in another factory in N_____. I said you go-but he had to have me with him.
Interviewer: Did he beat up the boys?
Vera: They never got touched. Well, he did push them around but nothing like what we went through. It was a female thing. You missed stuff in M______. He took our dog and swung her round he broke her nose and her leg. He hated my brother when he was born.
Katy: After I was two months pregnant with Don [their second son) I had a prolapsed uterus. We moved to N____ when I was eight months pregnant, and we sold the house that we built in M____.
Vera: We had very much beatings there. One time I forgot my report card and he tied my hair to the door. Then we moved to T_____. That's when I started turning him in (at school).
Katy: He had this new girl friend. When the phone rang we didn't answer the phone or talk. He started to be gone a lot. She lived in the next state.
Vera: I stayed with G'ma (Julio's mother) in seventh grade, in M______.
Katy: When she was gone one time, he started beating me with scissors. I took off running out the back. I said, 'that's it, I've had enough, kill me.' He left and he didn't come back. The next day I called a lawyer and got an order of protection.

While Katy was not the abusing parent there is a record of her arrest for that offense. Katy was marked as a violent woman by arrest statistics and punished by serving jail time for the sins of the father, Julio, as well as the stepfather from M_____. Katy acted consistently in a feminine manner. At age 48, she has long blond hair and dresses in a feminine style. She is obsessively neat and clean and makes a home wherever she lives, as does Vera, her daughter. As a result of domestic terrorism and patriarchy, Vera and Katy suffer from recurrent anorexia. Vera learned specific acts of violence from the foster home in which she stayed when she was two. Involved as an adult of 18 in an abusive and violent relationship, she burned her partner's arms with her cigarette when he attacked her at home. She subsequently separated from him. There is no official record of Vera's violence towards her partner, although he was arrested.

Twice shelters in M____ had betrayed Katy. When she moved to N____ she no longer trusted any agency. She eventually escaped from Julio but she was forced to leave her sons with him. He said he would kill her if she took them. In the family of Katy, Vera, and Julio patriarchy, power, and control were enacted. A father maintained power by physical violence, torture and domestic terror. He also maintained economic patriarchy by keeping Katy from accumulating any money or possessions of her own. Outside the family he had the ability to manipulate local law enforcement and shelter facility staff. Certainly this patriarchal power and control kept Katy submissive and non-violent to preserve her life. But this aggressive style was learned by Vera in her adult life. The sons remained with Julio who remarried and nearly killed his third wife several times in the presence of his teen-aged sons. There is no record of this patriarchal violence in arrests. Paradoxically, the non-violence of Katy resulted in a record of official violence and jail for the child abuse charge.

These stories show that women do choose non-violence despite horrendous victimization, but this choice is explained neither by their self-control or patriarchy. The ethic of caring for one another and maintaining family and relationship, on the other hand, was expressed throughout these women's stories. When officials ignore or normalize patriarchal and male violence, girls and boys violent responses and/ or running away are more likely. In much the same way "normalizing" male violence in our official accounts and responses tends to excuse it and to perpetuate it.

The dependent economic status of women in marriage, or in relationship with men, comes from their participation in a secondary labor market. This economic position, together with the vulnerability of motherhood, combine to place women and children at the mercy of men who may very well be insulated from any sanction of their abusive behavior. The recent qualitative studies of women and girls have shown how sexual and physical abuse are associated with the high prevalence of running away, substance abuse and criminality. The recent report by Snyder (2000) on the sexual assault of young children shows that 67 percent of all victims of sexual assault reported to law enforcement agencies were juveniles. One in seven of all victims of sexual assault found in this study was under six years old, and the peak age for victimization was fourteen. Eighty six percent of all victims were female, while 96 percent of the offenders were male. Snyder points out that "by design, the National Crime Victimization Survey is missing one third of all sexual assaults." These data support the qualitative findings from Chesney Lind (1997), and, combined with the autobiographies told here, indicate a need for a more reliable economic basis for the lives of mothers and their daughters. We need trustworthy shelters and adequate and loving childcare. Criminal justice and social service officials must act with compassion and humanity. Without these we may experience a continuation of the hidden victimization in families, which regenerates patriarchy and exacerbates violence.

In conclusion, choices in interaction are made in terms of specific interpretations of gender script, but they also follow what is more generally approved as "normal." Domestic patriarchy and the hegemonic masculinity of the state (Sumner 1990) only make the situation worse. "Enmeshed in the state apparatus of control and beholder to funding mechanisms criminology's very definition is suspect" (Klein 1995:228). In a feminist perspective and in a humanist perspective, our question should be how could we reduce harm to those who are increasingly dominated by domestic terror? It is clear from the Mary Smith, Katy and Vera stories that the systems we have in place function unjustly and may increase the domestic violence they are designed to prevent. The theory that patriarchy as power and control reduces female violence is refuted in each of the biographical accounts here. Mary Smith's view of acting as 'just folks' supercedes gender. Our first step must be to make known those harms, and tell the stories of those silenced, thereby giving them agency to define what is 'normal' and good action.

References

Adler, F. (1975). *Sisters in Crime: The Rise of the New Female Criminal,* New York, McGraw Hill.

Adler, F. (1981). *The Incidence of Crime in the Contemporary World,* New York, New York University Press.

Adler, F. and R. Simon. (1979). *The Criminology of Deviant Women,* Boston, Houghton Mifflin.

Bierne, P. and J. Messerschmidt. (2000). *Criminology,* Third Edition, Boulder, Colorado: Westview Press.

Braithwaite, J. And K. Daly. (1994). Masculinities, Crime and Communitarian Control, in Tim Newburn and Elizabeth A. Stanko (eds.), *Just boys doing business?* New York: Routledge.

Campbell, A. (1991). *The Girls in the Gang*, Oxford: Basil Blackwell.

Chesney Lind, M. (1986). Women and Crime: The Female Offender. *Signs: The Journal of Woman Culture and Society*, 12 (1) 78–96.

Chesney Lind, M. (1997). *The Female Offender, Girls, Women and Crime*, California, Sage.

Chesney Lind, M. and R. G. Shelden. (1998). *Girls, Delinquency and Juvenile Justice*, California: Wadsworth.

Daly, K. & M. Chesney Lind. (1988). Feminism and Criminology. *Justice Quarterly*, 4.

Elliot, D. (1994). 1993 Presidential Address. Serious Violent Offenders: Onset, Developmental Course and Termination, *Criminology*, 32 (1), 1–21.

Erez, E. (1988). The Myth of the New Female Offender. *Journal of Criminal Justice*, 16, 499–509.

Hagan, J., A. R. Gillis, and J. Simpson. (1985). The Class Structure of Gender and Delinquency: Toward a Power and Control Theory of Common Delinquent Behavior, *American Journal of Sociology*, 90, 1151–1178.

Klein, D. (1995). Crime Through Gender's Prism: Feminist Criminology in the United States, In N. Hahn Rafter and F. Heidensohn (Eds.), *International Perspectives in Criminology: Engendering a Discipline*, Bristol, PA, Open University Press.

Koss, M. P., C. Gidycz & N. Wishiewski. (1987). The Scope of Rape: Incidence and Prevalence of Sexual Aggression and Victimization in a National Sample of Higher Education Students. *Journal of Consulting and Clinical Psychology*, 55 (2) 162–170.

Messerschmidt, J. (1986). *Capitalism, Patriarchy and Crime: Toward a Socialist Feminist Criminology*, New Jersey, Rowman and Littlefield.

Miller, J. (1998). Up it up: Gender and the Accomplishment of Street Robbery, *Criminology*, 36 (1), 37–65.

Naffine, N. (1985). The Masculinity-femininity Hypothesis: A Consideration of Gender Based Personality Theories of Crime. *British Journal of Criminology*, 25 (4), 365–381.

Naffine, N. & F. Gale. (1989). Testing the Nexus: Crime, Gender and Unemployment. *British Journal of Criminology*, 29 (2), 144–156.

Siegel, L. (2000). *Criminology* seventh edition. USA. Wadsworth.

Simpson S. S. And L. Elis. (1995). Doing Gender: Sorting Out the Caste and Crime Conundrum. *Criminology*, 33 (1): 47–81.

Snyder, H. N. (2000). Sexual Assault of Young Children as Reported to Law Enforcement: Victim, Incident and Offender Characteristics. A Statistical Report Using Data From the National Incident-based Reporting System. *U.S. Department of Justice, Bureau of Justice Statistics*, NCJ 182990.

Steffensmeier, D. J. (1980). Sex Differences in Patterns of Adult Crime. *Social Forces*, 58 (4), 1080–1109.

Sumner, C. (1990). Foucault, Gender and the Censure of Deviance, in L. Gelsthorpe and A. Morris (Eds.), *Feminist Perspectives in Criminology*, Bristol, PA, Open University Press.

West, C. and S. Fenstermaker. (1995). Doing difference. *Gender and Society*, 9 (1), 8–37.

West, C. And D. Zimmerman. (1997). Doing gender. *Gender and Society*, 1 (2), 125–151.

Uniform Crime Reports. (1999). U. S. Federal Bureau of Investigation.

"You Can't Keep a Good Man Down: On Being a Man and Being a Victim"

Kathleen M. Burke, Ph.D.,
Simon Fraser University

Introduction

Perusing academic and popular criminological literature, it is obvious that the study of crime, criminals, victims, and the criminal justice system has been undertaken from a variety of angles. In particular, it is noticeable how these works examine diverse aspects of both the act of and the response to crime. However, there remains a glaring gap which may hold a key to how we understand and react to a significant portion of crime. What continues to be obscured and downplayed relative to their involvement in crime and the criminal justice system is the subject of men and masculinities. More specifically, we know little about how the state responds to male victims as "men."

The criminal justice system is an increasingly significant appendage of the state in terms of its size, influence and budgetary demands. Moreover, all facets of the criminal justice system are monopolized by males in positions ranging from patrol officesr to judicial seats. Yet, for the most part, the fact that they are gendered beings remains relatively underexplored. Although feminists have been variously effective in their endeavors to critically engender women's experiences of victimization, many of their insights have been marginalized as "women's issues" and overwhelmingly relegated to footnotes in mainstream criminological literature. Meanwhile, the links between masculinities[1] and victimizations have yet to undergo consistent, critical evaluation.

Although men are robbed, beaten and murdered every day, little is known about their experiences of victimization as "men." Furthermore, there may be

1. I purposively use the term masculinities here in order to capture what I view as the multiple and dynamic character of gender.

some types of victimization that men are more willing to acknowledge than others based on the extent to which the acts are perceived as threatening their masculine image. Male sexual assault is one example of abuse that men are hesitant to disclose. This paper examines masculinity as it is addressed within the context of male child sexual abuse under the tutelage of the state. I begin by examining two popular currents of thought in the area of men and masculinities as they are articulated within popular and academic literatures. Second, the male child sexual abuse literature is explored in terms of its portrayal of the impact of gender on males who have experienced this type of assault. Next, the role of the state is analyzed in terms of how relevant agencies respond to the needs of victimized males. Finally, suggestions are made for future analyses of the victimization of men and their relevance to academics and criminal justice practitioners.

Engendering Men

Feminists have prioritized the analysis of gender in studies of victims and victimization. Rooted in their scholarship and activism, feminists have emphasized gendered relations of power and their role in the process of victimization. At both the community and academic levels, feminists have been pivotal in naming and politicizing men's violence[2] against women and children. Their analyses of child sexual abuse, wife abuse, and sexual assault, to name a few, have exposed and engendered relations of power in the lives of women and children. Moreover, through highlighting the extent of violence in the lives of women, feminists have also provided an impetus to the problematization of men and masculinity.

Over the past 25 years, largely in response to feminist politics and practices, the literature on, by, and for men has grown exponentially. Both popular and academic literatures have taken a keener interest in men and their experiences of masculinity. As a result, while launching from similar venues, individual and collectivities of men have traversed very different courses in attempting to understand the "social reality of men". One of the most influential responses, particularly in North America, has been the development of a genre of writings on men that stresses the oppressiveness and fragility of the masculine "role" and the need for men's liberation.

---

2. I refer to "men's" rather than "male" violence to emphasize what I perceive to be the social, rather than the biological basis of this type of violence.

Masculinity and Men in Crisis

What I refer to as the "men in crisis" literature accentuates a particularistic representation of masculinity. Here, masculinity is referred to as essential, static, singular, and responsible for alienating men from their feelings and fathers, thereby leaving them insecure in their manhood. Writers working within this area have identified a variety of sources which constrain men from accomplishing a complete and secure sense of their masculinity. Among these, capitalism and Enlightenment modernism have been faulted for crippling men by removing the father (a boy's gender role model) from the home and tying masculine identity to employment status, denial of emotions, and self-control (Seidler,1991).

The wounded male has symbolized many of the popular writings on and by men in the late 1980s and early 1990s. This image is intended to capture not only men's alienation from their emotions, but also their disposability in times of war and replaceability in the workforce. Drawing primarily on the experiences of white, middle-class, heterosexual men, this literature heralds the message that men are hurting too and are in need of a safe space to express and confront their pain.

Across North America many men have sought solace and security in their masculinity at various "mythopoetic men's retreats" (Kimmel & Kaufman, 1994). However, all is not quiet on what the media has popularly dubbed the "men's movement" front. Much criticism has been directed toward the men-in-crisis thesis for its failure to problematize the relative power of men; for its uni-dimensional portrayal of masculinity; and for its reluctance to engage with the dynamic, non-linear, and contradictory processes of gender accomplishment.

Beyond One-Dimensional "Man"

Current scholarship, in contrast to the above, has tended to distance itself from the popular static, universal, and singular view of masculinity, instead emphasizing its dynamic, historical, and multiple representations. These "second generation" studies of masculinities are perhaps best exemplified by the works of Connell (1987), Brittan (1989), and Messerschmidt (1993). Through highlighting the complex and contradictory character of men's behavior, these theorists expose the wide gulf between images of masculinity and men's expressions of their masculine identity. According to Arthur Brittan, it is imperative to distinguish between masculinity and "masculinism," in which "masculinism is the ideology that justifies and naturalizes male dominance," while masculinity is the umbrella term for the variable character of men's behavior (1989, p.4).

The scholarship of R. W. Connell (1987) has been particularly influential in grounding a sociology of masculinities. He illuminates his view of the historical constitution of masculinities in the context of their hegemonic and subordinate forms. Connell uses the term "hegemonic masculinity" to refer to an idealized masculinity that has achieved ascendancy "in a play of social forces that extends beyond brute power into the organization of private life and cultural processes" (1987, p.184). For instance, as it is presently constituted, hegemonic masculinity harbors the ability to define femininity and various other types of masculinity through a multitude of processes and negotiations; including the nuclear family's regulation of desire, the sexual division of labor, and state complicity in establishing and enforcing regulations which reinforce a particular hegemonic form (e.g. policing homosexuality) (Carrigan, Connell, & Lee, 1985, pp.592–94). Key to Connell's understanding of hegemonic masculinity is its relational character. In other words, in its current form, hegemonic masculinity is signified in its heterosexuality: both its "difference from and desire for women" (Segal, 1990, p.99). Furthermore, along with Connell, scholars writing in the area of masculinities have also emphasized how masculine identities are mediated more generally through various relations of power. For instance, the strategies for accomplishing hegemonic masculinity will vary significantly depending on a male's race, class, age, able-bodiedness, and sexual orientation.

Scholarship by James Messerschmidt (1993) is singular in its exposure of the variable relationship between gender, race, and class in shaping and interacting with boys' and men's engagement in criminal activity. Applying theoretical groundwork laid out by Connell (1987), Messerschmidt explores how "doing gender" is often synonymous with doing crime. According to Messerschmidt, "Crime by men is not simply an extension of the 'male sex role.' Rather, crime by men is a form of a social practice invoked as a resource, when other resources are unavailable, for accomplishing masculinity" (1993, p.85). Hence, males are constrained by race and class from attaining certain masculine standards. Along with other scholars working within a social constructionist framework in analyzing gender, Messerschmidt begins with the notion that there is no single fixed masculine form, which all males aspire to and attain. Rather, he acknowledges the existence of masculinities and the hierarchically privileged dominant and subordinate versions comprised within. These understandings reinforce the importance of critically exploring the role gender plays in molding men's involvement in crime and their reactions to victimization.

Contradictions: On Being a "Man" and Being a "Victim".

As feminists have long noted, within a variety of contexts, the construct of masculinity and the identities and practices of men are far too often taken-for-granted and naturalized. Unfortunately, the criminological literature is no exception. For instance, conventional and left realist approaches to the study of victimization have been criticized for their tendency to portray victims and offenders as gender-specific and mutually exclusive categories while relying on and reinforcing hegemonic conceptions of masculinity (Newburn & Stanko, 1994, p.158). This propensity to equate men and masculine qualities with offending often results in the failure to explore and problematize gender as it pertains to male victims.

Although the fact that men are frequently on the receiving end of violent encounters is evident in criminological statistics and the media, there have been few attempts to explore how men define and respond to victimization. Newburn and Stanko attribute this lack of information on male victims to researchers "unproblematically assum(ing) that men are reticent to disclose vulnerability…,thus reinforcing the tendency to focus almost exclusively on women's experiences of physical and sexual assault" (1994:160). One of the few literatures to consider seriously, albeit not unproblematically, the impact of gender on boys' and men's experiences of victimization has been the research on male child sexual abuse.

Male Child Sexual Abuse

Prior to the mid to late 1980s, research addressing the sexual abuse of children mostly ignored or minimized the molestation of boys. Although a good portion of the research purported to examine "child" sexual abuse, the vast majority were based on all-female samples. The omission of males from numerous analyses often resulted because so few male victims came to the attention of professional and social service agencies, with the result being researchers who relied on these reported cases generally concluded that the sexual victimization of boys was an anomaly (Finkelhor & Baron, 1986, p.46). Consequently, researchers speculated that this underrepresentation of boys reflected the lack of any significant psychological or physical consequences experienced by male victims of this type of abuse (Watkins & Bentovim, 1992).

Feminists' interest and involvement in this area of research not only greatly influenced the direction of these inquiries, but also raised general awareness and action, thereby clearing a path along which many men would travel in naming their experiences of victimization in childhood. In addition, the expansion of men's consciousness-raising groups during the late 1970s and early 1980s offered many men a forum in which to begin sharing their own experiences of abuse. As a result, research and interest in the area of male child sexual abuse have noticeably grown over the last ten years.

Where it was once assumed that the sexual victimization of boys was a very rare occurrence, more recent scholarship has demonstrated the shortsightedness of this inference (Watkins & Bentovim, 1992). For instance, two of the most often cited national prevalence studies found that 8% of Canadian males (Committee on Sexual Offenses against Children and Youths, 1984) and 16% of the men in the U.S. (Finkelhor, Hotaling, Lewis, & Smith, 1990) reported unwanted or abusive sexual contact before the ages of 17 and 18 years, respectively. Commonly cited national and community-based studies indicate ratios of one boy for every two to five girls abused (Committee on Sexual Offenses Against Children and Youths, 1984; Finkelhor, 1984; Finkelhor, et al., 1990; Kercher & McShane, 1984). In-depth understandings of males' experiences of child sexual abuse, however, have largely emerged from small-scale clinical case studies of their clientele by therapists and clinical psychologists (Bolton, Morris, & MacEachron, 1989; Dimmock, 1988; Grubman-Black, 1990; Hunter, 1990; Lew, 1990).

Victimization as Emasculinization

The literature addressing male child sexual abuse is unique in its examination of the often profound and lasting impact of sexual molestation on males as masculine beings. Gender is enlisted to problematize the masculine "role" for inhibiting men from disclosing and coping with their experiences of this type of abuse. A common sentiment running through this literature is its insistence on the pivotal function of gender in keeping males silent about sexual abuse.

Within the research on male child sexual abuse, the association of a singular, unidimensional masculinity with emotional detachment, physical aggressiveness, heterosexuality, and sexual potency is reinforced. Principal among the reasons regarding why men rarely report this type of abuse are: (1) "boys grow up with the male ethic of self-reliance" (Finkelhor, 1985, p.102); (2) "our culture provides no room for a man as victim" (Lew, 1990, p.41); (3) masculine identity is coupled with sexual prowess so to "be preyed upon... is a phenomenon for which most males have little or no guidance" (Blanchard, 1987, p.19); (4) boys are not seen as needing protection (Bolton, et al., 1989; Pierce & Pierce, 1985); and (5) "emotional repression, as an effort to preserve one's masculine image, greatly limits a man in overcoming the sexual traumas in his past" (Blanchard, 1987, p.22). Gender then, becomes the thread that stitches together our frayed understandings of the sexual molestation of boys.

A key theme within this general critique of gender is the identification of the "stigma of homosexuality" as enhancing males' feelings of shame, guilt, and emasculinization. As Finkelhor observes, "(h)omosexuality is one of the more fearsome stigmas among many male peer groups, and boys may be concerned about earning the label 'queer' as a result of people finding out about a sexual abuse experience" (1985, p.103). Based on the fact that most reported sexual abuse of boys is committed by other males, studies have concluded that many boys and men shy away from disclosure and its potential consequences: "...to be less than a man is seen as feminization. The heterosexual survivor, clearly not a woman, worries about whether he is that even more shameful being—a feminized man, a homosexual" (Lew, 1990, p.57). The potential heavy price of disclosure, however, is not limited to the association of male child sexual abuse with homosexuality.

The extent and impact of female perpetrated child sexual abuse has been problematized as well. The relative inattention paid to the molestation of boys by women in the media and literature has been blamed for invalidating and isolating the experiences of those males who were abused by women during childhood (Lew, 1990, p.58; Mendel, 1995, pp.21–34). Recent scholarship has shown that male survivors often view themselves and are viewed by others as less than "men" for not enjoying early sexual encounters with women (Lew, 1990; Mendel, 1995). As one therapist who counsels male survivors observed,

> For the adolescent male that was abused by an older female and recounts this in later life, other males say, "oh you were lucky, you were lucky that an older woman was there to give you your first sexual experience." The experience is downgraded by other males.... (Burke, 1993, p.20).

Furthermore, popular notions of males as sexually aggressive and commanding of their sexual experiences have been identified as serving to obscure the potential for boys to be victimized. According to Finkelhor, "the male ethic itself has tended to portray youthful male sexuality in very positive, adventuresome terms...paint[ing] boys' experiences with older persons and adults as much less victimizing than it [sic] actually is" (1985, p.98).

Similarly, images of masculinity as omnipotent, self-commanding, and aggressive are also problematic in that they are often equated with offender characteristics. The resulting notion that the categories of victim and offender are gender-specific has been singled out as further compounding the reticence of some men to disclose the abuse. As one therapist illustrated,

> I have had guys who were obstinately referred to me as male survivors or in some cases they have been referred as both survivors and offenders...who would be much more willing to talk to me about being offenders than they have about being victims (Burke, 1993).

Research then, suggests that commonplace depictions of men as offenders and an association of masculinity with aggressivity serve only to magnify the extent to which men's experiences of child sexual abuse are invalidated and silenced. The significance of such stereotypes tends to be further inflated when victimized males turn to the state for assistance.

Official (In)Actions: The Role of the State

The state is not a reified, monolithic whole, rather it is comprised of a series of institutions and policies which are full of contradictions and contentions. However, the existence of inconsistencies should not underscore the way in which the structures and policies of the state reflect and reinforce structural inequalities on the basis of gender, class, race, ethnicity, sexual orientation and generation, to name a few. Feminists, in particular, have illuminated how the liberal notion of the state as a "neutral arbiter" and the separation of the social into public and private spheres obscure the ways in which hegemonic masculinity is institutionalized in the operation of the state. In recognizing the "state as a process" that changes historically, R.W. Connell (1990) stresses the importance of viewing the state as "historically patriarchal," in order not to conflate it with some essential maleness or patriarchy. Through extensive critique then, the state has been exposed as "part of a wider structure of gender relations" which organizes and reinforces relations of power based on gender (Connell, 1990:520).

The construction and operation of law and national/local governmental policies have received considerable attention regarding the extent to which they structurally disadvantage women and "other" men. For instance, the implementation of housing policies and tax laws, and the lack of adequate, publicly funded childcare have been exposed as privileging the nuclear family household (cf. Barrett, 1980; Pupo, 1988). In addition, feminists have emphasized the reluctance of and inconsistent manner in which the law and agencies of the state (e.g. police, social services, courts, etc.) "treat sexual violence as a 'real' crime" (Kelly and Radford, 1987:249). Several of the works theorizing men and masculinity have highlighted the ways in which the state maintains hegemonic masculinity. Principle among the strategies employed by the state to preserve and reinforce hegemonic images of masculinity is the "criminalization of male homosexuality" (Carrigan, Connell and Lee, 1985:594; cf. Brittan, 1989; Segal, 1990). The control and policing of homosexuality since the late 19th century and the resulting state-enacted legislation have reflected the state's bias in protecting and propagandizing heterosexual masculinity (cf. Brittan, 1989). Although the "state may no longer criminalize all forms of homosexuality...through legislation on the age of consent, welfare practice as regards adoption, and in all forms of taxation and benefit arrangements, it denies legitimacy to homosexual relations" (Segal, 1990:98). The state's tendency to actively devalue and regulate male homosexuality may have particular implications for the ways in which sexual violence against boys is viewed and responded to by state agencies and policies.

Research on the sexual abuse of boys has demonstrated the variable responses of state agencies in addressing this type of abuse. For instance, a study conducted by Pierce and Pierce (1985) comparing responses of a state protective services agency to sexually abused boys and girls observed that males were less likely to be removed from the home upon substantiation of the abuse. In addition, they found that when treatment was recommended, boys were released from therapy significantly earlier than girls. It was concluded that the state is less likely to perceive boys in need of protection or seriously traumatized as a result of sexual abuse. A survey of clinical psychologists, in which they were asked to hypothetically diagnose a case summary of an adult client where only the sex of the client was manipulated, further revealed that males were significantly less likely to be suspected of having been sexually abused (Holmes and Offen, 1996). Such examples of gender stereotyping serve to filter information and shape understandings regarding victim appropriateness. Moreover, the association of masculinity with certain behavioral expectations also isolate males from victim status.

Heterosexual prowess, physical potency, and invulnerability are among the defining characteristics currently associated with hegemonic masculinity. However, these very attributes simultaneously serve as antonyms of the qualities assigned to sexual assault victims. Victims (and women) are more commonly portrayed as weak, passive, and dependent; in need of and deserving state intervention. Such simplistic and dichotomized understandings of men/women and offender/victim limit our understanding of crime and obscure social and institutional recognition of male vulnerability to sexual assault. Moreover, sexually victimized males tend to be further thwarted from victim status due to the association of this type of abuse with homosexuality.

Given the same-sex character of most abuse of boys, many official reactions appear to be more concerned with issues of sexual orientation than with the actual incidence(s) of abuse. It is not uncommon for investigating officers to ask male complainants about their sexual orientation and reinforce heterosexual sentiments. One male survivor who was molested by his older brothers and filed charges as an adult complained,

> ...he(police officer) asked me about my own sexuality...and in the victim report I had to be very graphic about the type of acts that were committed. And as he was reading them back, he would say, 'oh you know, yeah this happened, but that doesn't necessarily make you a homosexual.' You know, like he is trying to comfort me for maybe not necessarily being gay...and my nephew was also abused by this brother and he is gay and in the same room with these officers (Burke, 1998).

Other research has also noted the reluctance of some therapists and police officers to believe accusations of male child sexual abuse; noting one officer's sentiment that "'a boy could prevent being raped if he really wanted to'" (Nasjleti, 1986:69). Presuppositions about gender, sexual orientation and sexual victimization can further hinder men who seek social services via sexual assault hotlines, crisis centers and counseling services which are primarily structured and staffed to treat women (Bolton, et al., 1989; Burke, 1993; Donnelly and Kenyon, 1996). However, there have been additional findings suggesting that the sexual abuse of boys is taken more seriously and responded to more punitively than the abuse of girls.

Several scholars have observed that same-sex child sexual abuse involving a man and a boy tend to be dealt with more harshly than the molestation of girls by men because of their (presumed) association with homosexuality (cf. Adler, 1992; Nava, 1984; Pierce and Pierce, 1985). According to her analysis of the current scope, implementation, and underlying assumptions of law on sexual offences against males in Britain, Zsuzsanna Adler found that "the law on sexual crimes involving male victims is primarily concerned with the control of homosexual behaviour" (1992:125). Similarly, Pierce and Pierce (1985) observed that in addition to receiving "harsh" sentences, men convicted of sexually assaulting boys were also more likely to be found "emotionally ill." Once again, the concept of "hegemonic masculinity" is useful to contextualize the state's tendency to use sexual assault laws pertaining to male victims as a way of policing and controlling anything that glints of male homosexuality.

However, the complex and contradictory manner in which the state operates should not be understated. Specifically, "once an issue is taken into the legal process, it is subject to a process of definition and redefinition that draws in various knowledge, and is pushed and pulled onto various agendas" (Bell, 1993:181). It is not absolute then, that the court will be used as an arena in which to severely admonish the (presumed) homosexual character of most sexual abuse of boys. For instance, in a British Columbia Supreme Court case involving the sexual assault of two teenage boys by an older male, Justice Howard Hamilton downplayed the impact the abuse had on the boys. During sentencing he opined,

> I don't think it changed their lives around.... It's very easy to blame what happens to yourself on someone else. But they were having difficulty coping themselves, otherwise they wouldn't have been there to be the victims (*Vancouver Sun*, April 16, 1994:A2).

In addition, as law enforcement and social service agencies continue to train officers in sex abuse awareness and sensitivity in dealing with victims, there is a greater likelihood that male victims will be heard, provided for, and validated. Some cities have even developed services specifically for male survivors of sexual abuse[3]. Therefore, the state's response to male child sexual abuse tends to vary considerably across time and space.

Conclusion

As we make our initial footprints in the twenty-first century and are confronted with increasingly complex issues in attempting to understand, prevent, and respond to crime, the consideration of gender is indispensable. Although decades of criminological inquiry have documented men's extensive involvement in criminal activity, more recent scholarship cautions us against the notion that men are unilaterally powerful and oppressive. As Kaufman warns,

> Our whole language of oppression is in need of overhaul for it is based on simplistic binary oppositions.... What is important for us here is not to deny that men, as a group, have social power... but that there are different forms of structural power and powerlessness among men (1994, p.153).

It is within a discourse of masculinities, then, that the language becomes available to critically theorize about and respond to men as victims.

As noted above, some literature has begun to seriously consider masculinity within the context of victimization. In these analyses men have identified

---

3. The British Columbia Society for Male Survivors of Sexual Abuse is one such program.

how "being a man" constrains their ability to disclose experiences of sexual abuse and often dulls the reactions of those to whom they confide. Alongside the accounts of women, male victims of sexual abuse problematize the role of the state in their ability to adequately respond to the offence and their needs. Too often, popular notions of males as naturally heterosexual and commanding of their sexual experiences overshadow the potential for them to be sexually victimized. Such inquiries hold significant promise for criminologists and criminal justice practitioners in that they reinforce the understanding that "gender does have consequences" (Stanko & Hobdell, 1993, p.413). Moreover, the above findings beg us to broaden essentialized understandings of both victim and gender. It is anticipated that continued work in the area of masculinities and victimization will yield more detailed insight not only into how men negotiate victimization, but also how police, lawyers, judges, jurors, and victim services variously respond to men as victims and victims as "men."

References

Adler, Z. (1992). Male Victims of Sexual Assault—Legal Issues. In G.C. Mezey and M.B. King(Eds.), *Male Victims of Sexual Assault.* Oxford: Oxford University Press

Barrett, M. (1980). *Women's Oppression Today.* London: Verson

Bell, Vikki (1993). Two Modes of Power? Foucault, Feminism and Child Sexual Abuse. *Journal of Gender Studies* 1(2), 168–185.

Blanchard, G. (1987). Male Victims of Child Sexual Abuse: A Portent of Things to Come. *Journal of Independent Social Work,* 1(1), 19–27.

Bolton, F., Morris, L., & MacEachron, A. (1989). *Males at Risk: The Other Side of Child Sexual Abuse.* Newbury Park, CA: Sage.

Brittan, A. (1989). *Masculinity and Power.* Oxford: Basil Blackwell.

Burke, K.M. (1993). *Getting Through: Selected Professional Perspectives on Male Survivors of Child Sexual Abuse in the Lower Mainland.* Paper presented at the meeting of the Western Association of Sociology & Anthropology, Vancouver, British Columbia.

_______. (1998). *Take it Like a Man: The Silencing of Men's Experiences of Sexual Abuse During Childhood.* Doctoral Dissertation, Simon Fraser University, Canada.

Carrigan, T., Connell, B. & Lee, J. (1985). Toward a New Sociology of Masculinity. *Theory and Society,* 14, 551–603.

Committee on Sexual Offenses Against Children and Youths. (1984). *Sexual Offenses Against Children: Report of the Committee on Sexual Offenses Against Children and Youth* (Vol 1). Ottawa: Canadian Government Publishing Centre.

Connell, R. (1987). *Gender and Power.* Cambridge: Polity Press.

_______. (1990). The State, Gender and Sexual Politics: Theory and Appraisal. *Theory and Society* 19(4), 507–544.

Dimmock, P. (1988). Adult Males Sexually Abused as Children: Characteristics and Implications for Treatment. *Journal of Interpersonal Violence,* 3(2), 203–221.

Donnelly, D. and S. Kenyon (1996). 'Honey, We Don't Do Men': Gender Stereotypes and the Provision of Services to Sexually Assaulted Males. *Journal of Interpersonal Violence,* 11(3), 441–448.

Finkelhor, D. (1984). *Child Sexual Abuse: New Theory and Research.* NY: Free Press.

_______. (1985). Sexual Abuse of Boys. In A. W. Burgess (Ed.), *Rape and Sexual Assault: A Research Handbook* (pp. 97–109). New York: Garland.

Finkelhor, D. & Baron, L. (1986). Risk Factors for Child Sexual Abuse. *Journal of Interpersonal Violence,* 1(1), 43–71.

Finkelhor, D., Hotaling, G., Lewis, I., & Smith, C. (1990). Sexual Abuse in a National Survey of Adult Men and Women: Prevalence, Characteristics, and Risk Factors. *Child Abuse and Neglect,* 14, 19–28.

Grubman-Black, S. (1990). *Broken Boys/Mending Men: Recovery From Childhood Sexual Abuse.* Blue Ridge Summit, PA: Tab Books.

Holmes, Guy and Offen, L. (1996). Clinicians' Hypotheses Regarding Clients' Problems: Are They Less Likely to Hypothesize Sexual Abuse in Male Compared to Female Clients? *Child Abuse and Neglect,* 20(6), 493–501.

Hunter, M. (1990). *Abused Boys: The Neglected Victims of Sexual Abuse.* Lexington, MA: Lexington Books.

Kaufman, M. (1994). Men, Feminism, and Men's Contradictory Experiences of Power. In H. Brod & M. Kaufman (Eds.), *Theorizing Masculinities* (pp. 142–163). Thousand Oaks, CA: Sage.

Kelly, L. and Radford, J. (1987). The Problem of Men: Feminist Perspectives on Sexual Violence. In P. Scraton (Ed.), *Law, Order and the Authoritarian State: Readings in Critical Criminology.* Philadelphia: Open University Press.

Kercher, G. & McShane, M. (1984). The Prevalence of Child Sexual Abuse Victimization in an Adult Sample of Texas Residents. *Child Abuse & Neglect,* 8, 495–501.

Kimmel, M. & Kaufman, M. (1994). Weekend Warriors: The New Men's Movement. In H. Brod & M. Kaufman (Eds.), *Theorizing Masculinities* (pp. 259–288). Thousand Oaks, CA: Sage.

Lew, M. (1990). *Victims No Longer: Men Recovering From Incest and Other Sexual Child Abuse.* New York, NY: Harper & Row.

Messerschmidt, J. (1993). *Masculinities and Crime: Critique and Reconceptualization of Theory.* Lanham, Maryland: Rowman and Littlefield Publishers.

Mendel, M. P. (1995). *The Male Survivor: The Impact of Sexual Abuse.* Thousand Oaks, CA: Sage.

Nasjleti, M. (1986). Suffering in Silence: The Male Incest Victim. In D.C. Haden (Ed.), *Out of Harm's Way: Readings on Child Sexual Abuse, its Prevention and Treatment.* Phoenix: Oryx.

Nava, M. (1984). Drawing the Line: A Feminist Response to Adult-Child Sexual Relations. In A.McRobbie and M. Nava (Eds.), *Gender and Generation.* Houndmills: Macmillan.

Newburn, T. & Stanko, E. (1994). When Men are Victims: The Failure of Victimology. In T. Newburn and E. Stanko (Eds.), *Just Boys Doing Business?* London: Routledge.

Pierce, R. & Pierce, L. (1985). The Sexually Abused Child: The Comparison of Male and Female Victims. *Child Sexual Abuse and Neglect,* 9, 191–199.

Pupo, N. (1988). Preserving Partriarchy: Women, the Family and the State. In N. Mandell and A. Duffy (Eds.), *Reconstructing the Canadian Family: Feminist Perspectives.* Toronto: Butterworths.

Segal, L. (1990). *Slow Motion: Changing Masculinities, Changing Men.* Brunswick, NJ: Rutgers University Press.

Seidler, V. (1991). *Recreating Sexual Politics: Men, Feminism and Politics.* London: Pandora Books.

Stanko, E. & Hobdell, K. (1993). Assault on Men: Masculinity and Male Victimization. *British Journal of Criminology*, 33(3), 400–415.

Vancouver Sun, April 16, 1994:A2

Watkins, B. & Bentovim, A. (1992). The Sexual Aabuse of Male Children and Adolescents: A Review of Current Research. *Journal of Applied Psychology & Psychiatry & Applied Disciplines*, 33(1), 197–248.

Section 4

Prostitution and Social Control

"Public Health and Social Policy: The Dilemmas of Street Sex, Crack, Heroin, and AIDS"

Gordon James Knowles,
University of Hawaii[1]

Abstract

The intent of the research was to conduct a replication study of a previous investigation in order to permit a comparative analysis of some aspects that might permeate overtime from the street sex trade of Honolulu. The design comprised the elements of (1) a longitudinal design, (2) a snowball sampling technique, (3) a survey instrument, and (4) ethnographic and field data collection. Data comparison utilized survey interviews obtained from a population immersed in the street sex trade at the same location, but from two different points in time. Both studies used Likert scale and semantic differential tests to target the prostitutes' attitudes toward the law, experiences with local social service agencies, as well as the other aspects of the streetwalkers' per-

1. Gordon James Knowles received his *Ph.D. in Sociology* with an emphasis in *Criminology* from the *University of Hawaii* and also holds an *M.S. in Criminal Justice Administration* with an emphasis in *Law Enforcement* and *Corrections Management* from *Chaminade University of Honolulu*. His main interests include *urban ethnography, applied sociology, criminology, criminal justice,* and *law*. Interested readers may contact him at *voice/fax (808) 696-3579* or via *E-mail at gordonknow@aol.com*.

sonal lives. Details included the use of drugs and alcohol, fear of sexually transmitted infections, and experiences with crime and victimization. Increases in highest educational level completed were noted, but decreases in the completion of high school were more significant. Self reported use of narcotics was relatively consistent across the two studies, but an overall decrease in frequency of use was found. The current subjects rated HIV and AIDS their main personal concern; whereas in 1974, the most commonly chosen concern was being arrested. None of the 1992 subjects reported that they had contracted HIV or the AIDS virus and stated that they primarily depended on regular military clients for their income. The overall analysis of both samples yielded the epidemiological themes of (1) drug addiction, (2) sexual exploitation, and (3) sexually transmitted infections among those within the street sex trade even though the time periods between them had spanned almost over twenty years.[2]

The Street Sex Market of Honolulu

Historically Honolulu, Hawaii's vice scene has sat at the center of the Chinatown district tightly bound by the streets of River, Beretania, Nuuana, Smith, and Hotel for over the last hundred years (Bailey and Farber 1992:95). Chinatown has been noted for vice crimes such as gambling and prostitution since 1880 (Krauss, 1995). Barley and Farber (1992:60) also cite that alcohol and drug addiction, especially heroin, was present in over one third of Chinatown's Hotel Street sex workers even by the 1940s. The prevalence of narcotic use within Honolulu's sex trade was described by a Hotel Street sex worker from that same era as simply, "with any red light district goes dope" (Barley and Farber, 1992:60).

By the early 1970s, the Hotel Street area became a popular target for research studies of street prostitution. One project entitled *The Honolulu Queens* examined the lifestyles of fifty transvestites who frequented the Hotel Street area. The findings revealed that most desired sex change operations and supported themselves economically through prostitution (Lubliner, Schmidt, Sefton, Spillane, Will, Wilson, Hansen, 1973). This investigation also provides a brief depiction of Hotel Street's past as follows:

2. An earlier version of this research was presented at the *American Sociological Associations* 1995 annual meeting held at the *Capital Hilton and Towers in Washington, D.C.* for the regular session panel on *Deviance and Social Control* on August 22nd, 1995.

> *At dusk, the dilapidated brick buildings come to life. Sailors, "respectable citizens" out slumming, prostitutes, pimps, police and vice squads' men converge in the tattoo parlors, pornography shops, movies, bars, and pool halls which line both sides of the streets (Lubliner, et al. 1973:1).*

Another study conducted in 1974, attempted to gain more knowledge about the experiences of Hotel Street streetwalkers in reference to the law, local social service agencies, and aspects of their personal lives regarding drugs, disease, and crime (Yoshimoto, 1983). The latter study was intended to assist social service agencies in becoming cognizant of problems encountered by prostitutes and in developing policies to address the many problems faced by prostitutes (Yoshimoto, 1983:9).

In the nearly 20 years since these studies, there have been some changes in the Hotel Street Area. Some old business have closed, particularly those catering to large numbers of Viet Nam era military personnel on R & R *(Rest and Recuperation)* leaves from combat. By the 1990s, considerable gentrification of shops on adjacent streets had occurred, but Hotel Street after dark remains an area of cheap, rough bars, marginally legitimate or disreputable businesses, drug trafficking, pornographic video and bookstores, curbside drinkers, and the focus of the present study—the street sex trade (Waite, 1995; Knowles, 1996).

Research Intent

The focus of the research design was to conduct a replication study of a previous investigation in order to permit a comparative analysis of some aspects that might permeate overtime from the street sex trade of Honolulu's Hotel Street. The design comprised the elements of (1) a longitudinal design, (2) a snowball sampling technique, (3) a survey instrument and (4) ethnographic and field data collection. Data comparison comprised two samples of survey interviews obtained from a population immersed in the street sex trade at the same location, but from two different points in time.

The intent of the data comparison was to uncover possible trends or patterns present among the two samples collected. The analysis of both samples yielded the epidemiological themes of (1) drug addiction, (2) sexual exploitation, and (3) sexually transmitted infections among those within the street sex trade even though the time periods between them had spanned almost over twenty years. The study also sought to compare the more recent data collected in Honolulu with other contemporary studies conducted at similar popular tourist destinations such as New York, Los Angeles, and Miami.

Survey Design and Research Methodology

Although, prostitution is by no means limited to Honolulu, the lack of previous prostitution studies in other areas besides Honolulu precluded the utilization of any type of comparative analysis or longitudinal study design. Based on this, the study site of Honolulu's Hotel Street district was chosen for the focus of the target population and eventual sample recruitment. The replication study in this area achieved intent of the design which was to not merely determine how things were at a single point in time, but rather assess how things had changed over time within the venue of Honolulu' s street sex trade.

The methodology that attempts to investigate how things are changing over time is referred to as longitudinal surveys. Studies often use longitudinal surveys that compare the results of the *same* sample obtained from two or more time frames, and this is known as *panel* longitudinal surveys (Ellis, 1998:175; Maxfield and Babbie, 1995:81). However, this research utilized a nonpanel longitudinal design which involved selecting two *different* samples within the same population at different points in time.

The advantage of a nonpanel longitudinal survey is that it provides estimates of how a population is changing over time without having to locate the same subjects again and again (Ellis, 1998:176). The nonpanel option was also preferred since panel designs that utilized surveying the same individuals overtime would be extremely difficult or impossible with this type of *hidden* or *hard-to-reach* population of street prostitutes (Kalton, 1993:70; Van Meter, 1990:31; Ellis, 1998:175; Maxfield and Babbie, 1995:209).

The data analysis compared a sample of street prostitutes collected in 1974 (Yoshimoto, 1983) with a similar sample acquired in 1992 (Knowles, 1992). The sample comprised two groups of twenty-five street prostitutes recruited from the same location at two different time periods spanning almost 20 years. This design attempts to compare and contrast the two samples in reference to (1) sociodemographic shifts, (2) socioeconomic status, and (3) epidemiological patterns in relation to sexual exploitation, drug addiction, and sexually transmitted infections.

The former study collected in 1972, and the latter in 1992, recruited subjects using a snowball sampling technique (Yoshimoto, 1983:11; Knowles, 1992:25). The 'snowball' method develops an ever-increasing set of observations by asking the participants under study to recommend others for interviewing and each subsequent participant is asked for other recommendations (Maxfield and Babbie, 1995:268; Knowles, 1996:2). The strategy of the snowball sampling technique is that members of *rare* or *hidden* populations know each other (Wolf, 1989; Kalton, 1993:71; Van Meter, 1990:31).

Although selecting prostitutes from a jailed population would permit utilization of a probability sampling design, arrestees would not fully represent the street population (Pettiway, 1995:506). Rather, a "snowball"sample of active street prostitutes probably reveals more accurate findings than those representative sampling designs drawn from inactive or static prison populations or rehabilitation programs (Pettiway, 1995:506). Further, it is more feasible and accurate to attempt to record the lifestyles of street prostitutes when they are actively involved in the behavior, which is not the case with jailed or treatment populations (Nurco *et al*, 1998:223).

Since no simple census of all prostitutes is available, it is difficult to impose some type of probability design on this population (Berry *et al*, 1990:2: Maxfield and Babbie, 1995:209). Additionally, because population parameters of street prostitutes cannot be reliably estimated, attempting to select a representative sample is impractical (Leonard, 1990:42). Snowball sampling has also been utilized extensively by other sociological and epidemiological studies of AIDS and drug use (Johnson *et al*, 1985; Kozel and Adams, 1986; Inciardi *et al*, 1991; Martin and Dean, 1993; Kalton; 1993:70)

Minimal modifications were made to the 1974 original survey instrument so that administered attempts retain the ability to conduct a direct data comparison among the two samples. However, one question addressing two prostitute organizations, Coyote and Dolphin, was omitted due to the inability to verify that these organizations existed or were accessible to Honolulu prostitutes in 1992. Additionally, questions in the previous survey that utilized the terms such as "Negro," "hooker," "john," and "cop" were replaced with more acceptable and professional terms of "black," "prostitute," 'client," and "police," respectively.

Questions using Likert scale design were also modified to offer respondents an "undecided"option which allowed for greater extremes in responses and also eliminated a forced choice dilemma. Finally, the 1992 survey also included questions relevant to current street prostitution trends such as AIDS and crack-cocaine that were omitted from collection in 1974 as the did not exist at that time. Other modifications to specific questions will be described as they relate to comparisons of results.

Reliability and Validity

The self-reports of criminal behavior are particularly suspect because of the deviant and illegal nature of the subject's lifestyles (Nurco *et al* , 1998:222). However, surprisingly studies have shown self-reports of criminal behavior *do not* distort or cover up the less desirable aspects of their lives on the street (Inciardi, 1986:121). Several studies have investigated this question by checking drug addicts' self-reported activities against other indicators and have consistently found that addict self-reports are surprisingly truthful and accurate (Aquilino, 1992, Anglin *et al*, 1993; Inciardi, Lockwood and Pottieger, 1993:66; Frendrich and Yanchun, 1994).

To determine intersubject reliability and internal validity, the subjects in both samples were asked the same questions and their responses were systematically checked against each other across respondents (Jacobs, 1996:415). Although the subjects may have conspired to respond only a certain way, their separation from each other in the interview process made this unlikely. Additionally, unobtrusive observations confirmed many of the issues or activities reported by the sample. In reference to external validity, the representativeness of a sample drawn from prostitutes at large in the community cannot be determined conclusively because the parameters of the total population are unknown (Jacobs, 1996:415; Berry *et al*, 1990:2). The purposive nature of the samples collected means these findings must be considered exploratory in nature and region-specific characteristics and that perceptions of street sex trade are likely to vary (Jacobs, 1996:415).

Findings

Demographics

Subjects from the initial 1974 sample ranged in age from 16 to 37, and were concentrated in the 22- to 29-year-old age bracket with mean, median, and mode at 25 years of age. The 1992 sample contained no minors, and nearly half the sample fell into the 22- to 29-year-old and 30- to 40-year-old brackets; mean age was 29.2. Mean age in prostitution studies on the mainland findings have generally been much lower than the Honolulu studies (U.S. Department of Justice, 1992; Weisberg; 1985): Inciardi's Miami study showed 15.6 as mean age (1989:691); another ranged from 15 to 23 (Coombs, 1974); a 1980 study of male prostitutes revealed a mean age of 16.1 (Allen, 1980:399); and a 1982 study of female prostitutes reported 70% under age 21, and 60% under 16. The 1992 "Crime in Hawaii" report by the State of Hawaii Attorney General notes only three arrests, all male, of prostitutes under the age of eighteen in the entire state (Department of the Attorney General, 1992:100). This may indicate that juvenile prostitution, especially female, in Hawaii is not as prevalent in comparison with other tourist destinations like Miami and Los Angeles (Inciardi, *et al*,1993; Boyle and Anglin, 1993; French, 1993).

The 1974 investigation showed a gross over representation of blacks: 62% of the subjects were black females, while a 1970 census had reported that blacks comprised only 0.7% of the state's population. Over-representation of blacks has been found in other studies as well (U.S. Department of Justice, 1987:52), but the 1992 study included no blacks in its sample. Caucasians were represented in proportion to the 1990 census, and Japanese, Hawaiian, and Samoan populations—absent or negligible in 1974—together made up 43% of the later sample. However, the later study also noted Caucasians were over-represented in reference to arrest data since 283 of the 367 females arrested for prostitution in 1992, were classified as white (Department of the Attorney General, 1993: 97). Reports of residency also reflect this shift in ethnicity; in 1974, 87% of the respondents were originally from other states, with almost one-half of the sample having lived in Hawaii for less than three years. In 1992, only 36% of respondents were from other states and most were born in Hawaii.

In both studies all respondents claimed affiliation with a religious faith, most being Catholic (though twice as many were in 1992 than in 1974). Almost all respondents in 1992 claimed a strong belief in God (92%) and 68% indicated irregular attendance at church. In general, subjects in 1992 reported attaining lower levels of education than the 1974 subjects. Although a drop was noted from 63% to 32% in the current study for the completion of high school, a rise from 7% to 36% was reported for the completion of some college courses.

All subjects in 1974 identified themselves as heterosexual, but in 1992 a majority reported being transsexual (40%*: noted as pre-op male to female transsexuals*), and only 32% heterosexual. Others were bisexual, "other," and homosexual. Most subjects in both studies were not married and never had been, however, the 1992 study found a higher percentage unmarried (1974: 62% 1992: 88%). The difference in marital status between the two samples was in the numbers of respondents who were married at the time of the study: 38% in 1974, but only 12% in 1992. However, with regard to dependents the two samples differed greatly: 65% of 1974 subjects had children, but in 1992 65% did not.

Attitudes Toward the Law and Police

Subjects in both studies were asked about their opinions on changing the legal status of prostitution. In 1974, only 19% favored legalization, 71% favored mere decriminalizing, and none favored penalizing clients more heavily than prostitutes—though at the time laws implicating clients in the crime of prostitution had yet to be made. The passing of such laws in 1990 may explain the very different attitudes of the 1992 respondents: 29% agreed that prostitution should be legalized, and only 30% felt that it should simply be decriminalized. Twenty-six percent felt that the criminal penalties should be equal for both participating parties, and only 9% desired a more severe penalty for the client. It should be noted that the 1974 study asked subjects to choose between "legalization," "decriminalization," and "no change," while the 1992 question asked subjects to indicate their degree of agreement to each of these options.

In the 1974 collection, most of the respondents indicated that they had been subjected to harassment by police officers—more so (and more frequently in physical ways) from uniformed than vice officers. Even higher percentages reported harassment in 1992 from uniformed officers, whereas other variations were negligible and not systematic. None of the subjects in the previous study reported being coerced into a sexual act by a uniformed police officer, but 44% reported this in the current study, and 92% reported being sexually approached by uniformed officers monthly. The percentage of subjects reporting this type of behavior by vice officers was also higher in 1992 than in the previous study.

Drug Use Frequency and Trend Analysis

In both studies, approximately 90% reported having used or experimented with alcohol, findings similar to Inciardi's 1985 study (Inciardi, 1989:691). Marijuana and hashish use was also consistently high across all three studies; use of inhalants increased from 1974 to1992, and use of amphetamines slightly decreased, but both were lower than Inciardi's study. Barbiturate, hallucinogen, and cocaine use were reported by more subjects in 1992, but heroin use decreased from the 1974 figures. Only 12% in 1992 reported use of crack. Frequent (5 to 7 times weekly) and moderate (3 to 4 times weekly) use of drugs decreased in all listed categories except cocaine, which increased only slightly in 1992. Percentages of subjects reporting never using each drug exhibit only slight variations between 1974 and 1992. Greater percentages of prostitutes indicated experimenting with every listed drug. Interestingly, in all categories except cocaine and heroine, reports of frequent use decreased while experimentation increased. Eighty-eight percent of the subjects indicated that they had had no prior use of crack-cocaine, and those who did indicate usage noted it as former or experimental. When the subjects were asked about crystal methamphetamine usage (called "ice" on the street), only one prostitute indicated experience with this drug.

Subjects in 1992 were asked at what age they first used each drug. Mean ages for alcohol, marijuana, and inhalants were 14.5, 14.4, and 13.4 respectively. For the rest of the drugs, age at onset of use was considerably higher: 18.4 and 18.8 for barbiturates and hallucinogens, 19.1 for amphetamines, 20 for heroin, 20.3 and 20.6 for crack and cocaine respectively. These are high in comparison to Inciardi's 1985 study. Inciardi (1989:692) reported a mean age at onset of cocaine use of 11.2, and for heroin use, 11.4. years.

In the 1992 study, subjects were asked to indicate on a Likert scale if they began using drugs before becoming prostitutes. Seventy-two percent responded with varying degrees of affirmation, ranging from "very strongly agree" to "somewhat agree"; only 12% disagreed (one subject "very strongly"). Inciardi (1986:160) also noted that drug use preceded prostitution for the vast majority of his sample. The subjects were next asked if their use of drugs had increased since entering prostitution: 36% very strongly agreed or simply agreed that it had, another 36% were neutral or had no opinion; and 28% disagreed or strongly disagreed that their drug use had increased. The researcher was told informally by some subjects that the use of speed (an amphetamine) had increased because of the long hours of hustling that were frequently necessary in order to make enough money.

In response to whether they primarily engage in prostitution to support their drug habit, 20% affirmed, 62% said no, and 18% were without an opinion. The researcher noted that common answers such as "I do it [prostitute] just to live"—is perhaps an indication of the high cost of living in Hawaii. The prostitutes were additionally asked to indicate whether most of the prostitutes they knew engaged in prostitution to support their drug habits, and to this question 80% answered in the affirmative, 16% disagreed, and 4% were without opinion. However, Knowles (1997:55) notes that the difference between engaging in "*sex for survival*" and "*sex for drugs*" is sometimes indistinguishable with populations such as prostitutes. A 31-year-old female heroin and crack-cocaine user describes:

> *Diane:* You see...I'm a heroin user...so sex for money...equals money for drugs...money for drugs in turn equals my survival. I can't survive without heroin, does that make sense? *(Field Station Interview: February 25th, 1997).*

Overall, the findings between the two studies support that drug and alcohol usage appears to precede prostitution, suggesting that the causal order is from drugs to prostitution, and that prostitution is continued to support existing drug habits even though this observation was made of other prostitutes and not admitted by the respondents themselves.

Sexual Abuse, Suicide, and Aids

Subjects in both studies were asked to respond to questions about their general impressions and attitudes about pimps, police corruption, crime, and sexually transmitted infections. The 1992 subjects felt that the presence of pimps was less common than did the 1974 subjects. In the later study, the prostitutes discounted the significance of their income supporting organized crime or paying for police protection. In 1992, twice as many subjects, and a significant majority felt that most prostitutes get robbed by their clients, and 68% (similar to 1974) believed that most prostitutes try to rob their clients.

Belief that prostitutes are satisfied with their lifestyle dropped considerably in 1992, and more (though still only 16%) felt prostitutes have a higher suicide rate than other occupational groups. A majority of the 1992 subjects believed most prostitutes drank heavily and had severe drug problems. The combination of drug and alcohol use, coupled with other occupational groups arguably like that of the sex trade, have been noted to be strongly associated with suicidal behavior (Adams and Overholser, 1992:344). Thirty-six percent (almost identical to 1974) stated that most of the prostitutes they knew had contracted a sexually transmitted infection. A majority of 84% (less than in 1974) agreed that most prostitutes who contracted a sexually transmitted infection would seek medical treatment promptly, and 56% agreed that most prostitutes would avoid engaging in acts of prostitution while infected with a sexually transmitted infection. Most subjects in 1992 frequently worried about contracting AIDS and agreed that they would not engage in sex without a condom. When asked if the majority of their clients took self-protective measures against sexually transmitted infections, 64% of the subjects responded affirmatively.

A question in 1974 that asked whether most prostitutes are "lonely, insecure, or afraid" was substantially modified for the 1992 study in order to isolate these feelings as separate variables. In all three categories, most of the subjects agreed that these terms characterized prostitutes. A question added to the 1992 study queried the prostitutes' experiences of early childhood and teenage sexual abuse. Nearly half of the respondents (44%) indicated they had never been sexually abused; 64% of those who did experience abuse indicated that the abuse was inflicted by a stranger (beginning at a mean age of 12.8 years). The remaining 36% of abused respondents were abused by a close relative (beginning at a mean of 7.7 years old). These findings were similar in respect to other studies (Silbert and Pines, 1983; Simons and Whitbeck, 1991).

In the 1992 study, subjects reported an average daily income from prostitution of $271.80 per day, a figure consistent with Barlow's study in 1982, conducted nearly a decade ago, which reported a range of income from $200 to $300 per day for even the classiest of New York's streetwalkers. From these figures, streetwalking prostitution may not be as profitable as it appears in theory. An issue raised by some prostitutes was that drug-addiction had driven the price down. One respondent states, "I try to hold out for $30 or $40 for a blow job [oral sex], but they got girls down here hooked on crack doing it for $7... how can I compete with that." The 1992 subjects reported that of these illegal revenues, an average of $121 per day was spent on narcotics and/or alcohol, and although income reports were relatively consistent, 24% of the respondents indicated that they were homeless and lived in Aala Park, a nearby sanctuary for the homeless.

Clients, Sex, Drugs, and Money

West (1993:263) contends the sex industry could not exist without a substantial demand for its services. Fifty-four percent of 1992 subjects reported that the service most often requested of them was intercourse, for which they charged on average $67. Forty-two percent were most often asked for oral sex at an average price of $49. Eighty-eight percent indicated this service was the most convenient to render. Four percent indicated that anal intercourse was most often requested, but was not granted at any price. It is important to stress that the subjects did not indicate the reluctance to engage in anal sex was due to the fear of AIDS. Rather, the prostitutes reported that anal sex was too intimate of a sex act to be performed with a client.

In 1992, the average age at which subjects had first engaged in prostitution for money was 18.7 years. Of the 1992 subjects who had engaged in prostitution in exchange for drugs (16%), average age of first incident was 21.2. (Inciardi's 1986 results with respect to age were only slightly lower, reporting 17.8 years old as average starting age for prostitution for money, and 19.2 years for prostitution for drugs (Inciardi, 1986:163).

Knowledge about the clients of female prostitutes is scanty and speculative, but information about the customers of male prostitutes is even more meager (West, 1993:263). West (1993:277) argues that clients, like sex workers, are of many kinds. They can be from any social class; they may be married or single, selfish or considerate, and may want only sexual release. They may be trying to relieve loneliness and want ordinary sex, or may desire special sexual rituals. The 1992 subjects' reported the age of their clients ranged from 16 to 55 (mean: 31.6 years). Fifty-four percent of subjects judged most of their clients to be military personnel, and 42% believed most of their clients were local residents. Only 4% believed most to be tourists. Subjects estimated that, on average, 65% of their clients were married, and 59.4% were "regulars" or frequent customers.

Silbert (1981:395) noted in his survey of 200 female street prostitutes that excessive victimization of both physical and sexual abuse coupled with learned helplessness were common.[3] Concerning the 1992 subjects victimization, 16%

3. Silbert (1981) noted that the 200 female street prostitutes interviewed (70% of whom were under the age of 21 years) showed extremely high levels of 'on-the-job' victimization. The subjects reported being physically abused and beaten up by both customers and pimps.

reported having been physically abused by their clients (average frequency: 0.84 times per month; 0.24 for rape). However, none of the subjects reported these assaults to the police.

This 1992 study also focused on determining if the subjects considered prostitution to be an "addictive" behavior like the other vice crimes of gambling and drug usage (Carson, Butcher, and Coleman, 1988:212) since the theory that prostitution may be addictive has been supported by previous research (Janus, 1977; Janus and Bess, 1977; Janus and Janus, 1993:130). Therefore, an additional question in the 1992 survey asked about the addictiveness of prostitution (to the subject and client), to which 60% reported feeling that the profession is addictive to prostitutes, and 92% felt that prostitution was addictive to their clients. Janus and Janus (1993:131) concluded that prostitution is a compulsive behavior beyond the control of the person and therefore must be considered a deviance. This "theory of addiction" may add insight into why the subjects and the clients continue to engage in the dangerous and self-destructive behavior of street prostitution which repeatedly exposes them to potential AIDS and HIV transmission (Cohen, 1987; Plant, 1990).

Personal Concerns and Personality

In response to a 1974 question asking subjects to select the single most worrisome concern from a list of nine, the two concerns selected by most of the initial subjects were police and client abuse. In 1992, responses to the modified question (having them rank each item rather than choosing from them, and adding AIDS as a tenth concern), 72% of the subjects indicated that contracting AIDS was their greatest concern. None of the subjects ranked police as their most worrisome problem, and only 12% selected abuse by client.

Finally, the subjects were asked to rate themselves, uniformed and vice police officers, and their clients on a series of thirteen semantic differential scales. Subjects ranked uniformed officers higher than themselves in terms of value and cleanliness, and equal to themselves in honesty. However, they rated their customers less honest than they rated uniformed officers, and rated vice officers lower than themselves in value, honesty, caring, and politeness. Comparing subjects' rankings of themselves to their customers, subjects viewed their clients as more worthless than themselves, but equally dirty, and felt

---

Other forms of victimization included customer rape, forced perversion, non payment, robbery, violence, clients going beyond the prostitution contract and unfair splits of the money with pimps. The subjects perceived no options for themselves, blamed themselves for their own victimization and therefore did not report victimization or avail themselves to any social agency support.

themselves more honest and moral than their clients. In contrast, the subjects rated themselves as less polite and caring than they rated their clients. Comparing the subjects' ranking of uniformed and vice officers, several significant differences were noted. The subjects rated vice officers as more worthless, cruel, and dishonest than uniformed officers.

Experiences with Social Services

Ninety percent of the 1974 subjects indicated they would seek professional help or guidance if it were necessary. By asking subjects to rank (from "very helpful" to "not familiar with agency") 22 different social service agencies operating on Oahu, the 1974 study found that 48% would initially approach friends and family members for help; the remainder would go to a psychiatrist, attorney, doctor, priest, or counselor. Many of the subjects were either unfamiliar with the organizations listed or viewed them as not helpful.

In 1992, a similar percentage (88%) indicated they would seek professional guidance, but many of these subjects informally told the researcher that they felt there were no such organizations for them to turn to. From a list of 19 currently existing and accessible agencies listed, doctors ranked highest as helpful designations at 84%. Other organizations receiving a majority of "helpful" rankings were the Diamond Head Health Clinic, the Salvation Army, the Welfare Department of Social Services, and Vocational Rehabilitation Services. Subjects in the 1992 study also listed other agencies they felt were helpful; mentioned were the Life Foundation, Castle Medical Group, the River of Life Mission (located in the Chinatown district), the Alakukie Hawaiian Program, and the Needle Exchange Program.

Comparative Trends and Patterns

The 1992 study based on the earlier 1974 study produced findings quite similar with respect to the age of sampled prostitutes (the later sample being somewhat older), dissimilar with respect to ethnicity and residency status, and similar with respect to religious faith. A greater proportion of the 1992 subjects were unmarried, and this group also reported having fewer children than subjects of the 1974 study did. Education among the 1992 subjects differed significantly from 1974, with a greater number having completed only grade 10 or 11, fewer having high school diplomas, more having taken some college courses, and fewer possessing college degrees.

Experience of harassment from uniformed and vice police officers remained relatively consistent; notable increases were found, however, in incidence of being sexually approached by uniformed officers and in incidence of verbal abuse from vice officers. Frequent use of narcotics generally decreased in 1992, though less frequent use and experimentation seems to have increased. In relation to national studies, the 1992 sample showed a later age at onset of drug use.

the advent of AIDS seems to have greatly changed what prostitutes worry about the most; in 1974, their main concern was being arrested, and in 1992 it was contracting the HIV virus. Most take protective measures against contracting and transmitting the disease, but a significant number reported that their clients did not. In light of the fact that prostitutes continue to have clients—regardless of the attention given by the public and the media in Hawaii to AIDS issues—it seems that prostitutes have taken the warnings much more seriously than have their clients. However, some subjects did admit that condoms were negotiable if the clients would not pay for sexual service if a condom was used, especially if the client increased the payment for services by ten or twenty dollars, which has also been noted in other studies (Leonard, 1990:47). This almost always applied for oral sex, and sometimes for intercourse. It was noted that the heterosexual prostitutes would be more open to condom negotiation than homosexual or transsexual prostitutes.

The research also shifted to ascertain why the subjects did not engage in the more profitable activity of drug dealing, as noted in other studies, instead of prostitution (Inciardi, 1986:164). Most subjects reported that they entered and remained in prostitution because narcotics trafficking resulted in heavier prison sentences than prostitution. A statement often heard was, "It's crazy to sell drugs, that just isn't a few days in jail like prostitution, it's long hard time." it would appear that the fear of long term incarceration has kept the subjects from entering into the drug selling business based on these statements.

The maintainment of the subjects in prostitution may also be compounded by the high cost of living and low wage jobs in Hawaii. The subjects did acknowledge some earnings went for the purchase of drugs or alcohol, however the question of remaining in prostitution out of economic "need" or "greed" still remains unclear because the subjects were reluctant to admit this about themselves, although they reported this association for the majority of their fellow prostitutes.

None of the subjects reported that they had contracted AIDS, which may be attributed to condom use *and/or* the lack of intravenous drug-use reported by the sample (Page *et al*, 1990:57; Taylor, 1993). However, many contemporary studies illustrate that AIDS, drug usage, and prostitution are entangled epidemics which pose caution in addressing policies regarding prostitution legalization (Johnson *et al*, 1985; Inciardi, 1989; Inciardi *et al*, 1991; Cottler *et al*, 1990; Larret and Zierler, 1993; McCoy and Inciardi,1995). Although the subjects appeared to be educated about the risk of AIDS, they tended to believe that condom usage would totally prevent the transmission of the AIDS virus or other blood borne pathogens during all types of sexual activity. The subjects did not acknowledge, or more probable, comprehend that their high frequencies of sexual activities also put them at a great risk for disease transmission, even with proper condom usage (Pleak and Meyer-Bahlburg, 1990).

Although only descriptive in nature, 1992 survey data produced a contemporary profile regarding the characteristics of those involved in Honolulu's street sex trade. This composite is provided to assist in identifying the population's needs in reference to social services, health care, and rehabilitation programs. The "average" street prostitute may be male or female and is about 29 years old. They will most likely be Caucasian and identify themselves as being heterosexual or transsexual. Although he or she has a strong belief in God and belongs to the Catholic faith, attendance at church is irregular. He or she was born in Hawaii, has received a high school education, and is single, without any children.

When working, they are frequently sexually approached by police officers. Although they have experimented with a variety of drugs, the preferred drug is alcohol, with the beginning drinking age of approximately 14. Because they primarily depend on regular military clients for a $271-per-day income, they do not regularly attempt to steal from clients and do not have a pimp or madam. They will try not to engage in sex without a condom, depending on the demands and price offered by the client. Additionally, they will seek medical treatment promptly in the event of contracting a venereal disease, and frequently worry about contracting the AIDS virus. Almost half of these prostitutes will have been sexually abused as children. When in need of medical treatment these subjects prefer to go to a private doctor rather than a social service agency.

Social Policy, Public Health, and the Common Good

The social concerns in reference to the street sex-trade of Honolulu's Chinatown are many. First, drug and alcohol addiction are present in both the current and previous samples. Second, the risk of HIV and AIDS transmission among the current sample is very high due to the potential transfer of bodily fluids associated with the sexual nature of the trade. Also, despite the attention given to AIDS, condoms are still negotiable if the "price is right," especially among the heterosexual prostitutes. Sexual abuse in adolescence and also adulthood is present and, although difficult to measure or assess, the issues of gender disorder and mental health problems appear to exist among the transsexual prostitutes.

Although, sex workers cannot be singled out for spreading AIDS or HIV, they are arguably a population that exhibits the behavior that puts them at the utmost risk for exposure, contraction, and transmission of the disease due to the sexual nature of the street sex trade. Admittedly, the illegality of prostitution could be considered to be an attempt to restrict or prevent the epidemiological matter of AIDS from broadening further. Proponents from the feminist perspective argue that the illegality of prostitution is a capitalistic construction that is merely patriarchal in nature (Messerchmidt, 1986:90; Faith, 1993:77). This argument is in spite of the fact that studies (over the last thirty years) have noted just as many men are exploited by the street sex trade as women (Ginsburg, 1967; Allen, 1980:399; Steward, 1991:1; West, 1993:3).

Despite this contradiction, this research contends, from a public health perspective the law may attempt to restrict behaviors strongly associated with fostering a strictly epidemiological concern. Thus, laws restricting the behavior of sex workers are not merely used to persecute those involved in socially unacceptable behavior, but rather the laws may be conceived as attempting to prevent a public health issue.

Structurally, the hotel street area has gone through numerous social, political, and economic changes (Bailey and Farber, 1992). However, during the almost twenty year period between surveys, both studies clearly indicate that drug and alcohol addiction are common denominators for prostitution in the Hotel Street area of Honolulu's Chinatown. An important aspect of this study is that it attempts to provide an accurate depiction of the individuals, behaviors, and activities of a population over time. It is hoped the information presented can be utilized by mental or public health agencies to develop practical intervention efforts and also assist government officials in forming public policy in addressing this social concern for the common good.

References

Adams., D., and J. Overholser. (1992). Suicidal Behavior and History Of Substance Abuse. *American Journal of Drug and Alcohol Abuse,* 18:(3):343–354.

Allen, D.M. (1980). Young Male Prostitutes: A Psychological Study. *Arch Sexual Behavior,* 9:5 Oct, 399–426.

Anglin, M. Douglas, Yih-Ing Hser, and Chih-Ping Chou. (1993). Reliability and Validity of Retrospective Behavioral Self-Report by Narcotic Addicts. *Evaluation Review,* 17:91–108.

Aquilino, William S. (1992). Telephone Versus Face to Face Interviewing for Household Drug Use Surveys. *International Journal of the Addictions,* 27:71–91.

Aquilino, William S., and Leonard A. Losciuto. (1990). Interview Mode Effects in Drug Use Surveys. *Public Opinion Quarterly*, 54:362–95

Bailey, B., and D. Farber. (1992). Hotel Street and the Politics of War. *Radical History Review*. New York: Cambridge University Press.

Barlow, H.D. (1982). *Introduction to Criminology*. 2nd Ed. Boston, MA: Little Brown.

Berry, Sandra H., Naihua Duan, and David E. Kanouse. (1990). *A Rand Note: Developing a Probability Sample of Prostitutes: Sample Design for the Rand Study of HIV Infection and Risk Behaviors in Prostitutes.* National Institute of Child Health and Human Development: N-3190 Nichd.

Boyle, K., and M.D. Anglin. (1993). *To the Curb: Sex Bartering and Drug Use Among Homeless Crack Users in Los Angeles*, in *Crack Pipe as Pimp: An Ethnographic Investigation of Sex-for-Crack Exchanges*, 1993 by Mitchell S. Ratner, New York: Lexington Press.

Carson, R.C., J.N. Butcher, and J.C. Coleman. (1988). *Abnormal Psychology and Modern Life.* 8th Ed. Glenview, IL: Scoot, Foresman and Co.

Cohen, J. (1987). Antibody to Human Immunodeficiency Virus in Female Prostitutes. *36 Morbidity and Morality Report*, 157:158–195.

Coombs, N. (1974). *Male Prostitution: A Psychological View of Behavior.* Am. J. Orthopsychiatry, 44:782.

Cottler, L.B., and J.E. Helzer, and J.E. Tip. (1990). Lifetime Patterns of Substance Abuse Among General Population Subjects Engaging in High Risk Sexual Behaviors: Implications for HIV. Risk. *Am J Drug Alcohol Abuse.* 16(3–4):207–222.

Department of the Attorney General, State of Hawaii. (1992). *Crime in Hawaii.* Crime Prevention Division: Honolulu, Hawaii.

Ellis, L. (1998). Research Methods in the Social Sciences. New York: McGraw-Hill.

Faith, Karlene. (1993). *Unruly Women: The Politics of Confinement and Resistance.* Press Gang Publishers: Vancouver.

Fendrich, Michael, and Yanchun Xu. (1994). The Validity of Drug Use Reports from Juvenile Arrestees. *International Journal of the Addictions* 29:151–70

French, John. (1993). *Pipe Dreams: Crack and the Life in Philadelphia and Newark*, in *Crack Pipe as Pimp: An Ethnographic Investigation of Sex-for-Crack Exchanges*, by Ratner, Mitchell S. New York: Lexington Press.

Ginsburg, K. (1967). *The Meat Rack: A Study of the Male Homosexual Prostitute.* American Journal of Psychotherapy. 21:170–185.

Inciardi, J.A. (1989). Trading Sex for Crack Among Juvenile Drug Users: A Research Note. *Contemporary Drug Problems*, Winter, 689–700.

Inciardi, J.A. (1986). *The War on Drugs, Heroine, Cocaine, Crime, and Public Policy.* Palo Alto, CA: Mayfield.

Inciardi, J., Pottieger, A., Forney, M., Chitwood, D., and D. McBride. (1991). Prostitution, IV Drug Use, and Sex-for-Crack Among Serious Delinquents: Risk for HIV Infection. *Criminology* 29:221–236

Inciardi, J.A., D. Lockwood, and A.E. Pottieger. (1993). *Women and Crack-Cocaine.* New York: Macmillian Press.

Inciardi, J.A. (1993). *Kingrats, Chicken Heads, Slow Necks, Freaks, and Blood Suckers: A Glimpse at the Miami Sex-for-Crack Market*, in *Crack Pipe As Pimp: An Ethnographic Investigation of Sex-for-Crack Exchanges*, 1993 by Mitchell S. Ratner, New York: Lexington Press.

Inciardi, J.A. , R. Horowitz, and A.E. Pottieger. (1993). *Street Kids, Street Drugs, Street Crime: An Examination of Drug Use and Serious Delinquency in Miami.* Belmont, Calif: Wadsworth Publishing

Janus, S. (1977). Prostitutes Emotional Needs. *Med. Asp. Hum Sex* (11)11:102.

Janus, S. and C. Janus. (1993). *The Janus Report on Sexual Behavior.* John Wiley & Sons: New York.

Janus, S. and B. Bess. (1977). *Prostitution: Option or Addiction?* Paper Presented at the National Convention of the American Psychiatric Association. Toronto, Canada.

Johnson, B., Goldstein, P., Preble, E., Schmeidler, J., Lipton, D., Spunt, B., and T. Miller. (1985). *Taking Care of Business: The Economics of Crime by Heroin Abusers.* Lexington, Maine: Lexington Books.

Kalton, G., (1993). *Sampling Considerations in Research on HIV Risk and Illness,* in *Methodological Issues in AIDS Behavioral Research,* by D. Ostrow and R. Kessler. New York: Plenum Press.

Knowles, Gordon James. (1992). *A Study on the Prostitutes of Hotel Street in Honolulu, Hawaii.* Graduate Thesis. Department of Criminal Justice, Chaminade University, 3140 Waialae Ave, Honolulu, Hawaii, 96818.

Knowles, Gordon James. (1996). "Dealing Crack Cocaine: A View from the Streets of Honolulu" *FBI Law Enforcement Bulletin.* 65(7):1–8.

Knowles, Gordon James. (1997). *Sex, Crack, Ice, Heroin, and AIDS: An Ethnographic Study of "Chinatown" Street Addicts in Honolulu, Hawaii.* Doctorate Dissertation, Department of Sociology, University of Hawaii, 2424 Maile Way, Honolulu, Hawaii 96822.

Kozel, N., and E. Adams. (1986). Epidemiology of Drug Abuse: An Overview. Science 234:970–974.

Krauss, Bob. (1995). "Chinatown's Diversity is the Core of its History." *The Honolulu Advertiser.* January 29th, Section A3.

Larrat, P., and S. Zierler. (1993). Entangled Epidemics: Cocaine Use and HIV Disease. *Journal of Psychoactive Drugs* 2:(3) 207–221.

Leonard, Terri L. (1990). *Male Clients of Female Street Prostitutes: Unseen Partners in Sexual Disease Transmission.* Medical Anthropology Quarterly. March Vol. 4, 42–55.

Lubliner A., R. Schmidt, S. Sefton, E. Spillane, G. Will, E. Wilson, R. Hansen. (1973). *The Honolulu Queens.* School of Social Work, University of Hawaii at Manoa, Honolulu, HI: Graduate Thesis.

Martin, J., and L. Dean. (1993). *Developing a Community Sample of Gay Men for an Epidemiological Study of AIDS,* in *Researching Sensitive Topics,* by C. Renzetti and R. Lee. Newbury Park: Sage.

Maxfield, M., and E. Babbie. (1995). Research Methods for Criminal Justice and Criminology. Belmont, California: Wadsworth

McCoy, Clyde B., and J.A. Inciardi. (1995). *Sex, Drugs, and the Continuing Spread of AIDS.* Los Angeles, California: Roxbury Publishing Company.

Messerschmidt, J. 1986. *Capitalism, Patriarchy, and Crime: Towards a Socialist Feminist Criminology.* New Jersey: Rowman and Littlefield.

Nurco, D., Kinlock, T., and Hanlon. (1998). The Drugs-Crime Connection" in J. Inciardi and K. McElrath (Eds.), *The American Drug Scene: An Anthology,* 220–234. Los Angeles, California: Roxbury Publishing Company.

Page, J., D. Chitwood., P. Smith., N. Kane., and D. McBride. (1990). Intravenous Drug Use and HIV Infection in Miami. *Medical Anthropology Quarterly*. March Vol. 4, 56–71.

Pettiway, L. (1995). Copping Crack: The Travel Behavior of Crack Users. *Justice Quarterly*, Vol. 12 (3).

Plant, M. (1990). *AIDS, Drugs, and Prostitution*. London: Tavis/Routledge.

Pleak, R.R., and Meyer-Bahlburg Hfl. (1990). Sexual Behavior and AIDS Knowledge of Young Male Prostitutes in Manhattan. *J Sex Research*. 27(4):557

Silbert, M.H, and A.M. Pines. (1981). Occupational Hazards of Street Prostitution. *Crime Just. Behavior*. Dec 8(4):391–395.

Silbert, M.H., and A.M. Pines. (1983). Early Sexual Exploitation as an Influence in Prostitution. *Social Work* 28(4):285–289.

Simons, R.L., and L.B. Whitbeck. (1991). Sexual Abuse as a Precursor and Victimization Among Adolescent and Adult Homeless Women. *J Fam Iss*. 23(3):361–379.

Steward, S. (1991). *Understanding the Male Hustler*. New York: Haworth Press.

Taylor, A. (1993). *Women Drug Users: An Ethnography of a Female Injecting Community*. Oxford: Clarendon Press.

U.S. Department of Justice, National Obscenity Enforcement Unit, National Center for Missing & Exploited Children. (1987). *Child Pornography and Prostitution*.

U.S. Department of Justice, National Obscenity Enforcement Unit, National Center for Missing & Exploited Children. (1992). *Female Juvenile Prostitution: Problem and Response*.

Van Meter, K. (1990). *Methodological and Design Issues: Techniques for Assessing the Representatives of Snowball Samples*, in *The Collection and Interpretation of Data from Hidden Populations* edited by E. Lambert. NIDA Research Monograph 98.

Van Meter, K. (1990). *Methodological and Design Issues: Techniques for Assessing the Representatives of Snowball Samples*, in E. Lambert (Ed.) *The Collection and Interpretation of Data From Hidden Populations: Research Monograph* 98:31–43, Rockville, MD: National Institute on Drug Abuse.

Waite, David. (1995). "Trouble in Chinatown: Crime Pollutes Neighborhoods's Life." *The Honolulu Advertiser*. January 29th: Section A1.

Weisberg, D.K. (1985). *Children of the Night: A Study of Adolescent Prostitution*. Toronto: Lexington Books.

West, Donald J. (1993). *Male Prostitution*. New York: Haworth Press.

Wolf, J. (1989). *Gay Priests*. New York: Harper and Row.

Yoshimoto, Glenn Y. (1983). *Prostitutes of Hotel Street*. School of Social Work, University of Hawaii at Manoa, Honolulu, HI: Graduate Thesis.

"Hustling for Money: Male Prostitutes' Experiences of Social Control"

Ann M. Lucas,[1]
San Jose State University

Introduction

This paper presents preliminary findings from ten interviews with indoor (i.e., non-street) male prostitutes from the east and west coasts of the United States. The purpose of this research is to explore prostitutes' experiences of law, criminal justice, social stigma and social control, among other themes.

This research project grew out of a prior study which included interviews with 30 female prostitutes, primarily escorts and call girls, in the United States (Lucas, 1998). The focus of that project, however, was to explore whether and how the criminalization of prostitution and demonization of prostitutes contributed to the social construction of gender. I was particularly interested in the role of law in marking certain behaviors as disfavored and deviant to encourage socially acceptable behavior. In the case of women, the criminalization and stigmatization of prostitution appeared to be designed, in part, to encourage women to be chaste and avoid promiscuity, to seek the protection of males (in the form of husbands) and thereby accept emotional, social and financial dependence on men, and to encourage women to be good wives and mothers. The study on which this paper is based addresses two questions left unanswered in the previous project: what is the social significance of *male* prostitution, and what is its significance in regard to gender? In this paper, I address these questions through an exploration of male prostitutes' experiences of formal and informal social control. Although I cannot fully answer

---

1. Assistant Professor, Administration of Justice Department, San Jose State University, One Washington Square, San Jose, CA 95192-0050; alucas@email.sjsu.edu. The author gratefully acknowledges a grant from the University Research Institute at the University of Texas, El Paso, which supported the initial phases of this research project. The author also thanks Laura Beth Nielsen and Amy Toro for their thoughtful comments and suggestions on early drafts of this article, and Nancy Flores and Georgina Romero for their invaluable research assistance in developing the project and transcribing the interviews.

these questions here, my informants' insights do provide a starting point to address them. I conclude with some observations about how the social control of female and male prostitutes is similar and different, and what the significance of those similarities and differences is in regard to my two broad questions.

Law, Prostitution, and Social Control

Background

Male prostitution is an under-studied phenomenon (Weitzer, 2000a; Davies and Feldman, 1997; Prestage, 1994; McNamara, 1994a; van der Poel, 1992; Waldorf and Murphy, 1989), particularly in regard to the social control of male prostitutes (partial exceptions include Calhoun and Weaver, 1996; McNamara, 1994a and 1994c; Calhoun, 1992).[2] Indeed, most scholarship on male prostitution focuses on the medical and public health aspects of this practice (see e.g., Minichiello, Mariño, Browne, Jamieson, Peterson, Reuter and Robinson, 2000; Aggleton, 1999; Longo, 1998; Miller, Klotz and Eckholdt, 1998; Boles and Elifson, 1994a; Boles and Elifson,1994b; Simon, Morse, Balson, Osofsky and Gaumer, 1993; Morse, Simon, Balson and Osofsky, 1992; Morse, Simon, Osofsky, Balson and Gaumer,1991; Bloor, McKeganey and Barnard, 1990; Pleak and Meyer-Bahlburg, 1990; Waldorf and Murphy, 1989), in part because of the priorities of institutions which fund scholarly research. There are also many strong studies and accounts of prostitution outside of this body of literature, but most consider female prostitutes exclusively, or devote only limited attention to male prostitution (see e.g., Weitzer, 2000b; Dank and Refinetti, 1999; Delacoste and Alexander, 1998; Kempadoo and Doezema, 1998; Chapkis, 1997; Hodgson, 1997; Nagle, 1997; McKeganey and Barnard, 1996; Pheterson, 1996; Bell, 1995; Bell, 1994; *Social Text,* 1993; Pheterson, 1989; Bell, 1987; Millett, 1976; see also Lucas, 1998).

In recent years, a few social scientists and others have begun to pay more attention to both male and female sex workers (see e.g., Sycamore 2000; Elias, Bulloughs, Elias and Brewer, 1998; Scambler and Scambler, 1997; Perkins, Prestage, Sharp and Lovejoy, 1994; Lindquist, White, Tutchings and Cham-

---

2. Humphreys (1970) is occasionally cited as a classic work in this area (see e.g., Calhoun, 1992; McNamara, 1994b), perhaps because it refers to "trade" in its title. However, while *Tearoom Trade* is indeed a notable, classic work in the sociology of deviance, its subject is, as its subtitle says, "impersonal sex in public places"; it discusses *non-monetized* homosexual sexual encounters in public places, not male prostitution.

bers, 1989), and some scholars have focused exclusively on male sex workers outside the arena of public health (Kulick, 1998; Calhoun and Weaver, 1996; McNamara, 1994a, 1994b, and 1994c; Calhoun, 1992; van der Poel, 1992; Earls and David, 1989). Male prostitution is also discussed in the context of studies of male transvestites (Kulick, 1998; Prieur, 1998), but while the question of social control is more likely to figure prominently in these analyses, the focus tends to be the subjects' "deviant" lifestyles (i.e., cross-dressing and same-sex attraction) rather than a more narrow focus on their means of economic survival.

In the past two decades, first-person accounts of female prostitution (Sycamore, 2000; Delacoste and Alexander, 1998; Nagle, 1997; Almodovar, 1993; Adams and Stadiem, 1993; French, 1988; Barrows, 1986) and male prostitution (Sycamore, 2000; Lawrence, 1999; Whitaker, 1999; Goodley, 1994) have also appeared; as in the scholarly work, memoirs by women in prostitution are more likely to discuss law and social control than are memoirs by men. Similarly, historical work on the practice of prostitution also emphasizes female prostitution (Roberts, 1993; D'Emilio and Freedman, 1988; Hobson, 1987; Rosen, 1982), although the practice of male prostitution in various historical periods and locations is acknowledged by several writers (Chauncey, 1994; Roberts, 1993; Sanger, 1937).

Methodology and Interview Subjects

These male interview subjects were identified through chain referral, also known as snowball sampling, with initial contacts made by female friends or colleagues of these subjects (most of these women were identified in the previous study of female prostitution). While snowball sampling has been criticized as lacking "independent verification that the subjects were accepting money for sexual services" (Earls and David, 1989: 403), this shortcoming is evident primarily where the researcher seeks superficial or standardized answers to close-ended questions, such that a subject could easily pretend membership in a group to which he/she does not belong.[3] In qualitative studies, this concern is readily overcome if interviewers have sufficient knowledge of their topic and interview

3. Earls and David (1989) utilized several such questions—age, education completed, number of siblings, etc.; age at first sexual relation, sex of first partner, age at first sexual act for money, etc.; number of arrests, employment history outside prostitution, frequency of drug and alcohol use, etc. They also paid subjects for their participation. Use of this methodology indeed warranted their independent verification of subjects' involvement in prostitution.

subjects carefully. That is, it is extremely difficult for non-prostitutes to feign the detailed familiarity with prostitution derived from experience which would be necessary to fool a knowledgeable interviewer/ethnographer.[4]

Moreover, even absent astute researchers, without payment or other material reward for participation, few people would be motivated to feign a prostitution history and participate in lengthy interviews, particularly where risks of disclosure could have negative consequences. While human subjects protocols are designed to protect subjects from such consequences, and usually succeed in doing so, the difficulties in obtaining informed consent from research subjects involved in criminal activity indicate that many subjects are doubtful whether the protections are sufficient.

As is evident from the method of subject identification, this group of male prostitutes was not a random or representative sample. Indeed, in the current legal situation, it is essentially impossible to obtain random or representative samples of male or female prostitutes, since the size of and range of characteristics possessed by these populations are unknown. While it may be possible to draw random samples of some subpopulations—for example, Lever and Dolnick (2000) report drawing a probability sample of nearly 1,000 Los Angeles street prostitutes while using snowball sampling for off-street prostitutes—it is difficult to do so consistently. Prostitution is not an occupation its practitioners list on census forms, tax records, job or loan applications, or the like, due to its illegality and stigma. Moreover, the number of prostitutes and the locations where prostitution is practiced, for both street and indoor prostitutes, often vary or change over time in response to the actions of law enforcement (see, e.g., Hampton, 1988). For these reasons, the size and contours of the prostitute population in the United States are impossible to determine with precision,[5] which means that nearly all prostitution studies involve non-random samples.

---

4. Hampton (1988: 162–163) provides an example. Working with the Centers for Disease Control, the Georgia Department of Human Resources and HIRE (Hooking Is Real Employment), a prostitutes' rights advocacy group in Atlanta, Hampton did outreach and HIV testing of female street prostitutes. In interviewing two prostitutes who agreed to cooperate, Hampton quickly realized (without their saying so) that they were male-to-female transsexuals; although they were tested for HIV, their HIV statuses were not included in the reported results of the study of female prostitutes.

5. While it is theoretically possible that a researcher might obtain a representative sample of prostitutes, there would be no way under current legal and social conditions for her or him to know or to demonstrate, scientifically and conclusively, that the sample is representative of the population.

After the initial conversation with a current or former colleague or friend, potential subjects who had consented to further communication were contacted by the author. Those who provided informed consent to participate in the study were later interviewed by telephone, and the interviews were tape-recorded. The interviews lasted from about 45 minutes to about three hours, with most lasting about an hour. The interviews involved open-ended questions relating to the subjects' experiences with and opinions about prostitution as work; clients; law enforcement; regulation; HIV/AIDS and safer sex practices; prostitution compared to "legitimate" jobs; work settings and locales; violence; drug use; the rewards and costs of engaging in prostitution; stigma; social attitudes toward prostitution; and relations with intimates.

The ten men I interviewed were currently working or had worked as escorts, "call boys," and bar hustlers. That is, each solicited male clients[6] in an indoor setting which offered more privacy and safety than street solicitation usually does.[7] As discussed below, this group of prostitutes had relatively few direct encounters with law enforcement, particularly in comparison to street prostitutes. Thus, this group's views of law and social control may well differ from the views of male street prostitutes, because of the significant difference in working conditions.[8] In this regard, indoor male prostitutes provide an im-

---

6. In the overwhelming majority of cases, both male and female prostitutes serve male clients. Although there are occasional instances of prostitutes being hired by a heterosexual couple, these are relatively rare. Even more unusual is a woman hiring a prostitute (of either gender) alone. While this practice may be gradually increasing, women customers are still an insignificant portion of prostitutes' clientele (Monto, 2000; Meier and Geis, 1997; Pheterson, 1996; Prestage, 1994). However, Chiasson, Lifson, Stoneburner, Ewing, Hildebrandt and Jaffe did report identifying 52 male prostitutes who claimed to serve only women (Chiasson, Lifson, Stoneburner, Ewing, Hildebrandt and Jaffe, 1988, discussed in Waldorf and Murphy, 1989: 110–111). In addition, female tourists' patronage of male prostitutes appears to be increasing in some developing countries (de Albuquerque, 1999; de Moya and García, 1999; Ratnapala, 1999).

7. In some cases, these indoor venues undoubtedly also brought them into contact with a different group of potential clients than the street would have. However, there is no absolute distinction between clients who patronize street hustlers and clients who patronize indoor prostitutes; while the stereotype is that indoor workers, both male and female, reach a "better class" of clients, it cannot be presumed that all clients restrict themselves to one or another setting. Indeed, the arrest of prominent, wealthy individuals, such as actors Hugh Grant and Eddie Murphy, for soliciting street prostitutes suggests that some high-status clients are attracted to the perceived high risk, high taboo, low cost, easy accessibility, and/or "sleaze" commonly associated with street prostitution.

8. However, this caveat is not meant to suggest that one should expect no overlap in the opinions or experiences of street and non-street workers. Despite differences in the manner of solicitation and the attention received from law enforcement, anyone who ex-

portant and interesting comparison group to the more academically and popularly familiar group of female escorts and call girls, whose working conditions are also safer and more private than those of female street prostitutes, but who nonetheless receive more attention from law enforcement than do their male counterparts.

My informants usually began working in prostitution in their mid- to late adolescence or early twenties, and worked or have worked as prostitutes for as little as a year to upwards of 15 years. Most of them self-identified as gay, although there is no necessary correlation between one's sexual orientation/preference in one's intimate life and the gender of his or her commercial sex partners (for heterosexual men working as prostitutes with male clients, see McNamara, 1994a and 1994c; Goodley, 1994; Bloor, et al., 1990; Waldorf and Murphy, 1989; for lesbian women working as prostitutes with male clients, see Sycamore, 2000; Delacoste and Alexander, 1998; Nagle, 1997; Queen, 1997; Bell, 1987). Thus, my informants' perceptions of social attitudes and their investment in social approval are undoubtedly quite different than those of heterosexually-identified men who work as prostitutes with male clients. Heterosexual male prostitutes[9]—particularly, perhaps, young ones—may feel conflicted about their work and therefore may dedicate considerable energy to avoiding being labeled as gay, or considering themselves as gay (Calhoun, 1992; cf. Longo, 1998). In other words, by virtue of their work they may often be challenged (or perceive challenges) in regard to their masculinity and sexual prowess, and thus expend much psychic and physical energy in defending their self-images and reputations as tough, heterosexual men.

In contrast, my subjects did not report these problems. Comfortable with their sexual identity, and not experiencing any significant disjuncture between private and commercial sexual activity, my informants were much more concerned about acceptance within the gay community than in disavowing any connection with that community. Heterosexual male prostitutes may feel no sense of solidarity with either a gay community or a community of sex workers; thus, while they may resent police attention and social stigma when these are focused on them as individuals, they may also perpetuate negative atti-

---

changes money for sex in the United States, with the partial exception of brothels in some rural counties in Nevada, is violating prostitution laws. This fundamental commonality, and the shared stigma and risks that come with it, suggest that different working conditions may not completely determine prostitutes' attitudes toward their work and toward the society in which they live.

9. "Heterosexual male prostitutes" henceforth refers to heterosexually-identified men who work as prostitutes with men as clients.

tudes toward, and treatment of, gay men and other male prostitutes (cf. Calhoun, 1992: 42; Calhoun and Weaver, 1996: 220; Longo, 1998: 232–234). In contrast, openly gay men who work as prostitutes are likely to understand and experience social control as directed at them as individuals *and* as "representatives" of these two stigmatized groups with which they willingly affiliate, and thus to be more critical of social control efforts as emblematic of unwarranted and discriminatory hostility toward sexual "deviants."

Formal Social Control: Social Control by the State

Law and Law Enforcement—As a sociologist of law, I was interested in how my interviewees viewed the law and the criminal justice system. Had they had negative experiences with police? Did they structure their lives in certain ways to avoid coming to the attention of law enforcement? How did they feel about the criminalization of prostitution—would they change it if they could?

In large part, the men told me that they felt reasonably safe from police stings, and attributed it to homophobia in the police force and in society, and to the visibility of female prostitutes. As one said, "I often did not remember that [it was illegal], it didn't even cross my mind." Another one said:

> Thankfully cops are homophobic, and they would hate a man, well, let's all face it.... I think that they would not like to be naked in front of a man to entrap a man for the sake of prostitution laws. Or for whatever action the prostitute needed to take to show that the prostitute was trying to solicit, I don't believe that the majority of male police would be willing to do that.... [P]olice will crack down on women before men, because...homophobia acts as...some protection for male prostitutes....

This relative safety from police was, of course, not absolute; one subject reported being raped by a police officer when he was sixteen or seventeen.

Yet even without direct contact with law enforcement, criminal (and civil) laws certainly shaped my subjects' working lives. One subject was an undocumented immigrant when he worked as a prostitute in this country, and felt that the immigration and criminal laws worked in tandem to make him lie or change his life.

> [A]t the time I was working I was an illegal immigrant, so I knew that I could be deported...But also just, as someone coming into America, America has this damn piece of paper that you need to sign to say that you...[do not] have a transmittable disease,...[and they also

> ask you] if you have a history or are you currently prostituting, and if you are or have you ever been an armed terrorist.... [S]o that immediately makes you have to lie if you have got the hepatitis C, if you are a prostitute and if you intend to be a prostitute or if you have been a prostitute.

Thus, although the men I talked with were not as vigilant about police as one might expect, they were still aware and resentful of law's actual or potential use in social control. In order to avoid the penalties imposed for law violations, these men felt compelled to lie or to alter their behavior, actions they would not have taken but for the existence of the law.

The Collateral Effects of the Criminalization of Prostitution—Obviously, however, investigation and arrest are not the only effects of the criminal law on law-breakers. My informants, while feeling relatively secure in regard to the police, nonetheless recognized other impacts the law had on their lives. One referred to the "hurdles" he had to jump because of his vocation, mentioning "having to show tax forms to get financial aid at school, so having to make up this whole career that...didn't give me W-2s." Another said that he felt "[t]he laws force people underground" in such a way that prostitutes could not go to the police if they had been *victims* of crime, simply because of their status as prostitutes:

> I don't believe that the prostitutes I meet would be likely to go to the police in case of a rape, or if a trick failed to give them the money.... [I]f, you know,...a prostitute...would go to the police and say, "this wrong has been done against me," they're going to be seen as a prostitute....And so rather than just acknowledging that prostitution is a career, a vocation, a job, and looking at ways that that industry can survive in a healthy manner, the current laws in [state], actually in every...state, continue to drive people underground which makes them unsafe.... [I]t encourages people to be very...isolated in terms of their work, in terms of social support, and it's very...detrimental.... [B]ecause of the lack of social support and ability to go to the police for support, I think prostitutes are more at risk of not having people to look out for them....

This individual expresses a sentiment which is nearly uniform among both my male and female interviewees, suggesting here that prostitution is not an inherently unsafe enterprise, but is made unsafe by the punitive measures of the state, which result in isolating prostitutes from one another, separating them from society's mainstream, and denying them formal and informal protection from harm.

The subject who worked in prostitution as an undocumented immigrant in the U.S. had also worked in prostitution in his home country. Although prostitution was illegal there as well, law enforcement practices were targeted more toward abusive practices rather than everyday consensual prostitution, so he experienced more "camaraderie," as he called it, in his former home. In the U.S., he experienced "hurdles" similar to those experienced by American citizens, reporting that:

> when I first came here, I was trying to work out the difference between what is "body work" versus prostitution.[10] And I went to [a local prostitutes' rights group], and I asked them. And *no one* was willing to talk to me about that. They were fearful of it being reported, because that would be basically procuring me into work.[11] And so I was forced to go and learn on my own. Which I thought was extremely fucked up, that hookers could do that to another hooker....

---

10. Although there is no exact definition of "body work," this term in essence refers to therapeutic massage, sensual massage and other practices on the legal side of the line dividing prostitution and other criminalized forms of sex work from those practices which are clearly or arguably legal, such as stripping, domination, etc. Waldorf and Murphy's (1989: 112) discussion of "[e]rotic [m]asseurs...who provide some elements of the legitimate massage business with an erotic twist [and] are often certified by licensed massage schools and...guided by well-developed philosophical rationales for their work" provides one example of possibly legal "body work." The line between legal and illegal sex work depends on the laws of the particular jurisdiction; in some places, for example, the line is crossed when the worker touches the genitals of the client for purposes of sexual stimulation or release. Thus, my informant was asking his colleagues where this line is drawn in that particular American state.

11. Procurement is a felony, while simple prostitution is a misdemeanor. The line commonly drawn in this area of criminal law is between sole operators and organized enterprises, understood as any two or more prostitutes working together to benefit from prostitution. Many prostitutes' rights groups are familiar with one woman's account (Almodovar, 1993) of being "set up" for procuring and put in prison in California, and are also aware of more recent high-profile prosecutions of Southern California "madams" like Heidi Fleiss and "Baby Doll" Gibson. This fact likely explains the wariness my informant encountered when he asked for guidance from other workers; to be on the safe side, many prostitutes do not refer clients, give advice, or discuss business-related strategies with other prostitutes in order to avoid being charged with pimping, pandering and procuring (all felonies), i.e., to avoid any perception that they are working in concert with others (Scott, 1987: 102; Pheterson, 1989: 78, 93; cf. Alexander, 1998: 210; Pheterson, 1996: 43; French, 1988: 283).

> [T]hey were so fearful of being reported... [T]he one bizarre thing about prostitution is that there can be an amazing solidarity,... but we are individuals and we have our insecurities. And one of the insecurities to do with prostitution is being busted, I guess.

In other words, while angry that his sex work colleagues would not answer his questions, this subject attributes their reluctance not to feelings of hostility or competition, but rather to fear induced by the criminal law. Absent concern about being charged with procuring, his peers, he believes, would have willingly advised him. Thus, the social control exercised by the law, while not preventing these individuals from engaging in prostitution, did mitigate their solidarity with one another.

When I asked my subjects if they thought prostitution should be legal, those who were aware of the distinction between decriminalization and legalization[12] tended to favor decriminalization, given their general distrust of the government. As one explained, "if it is decriminalized, there should be no zoning of prostitution that can allow police and the state to have a negative impact on prostitutes' lives in terms of cracking down again. [Zoning] can also create negative enclaves, which can further stigmatize people who work in a certain area..." As another said:

> It's ok, perhaps, to register with the police, on one level. But that ignores the fact that your name is known, your address is known, and at any time, with a change of political administration, people have your name and your number, your address, and you can be cracked down on, you know. And we don't know who that information is going to.

This subject clearly recognizes that legal changes may not be permanent, and that intentions motivating law reform may be subverted. Thus, even though as a philosophical matter he might support a law requiring the state registration of prostitutes—perhaps, as he later mentioned, to prevent the sexual exploitation of juveniles—as a political realist he is wary about how seemingly benign laws may be put to punitive purposes once they are on the books.

While support for decriminalization was common and is perhaps to be expected, I was surprised that many of my subjects also discussed the possibility of limited regulations. Most commonly discussed were health (i.e., sexu-

12. Legalization implies state regulation, e.g., zoning laws, special taxes, health and safety regulations, etc. Decriminalization refers to the de facto or de jure removal of criminal penalties, but without any additional state intervention.

ally transmitted disease) checks for prostitutes and age limitations. Several also mentioned the need for prostitutes to be eligible for healthcare and other benefits. The following comments are representative of this viewpoint:

> I would regulate [prostitution] to the extent that I would want healthcare rights for prostitutes, I would want benefits, I would want health checks put into place so that some of the dangers to prostitutes could be eliminated. I think health care issues just in terms of getting tested regularly so that the client is protected as well, if those are considered regulations, yes, I think that would be a good idea. [*Interviewer: So you would make the health checks mandatory?*] Yes, I think in the same way that I would want a doctor who is treating me to also have mandatory functional tests.

Thus, despite their distaste for the law as an instrument of social control, several of my informants also displayed an awareness of, and in some cases an appreciation for, the benefits that may accompany legal regulation. However, it was more common for my subjects to reject any form of regulation, out of concern that it would have detrimental effects similar to those created by criminalization.

Illegality and Stigma: Informal Social Control

Social Control by the "Mainstream"—In most of my interviewees' minds, prostitution's illegal status and the social stigma associated with it were closely coupled, and discussions about the law often segued into discussions about the effects of stigma. Certainly, these men often professed pride in their deviance—pride in their work, pride in their identity, pride in their integrity and "following [their] own path[s]." As one prostitute explained:

> there can be a phenomenon within sex work that a lot of sex workers like the fact that they are... walking on the edge of the line between good and bad. [T]hey can have a good lifestyle during the day, but at night... turn into another person... [S]ome people might say being the criminal person actually is quite a buzz....

Another made a similar point: "[S]tigma... can be a driving force for you to actually do your work, because it can be a satisfaction... [in] being different.... I'm on my own path." And, of course, they recognized that prostitution's taboo status also made it an "alluring adventure" for many of their clients, particularly the "straight-job," married, businessman type.

Yet they also keenly felt that the stigma associated with prostitution often caused or enabled others to deny their full humanity. Some male prostitutes mentioned how the stigma of prostitution made them censor themselves. One who worked off and on in prostitution for fifteen years made the following comment.

> [Male and female prostitutes] I know are very good at marketing, balancing their books,...customer satisfaction, providing a service, you know, all those things that are involved in business.

He says he felt "very professional," but finds that fact "disappointing." As he explains:

> Sadly, these aspects of our work cannot be transferred...to straight [legitimate] work. And so we can't put on our résumé, I did this, and that I'm very, very good at marketing, or, like, filling a gap. I mean, so many [female prostitutes] I know will move from being an escort to being a dominatrix, simply within a particular city because there is a need for that....I mean, we fill gaps and we are very, very astute, generally....And [yet] that is something that can't be generalized over [to other forms of employment].

Thus, the need to hide a criminal history in order to secure legitimate employment may also mean concealing relevant skills, talents and qualifications. As discussed further below, this phenomenon demonstrates that the social control effects of law and mainstream attitudes continue even after involvement in prostitution ends.

Another subject feels he could be more effective in his current job if he could reveal his sex-work history to his boss, but he feels he cannot:

> I find it very hard not to say to people, like, managers at work, when they sort of assume that you haven't done certain things,...I find it very hard not to say, "well, actually, I know this because of this." I find that really, really frustrating.

At the time of our interview he worked with a drug rehabilitation agency and felt he had some insights into his clients' risk behavior, their potential for relapse, and the like. But his co-workers assumed he had no personal knowledge of deviant behavior and lifestyles, so he felt his observations were given less credibility than they would have earned had he felt able tell his co-workers the truth. He explained that he felt constrained to lie because he believes he once lost a similar job after revealing his past in sex work:

> I applied for a job at [organization], and I made the mistake of telling someone there that I'd been a [prostitute]. I never got the job. And

> they've never contacted me about any other jobs. But this person was working with junkies, and he's an ex-junkie, and that was fine for him to be known in the field as an ex-junkie, but it's not o.k. for me to be known as an ex-prostitute. You know? So, like, when it comes to stigma,...I think that it's *not* o.k. to say that you've been, you're an ex-prostitute, and expect to have an amazing, for having the straight world open up their arms and say "please come and work for us."... And...the fact that [organization] is supposedly progressive...you know...I felt that he lulled me into a false sense of security.

As all of these comments illustrate, male prostitutes are acutely aware of the stigma associated with prostitution in the larger society. They know that avoiding criminal charges is not their only concern. Both the formal criminal penalties and the stigma associated with prostitution act as instruments of social control for these men; indeed, the informal social control exercised by stigmatization appears, in these accounts, to be the more onerous form.

It is certainly true that these men are not always effectively controlled—they have engaged or did engage in prostitution for significant periods of time, and many expressed pride in their ability to make their own choices despite state sanctions—but they nonetheless knew they were targets of social control efforts. Equally important, for those who have left prostitution to work in the "legitimate" world, informal social control is even more effective today than formal social control once was. As former prostitutes, these men's risk of arrest and punishment for prostitution is virtually nil—the statute of limitations has passed for most, and for the rest, it is highly unlikely that police and prosecutors would be interested and successful in arresting and prosecuting these men for misdemeanor prostitution offenses that took place in the past, even the relatively recent past. However, informal sanctions—loss of jobs, respect, status, acceptance, and the like—remain real possibilities if these men reveal that they once worked as prostitutes, and thus the informal social control continues even after their participation in this form of deviant behavior has ceased.

Social Control Within "Deviant" Subcultures—Those who self-identified as gay mentioned that they felt stigma from the heterosexual world, but also from the gay community, on account of their status as sex workers. Being shunned by those they cared about was, not surprisingly, the most important effect of stigma for a majority of them. As one of my informants explained:

> [For] a lot of prostitutes, not only do [they] have a double life to evade the...police...[or they have] to hide...to protect [themselves] from losing [a] straight job, but they also have to engage in a lot of activities to not let their family and friends know that they are [pros-

> titutes]. And so there's a huge social cost there...this is the greatest social cost. It's not actually...getting busted for being a prostitute. Because in itself that's just being busted. But what is the cost of being busted, and that's generally beyond possibly going to jail..., [it's] losing friends and family. That just can't be quantified in terms of what that means.

Others were more specific in their concern about *gay* reaction to sex work:

> Working in a small city...is very, very difficult because you lose your anonymity, and you can become known very, very quickly. And the gay community can be very, very scathing of male sex workers. And...in the majority of cities I've lived in, the gay community...quite quickly, will shun you if they find out that you're a [prostitute, and that's] a whole other line of questioning as to why gay men would be so negative towards their own kind. And with all this, sexual identity politics stuff, free love and everything else,...they turn on people who want to charge for it.... [S]o that's one of the difficulties [of] being a *gay* man and being a sex worker at the same time, male-to-male sex worker,... the gay community won't embrace you or at least offer you some support, on finding out that you're a prostitute. But straight people within the community, I mean, it's never really worried me, because it's like,... I have not aligned myself with straight people that much.

Another man who worked in prostitution for five years and then worked in a large private sector organization had a similar experience:

> There was a lot of judgment just across the board in both [work] situations; a lot of my gay friends had a great deal to say about it, very negative, when I was in sex work, but these weren't people in the sex industry, they were just gay friends who I saw as incredibly promiscuous compared to me. Then some of the same friends couldn't believe that I had sold out and gone to a [legitimate job]. I was a punk rocker for awhile and [the reaction was,] "what, you're in a suit and tie?" You know, they wouldn't forgive me for having a nine-to-five job, so you know I just assumed that everybody's gonna be down in whatever I do and I really pay it no mind.

Yet the reaction from the gay community to prostitution involving gay men is by no means monolithic or identical to the dominant society's response to female prostitution. As several subjects reported, their male clients were often respectful and appreciative. According to the undocumented immigrant:

> The American clientele is more likely to treat a male prostitute with respect.... [M]y male clientele have not assumed that I'm deficient because I'm doing this sort of work. Like I remember telling...all my clients in [U.S. city that I'm here] "chasing my rainbow." And they ask me my qualifications and I'll say, "I have a Ph.D.," and...very few of them gave me a vibe or a statement which said that they didn't believe that. Whereas, I know when I was embarking on my Ph.D. in [country], when clients asked me what I was doing, and I told them a Ph.D., every one of them said, "Oh, come on. Don't spin me the shit."...I believe it was manifesting a viewpoint that prostitutes are losers, prostitutes are stupid, prostitutes don't want a career or entree to a career, and so why would you, one, be studying, and how could you have the intellectual capacity to do a Ph.D. So, in that, on that level I believe that clients are more respectful in [U.S. city], at least, of male sex workers.

Another commented about his clients' motivations for hiring him:

> [A] lot of it is about either recapturing youth or something that you idolized that you can't get anymore. It's much more of a, I don't know if respect is the right word, but it's much more of a desire relationship....I think that the man tends to think he's buying something that he no longer has the power to get on his own good looks or that they're in a situation where they can't come out of the closet because they're either famous or they're married or whatever. They're seeing it much more of a favor that they are paying for.

In other words, at least in the context of the prostitution transaction, male prostitutes may well feel accepted and appreciated by some of their male clients (Goodley, 1994: 126, 131; Davies and Feldman, 1997: 42), many of whom self-identify as gay.[13] Outside the prostitution transaction, however—i.e., when interacting with gay men who are not their clients—gay male prostitutes may encounter more judgment and stigma. Prostitutes are also frustrated by these reactions when encountered in mainstream society, as discussed above, but my subjects often found these attitudes within the gay community to be particularly upsetting, since they are more likely to expect, desire and value interpersonal acceptance and support from other gay men than from society at large.

---

13. However, many clients of male prostitutes are married and consider themselves heterosexual. Indeed, some male prostitutes believe that heterosexual married men are a majority of their customers (Bloor, et al., 1990: 22; Goodley, 1994: 128; Prestage, 1994: 182; see also Waldorf and Murphy, 1989: 109–110).

Male and Female Prostitution Compared

So what does all this add up to, if anything? Taken as a whole, the interviews revealed several things. First was that for men, prostitution may be an illegal vocation like it is for women, but the effects of the law are more "administrative hassles," as one of my subjects said, than needing to keep an attorney on retainer, have a pimp to bail them out of jail, or similar things that women experience. The women I interviewed, in contrast, spent much more time discussing their arrests, their tactics to avoid police, their tactics to soothe their neighbors so they wouldn't be reported, and the like.

The second common theme that arose in the interviews with male prostitutes was that they, like the women, deeply resented the social stigma associated with the work. They kept explaining in different ways that prostitution was just work, nothing more, nothing less, an honest service, and/or a way to make money to put themselves through school. Many were critical of what one called the "Judeo-Christian morality" that resulted in judgment and condemnation. Those who were gay often felt particularly upset with condemnation in the gay community. As members of that community, the community's opinion was more important to them; but also they felt it hypocritical that one sexual minority would condemn another for consensual sexual activity between adults. Although the women I interviewed were also extremely agitated about what they felt was their unfair stigmatization, it did not seem so personal to many of them. Most of them were heterosexual, and so to them the stigma against prostitution seemed to come from society at large, not from a community where they had hoped for and expected more acceptance.

The third common theme I heard was that, taken as a whole, prostitution compared quite favorably to other work my subjects had performed (see also Davies and Feldman, 1997: 32). Since many of them have "retired" from sex work it may be appropriate to question their rosy view of the past versus their dismal lives in the legitimate world, but their comments still offer food for thought. Those who were retired all said they missed the work: the flexible hours, being their own bosses, the easy money (when it was easy, which it sometimes was not). In contrast, one said that when he worked in a corporation "the managers were... treating the staff as expendable." He argued that in legitimate jobs he was more likely to lose his autonomy than in prostitution, because as an escort he could easily quit one agency and go to another or work on his own, but "unfortunately in the straight world it's much harder to get a job. You just can't walk from one job to another. Unless McDonald's is an option, which it isn't." Another made a similar comment relating to autonomy, comparing where he works now, a social service agency, with his work as a prostitute. The agency has a dress code that covers hairstyles and hair lengths, whether men can wear earrings, and how long women's fingernails can be. In contrast:

> the independent operator [prostitute]...can wear whatever you... want. And you don't have someone telling you that it's not appropriate...you know damn well what's appropriate because you need to go to get into that hotel, and not be stopped, so you wear very good clothes. But underneath you have whatever clothes you...you know?...turn someone on.

Still another says prostitution is "probably the most honest and fair profession" that he's had. He worked as an escort/call-boy for six years to put himself through an Ivy League university, and then moved on to pursue other work. For ten years, he ran a computer department with a staff of 100 people in a prestigious office in one of the leading financial cities in the U.S. He says the partners in the firm where he worked had a "far, far, greater...desire to humiliate the staff" than his prostitution clients ever did; the partners "really treated their staff far worse than I've seen a date treat a prostitute." While working there he saw himself as "just pretty much labor in somebody else's dream," just a "slave."

The women I interviewed made similar comments about prostitution versus legitimate work. While some, particularly activists, may have had a habit of defensiveness about prostitution, the terms they used to describe boring, degrading, minimum wage legitimate work were quite sobering. They discussed lecherous bosses, noxious chemicals and solvents, petty back-stabbing office politics, mind-numbing days of photocopying, irate customers, and the like (Lucas, 1998). Certainly their work as prostitutes was not all adventure and excitement, either, but the element of autonomy and the significantly higher pay may indeed have combined to make prostitution a genuinely more attractive option to them, at least while they were of an age to be willing to risk criminal sanction, and to be able to earn top dollar.

Conclusion: Social Control and Prostitution's Social Significance

In regard to the questions which began this paper, the social significance of male prostitution seems to be largely subsumed within social attitudes toward "deviant" sexual practices and lifestyles. Although male prostitution involves the exchange of sex for money, in the eyes of many it is not "real" prostitution. People rarely even think about male prostitution, but when they do they either think of gigolos—not common, and not likely to spark a huge moral crusade—or street hustlers. When they think of the latter, their objection is usually based on the fact that both parties to the sex act are men; the money is irrelevant. In contrast, in regard to female prostitutes, the exchange of money is central to social attitudes: the social objection to female prostitution centers on the fact that women *sell* sexual services.

Yet, of course, what turns sex into prostitution is precisely the money. And this fact explains why male prostitution *is* technically prostitution, but not viewed as the social evil female prostitution is—because most people who object are not really objecting to the *commercialization* of sex when both parties are men.[14] Nor, of course, are they quite as judgmental of male customers of female prostitutes as they are of the prostitutes themselves. It seems that buying and selling sex is a behavior expected, or at least understood, in men,[15] while for women it is a sign of larger problems (moral decay, the commodification of bodies, etc.). And so in terms of the social construction of gender, I believe that female prostitution and its criminalization are highly significant, but male prostitution and its criminalization are not. Thus, while both male and female prostitutes experience severe forms of social control in the course of engaging in prostitution, the motivations behind the various forms of social control differ in the two cases.

The evidence suggests that society uses formal and informal social control in an intentional, direct effort to deter women from engaging in prostitution and to minimize the prevalence of female prostitution. However, male prostitutes experience similar forms of social control not because most leaders or

---

14. Although it is unclear whether the view is his or his subjects', Calhoun (1992), for example, argues that male hustlers hide their involvement in prostitution in order to avoid stigmatization as *gay*: "Given society's negative views toward those who engage in *homosexual* activity, a hustler usually prevents others from learning of his participation. Should his *homosexual* activities become known, the hustler risks others important to him redefining him negatively. He may face social and familial ostracism" (pp. 35–36) (emphasis added). See also Calhoun and Weaver, 1996: 220.

15. However, as many social scientists have noted, it is very difficult to study prostitutes' clients, as few men are willing to identify themselves as such, even anonymously, due to fear of exposure of deviant behavior (see e.g., Prestage, 1994) and/or shame at being seen as "having to pay" for sex (Weitzer, 2000a: 7; McKeganey and Barnard, 1996: 14–16, 48; Bloor, et al., 1990: 22). Thus, while it may be expected that men will buy and sell sex, clients' secretiveness suggests that they do not see paying for sex as a badge of honor (but see Prestage, 1994: 178 (suggesting clients of male prostitutes have their masculinity enhanced by the transaction)).

community members see male prostitution as a serious social problem, but rather because they see *female prostitution and male homosexuality* as social ills needing eradication. Male prostitutes suffer the double whammy of societal disapproval of (primarily female) prostitution and of homosexuality, but suffer primarily *indirectly*, since social attention is not focused on male-male commercial sex. Female prostitutes suffer the brunt of prostitution-related law enforcement efforts (Weitzer, 2000a: 8–10; Alexander, 1998: 205–207; Rhode, 1989: 261; French, 1988: 149; Tong, 1984: 55–56) and social stigma, but are largely free of the effects of heterosexism/homophobia, at least in regard to their work. In other words, what male prostitutes experience appears to be an artifact of the attempt to channel women's sexual behavior into socially "appropriate" (non-commercial) forms, and to channel men's sexual behavior similarly (i.e., into heterosexual expression); male prostitutes are at the intersection of these two other concerns, but are the primary emphasis of neither.

This is not to suggest that prostitutes of any gender are simply objects of state control. Obviously, these people engage in a socially-disfavored behavior *despite* the existence of legal and social penalties. Moreover, both the female and male prostitutes I interviewed frequently expressed pride in their work and their choices, and some overtly stated that engaging in prostitution was, for them, a form of political resistance to rules they felt to be overly moralistic and oppressive to full individual autonomy (see Lucas, 1998). Yet this resistance does not suggest the absence of social control, or even, necessarily, its ineffectiveness—rather, it suggests the opposite. Resistance only exists when control, or an attempt to control, also exists.[16] Acts of resistance, then, indicate that the individuals resisting are the targets of various control efforts.

A comparative examination of female and male prostitutes' differential experiences of social control thus has broader implications for our understanding of the social construction of gender, both male and female,[17] and of sex-

16. I thank Laura Beth Nielsen for reminding me of this point.

17. Although beyond the scope of this study, transgender prostitution also warrants scholarly examination, both in its own right and because it is likely to add further nuance and complexity to our understanding of gender orientations and gender construction. Transgender prostitutes (particularly male-to-female (MTF) transsexual and male transvestite prostitutes, who appear to be much more numerous than female to male (FTM) prostitutes) may be expected to have unique perspectives on both male and female gender identities, as they generally have lived in and tried to conform to both at different points in their lives, and as prostitutes have tried to use at least one gender identity to attract clients. Clients who intentionally hire transgender prostitutes to provide sexual services also merit scholarly consideration, as their appreciation of gender and sexuality also may well differ from clients who prefer prostitutes with more "stable" gender identities (cf.

uality, whether heterosexual, homosexual, or bisexual, monogamous or non-monogamous, commercial or non-commercial, socially approved or "deviant," etc. Whether formal or informal, the penalties imposed on prostitutes for engaging in their vocation have implications for everyone, given that one primary purpose of penalization is to deter others through example. The study of social control in the context of prostitution tells us much about the dominant understanding of "good" sexuality and "good" female and male behavior in our society, and about the effectiveness or ineffectiveness of various mechanisms of social control attempting to achieve these ends. It also instructs us about the methods and efficacy of resistance to state or social control. While this paper has been able only to scratch the surface of these complex issues, it succeeds if it provokes more scholarship in this area.

References

Adams, A. & Stadiem, W. (1993). *Madam 90210: My Life as Madam to the Rich and Famous.* New York: Villard Books.

Aggleton, P. (Ed.) (1999). *Men Who Sell Sex: International Perspectives on Male Prostitution and HIV/AIDS.* Philadelphia: Temple University Press.

Alexander, P. (1998). Prostitution: *Still* a Difficult Issue for Feminists. In F. Delacoste & P. Alexander (Eds.), *Sex Work: Writings by Women in the Sex Industry,* 2d ed. pp. 184–230. San Francisco: Cleis Press.

Almodovar, N.J. (1993). *Cop to Call Girl: Why I Left the LAPD to Make an Honest Living as a Beverly Hills Prostitute.* New York: Simon & Schuster.

Barrows, S.B. with Novak, W. (1986). *Mayflower Madam: The Secret Life of Sydney Biddle Barrows.* New York: Arbor House.

Bell, L. (Ed.) (1987). *Good Girls/Bad Girls: Feminists and Sex Trade Workers Face to Face.* Seattle: The Seal Press.

Bell, S. (1994). *Reading, Writing & Rewriting the Prostitute Body.* Bloomington & Indianapolis, IN: Indiana University Press.

Bell, S. (1995). *Whore Carnival.* Brooklyn: Autonomedia.

Bloor, M., McKeganey, N., & Barnard, M. (1990). An Ethnographic Study of HIV-Related Risk Practices Among Glasgow Rent Boys and Their Clients: Report of a Pilot Study. *AIDS Care, 2,* 17–24.

Prestage, 1994).

Transgender prostitutes may also suffer severe forms of social control. As one of my subjects commented,

> because the police...are very fucked in terms of their homophobia and their machismo, transgendered sex workers are often the first to get beaten up by the police, because of [the police's] own inability to understand a different lifestyle. Then not only will that transgendered sex worker be raped or fucked, and have money extorted, but they're also beaten as well.

Boles, J., & Elifson, K.W. (1994a). Sexual Identity and HIV: The Male Prostitute. *Journal of Sex Research, 31,* 39–46.

Boles, J., & Elifson, K.W. (1994b). The Social Organization of Transvestite Prostitution and AIDS. *Social Science and Medicine, 39,* 85–93.

Calhoun, T.C. (1992). Male Street Hustling: Introduction Processes and Stigma Containment. *Sociological Spectrum, 12,* 35–52.

Calhoun, T.C., & Weaver, G. (1996). Rational Decision-Making Among Male Street Prostitutes. *Deviant Behavior: An Interdisciplinary Journal, 17,* 209–227.

Chapkis, W. (1997). *Live Sex Acts: Women Performing Erotic Labor.* New York: Routledge.

Chauncey, G. (1994). *Gay New York: Gender, Urban Culture, and the Making of the Gay Male World, 1890–1940.* New York: Basic Books.

Chiasson, M.A., Lifson, A.R., Stoneburner, R.L., Ewing, W., Hildebrandt, D., & Jaffe, H.W. (1988). HIV-1 Seroprevalence in Male and Female Prostitutes in New York City. *Abstracts from the Sixth International Conference on AIDS.* Stockholm, Sweden (June). Cited in D. Waldorf & S. Murphy (1989), Intravenous Drug Use and Syringe-Sharing Practices of Call Men and Hustlers. In M. Plant (Ed.), *AIDS, Drugs and Prostitution,* pp. 109–131. London: Routledge.

Dank, B.M. & Refinetti, R. (Eds.) (1999). *Sex Work & Sex Workers* (special issue of *Sexuality & Culture, 2* (1998)). New Brunswick, NJ: Transaction Publishers.

Davies, P. & Feldman, R. (1997). Prostitute Men Now. In G. & A. Scambler (Eds.), *Rethinking Prostitution: Purchasing Sex in the 1990s,* pp. 29–53. London: Routledge.

De Albuquerque, K. (1999). Sex, Beach Boys, and Female Tourists in the Caribbean. In B.M. Dank & R. Refinetti (Eds.), *Sex Work & Sex Workers* (special issue of *Sexuality & Culture,* 2 (1998)), pp. 87–111. New Brunswick, NJ: Transaction Publishers.

De Moya, E.A. & García, R. (1999). Three Decades of Male Sex Work in Santo Domingo. In P. Aggleton (Ed.), *Men Who Sell Sex: International Perspectives on Male Prostitution and HIV/AIDS,* pp. 127–139. Philadelphia: Temple University Press.

Delacoste, F., & Alexander, P. (Eds.) (1998 (1987)). *Sex Work: Writings by Women in the Sex Industry,* 2d edition. San Francisco: Cleis Press.

D'Emilio, J., & Freedman, E.B. (1988). *Intimate Matters: A History of Sexuality in America.* New York: Harper & Row.

Earls, C.M. & David, H. (1989). A Psychosocial Study of Male Prostitution. *Archives of Sexual Behavior, 18,* 401–419.

Elias, J.E., Bullough, V.L., Elias, V., & Brewer, G. (Eds.) (1998). *Prostitution: On Whores, Hustlers, and Johns.* Amherst, NY: Prometheus Books.

French, D., with Lee, L. (1988). *Working: My Life as a Prostitute.* New York: E.P. Dutton.

Goodley, S. (1994). A Male Sex Worker's View. In R. Perkins, G. Prestage, R. Sharp, & F. Lovejoy (Eds.), *Sex Work and Sex Workers in Australia,* pp. 126–131. Sydney: University of New South Wales Press.

Hampton, L. (1988). Hookers with AIDS—The Search. In I. Rieder & P. Ruppelt (Eds.), *AIDS: The Women,* pp.157–164. Pittsburgh, PA & San Francisco: Cleis Press.

Hobson, B.M. (1987). *Uneasy Virtue: The Politics of Prostitution and the American Reform Tradition.* New York: Basic Books.

Hodgson, J.F. (1997). *Games Pimps Play: Pimps, Players and Wives-In-Law: A Qualitative Analysis of Street Prostitution.* Toronto: Canadian Scholars' Press.

Humphreys, L. (1970). *Tearoom Trade: Impersonal Sex in Public Places.* Hawthorne, NY: Aldine de Gruyter.

Kempadoo, K. & Doezema, J. (1998). *Global Sex Workers: Rights, Resistance, and Redefinition.* New York: Routledge.

Kulick, D. (1998). *Travesti: Sex, Gender and Culture among Brazilian Transgendered Prostitutes.* Chicago: University of Chicago Press.

Lawrence, A. (1999). *Suburban Hustler: Stories of a Hi-Tech Callboy.* Warren, NJ: Late Night Press.

Lever, J. & Dolnick, D. (2000). Clients and Call Girls: Seeking Sex and Intimacy. In R. Weitzer (Ed.), *Sex for Sale: Prostitution, Pornography, and the Sex Industry*, pp. 85–100. New York: Routledge.

Lindquist, J.H., White, O.Z., Tutchings, T., & Chambers, C.D. (1989). Judicial Processing of Males and Females Charged with Prostitution. *Journal of Criminal Justice, 17,* 277–291.

Longo, P.H. (1998). The Pegação Program: Information, Prevention and Empowerment of Young Male Sex Workers in Rio de Janiero. In K. Kempadoo & J. Doezema (Eds.), *Global Sex Workers: Rights, Resistance, and Redefinition*, pp. 231–239. New York: Routledge.

Lucas, A.M. (1998). *The Dis(-)ease of Being a Woman: Rethinking Prostitution and Subordination.* Unpublished doctoral dissertation, University of California, Berkeley.

McKeganey, N., & Barnard, M. (1996). *Sex Work on the Streets: Prostitutes and Their Clients.* Buckingham, England & Philadelphia: Open University Press.

McNamara, R.P. (1994a). Hustlers in a Shifting Marketplace: The Effects of Displacement on Male Prostitution. *American Journal of Police, 13,* 95–117.

McNamara, R.P. (1994b). Vials and Tribulations: The Effects of Crack Cocaine in Male Prostitution. *Sociological Viewpoints, 1994,* 16–24.

McNamara, R.P. (1994c). *The Times Square Hustler: Male Prostitution in New York City.* Westport, CT: Praeger.

Meier, R.F. & Geis, G. (1997). *Victimless Crime? Prostitution, Drugs, Homosexuality, Abortion.* Los Angeles: Roxbury.

Miller, R.L., Klotz, D., & Eckholdt, H.M. (1998). HIV Prevention with Male Prostitutes and Patrons of Hustler Bars: Replication of an HIV Preventive Intervention. *American Journal of Community Psychology 26,* 97–131.

Millett, K. (1976). *The Prostitution Papers: A Quartet for Female Voice.* New York: Ballantine.

Minichiello, V., Mariño, R., Browne, J., Jamieson, M., Peterson, K., Reuter, B., & Robinson, K. (2000). Commercial Sex Between Men: A Prospective Diary-Based Study. *Journal of Sex Research, 37,* 151–160.

Monto, M. (2000). Why Men Seek Out Prostitutes. In R. Weitzer (Ed.), *Sex for Sale: Prostitution, Pornography, and the Sex Industry*, pp. 67–83. New York: Routledge.

Morse, E.V., Simon, P.M., Balson, P.M., & Osofsky, H.J. (1992). Sexual Behavior Patterns of Customers of Male Street Prostitutes. *Archives of Sexual Behavior, 21,* 347–357.

Morse, E.V., Simon, P.M., Osofsky, H.J., Balson, P.M., & Gaumer, H.R. (1991). The Male Street Prostitute: A Vector for Transmission of HIV Infection into the Heterosexual World. *Social Science and Medicine, 32,* 535–539.

Nagle, J. (Ed.) (1997). *Whores and Other Feminists.* New York: Routledge.

Perkins, R., Prestage, G., Sharp, R., & Lovejoy, F. (Eds.) (1994). *Sex Work and Sex Workers in Australia.* Sydney: University of New South Wales Press.

Pheterson, G. (1996). *The Prostitution Prism.* Amsterdam: Amsterdam University Press.

Pheterson, G. (Ed.) (1989). *A Vindication of the Rights of Whores.* Seattle: The Seal Press.

Pleak, R.R., & Meyer-Bahlburg, H.F.L. (1990). Sexual Behavior and AIDS Knowledge of Young Male Prostitutes in Manhattan. *Journal of Sex Research, 27,* 557–587.

Prestage, G. (1994). Male and Transsexual Prostitution. In R. Perkins, G. Prestage, R. Sharp, & F. Lovejoy (Eds.), *Sex Work and Sex Workers in Australia,* pp. 174–190. Sydney: University of New South Wales Press.

Prieur (1998). *Mema's House, Mexico City: On Transvestites, Queens, and Machos.* Chicago: University of Chicago Press.

Queen, C. (1997). *Real Live Nude Girl: Chronicles of Sex-Positive Culture.* Pittsburgh, PA: Cleis Press.

Ratnapala, N. (1999). Male Sex Work in Sri Lanka. In P. Aggleton (Ed.), *Men Who Sell Sex: International Perspectives on Male Prostitution and HIV/AIDS,* (pp. 213–221. Philadelphia: Temple University Press.

Rhode, D.L. (1989). *Justice and Gender: Sex Discrimination and the Law.* Cambridge, MA: Harvard University Press.

Roberts, N. (1993). *Whores in History: Prostitution in Western Society.* London: Grafton.

Rosen, R. (1982). *The Lost Sisterhood: Prostitution in America, 1900–1918.* Baltimore: Johns Hopkins University Press.

Sanger, W.W. (1937). *The History of Prostitution: Its Extent, Causes and Effects Throughout the World.* New York: Eugenics Publishing Company.

Scambler, G., & Scambler, A. (Eds.) (1997). *Rethinking Prostitution: Purchasing Sex in the 1990s.* London: Routledge.

Scott, V. (1987). C-49: A New Wave of Oppression. In L. Bell (Ed.), *Good Girls/Bad Girls: Feminists and Sex Trade Workers Face to Face,* pp. 100–103. Seattle: The Seal Press.

Simon, P.M., Morse, E.V., Balson, P.M., Osofsky, H.J., & Gaumer, H.R. (1993). Barriers to Human Immunodeficiency Virus Related Risk Reduction Among Male Street Prostitutes. *Health Education Quarterly, 20,* 261–273.

Social Text, 37, pp. 1–185 (special section on the sex trade) (1993).

Sycamore, M.B. (Ed.) (2000). *Tricks and Treats: Sex Workers Write About Their Clients.* Binghamton, NY: Harrington Park Press.

Tong, R. (1984). *Women, Sex, and the Law.* Towowa, NJ: Rowman & Allanheld.

Van der Poel, S. (1992). Professional Male Prostitution: A Neglected Phenomenon. *Crime, Law and Social Change, 18,* 259–275.

Waldorf, D., & Murphy, S. (1989). Intravenous Drug Use and Syringe-Sharing Practices of Call Men and Hustlers. In M. Plant (Ed.), *AIDS, Drugs and Prostitution,* pp. 109–131. London: Routledge.

Weitzer, R. (2000a). Why We Need More Research on Sex Work. In R. Weitzer (Ed.), *Sex for Sale: Prostitution, Pornography, and the Sex Industry,* pp. 1–13. New York: Routledge.

Weitzer, R. (Ed.) (2000b). *Sex for Sale: Prostitution, Pornography, and the Sex Industry.* New York: Routledge.

Whitaker, R. (1999). *Assuming the Position: A Memoir of Hustling.* New York: Four Walls Eight Windows.

Section 5

Life, Liberty, and the Pursuit of Happiness: Law and Social Control

"Employee Drug Testing: A Question of Rights"

Alberta B. Thrash,
Central State University

Introduction

Does employee drug testing work "for the common good"? It is often suggested that there was a time in the United States when your business was also your boss' business. At the turn of the century, company snooping was pervasive and privacy almost nonexistent. At that time, your boss had the right to know with whom you lived, what you drank, when you went to church, and the political groups to which you belonged. With the growth of the trade union movement and heightened awareness of the importance of individual rights, American workers came to insist that life off the job was their private affair and not to be scrutinized by employers. The pendulum began swinging back toward greater surveillance when drugs were deemed a major problem in this country. Given this history, this paper will explore various types of tests and programs in an informational manner, ways employees beat drug tests, privacy issues, and finally the influence of the drug testing market on policymakers.

Recent History

In the 1980s, America started a war on drugs. In 1986 President Ronald Reagan signed Executive Order 12564, which required federal agencies to develop anti-drug programs that included requirements for testing of employees for drug use. And in fact, President Ronald Reagan's attitude towards drug use had been clear since 1969 when he and his staff attested to a link between marijuana use, radicalism, and anarchy (Fay, 2000).

In the 1990s, a drug czar was appointed who went after major drug dealers using the military. Search and seizure laws were relaxed and the population of jails and prisons increased. The United States now has the highest rate of incarceration in the world, with over 5.6 million adults under the supervision of the correctional system. The average annual cost of maintaining an inmate is over $20,000 per year. The Justice Department links the bulk of increasing population to drug enforcement convictions (Seattle Times, 1990).

In recent years, factors such as safety, security and productivity of the workplace have led to the increased frequency of drug testing in the workplace. Employers also use drug testing to protect themselves from any liability that may result from an incident involving an impaired employee.

Increased security is another tool used by employers in fighting drugs in the workplace. In an effort to restrict the influx of drugs into the workplace, search policies may be instituted that include searches of packages, lunch boxes, automobiles, and any objects that may be used for drug transport. Consequently, lockers and other places in the workplace are subject to search.

As a result of the war on drugs, many American workers have been made to prove their abstinence from illegal drugs by urinating into small bottles. This practice has since become known as employee drug testing (Gilliom, 1994).

Everyone Is Suspect

By testing all applicants, employment begins with suspicion. Employers believe that by drug testing all employees when hired, and subsequently those involved in accidents, the use of drugs will be deterred.

The American Civil Liberties Union is opposed to random drug testing. Random or mass urine testing reverses the presumption of innocence upon which much of our jurisprudence is built, and violates the strong prohibition of dragnet searches sweeping in the many who are innocent in order to find the few who are guilty which is the hallmark of a free and democratic society (Banta and Tennant 1989).

Types of Drug Tests

There are six main types of drug tests in use today. There are the (1) urine screen, (2) blood test, (3) saliva test, (4) sweat test, (5) hair test and (6) breath alcohol test.

Urine Screen

Urine screen is the most popular and widely used method of drug testing. Enzyme Multiplied Immunoassay Technique (EMIT) is the most commonly used test for urine drug screening. Radioimmunoassay (RIA), a highly sensitive test, is primarily used in the military. Urine screening is used by 92 percent of the organizations testing employees. It is also considered one of the most intrusive of the testing procedures. Tests differ in regards to sensitivity, costs, accuracy, analysis time, and requirements for expertise in interpretation of results.

Urine testing not only reveals the presence of illegal drugs, but also the existence of any other physical and medical conditions, including pregnancy or genetic predisposition to disease. In 1998, the Washington, D.C. Police Department admitted it used urine samples collected for drug tests to screen female employees for pregnancy—without their knowledge or consent (American Civil Liberties Union Freedom Network, 2002). Urine tests are unable to determine when drugs were taken, only what type of drugs were used. Drugs have different live spans in the urine, ironically cocaine, the culprit of the war on drugs, has one of the shortest period of time in the urine.

Blood Tests

Unlike urine screening, blood tests measure the actual amount of alcohol or other drugs in your blood at the time of the test. It is difficult to evade detection with this type of test, however it is highly invasive. Problems arise because of the fear of blood borne, infectious diseases. Drug testing with blood is not the preferred method and is the least used form. This method is also more expensive because of the need for skilled sample takers.

Saliva Test

A saliva test for marijuana can presumably detect recent use. Intravenously administered THC or tetrahydrocannabinol, the primary psychoactive ingredient in marijuana does not appear in significant amounts in human saliva. Thus, cannabinoids that are detected in saliva probably result from recent smoking of marijuana (Potter and Sebastian, 1995).

Sweat Test

Sweat Tests may prove to be cost effective. Testing could be done on a less frequent basis and with less invasion of privacy than urine tests. According to the National Institute of Drug Abuse, testing human sweat for drugs can be an effective method of monitoring drug use over extended periods. Sweat is collected over several days or weeks by a small patch worn on the skin. The participants said that the patch could be worn for up to four weeks with minimal discomfort (See the National Institute of Drug Abuse Website). The patch can detect cocaine, PCP, marijuana, opiates, including heroin, and amphetamines, including methamphetamine (Potter and Sebastian, 1995).

Refinements in the test that use hair or sweat may provide a reliable drug-use monitoring process that could be performed less frequently and with less invasion of privacy than urine tests. Drugs and their chemical byproducts of metabolism, called metabolites, are excreted into sweat and then bind to hair, where they remain detectable for months. Research has determined that residues of a number of drugs can be detected in human sweat, including alcohol, amphetamine, cocaine, heroin, morphine, methadone, methamphetamine and PCP phencyclidine(See the National Institute of Drug Abuse Website).

Hair Tests

Hair tests are less intrusive and are less subject to cheating than urinalysis. Hair samples are examined using radioimmunoassay, then confirmed by gas chromatography or mass spectrometry. The same techniques are used to test urine samples. Chemicals, residues from drugs, legal or illegal, are left behind in the hair as it grows and provide a record of past drug use. The type of drug in a relatively small sample can provide a long record of drug use. This type of test is accepted by courts in criminal trial and provides a detailed record of past drug use. Hair tests cannot be avoided as easily as urinalysis and are less awkward (Segal, 1992). Advocates claim that hair testing can detect the frequency and quantity of drug use (Campbell and Graham, 1990). Hair testing, however, cannot give an indication of whether drug use was current or recent.

There is controversy surrounding hair testing. Critics of hair testing believe that it suffers from many of the problems associated with urine testing. The testing of hair enables employers to learn a great deal about an individual's medical history. Many legal drugs detectable by hair testing are used to treat expensive illnesses, like AIDS, epilepsy, depression, cancer and heart conditions. (American Civil Liberties Union Freedom Network, 2002). With this knowledge, if they choose to do so, employers can discriminate against individuals with certain medical problems. Critics believe hair tests can be affected by passive exposure to drugs (Baily, 1989). Critics also express concern that different types of hair (coarse hair versus fine hair) may differentially retain traces of drugs (Holden, 1990). They believe that drugs bind to African-American hair in amounts 10–50 times greater than they do to Caucasian's hair and this difference can influence the likelihood of a positive drug test (Potter, et. al., 1995). In turn, this concern has led to speculation that hair tests could discriminate against blacks and other minorities.

Table 1. Comparison of Urine, Sweat and Hair Testing for Cocaine and Heroin

Issues	Urine	Sweat Patch	Hair
Type of Measure	Incremental	Cumulative	Cumulative
Invasiveness	High	Low	Low
Detection Period	2–3 days	Weeks	Months–Years
Risk of False Positives*	Low	High	High
Risk of False Negatives**	High	Undetermined	Undetermined

*False Positives resulting from environmental contamination of biological specimen during collection and handling and from passive drug exposure as a result of, for example, contact with skin or exposure to cocaine vapors.

**False negatives resulting from the drug detection "window" of the biological specimen. (Adopted from the National Institute of Drug Abuse website.)

Breath Alcohol Test

The most common test used for finding out how much alcohol is in the blood is the breath alcohol test. A breath alcohol test tells if the person is impaired by alcohol at the time of the test. Alcohol use while on the job is not new. It has been estimated that 10% of the workforce is alcoholic. Half of all industrial injuries can be linked to alcohol abuse. Do your employees have a drug or alcohol problem? The self-assessment test (figure 1) may enlighten employers and employees to the problem.

Figure 1. Self-Assessment Test

Has anyone ever questioned you about your alcohol or drug use?

Have you ever-used alcohol or other drugs alone?

Have you ever missed work because you were sick form using too much alcohol or other drugs?

Have you ever had legal problems because of your alcohol or other drug use?

If you can't use alcohol or other drugs, do you get jumpy, shaky, cranky, nervous, or have cravings?

Are you in debt because of your alcohol or other drug use?

Does it now take more alcohol or other drugs to get the same effect?

Have you ever-used alcohol or other drugs in the morning?
Have you ever been in the hospital as a result of your drinking or drug use?
Have you ever-used alcohol or other drugs at work?

If you answered "yes" to more than one of these questions, there may be reason for concern about abuse or addictions. (National Institute for a Drug-Free Workplace website.)

Illicit Drug Users

Who uses drugs on the job? Most employee users are white, young and have limited seniority. Seventy four percent of all users (9.7 million) are white, 14 percent (1.8 million) are black and 8 percent (1.1 million) are Hispanics. In a study by Halpern reported to the American Management Association, no relationship was found between minority-group employment and increased drug use. According to Mental Health Service Administration research, drug use cuts across ethnic, racial, class and educational lines. However, being unmarried, divorced, separated or never married puts workers at greater risk of illicit drug and heavy alcohol use. Women have lower rates of drug use than do men.

According to the National Institute of Drug Abuse it is estimated that nearly two-thirds of those entering the workforce in the mid to late 1990s have used illegal drugs at least once. Seventy four percent of all drug users are employed (National Institute of Drug Abuse Website).

The U.S. Department of Labor estimated that drug use in the workplace cost employers between $75 billion to $100 billion annually in lost labor time, accidents, health care costs and workers compensation. According to Dr. Nelba Chavez, Administrator of the Substance Abuse and Mental Health Services Administration (see website), marijuana use damages short-term memory, distorts perception, impairs judgement and complex motor skills, alters the heart rate, can lead to severe anxiety, and can cause paranoia and lethargy.

When compared with non-abusing employees, substance abusers have been found to take three times as much sick leave, file five times more workers' compensation claims, have four times more accidents on the job and make twice as many mistakes (DeBaernardo, 1994).

Drug Tests by Employers

Employers choose to use drug tests to determine employee drug use based on five basic categories; pre-employment, reasonable suspicion and for cause, random, post-accident and post-treatment. Those categories will be described here.

Pre-Employment Tests

In order to decrease the chance of hiring a current drug user, some employers test job applicants at the time of a job offer. The offer is contingent on negative drug test results.

Reasonable Suspicion and For Cause Tests

When an employee shows obvious signs of not being fit for duty (for Cause), or has a documented pattern of unsafe work behavior (Reasonable Suspicion), the employee may be asked to take a drug test.

Random Tests

In an effort to discourage drug use among all employees, employers may ask employees to take drug tests at random and unpredictable times.

Post Accident Tests

After an employee has had an accident or there has been an unsafe practice incident, an employer may use a post-accident drug test to find out if alcohol or other drug use was a contributing factor to the incident.

Post-Treatment Tests

When an employee has taken time off work to go through an inpatient drug or alcohol treatment program, or when an employee is participating in some form of outpatient drug or alcohol treatment program an employer may arrange for random testing to ensure the employee remains sober (Fay, 2000).

Drug-Free Workplace Program

Some employers are required to have a drug free workplace program. Those who have a federal grant or a federal contract valued at $25,000 or more, or subcontracts that include drug-free workplace requirements are usually required to maintain a drug free workplace program. Employers who are subject to any federal agency regulations, such as those of the Department of Transportation or the Department of Defense are also likely to be required to maintain such a program (Fay, 2000).

The drug-free workplace program requires that the employer have a written policy that explains what is prohibited and the consequences of violating that policy. Employees must read and consent to the policy as a condition of employment on the project. The employer must have an awareness program to educate employees about alcohol and other drug abuse and addiction, the employer's policy, and available help, counseling, and assistance. Employees must disclose any conviction for a drug-related offense in the workplace to the employer within five days after such conviction. Employers must disclose any conviction for a drug-related offense in the workplace to the Federal agency with which the employer has a grant or contract within ten days after receiving notice from the employee or others. Employers must make an ongoing effort to maintain a workplace free of drugs (Banta and Tennant, 1989).

Employee Assistance Programs

Employee Assistance Programs (EAPs) have been around since the 1940s. They were originally formed to combat alcoholism affecting the performance of white-collar workers. Recovering alcoholics and other non-professionals staffed the early EAPs, where they mainly referred employees to community treatment programs.

EAPs have enjoyed success and growth because they benefit both the employee and the organization. Employers offer EAPs in an attempt to improve performance and retention by helping employees solve personal problems. Additionally, EAPs temper discipline for impaired employees with an opportunity for treatment and rehabilitation. Employees benefit from confidential assistance with various types of problems. More than 75% of all fortune 500 companies have EAPs (Banta and Tennant, 1989).

Table 2. Growth of Employee Assistance Programs

Growth of EAPs	# of US Workers With Access To EAPs
1980	12%
1991	over 36%
1998	over 50%
Services offered by EAPs	**% of employers offering Counseling in Specific Areas**
• Alcohol abuse treatment	46%
• Drug abuse treatment	46%
• Emotional problems	43%
• Marital/family problems	40%
• AIDS	33%
• Outplacement services	23%
• Personal finance	22%
• Retirement	22%
• Legal Matters	17%

Source: 1994 Survey of Employee Benefits, Business & Legal Reports, Inc.

The Family Medical Leave Act

President Clinton signed the Family Medical Leave Act (FMLA) into law on February 5, 1993. The law allows eligible employees to qualify for up to 12 weeks of unpaid leave during a twelve month period for one of the following circumstances: the birth of a child of an employee and the need to care for the child; adoption or foster care of a child; caring for a spouse, child or parents with a health condition; or the employee's own serious health condition. This could include employee leave of absence in order to receive treatment for substance abuse. Once an employee returns to work he or she is entitled to return his or her former position or an equivalent position with equal pay, benefits and working conditions.

The Employees Right to Privacy

Almost all states recognize the individuals' right to bring suit against an individual or organization for invasion of privacy. The suit must prove that there was an intrusion upon the individuals' privacy in a way that a "reasonable person" would find highly offensive. Cases have been brought against employers regarding drug testing. "By in large, courts are upholding the drug testing," says Mark de Bernardo, executive director of the Institute for a Drug-Free Workplace in Washington, D.C. "When you do it right, courts apply a balancing test between individual privacy and the safety of other workers—they generally side with employers trying to eliminate drug use to protect the safety of other workers," he says (DeBernardo, 1994).

Can a prospective employer conduct a test without the applicant's knowledge? The law on testing varies from state to state, but generally it is a good business practice for employers to test for drug use, and some require the applicant be informed beforehand. An employer can reject an applicant who tests positive for current drug use (for further information, see the Court Law Center Website). However, inappropriate inquiries into legal prescriptions, pregnancy or illness may be construed as an invasion of privacy.

How Employees View the Test

Researchers have evaluated job candidates' attitudes toward drug testing. They found that drug users are more negative than non-users to the idea of drug testing, but that most candidates say they are less likely to apply to an organization that requires drug testing than to one that does not. Attitudes toward testing also vary with the job involved. Testing is much more strongly approved for jobs involving danger to the incumbent or risk to others, such as airline pilot, surgeon, police officer, firefighter, air traffic controller, nuclear engineer, and truck driver, than it is for jobs less likely to put other peoples' lives in jeopardy, such as janitor, salesperson or secretary (Crant and Bateman, 1990). Studies have shown that the majority of Americans are in favor of drug testing, others, however wonder "is Big Brother becoming involved in our lives?" (Konovsey and Cropanzano, 1991).

Statistics

According to Bahls, (1998) SmithKline Beecham Clinical Laboratories, the publisher of the semiannual drug-testing index, suggests that workplace drug use has been declining. The overall rate of positive tests among more than 2.2 million done in the first six months of 1997 was 5.4 percent, down from 5.8 percent in 1996. The rate of positive tests has declined steadily since it hit 18.1 percent in 1987 (Bahls, 1998).

Marijuana use is increasing according to SmithKline Beecham, fifty nine percent of all positive test results in the first half of 1997 revealed marijuana use, compared with 52 percent for the same period in 1996. The tests that detect cocaine use, has stayed about the same at 24 percent over the past few years but, declined to less than 18 percent in early 1997 (Bahls, 1998).

Prescription drugs account for 25–30 percent of the drug abuse in the work place. Much of this abuse is not detected by standard drug tests. Prescription drugs that are often abused include Demerol, Darvon, Tylenol with codeine, Zanax and Valium (anti-anxiety drugs) and stimulants such as Ritalin.

Beating the Test

The best way to avoid detection is to abstain from drug use. Those who choose this method clear the drugs out of their systems during the test period.

Table 3 lists the average detection period as published by PharmChem Laboratories headquarters in Menlo Park California. Urine tests are unable to determine when drugs were taken, only what type of drugs were used. Drugs have different life spans in the urine.

Table 3. PharmChem's Drug Detection Periods for Urine

Drug	Detection Period
Amphetamines-Stimulants	
Ethanol-Sedatives Hypnotics	
Amphetamine	Up to 72 hours
Alcohol Very Short**	
Methamphetamine	Up to 72 hours
Methadone-Narcotic Analgesics	
Barbiturates-Sedative Hypnotics	1–4 days
Amobarbital	2–4 days
Methaqualone-Sedative Hypnotics	
Butalbital	2–4 days
Quaalude	2–4 days
Pentobarbital	2–4 days
Opiates-Narcotic Analgesic	
Phenobarbital	Up to 30 days
Codeine	2–4 days
Bensodiazepines-Sedative Hypnotic	
Hydromorphone	2–4 days
Morphine for Heroin	2–4 days
Chlordiazepoxide	Up to 30 days
Cannabinoids-Euphoriants	
Casual Use	Up to 5 days
Marijuana	
Chronic use	Up to 14 days*
Casual use	1–4 days
Cocaine-Stimulants	
Benzoylecgorine	Up to 72 hours

**In rare instances, an individual may be at a detectable level for up to 30 days.*
***Alcohol is excreted at the rate of approximately one-ounce per hour.*

Drug users learn of the "detection periods" and avoid usage during this time. The detection period varies depending on the individuals' fat level and speed of metabolism as well as frequency of use. Another method used to avoid detection is the use of diuretics. Diuretics such as furosemide and caffeine cause the kidneys to increase their secretions. Employees who use this technique increase the amount of water ingested.

A favorite strategy for beating the test is masking. Employees ingest a substance that masks the drug in the urine. The effectiveness of this technique is questionable. Products such as goldenseal, cranberry juice, vinegar, and aspirin are often used. Internet companies such as Byrd Laboratories of Austin provide guaranteed 100% substance free urine by mail for $49.99, delivered freeze dried, just add water. A California company markets easily concealable carrying devices, hidden even when the subject is disrobed These deceptive techniques are successful because the majority of companies do not observe the urine collection, only 29 percent do.

According to Holtorf and Vandaele (1998), author of Ur-Ine Trouble, an underground beat the test book, vitamin C masks marijuana. Large doses of vitamin C acidifies urine, however, it increases the excretion of cocaine and amphetamines (Holtorf and Vandaele, 1998).

Other Methods to Avoid Detection

Bleach and ammonia are used to adulterate the sample. Once added to urine it will oxidize & destroy the cannabinids. Liquid Drano can cause false negative results for cocaine, opiates and marijuana. Adulterating the sample with vinegar can cause false negative results for marijuana. Blood in the sample is another way to create a false negative for cannabis (Holtorf and Vandaele, 1998).

Who Gets Caught in Drug Testing?

An estimated 65 to 90 percent of people who get caught on drug tests are caught for marijuana use. This is due to two factors. First, the number of marijuana users is far greater than the number of cocaine or heroin users. Second, marijuana is easier to detect than cocaine or heroin because it is the drug that leaves metabolites in your body the longest (Julin, 1993).

Drug users are gravitating to small businesses. Ninety-five percent of Fortune 500 companies now conduct pre-employment drug testing. Most U.S. workers, however, work for small to mid-size firms, many of which do not perform drug testing (Bahls, 1998).

Jobs Associated with Drug Use

Certain professions are especially prone to drug use. These include shift work between 5 p.m. and 8 a.m., and those who work in boring or tedious jobs. Professionals who are most likely to use drugs include nurses, physicians, pharmacists and dentists. These professionals have access to drugs, work shifts and are under stress (Potter et. al, 1995). Those working in construction, food preparation, and food service, according to statistics from the Substance Abuse and Mental Health Services Administration (SAMHSA) report the highest rates of drug use (see this website for more information).

Why Use Drugs at Work?

The motivation for drug use varies. Some reasons for drug use at work include relief of stress, boredom and pain, self-medication and self-treatment for a hangover from other drugs.

Some workers use drugs in an attempt to increase performance. Executives might use stimulants to enhance performance and endurance. Truck drivers may use drugs to combat fatigue.

Drug Costs and Sales in the Workforce

In order to continue to afford their drug use, some employers sell drugs to fellow employees. The cost of drugs in the workplace includes wages paid for unproductive work hours, the cost of repairing damaged or replacing stolen items, the cost of hiring security services, legal fees, court fees, investigative costs and travel costs.

False Positives Results

What are false positives? False positives means that a drug free sample was reported positive for drug use. How many employees are the victims of false positives? It depends upon the test and the lab, however civil libertarians say five percent is a conservative estimate (Hicks, 1999). What causes false positives? Mishandling or tampering with the sample or test results. Substances such as poppy seeds can produce a false positive test for heroin, and cold medicines can suggest methamphetamine. Clerical and laboratory errors can cause false positives and false negatives. False negative means that a sample containing drugs was reported as being drug free (Potter and Sebastian, 1995).

Employers must take the necessary steps to avoid false positive results. Accuracy is a concern as private-sector employers gain more power to test employees for drugs. Critics say the law favoring drug testing gives employers more power than is given to the police.

Americans with Disabilities Act of 1990

The Americans with Disabilities Act (ADA) of 1990 is a significant piece of civil rights legislation that extends the prohibition against discrimination on the basis of race, sex, religion and national origin to persons with disabilities. The employment provisions in Title I of the Americans with Disabilities Act prohibits discrimination against persons with disabilities in recruitment, pre-employment screening, hiring, promotions, layoffs and terminations, and any other term, condition, or privilege of employment. Title I covers private employers, state and local governments, employment agencies, and labor unions.

Is drug testing prohibited under the ADA? The ADA neither requires nor prohibits drug testing. Testing for illegal use of drugs is not considered to be a "medical examination". You may test applicants prior to making an offer of employment. It is best to test all applicants (or all applicants for certain positions) and not just those who "look" as if they take drugs. The ADA protects those who are "perceived" as having a disability, as well as those who actually have one. Drug testing does not have to be related either to job duties or business necessity. If employers do test for drugs they must be sure that the procedures used conform to all applicable federal, state and local laws. The ADA considers a positive drug test indicative of current drug use (see the ADA Technical Assistance Program Website).

People with past drug or alcohol problems are protected from job discrimination by the ADA, as are persons with current alcohol problems who are able to perform their job. The only individuals with drug and alcohol problems who do not have the same rights as others with disabilities are those who are currently using drugs illegally. The ADA specifically excludes from the definitions of "individual with a disability" any employee or applicant who is currently engaging in the illegal use of drugs, when the covered entity acts on the illegal use (ADA Technical Assistance Program Website).

Even if an applicant or employee has a disability as defined by the ADA, an employer must determine if the individual can perform the essential functions of the job, with or without reasonable accommodation. Reasonable accommodation may include periodic alcohol or drug testing, counseling, modification of job responsibilities and/or increased supervision (Guhr, 1997).

The Americans With Disabilities Act makes it clear that an individual with an alcoholism problem has a disability, which is protected under the ADA. It also states that an employer may not refuse to hire a qualified individual because of his or her alcoholism, and may not punish an alcoholic employee more severely than non-alcoholic employees for the same conduct.

Alcohol

According to a mid 1990s study, conducted by the National Institute on Drug Abuse (NIDA), the most serious drug abused at work is alcohol (Fay, 2000). The study reported that 7.5 percent of Americans employed full-time reported drinking five or more drinks per occasion on five or more days in the previous month, which was classified, as "heavy drinking."

Another study conducted over a four-year period at seven Fortune 500 companies by JSI Research and Training Institute in Boston and researchers from the Harvard and Boston University Schools of Health, showed that social drinkers, not alcoholics, are the bigger drain on productivity. Social drinkers are responsible for most of the estimated $67 billion worth of lost productivity that is attributed each year to alcohol related problems. The study found that even a glass of wine or beer with a burger impaired worker productivity (Marks, 1998).

Contrary to popular belief, the study showed that it was managers, not hourly employees, who most often drank during the workday. Twenty-three percent of upper management and eleven percent of first-line supervisors said they had a drink during the workday, compared to only eight percent of hourly employees (Marks, 1998). As a result of this study, researchers say they should start educating every worker about the negative "stealth effects" of even low levels of drinking at work and any heavy drinking off the job. The Robert Wood Johnson Foundation funded a study that found twenty-one percent of employees recognize their own productivity was affected because of a co-worker's drinking. Most drug tests do not test for alcohol consumption. As a result of this study, consultants and company representatives are looking at changing drug and alcohol policies.

Employer Liability and Legal Issues

Obviously, employers feel they must test for drugs to protect their interests. Employee accidents on the job caused by drug use can legally be considered an extension of their employment. Examples of employer liability are shown in the following cases as described by Potter and Sebastian (1995).

In the case of Otis Engineering Corp. v. Clark, a wrongful death action was allowed against the employer when a supervisor sent an intoxicated employee home. On the way home, the employee had an accident, which killed two individuals.

In Brockett v. Kitchen Boyd Motor Company, cause of action for an automobile accident was permitted against the employer. An intoxicated employee left a Christmas party and caused an accident. The above mentioned cases demonstrate how employers can be held liable for employee actions after leaving the workplace (Potter and Sebastian, 1995).

An employer who does not act reasonably when such information is available or could have been available is exposed to substantial legal liability issues (Potter and Sebastian, 1995).

Opponents of drug testing argue that random urine testing violates the Fourth Amendment to the Constitution, which requires individualized suspicion based upon probable cause before conducting a search. Since no urine test is one-hundred percent accurate, people are losing their careers unfairly. Critics also argue that urine tests by employers do not indicate impairment, intoxication, on the job drug use or competence (see the Common Sense Series Website for more information).

Politicians are jumping on the testing bandwagon. During the 1996 presidential campaign, President Clinton advocated requiring that the states make teenagers pass a drug test before they can get a driver's license. Bob Dole, a 1996 presidential candidate, proposed compelling all welfare recipients to submit to drug tests. On the national level the welfare idea died, however, state legislatures are looking closely at the idea.

Federal law allows people in certain jobs, such as airline pilots, long-distance drivers and transit workers, to be tested at random as a condition of their employment. A boss can demand a specimen, and if workers refuse, they can be fired for insubordination. In many jurisdictions, people in other jobs where safety is a factor, (including firefighters and prison guards) can be tested only if the employer has a "reasonable basis" to believe the workers performance has been impaired by drugs. Examples of reasonable basis would include accidents or violent behavior. Employers must use caution when asking an employee to take a drug test. In many jurisdiction the employee can sue for invasion of privacy or wrongful discharge if the testing isn't handled properly (Court Law Center Website).

According to the American Civil Liberties Website, in the 1997 case of Chandler v Miller, the U.S. Supreme Court held that Georgia's requirement that candidates for state office pass a drug test did not fit within the closely guarded category of suspicionless searches. While recognizing the state's commitment to the so-called "war on drugs," the Court said that subjecting public officials or candidates to such a search is unreasonable because Georgia asserts no evidence of a drug problem among the state's elected officials. Such officials, the Court said, typically do not perform high-risk, safety-sensitive tasks, and the urine test did not immediately aid interdiction efforts. The need revealed, in short, was symbolic, not "special" as that term's meaning comes from case law. Because public safety is not genuinely in jeopardy from drug-using candidates, the drug test "diminishes personal privacy for symbol's sake" is shielded by the Fourth Amendment (see the ACLU Website).

In New York, the Legal Activities Law prohibits an employer from refusing to hire or dismiss an employee for the use of alcohol and prescription drugs during off-duty hours. Employers may take action under the statue, but only if they have "an established substance abuse or alcohol program or workplace policy." (ACLU Website).

The case of Luck *v.* Southern Pacific Transportation Co. (1987) challenged the random drug-testing policy. The case involved a computer operator (Luck) who was fired in July 1985 for refusing to participate in a random testing program imposed by the employer. The California jury unanimously decided in favor of Luck on her claims of wrongful discharge and violation of public policy, breach of the implied covenant of good faith and fair dealing, and intentional infliction of emotional distress. They awarded her $485,000 in damages. Luck's attorney stressed that Luck's job had no direct public safety implications and that the company was wrong to order testing without some cause to believe that a substance abuse problem existed. The appeals court affirmed the jury verdict (ACLU Website).

Employers in California, as well as other states, are required to reasonably accommodate employees who wish to voluntarily enter drug, or alcohol rehabilitation programs. Generally, the employer must allow the workers time off to participate in such programs unless this imposes an undue hardship (ACLU Website).

The Influence of the Drug Testing Market

A report released in January of 1997, by Business Communication Company of Norwalk, Connecticut, entitled "The Drug Monitoring and Abuse Testing Business," explains that revenue for drug testing products and services grew as high as 15 percent annually during the first half of the 1990s. The U.S. market was about $628 million in 1996 and is projected to increase to about $900 million in 2001, the report estimates. In other words, throughout the 1990s, drug testing has become a booming industry.

Along with this boom has come a growing acceptance. In some industries, taking a drug test is as routine as filling out a job application. Workplace drug testing is up 277 percent from 1987 (ACLU Website). This despite the fact that a positive drug test only reveals that a drug was ingested at some time in the past. It does not distinguish between occasional or habitual use (ACLU Website).

Perhaps because of this ambiguity, as of mid 1997, a handful of states banned testing that is not based on individual suspicion like Montana, Iowa, Vermont, and Rhode Island. Minnesota, Maine and Connecticut permit not-for-cause testing, but only of employees in safety-sensitive positions. These laws also require confirmation testing, lab certification and test result confidentiality. Hawaii, Louisiana, Maryland, Nebraska, Oregon and Utah regulate drug testing in some fashion. Florida and Kansas protect government employee rights, but not those of private sector workers. Only in California, Massachusetts and New Jersey have the highest courts ruled out some of the forms of drug testing on state constitutional or statutory grounds (ACLU Website).

Conclusion

Giving up individual rights for the "good of the whole" appears to be the theme underlying the use of drug testing. One the one hand, it puts employers in a precarious situation. If the employers do not drug test they open themselves up to negligence law suits. If they do drug test, they start the employment process off on a suspicious note, and obviously employers have the right to expect sober and drug free employees. Toward this end, the programs that have been briefly described here are even mandated by the government for certain companies. Proponents of testing have portrayed the U.S. work force as being so engulfed by the surge of illegal drugs and have deemed drug testing as the "laboratory savior" of the nation. There is one glitch—there is no empirical data proving drug testing deters drug usage.

The rights of employees and indeed citizens are challenged by these market-driven practices—especially since the belief that if you do not use drugs means that you do not have anything to worry about is not necessarily true. Quite simply, since no drug test is infallible, and problems and flaws can arise in any testing program, it is difficult to make a blanket justification for drug testing. Whatever opinion one might hold, drug testing is here and will be for the foreseeable future—causing many of us to ask, does employee drug testing work "for the common good"?

> Malcolm Forbes, for one, would disagree, "Blood, urine and lie detector employee tests as a general rule should be illegal. they are outrageous invasions of privacy" (as cited in Banta and Tennant, 1989).

References

ACLU Testimony on Drug Testing in Congress. American Civil Liberties Union Freedom Network. http://www.aclu.org/congres/t051498a.html

ACLU in Brief: Privacy in America: Workplace Drug Testing. http://www.aclu.org/library/pbr5.html

ACLU of Louisiana Sues Over "Clean Urine Loyalty Oath. http://www.aclu.org/new/n092398b.html

ADA Technical Assistance Program. Employing & Accommodation Individuals. http://janweb.icd.wvu.edu/kinder/pages/alcohol_and_drug.html

Bailey, D. (1989). Drug Screening in an Unconventional Matrix. *Journal of the American Medical Association*, 262:331.

Bahls, J.E. (1998). Drugs in the Workplace. *HR Magazine.* http://www.shrm.org/hrmagazine/articles/0398drug.htm

Banta, W.F. and F. Tennant. (1989). *The Complete Handbook for Combating Substance Abuse in the Workplace.* Lexington Books.

Campbell, D. and M. Graham. (1990). Drugs and Alcohol in the Workplace: a Guide for Managers. NY: Facts on File, Inc.

Common Sense Series. The Common Sense Series—Urine Testing, http://www.timesoft.com/ncnorml/common/urine.htm

Court Law Center. Little & Brown Editors. Hiring a New Employee? What You Can and Cannot Ask. http://www.courttv.com/legalhelp/lawguide/smbusiness/g10.html

Crant, M. and T. Bateman. (1990). An Experimental Test of the Impact of Drug-Testing Programs on Potential Job Applicants' Attitudes and Intentions. *Journal of Applied Psychology,* April. 127–131.

DeBernardo, M. (1994). *Workplace Drug Testing: An Employers Development and Implementation Guide.* New York: Institute for a Drug-Free Workplace.

Dubowski, K.M. and S.L. Tuggle. (1990). *Drug-Use Testing in the Workplace: Law and Science (Employment Law Library).* Wiley Law Publications.

Fay, J.J. (2000). *The Drug Free Workplace: How to Get There and Stay There.* Butterworth-Heinemann.

Gilliom, J. (1994). *Surveillance, Privacy and the Law. Employee Drug Testing and The Politics of Social Control.* University of Michigan Press.

Guhr, L. (1997). Hidden Costs Involved With and On-The-Job Alcoholic. *Wichita Business Journal* http://www.amcity.com/wichita/stories/111097/focus1.html

Hicks, L. (1999). Drug Tests Bring Worries of Accuracy. *The Des Moines Register,* page 10s.

Holden, C. (1990). Hairy Problems for New Drug Testing Method. *Sciences,* 249: 1099–1100.

Holtorf, K. and A. Vaneaele. (1998). *Ur-Ine Trouble.* Vandalay Press.

Julin, B. (1993). Clear Test Drug Testing Facts: Drug Testing: Is It Worth It? http://www.cleartest.com

Konovsey, M. and R. Cropanzano. (1991). Perceived Fairness of Employee Drug Testing as a Predictor of Employee Attitudes and Job Performance. *Journal of Applied Psychology,* October, 698–707.

Marks, A. (1998). How Drinking Harms On the Job Efficiency. *Christian Science Monitor,* http://csmonitor.com/durable/1998/12/12p2sl.htm

National Institute of Drug Abuse. Sweat Testing May Prove Useful in Drug Use Surveillance. http://www.nida.hih.gov/NIDA_Notes?NNVVoll0N5/Sweat.html

Potter, B.A., J. Orfali, and J. Sebastian. (1995). *Drug Testing at Work: A Guide for Employers.* Ronin Publishing.

Seattle Times. (1990). Staff Reporter, May 21.

Segal, J.A. (1992). To Test or Not to Test *HR Magazine,* 37, No. 4.

Zurer, P. (1997). Drug Abuse Testing Policy Not as Defensible as Testing Technology. *Chemical Engineering News.*

"A Review of the Debate Over Hate Speech Legislation: Can Criminalizing Statutes Work for the Common Good?"

Kellina M. Craig-Henderson, Ph.D.,
Howard University

Abstract

This paper considers the degree to which sentencing strategies aimed at hate-motivated offenses permit justice for all. The issue which continues to be the focus of ongoing debate concern the extent to which regulation of hate, including speech as well as criminal behaviors, compromises fundamental rights ensured by the constitution, as well as the extent to which such actions warrant enhanced penalties. An overview of current penalty sentencing strategies for hate speech and hate crime is presented. The paper cautiously concludes that hate speech regulation and hate crime sentencing strategies are consistent with the spirit of the constitution, i.e., can work for the common good.

Hate-Based Offenses

A hate crime is an illegal act involving intentional selection of a victim based on a perpetrator's bias or prejudice against the actual or perceived status of the victim. Crimes that are motivated by hate can include vandalism, intimidation, harassment, physical and verbal assaults, and in some extreme cases, murder. Victims of hate crime may be racial, ethnic, and religious minority persons, gays, lesbians, bisexuals, women, as well as the physically and mentally disabled (see Craig, 2002 for a comprehensive review of hate crimes, victims and perpetrators). Although some profiles suggest that most offenders are male and young, people who commit hate crimes may hail from a diversity of backgrounds (Dunbar, 1999; & Garofalo, 1997).

Interestingly, although the effects of hate-based actions are often egregious, more legislative attention has focused on hate speech. This is presumably because hate speech occurs more frequently than hate inspired actions, and there is a correspondingly greater amount of ambivalence about legislation aimed at it. Few people contest the necessity of penalties for hate crimes, and when dissension about hate-based action penalties occurs it is usually about the degree of the penalty. People generally agree that those who carry out hate-based actions should be punished. However, the situation is less clear when hate speech is the focus, and although some advocate hate speech regulations (e.g., Delgado, & Yun, 1994), others do not (e.g., Cole, 1992). Individuals representing both sides of the ideological spectrum each contend that their own position is most consistent with constitutional prescriptions.

This paper considers the existing debates about hate speech, and to a lesser extent hate crime legislation, as well as the extent to which this legislation raises fundamental questions about civil liberties and civil rights. In order to accomplish this, a brief review of current penalty sentencing strategies for hate speech and hate crime is presented. This is followed by discussion of the philosophical and juridical issues that arise when one undertakes the task of regulating "hate." How these issues can be reconciled in light of the first and fourteenth amendments is also considered. By carefully considering each of these issues, this paper seeks to determine whether hate legislation can work for the common good. Throughout this discussion hate speech and hate crime will be viewed as actions located along a continuum of actions expressing outgroup hatred.

Sentencing and Pentalties for Hate-Based Offenses

Since 1981, the Anti-Defamation League of B'nai B'rith (ADL) has promoted a model of hate crime statutes that penalizes convicted hate crime offenders who victimize others because of their "...race, religion, national origin or sexual orientation." The ADL statute also ensures that institutional vandalism directed at "houses of worship, cemeteries, schools and community centers..." will also be punished (ADL, 1994, p.2). In addition to the criminal provisions, the statute also creates a private right of civil action.

Many states have based their sentencing strategies for hate crime on the ADL model. As such, these strategies have been the subject of debate—a debate which is often construed as a battle between civil liberties and civil rights. Legal scholars and civil libertarians are represented on both sides of this debate. Although much of the discussion in the lower courts has focused on the appropriateness of the legislation aimed at curtailing the verbal form of hate, i.e., hate speech, on at least two occasions the Supreme Court has actually addressed hate-based actions, i.e., hate crime.

Constitutional Challenges to Hate Legislation

On two separate occasions the Supreme Court intervened (R.A.V. v City of St. Paul, 1992; Wisconsin v. Mitchell, 1993), and in both instances, the Court's decision resulted in significant changes to existing state-level hate crime statutes. In the first case, the defendant and a group of teenagers burned a cross on the yard of an African American family who lived across the street from the defendant's home. After being charged and convicted under the city's hate crime ordinance, the case was appealed to the United State Supreme Court. The Court reversed the conviction, and struck down the city's ordinance because it violated the First Amendment.

As a result of this decision, constitutional challenges to existing hate crime laws were considerable and not until the following year when the Supreme Court ruled on a second case (Wisconsin v. Mitchell, 1993) was the issue clarified. In this case, a group of African American teens attacked a White youth who was beaten until he was unconscious. One of the teens, Mitchell, instigated the attack on the youth by inciting the group toward violence. Mitchell was tried and convicted, and because the jury found that he intentionally selected his victim because of his race, he received an enhanced penalty of from 2 to 7 years. Ultimately upon appeal the Supreme Court ruled on the case and held that the defendant's First Amendment rights were not violated. It stated that the application of penalty-enhancing statutes designed to deter bias crime during sentencing was permissible and did not punish a defendant's beliefs. The critical issue for the Court, and the reason why the First Amendment was not compromised was because the punishment targeted the prejudiced conduct in selecting the victim, not the ideology of the offender.

Although the Supreme Court's decision in Wisconsin v Mitchell (1993) effectively obviated the specific claims of constitutional compromise advanced in the case, debate surrounding the legitimacy of hate legislation continues (Wallace, 1999). This debate is not only juridical, but also philosophical and evokes issues of protection, freedom and safety, and when these issues are viewed collectively the question "Can hate legislation work for the common good?" seems especially reasonable.

This debate has been waged across a wide variety of forums (Delgado and Stefanic, 1994; Gates, 1993; Gellman, 1991). On one side of the debate are supporters of hate statutes who believe them to be an effective deterrent to hate speech and hate-based actions (Cotter, 1993; Delgado & Stefanic, 1994; Greene, 1995). On the other side are those who see such protections as infringing upon individual civil liberties (Cole, 1992; Kelley, 1992). For example, according to those who argue against hate speech regulations, the criminal sanctions targeting the presence of bias or hate among offenders are unsettling in a country committed to freedom of thought. Here, the debate focuses on the relative compatibility of the First and Fourteenth Amendments.

Legislation for Hate Speech

Generally when the topic is hate speech (and to a lesser degree hate-based actions) and possible remedial regulations, the question arises as to what many perceive as a direct conflict between the First and Fourteenth Amendments. Among other things, the First Amendment protects freedom of speech, freedom of the press, as well as the right to petition. With respect to freedom of speech, this amendment requires that the government of the United States make no law abridging individuals' right to free speech. According to proponents of hate speech regulation, hate speech is not free speech and should not be afforded the same protections ensured by the constitution. In contrast, those who oppose hate speech regulations see them as an infringement upon one of the greatest rights ensured by the Constitution. As for the Fourteenth Amendment, not only does it ensure the right of citizenship, the right to pursue life, liberty and own property, but it also ensures equal protection and due process. In short, according to the Fourteenth Amendment, every individual has a right to exist freely without harm and to be equally protected by the law.

The potential conflict between the two amendments concerns the extent to which the protection of one individual's (or group's) right to free speech may compromise another individual's (or group's) right to exist freely without harm. Finding a common ground within our current system of justice that satisfies supporters and opponents of hate speech regulations is complicated. Those who oppose regulations invoke reasonable arguments reminding us of the efforts of tyrannical figures in history who sought to limit the freedoms of the populace (Cole, 1992; Kelley, 1992). They caution against the danger posed by the risk of censorship. Equally as sound are the arguments of supporters of hate speech statutes who invoke arguments describing minority quests for equality and inclusion as the leading narrative (Delgado and Yun, 1994; Gates, 1993).

Where these 2 perspectives collide exists the individual (or group) that is the frequent or potential target of bigotry, insult and name-calling. At odds is the individual's desire to avoid expressions of bigotry which target them because of their membership within a particular social category, and the desire that someone else may have to express bigoted or hateful sentiments. For some legal scholars and judges, these desires are seemingly incompatible and one desire must outweigh the other. Many scholars within the legal community see this as a challenging task at best, and an irreconcilable one at worst given the usual tendency within the current system to balance competing values.

Legislation for Hate-Based Actions

Penalties for hate crime usually assume one of two forms—those that enhance penalties for certain criminal conduct when it is hate-motivated, and those that criminalize the behavior of the offender. With respect to the former, when the commission of a given list of offenses (e.g., assault) is motivated by bigotry, that is, the victim is intentionally selected because of their association with a particular category, the offense is more heavily punishable. The net effect of this type of a statute is that it punishes ordinarily criminal conduct in the usual way, and adds an additional penalty for the offender's intentional selection of the victim, i.e., the offender's hate motive.

The other form that penalties can take treat the combined effect of the criminal conduct and the bias motive as qualitatively greater than the sum of its parts. According to this approach, the presence of the bias motive makes a qualitative change in the conduct itself so that a completely different action is regarded as having been committed. This "new" action has different and presumably more far-reaching consequences. This approach to punishment of hate crime offenders regards hate-based actions as especially pernicious because they are not limited to the immediate victim's geographic and temporal locale, but instead have implications for non-victims who share association with the actual victim's social category.

How Might Existing Debates Be Resolved?

The enactment and implementation of hate speech regulation puts two seemingly reasonable quests at odds. Hate speech regulations make explicit the potential conflict of interest that exists in a society which values civil rights such as equal protection and due process, and civil liberties such as freedom of speech. According to some writers in this area (Delgado & Stefanic, 1994), resolution of this conflict must necessarily involve revision of the existing speech paradigm. These writers suggest that this can only come about when the potential sides of the debate, those arguing for speech and those arguing for equality, are viewed as what they really are—"two sides of the same coin" rather than as two separate values.

According to these authors and others, speech and equality are interdependent with one another to the extent that both are integral aspects of "community." Thus, speech requires community in the same way that community requires speech. Furthermore, the type of community envisioned by this country's earliest social architects, and one which is aspired to even now is one in which all members of society are equal (at least ostensibly so).

The one way to resolve the conflict between hate speech regulation advocates and opponents is to consider that hate speech regulation is *not synonymous* with compromising the First Amendment, and strong endorsement of the Fourteenth Amendment does not require subjugation of civil rights. Hate speech regulation can, and should be consistent with the First Amendment, and, so too can it be consistent with the Fourteenth Amendment.

Conclusion

The present discussion has focused on the extent to which hate crime law as it is currently applied can work for the common good. Hate crime laws, though still controversial, can protect the rights of minority communities. Contrary to what opponents of hate rules contend, these laws do not require that others' rights to freedom be stifled. Instead, by recognizing and considering the communal quality of speech and equality, judges and lawmakers can construct hate-based laws which work for all.

References

Anti-Defamation League of B'nai B'rith (1994). Hate Crime Laws. A Comprehensive Guide. New York: Author.

Cole, D. (1992). Neutral Standards and Racist Speech. Reconstruction, 2(1).

Cotter, W.R. (1993). Hate Speech-How to Handle It. Nieman Reports. Cambridge MA: Nieman Foundation at Harvard University.

Craig, K.M. (2002). Examining Hate-Motivated Aggression: A Review of the Social Psychological Literature on Hate Crimes as a Distinct Form of Aggression. *Aggression and Violent Behavior*, 7, 85–101.

Delgado, R. and Stefanic, J. (1994). Hateful Speech, Loving Communications: Why Our Notion of "A Just Balance" Changes So Slowly. *California Law Review*, 82, 847–868.

Delgado, R. and Yun, D.H. (1994). Pressure Valves and Bloodied Chickens: An Analysis of Paternalistic Objections to Hate Speech Regulations. *California Law Review,* 82, 871–892.

Dunbar, E. (1999). A Psychographic Analysis of Violent Hate Crime Perpetrators. Aggressive, Situation and Ideological Characteristics of Bias-Motivated Offenders. Manuscript currently under review.

Garofalo, J. (1997). Hate Crime Victimization in the United States. In R.C. Davis, A.J. Lurigio, and W.G. Skogan (Eds.), *Victims of Crime* (pp. 134–145). Thousand Oaks, CA: Sage Publications, Inc.

Gates, H.L. (1993, September). Let Them Talk. Why Civil Liberties Pose No Threat To Civil Rights. *The New Republic,* pg. 20, 27, 37–47.

Gellman, S. (1991). Sticks and Stones Can Put You in Jail, But Can Words Increase Your Sentence? Constitutional and Policy Dilemmas of Ethnic Intimidation Laws. *UCLA Law Review,* 39, 333–396.

Greene, L.S. (1995, Spring). Racial Discourse, Hate Speech, and Political Correctness. National Forum: *The Phi Kappa Phi Journal,* 75(2).

Kelley, K. (1992, Winter). Free Speech/ Hate Speech: A Student's View. *Peace and Democracy News.*

R.A.V. v City of St. Paul, 505 U.S. 377, 381 (1992).

Wallace, P.S. (1999). Hate Crimes: Legal Issues. CRS Report for Congress. Washington, DC: Library of Congress.

Wisconsin v. Mitchell, 113 S. Ct. 2194 (1993).

Section 6

The Wars: Drugs, Crime, and the Role of the Law

"Women in the Wars: The Processing of Women Through the Criminal Justice System"

Gail Hurst,
Southern Illinois University

Introduction

The number of women arrested and processed through the justice system has steadily risen over the past three to four decades. While the share of females found within the criminal justice system still remains substantially lower than males, the number of female defendants grew at two and a half times the rate of increase of males between the years of 1990 and 1996 (Bureau of Justice Statistics, 1999). These numbers are mirrored by prison figures, which show that between the years 1990 to 1998 the number of women confined in prison increased by an annual 8.5 percent. During these same years however, the prison population grew only by an averaged 6.7 percent annually (Bureau of Justice Statistics, 1999).

While the number of women processed through the system has increased, their overall profile remains relatively the same. The average woman incarcerated is still likely to be African-American, with an average of two children to whom she held custody prior to incarceration. Moreover, the majority of these women continue to be convicted of property and, in recent years, drug related offenses as opposed to violent offenses (Bush-Baskette 1998; Bureau of Justice Statistics, 1999). About half of female offenders also used alcohol or drugs at the time of their offense. In fact, recent statistics reveal that female offenders in state prisons reported higher usage than males (Steffensmeier and Allan, 1998; Bureau of Justice Statistics, 1999). Also, female offenders frequently report childhood or adult abuse. Bloom and Chesney-Lind (2000) report that 43 percent of female inmates have reported either physical or sexual abuse in their lives.

The increased rates of women within the system can not merely be explained by changes in the nature of female offending. In fact, their rates of imprisonment for violent offenses have declined (Bloom and Chesney-Lind, 2000; Steffensmeier and Allan, 1998). With this point in mind, during the last three to four decades, researchers have also explored possible reasons for the increased number of women processed through the system. One of the first group of theories linked this pattern of increase to the woman's newly acquired liberation in the 1970s. This view however, has been criticized on a number of levels. For example, the social profile of the female offender would indicate that she is a woman experiencing economic inequality, rather than liberation (for full discussion see Pollock, 1999 and Steffensmeier and Allan 1998). Today, a number of other possible theories are offered, and debated, to explain increased rates of women within the system.

The Chivalry Hypotheisis

Research has shown that the criminal justice system treats females more leniently than males. Spohn, Gruhl, and Whelch (1987) examined prosecutors' decision making as related to rejections and dismissals and found gender differences in favor of females at both stages. Moreover, females were less likely to be prosecuted. Whether leniency has been extended because of the woman's family obligations, or the belief that she is less dangerous and more amendable to treatment, women it is argued, have traditionally been afforded preferential treatment for their wrongdoings. Those who believe in the chivalry hypothesis contend that increases in the rate of female arrest and processing may, in part, be due to the fact that chivalry is now dead. These proponents link these increases to the feminist movement, believing that the fight for the political, economic, and social equality of women has also meant that the leniency once reserved for females has now ceased to exist. Chesney-Lind and Pollock (1995), best explains this contention. They write:

> ...some feminist scholars argue that the only way to eliminate the discriminatory treatment and oppression that women have experienced

> in the past is to push for continued equalization under the law. (pg. 155).

Many proponents on this side of the debate also argue that while there has been leniency based upon one's gender, a gender "benefit-of-the-doubt" has not been afforded to black women. Women of color have been less likely to receive preferential treatment as compared to white women (see Kratcoski and Scheuerman 1974; Bush-Baskette 1998).

It is also important to note that there is research suggesting that leniency afforded to women may not necessarily be due to chivalry. Daly (1989) states that the idea of paternalistic treatment of women was developed out of thin air, and was not based upon how court officials truly reach their decisions. A defendant's family situation (i.e. having dependants and marital status), and not gender best explains sentence outcome (Daly 1987; Daly 1989). Moreover, the leniency women have traditionally received is due to the fact that they are less likely to engage in the same types of offenses as men. Therefore, what on the surface may appear to be chivalry is in fact leniency because of other variables such as less crime seriousness on the part of women. To illustrate, Steffensmeier, Kramer, and Streifel (1993) found that gender had only a small or negligible effect on the likelihood of imprisonment or length of imprisonment decisions in Pennsylvania. Sentences instead were based upon factors such as the type and seriousness of the crime, and prior record. In fact, men and women similarly situated were charged with similar offenses and sentenced in a like manner, calling the chivalry hypothesis into further doubt.

The War Against Drugs

Less debate exists regarding the effects that the war on drugs and other crime control policies have had on women. Danner (1998), using an analogy with "three strikes and you're out" laws, shows how all women are impacted. First, she states that such laws have a hidden cost to women in general. For example, to pay for criminal justice expansion (prison space) social service programs, especially those likely to be used by poor women with children, are sacrificed. A common approach is to pass legislation which reforms programs such as welfare, while at the same time laws and policies that increase sentence lengths are implemented. Second, there is also a cost to those employees, most of whom are women, who will likely lose their jobs once social services are cut. Finally, according to Danner, strike three is the hidden cost to those women, mostly grandmothers, who must care for the children of women who are incarcerated under these crime control policies (Danner, 1998). This line of argument can just as easily be applied to drug laws, which have dramatically contributed to the number of women under confinement.

Price and Sokoloff (1995) state that the war on drugs has created a new and larger wave of offenders. These offenders are convicted of either drug possession, selling small amounts of narcotics, or other crimes to support their habit. Moreover, women have been severely affected by these drug laws. Between 1990 and 1996 the number of women convicted of drug trafficking grew by 34 percent, and the number of convictions for drug possession grew by 41 percent (Bureau of Justice Statistics, 1999). Nowhere is the war on drugs more dramatically felt than on the federal level. Federal sentencing guidelines designed to reduce disparities in race and class for example has meant that more women are now under federal confinement. On the federal level, the average time served for female drug offenders rose from 27 months in July of 1984 to 67 months in June of 1990. Likewise, 72 percent of women under federal confinement are there because of a drug law violation (Bureau of Justice Statistics, 1999).

Among states, Chesney-Lind and Pollock (1998) documents the rate of change in the number of women incarcerated, largely because of drug related offenses. Within a five year period the number of women incarcerated in Rhode Island rose from 20 to 250. Nearly half of the women imprisoned in Massachusetts are there because of a drug offense. Women of color have been hardest hit by these increases. In fact, the war on drugs could be viewed as a war against women, more specifically against black women. Black women are 3 times more likely to be incarcerated than white women (Bush-Baskette, 1998). Under the Federal Sentencing Guidelines, 50% of women sentenced for drug offenses in 1995 were black. Such figures are mirrored in many states. In New York, for example, black females represent 58 (Bureau of Justice Statistics, 1999). of women confined, and a great portion of these women are there because of drug offenses (Hendriques and Jones-Brown, 1999; Bush-Baskette 1998). Currently, black women represent a larger percentage of the incarcerated female population than black males represent of the incarcerated male population.

Also specific to black females is the move in some states toward prosecuting addicted pregnant women with crimes against the fetus. Humphries (1993) discusses how pregnant women, most of whom are women of color, are scapegoats for the lost battle against drugs. The addicted, poor, black woman draws upon class, race, and gender biases. This new type of criminal is easy to target under new crime control policies because she reinforces the stereotype held of the addicted woman who is living in poverty and ignoring her children to support a habit, at taxpayer's expense. These laws are even more troubling because aside from her drug use, which many see as an illness rather than a crime, many of these women have not engaged in any other types of offenses.

Economic Marginalization, Drug Use and Increased Formal Social Control

Females are in worse financial shape today than they were 30 years ago. The impact of poverty, unemployment and underemployment cannot be ignored when examining reasons for increased female processing. Economic marginalization theory posits that female involvement in crime is rising not because of employment opportunities, but because of decreased economic stability (Pollock, 1999). Steffensmeirer and Allan (1998) assert that it is not equality that has contributed to female offending patterns, but female inequality and economic vulnerability. While the educational attainment of women has increased, they have yet to reach parity with men. Moreover, females still tend to work in "pink ghetto jobs", that is positions labeled as technical sales and administrative support, where the pay is lower than men (Pollock 1999; Merlo 1998). This problem is further exacerbated when one considers the fact that more women today are single heads of households. Divorce, separations, and illegitimacy have created more responsibility for females. This point is particularly true for African Americans, were a large portion of all births are to unmarried women. Still, regardless of race or ethnicity, families headed by women are generally characterized by poverty, underemployment, limited education, and depression (Merlo, 1998). This profile may likely explain female arrest figures for property crimes such as larceny, check and welfare fraud, and forgery of credit cards. Females may be engaging in these types of crimes to meet their families' financial needs. Merlo, (1998), provides a study which found that twice as many women than men reported that meeting family financial needs was the major reason for their offending.

An issue related to the economic marginalization of women is the high level of drug use among female offenders. Pollock (1999) contends that drugs play a crucial role in female criminality. She states that while drug use may not be the sole and necessary cause of criminal choices, addicted women are much more likely to engage in crime at a more frequent rate. While one usually assumes that the female drug user supports her habit through prostitution, research reveals that these women are more likely to become involved in property crimes. Research performed in Miami of crack abusers, found that over 70 percent of the women in the sample violated drug and minor property offenses (cited in Merlo, 1998). Women who report drug use are also increasingly becoming involved in more serious crimes such as robbery, burglary, weapons possession, and assault (Merlo, 1998; Steffensmeirer and Allan 1998). This presents the recognition that increased arrest and processing of females may be due to changes in formal social control. For instance, formal policing has lead to increased documentation and better manners of apprehending offenders, and research performed by Steffensmeier and Streifel found that between the years of 1960 and 1985, increased social control best explained the number of female arrests (cited in Merlo 1998).

For the Common Good

This chapter has already discussed many of the commonly cited reasons used to explain the increased criminal justice processing of females in this country and the effects such reasons have on women, particularly women of color. To end, perhaps one of the most devastating effects of this rise is the impact of imprisonment on females and their children.

An estimated 75 to 80 percent of incarcerated women are mothers (Bloom and Chesney-Lind, 2000). Likewise, over half of these women had custody of their children prior to incarceration. With these points in mind, the imprisonment of the mother has much more of a devastating impact on the child, since she was the primary caretaker prior to incarceration. Zaplin and Doughtery (1998) state that fathers can be reasonably sure that upon incarceration the mother will provide for their child. Most often this assurance is not a reality for women. In the majority of instances, when women are incarcerated, their children are left to the care of parents, relatives, or friends (Bloom and Chesney-Lind, 2000). Often when these people are unable to provide care, the child is placed in foster care. Of course, female inmates may also face issues surrounding parental rights. In fact, women run a greater risk of losing their parental rights while incarcerated (Zaplin and Doughtery, 1998).

Because women are generally the primary caretakers, children play an intricate role in their ability to adjust to incarceration. Owen's (1998) quasi-ethnographic study of women in Central California Women's Facility (CCWF) shows this. She writes:

> Children are part of the prison culture in two distinct ways. First, women maintained ties with their children through a variety of means: phone calls and letters were the most common, with regular visits and family visits.... the least common.

> second, for many women, reuniting with their children becomes a primary goal and acts as a form of informal social control during their days in prison.

Children are also much more likely to have problems with adjustment once the mother is incarcerated. These children exhibit many of the psychological and behavioral problems seen among children who have been separated from a parent because of divorce or death. These problems include: depression, poor school performance, truancy, anger, sleep disruptions, and poor social skills (Snyder-Joy and Carlo 1998; Zaplin and Doughtery, 1998). Moreover, girls whose mothers are incarcerated and who lack a stable home life, are more likely to become pregnant as teenagers (Snyder-Joy and Carlo, 1998).

One of the largest hindrances in the adjustment of both the female inmate and her child is the lack of visitation between the two. Many women never see their children while incarcerated. Several reasons have been given for this lack of visitation. Zaplin and Doughtery (1998) point out that most children live very long distances away from the correctional facility which generally is located in a rural area. Transportation to these areas tends to be difficult because of a lack of public transportation. Moreover, limited finances pose a barrier in visitation (Bloom and Chesney-Lind, 2000). One must also consider the reality that because of shame many incarcerated women may not want their children to see them incarcerated.

In conclusion, there are those who might argue that having children is not a circumstance that should somehow mitigate or excuse criminal behavior. Moreover, one might argue that the female offender is not necessarily a good role model for her children. However, given the mood of the country to put families first we must consider whether the move to process and incarcerate more and more women serves the common good. Given the less serious nature of her crimes and the circumstances that generally surround them, many female offenders would be better helped in the community; where ties to her family can be maintained. Likewise, when one considers the large number of women who offend because of factors such as addiction and economic marginalization, it seems clear that it is community treatment and programming that is needed, not prisons.

References

Bloom, B. and M. Chesney-Lind. (2000). Women in Prison: Vengeful Equality. In R. Muraskin *It's a Crime: Women and Justice 2nd. Edition*. Upper Saddle Rive, New Jersey: Prentice-Hall, Inc.

Bureau of Justice Statistics. (1999). *Women Offenders.* Washington, DC: Department of Justice.

Bush-Baskette, S. R. (1998). The War on Drugs as a War Against Black Women. In S. L. Miller (Ed.), *Crime Control and Women: Feminist Implications of Criminal Justice Policy.* Thousand Oaks, CA: Sage Publications, Inc.

Chesney-Lind, M. (1998). Rethinking Women's Imprisonment: A Critical Examination of Trends in Female Incarceration. In Price B.R and N.J. Sokoloff (Ed.), *The Criminal Justice System and Women.* New York: McGraw-Hill, Inc.

Chesney-Lind, M., and J.M. Pollock (1995) Women's Prisons: Equality with a Vengeance. In A.V. Merlo and J.M. Pollock (Eds.) *Women, Law, and Social Control.* Boston, MA: Allyn and Bacon.

Danner, M. J. E. (1998). Three Strikes and It's Women Who Are Out: The Hidden Consequences for Women of Criminal Justice Policy Reforms. In S. L. Miller (Ed.), *Crime Control and Women: Feminist Implications of Criminal Justice Policy.* Thousands Oak, CA: Sage Publications, Inc.

Daly, K. (1987). Discrimination in the Criminal Courts: Family, Gender, and the Problem of Equal Treatment. *Social Forces.* 66(1), 152–175.

Daly, K. (1989). Neither Conflict Nor Labeling Nor Paternalism Will Suffice: Intersections of Race, Ethnicity, Gender, and Family in Criminal Court Decisions. *Crime and Delinquency.* 35(1), 136–168.

Henriques, Z.W. and D. Jones-Brown. (1999). Self-Taught Empowerment and Pride: A Multimodal/Dual Empowerment Approach to Confronting the Problems of African American Female Offending. In R. T. Zaplin (Ed.), *Female Offenders: Critical Perspectives and Effective Interventions.* Gaithersburg, MD: Aspen Publishers, Inc.

Humphries, D. (1993). Crack Mothers, Drug Wars, and the Politics of Resentment. In K.D. Tunnel (Ed.), *Political Crime in Contemporary America: A Critical Approach.* New York: Garland Publishing.

Kratcoski, P.C. and K. Scheuerman. (1974). Incarcerated Male and Female Offenders' Perceptions of Their Experiences in the Criminal Justice System. *Journal of Criminal Justice.* 2: 73–78.

Merlo, A. V. (1998). Female Criminality in the 1990s. In A. V. Merlo and J. M. Pollock (Eds.), *Women, Law, and Social Control.* Boston, MA: Allyn and Bacon.

Owen, B. (1998). *In The Mix Struggle and Survival in a Women's Prison.* Albany, NY: State University of New York Press.

Pollock, J. M. (1999). *Criminal Women.* Cincinnati, OH: Anderson Publishing Co.

Price, B.R., and N. J. Sokoloff (Eds.). (1995). *The Criminal Justice System and Women: Offenders, Victims, and Workers.* New York: McGraw Hill.

Snyder-Joy, Z.K. and T.A. Carlo. (1998). Parenting Through Prison Walls Incarcerated Mothers and Children's Visitation Programs. In A.V. Merlo and J.M. Pollock (Eds.) *Women, Law, and Social Control.* Boston, MA: Allyn and Bacon.

Spohn, C., J. Gruhl., and S. Welch. (1987). The Impact of the Ethnicity and Gender of Defendants on the Decision to Reject or Dismiss Felony Charges. *Criminology* 25(1), 175–187.

Steffensmeier, D. and E. Allen (1998). The Nature of Female Offending: Patterns and Explanation. In R. T. Zaplin (Ed.), *Female Offenders: Critical Perspectives and Effective Interventions.* Gaithersburg, MD: Aspen Publishers, Inc.

Steffensmeier, D., J. Kramer, and C. Streifel (1993). Gender and Imprisonment Decisions. *Criminology*. (31)3: 411–443.

Zaplin, R.T. and J. Dougherty (1998). Programs that Work: Mothers. In R. T. Zaplin (Ed.), *Female Offenders: Critical Perspectives and Effective Interventions.* Gaithersburg, MD: Aspen Publishers, Inc.

"Drug War Prisoners: Incapacitation and the Limits of Drug Policy"

Jeanette Covington,
Rutgers University

Introduction

Since 1914, the United States has insisted on outlawing the use and sale of a wide variety of drugs. Yet in the course of this 87-year experience with drug prohibition, it has become increasingly clear that prohibition results in certain unintended consequences. For one thing, it requires that the state criminalize many otherwise law-abiding Americans, who use and/or sell drugs. For example, in 1999, an estimated 27 million people used and/or sold drugs and were thereby deemed criminals eligible for some type of punishment (Office of Applied Studies, 2000). It is obvious that zero-tolerance policies are not possible with such a huge pool of drug users and user-sellers as the criminal justice system simply does not have the capacity to punish or monitor the behavior of all those who violate drug laws. Hence, it has been necessary to be very selective about which drug users and sellers will be drawn from this huge pool of offenders and subjected to punishment and prolonged surveillance. Yet for many, the fact that a mere handful are punished for drug law violations, while most go free, is likely to be an unacceptable cost of insisting on drug prohibition.

Drug prohibition exacts other social costs as well as it raises the price of drugs and thereby causes crime to spiral upwards as some drug users initiate or escalate their criminal behavior in order to support expensive drug habits. Even worse, disputes among illegal drug users and sellers sometimes end in violence simply because they are required to take the law into their own hands. Therefore, prohibition virtually guarantees that some drug epidemics will be accompanied by homicide epidemics as disputes over illegal drugs temporarily raise the intensity of conflict in a neighborhood.

While these harms brought about by the illegality of drugs are considerable, defenders of the status quo seem to think that at least some of the drug-related offending that stems from prohibition can be prevented by incapacitating those drug offenders at greatest risk of engaging in crime and violence.

Incapacitation is promoted as an effective crime prevention strategy based on the straightforward assumption that locking up those drug offenders at greatest risk for criminal or violent behavior for extended periods makes them incapable of preying upon law-abiding members of the community. Therefore, much of the research on incapacitation is geared towards identifying the handful of drug users most prone to crime and violence among the 87 million Americans who have used drugs in their lifetime or the 27 million who have used annually in recent years (Office of Applied Studies, 2000). Because incapacitation is meant to prevent crime, its proponents argue for the legitimacy of locking people up not simply because of the crimes they have committed (i.e., nonviolent drug law violations), but also because of the crimes they *might* commit (i.e., predatory crimes and violence). It is left to researchers who are expert in predicting who is most likely to commit acts of crime and violence to identify the few most dangerous users among the millions of drug law violators.

The notion of using incapacitation as a crime prevention tool has generated a good deal of criticism. Some of its detractors include those who argue that two people who have both used and/or sold illegal drugs should both get the same punishment. Such critics object to incapacitation because it means that the state no longer punishes drug law violators for the nondrug crimes they have actually committed, it also punishes some for the future violent and criminal acts they *might* yet commit. For those who object to incapacitation on these grounds, it is morally repugnant to think that a handful of drug criminals could be punished for crimes they *had not yet committed and might never commit.* Yet, incapacitation with its focus on crime prevention means that it is no longer just a crime to actually use and sell drugs; it also becomes a crime to have background characteristics that suggest one may be at risk of committing future crimes or homicides. In essence, incapacitation divides the drug law violating population into those who come before the criminal justice system with drug crimes and what is deemed low risk for future crime and those who present with drug crimes and are labeled as high risk.

Other critics might object to incapacitation on political grounds because they fear that the populations who will be most likely to be labeled high risk for future crimes will be minority and of low income. In this view, incapacitation theory might be used to explain away gross racial disparities in who gets locked up for drugs. As it stands, blacks are believed to make up 15.4 percent of monthly drug users and 16 percent of drug sellers, but they make up a whopping 54 percent of those in prison for drug law violations nationwide. Even worse, in 7 states, they make up 80–90 percent of those behind bars for drug crimes (Office of Applied Studies, 2000, Human Rights Watch, 2000,

Justice Policy Institute, 2000, Covington 2001). Incapacitation theory could easily be used to justify these gross disparities by suggesting that few white drug law violators go to prison for drug crimes simply because they do not have the background characteristics that make them high risk for future crime. On the other hand, black drug law violators, presumably, do have these high-risk characteristics and their overrepresentation among those in prison for drug crimes can thereby be justified.

Yet even though these legal, ethical and political objections to incapacitating drug criminals can be quite persuasive, they ultimately fail to address the utilitarian claims made by proponents of incapacitation.

In fact, those who favor incapacitation easily sidestep these moral and ethical objections to the harms associated with punishing some and not others by claiming that incapacitation can improve public safety by preventing crime and violence. This has led a number of criminologists to turn away from legal, moral and ethical objections and examine the utilitarian claims made in the incapacitation literature by attempting to determine if incapacitation can be shown to prevent crime and violence.

Most of the research on whether incapacitation actually prevents crime is based on studies of predatory criminals like robbers and burglars that were conducted in the 1980s. Hence, the degree to which any findings on the incapacitation of robbers and burglars might reasonably be applied to incapacitation's likely effects on a population of nonviolent drug-law violators is unclear. Yet the need to focus on nonviolent drug law violators could not be more urgent as they have come to make up a larger and larger share of the prison population since 1980. Therefore to assess claims that incapacitation reduces crime and violence requires that this chapter start with some review of the literature on the effectiveness of incapacitation in preventing predatory crimes like robbery and burglary before going on to describe its likely impact on nonviolent drug law violators.

In the next section, I will begin by discussing the claims of proponents of incapacitation who argue that it can prevent crime, and then review research examining its capacity to prevent crimes like robbery and burglary. Those who question its capacity to prevent robberies and burglaries typically point to the fact that, to date, efforts to predict which offenders are likely to recidivate have failed. For them, the failures of criminal forecasting have much to do with the background characteristics used to predict future crime. Hence, two sections will be devoted to a review of research that explains why background characteristics like a criminal history or a history of drug use have failed to predict future involvement in robberies and burglaries.

Even today, much of the thinking about incapacitation is based on studies conducted with robbers and burglars in prison in the 1980s. Yet, as noted, the prison population has changed and now includes many more inmates who have been incarcerated for nonviolent drug law violations. Moreover, many of these new prisoners have been incapacitated for their use or sale of crack-cocaine or powder cocaine. Hence, I will consider whether the rise in this new prison population, in which crack and cocaine drug law violators predominate, makes criminal forecasting easier or more difficult.

Finally, because the incapacitation of drug law violators is also thought to prevent drug-related homicides, the likely impact of locking up drug offenders on homicide will also be considered. This argument seems all the more important today because of evidence indicating a strong association between the use and sale of crack and homicide. Hence one of the closing sections will be devoted to examining whether the recent rise in the incapacitation of crack users and sellers might have brought about a reduction in drug-related homicides.

Review of Research on Incapacitation

As noted, much of the research on incapacitation was conducted in the 1980s on samples of robbers and burglars. In this older research, locking up robbers and burglars was described as an effective crime prevention tool because while these criminals were locked up, they were incapable of preying on the community. Those who argued that incapacitation could prevent crime assumed that if an offender did 100 robberies in the year before coming to prison and then was locked up for a year, 100 robberies would be prevented during the year in which the offender was incapacitated.

Furthermore because only a handful of criminals were likely to engage in such high rate criminal activity, a good deal of effort was put into distinguishing the most criminally active offenders from those inclined towards less frequent offending. It is easy to see why there was such an interest in identifying high rate offenders as research indicated that the handful of criminals who were most active committed a considerable amount of crime. For example, research suggested that high rate robbers averaged 31 robberies per year and high rate burglars averaged 156 burglaries per year in the years before their imprisonment (Walker, 1994). By contrast, low rate robbers and burglars respectively averaged only 2 robberies and 13 burglaries per year before coming to prison.

In light of such evidence, "get tough" policies like incapacitating these prospectively high rate offenders for longer periods of time were promoted. The thinking was that lengthy incapacitation of high rate offenders could lead to major reductions in crime while conserving prison space.

At least some of the research suggested that high rate offenders could be distinguished from medium or low rate offenders based on 7 background characteristics that indicated: 1) a history of involvement in predatory crimes; and/or 2) a history of involvement in drug use (Greenwood and Abrahamse, 1982). These characteristics are listed in Table 1.

Table 1. Predictors of Criminal Recidivism

- Prior convictions for robbery or burglary
- Being incarcerated for more than half of the preceding 2 years
- A delinquency conviction prior to age 16
- Commitment to a state or federal juvenile institution
- Being employed for less than half of the preceding 2 years
- Heroin or barbiturate use in the prior 2 years
- Heroin or barbiturate use as a juvenile

In order to assess how well these background characteristics predicted the risk of involvement in high rate criminal activity upon release, one point was assigned to each of the seven characteristics. It was then predicted that those who scored 4–7 points on this scale (i.e., had 4–7 of the background characteristics) would be most likely to be high rate recidivists. However, when the actual reported criminal activity of those predicted to be high risk is examined, the above prediction scale is accurate only 51 percent of the time (Walker, 1994, Visher, 1995). A recent effort to replicate this prediction scale with proxy measures also results in inaccurate predictions—particularly for the high rate offenders (Auerhahn, 1999).

The dramatic inaccuracies of these prediction scales were attributed to two types of error—namely false positive error and false negative error. With false positive errors, the prediction scales suggest that an individual inmate will recidivate at a high level and that individual, in fact, does not re-offend. Hence if they are imprisoned longer, based on these predictors, inmates and their families suffer needlessly as they are punished for crimes they never commit. Moreover, if they are kept in prison longer based on these background characteristics, limited prison space is wasted without reducing crime rates.

These prediction scales also produce false negative errors. This occurs when scores on the prediction scales suggest that an individual is not likely to re-offend at a high rate and thus indicate only a short stint in prison is required. Yet, inmates who are false negatives do re-offend at higher than predicted levels when released to the community. Hence they can continue to wreak havoc in the community because these prediction scales do not indicate a need for lengthy prison sentences because, presumably, these people do not pose much of a threat.

Many criminologists have concluded from this research that there is little reason to believe that background characteristics that include: 1) a prior history of predatory crime; or 2) a prior history of drug use, allow for the selection of those high rate offenders who most need to be incapacitated. Indeed because the research on incapacitation has not yet produced accurate predictors of future criminal behaviors, some have begun to consider the reasons why it is so difficult to predict who will and will not recidivate. In the next section, I will consider why background characteristics indicating that an inmate has a prior history of extensive involvement in predatory crime may not predict future involvement in serious offending. A section that considers why a prior history of drug use may also fail to forecast serious offending will follow.

Problems in Predicting Recidivism Using Prior Criminal History

The notion that high-risk populations can be accurately identified based on a prior record of frequent offending, depends on certain assumptions about the nature of criminal careers. To identify high-risk inmates and accurately forecast their future crimes, criminal careers must be predictable in the sense that those who do 100 robberies in the year 2000 must also do 100 robberies in 2001. If this assumption is correct, then locking them up in 2001 allows one to conclude that 100 robberies have been prevented while they are incapacitated.

However, this assumption about the nature of criminal careers is often incorrect, in part, because the dynamics of criminal careers are not well understood. In other words, knowing that a criminal has a history of frequent robberies before coming to prison is not a sure indicator that he would have persisted in these crimes if he had not been locked up. It is possible that the offender might have shifted to minor crimes during the year that he was locked up and thus no serious crime would have been prevented (false positive error). Conversely some of those with a history of minor, nonviolent crimes before coming to prison might suddenly escalate to frequent serious offending and yet their criminal histories would cause them to be released and thereby allow them to prey on the community (false negative error). Poor understanding of the peaks and valleys of criminal careers makes it difficult to develop accurate career trajectories simply by looking at an offender's prior bad acts. It is this limited understanding that also assures that there will be a large number of false positive and false negative errors.

Not only is it difficult to predict which offenders will escalate or curtail their criminal activities from year to year, it is also difficult to make accurate forecasts about when a criminal career will end. Much of the literature on criminal careers suggests that adult criminal careers last six years on average. This means that by the time an offender enters prison, much of his criminal career may be over. Hence, despite a history of frequent offending, if an offender is maturing out of crime when she is imprisoned, no crime will be prevented while she is incapacitated. Because it is unclear how many years of offending are left for any given criminal who enters prison, it is impossible to say how much crime will be averted while they are incapacitated. Hence, limited understanding of when offenders are likely to desist from crime also assures a large number of false positive and false negative errors.

Problems in Predicting Recidivism Using A History of Drug Use

While a history of frequent and serious offending ultimately turns out to say little about the likelihood that an offender will recidivate, a history of drug use might seem to be a more promising predictor of recidivism. For one thing, it was assumed that a history of drug use could predict a future of high level criminal offending because the inflated prices of illegal substances (e.g., heroin) might cause some drug users to initiate a career in moneymaking crime in order to finance their expensive drug habits.

However, empirical research indicates that use of an expensive illegal drug does not so much cause heavy users to turn to moneymaking predatory crime but rather amplifies pre-existing criminal careers. In other words, many studies indicate that delinquent and criminal careers are more commonly initiated before offenders began to use hard drugs. However, once these career criminals began to use expensive drugs like heroin regularly, their criminal activity tends to escalate. Conversely, when they are not involved in regular drug use—such as occurs when they are in treatment—they are considerably less likely to commit crimes (Nurco, Kinlock and Hanlon, 1998, Gentry, 1991, White and Gorman, 2000). In this view, then, the regular use of expensive drugs seems to more frequently amplify criminal behavior rather than cause it.

However, the links between regular drug use and criminality do not stop there; drugs can also be linked to the prolonging of criminal careers (White and Gorman, 2000, Gentry, 1991). The thinking here is that offenders, who might otherwise age out of criminal careers between age 17 and 22 (Steffensmeier and Allan, 1995) persist in crime because of their need to support an expensive drug habit that would be likely to last longer than a criminal career. Indeed early research suggests that drug careers tend to outlast criminal careers as 40 years ago, heroin addicts often did not age out of their addictions until age 35 (Winick, 1962). More recent survey research on drug users, who begin experimenting in high school, also indicates that many do not age out of drug use till their late twenties and early thirties (Bachman, Wadsworth, O'Malley, Johnston and Schulenberg, 1997). Since individuals may age out of drugs so late, it is conceivable that drug dependence could lead to an extended career in crime.

Based on this evidence of a strong link between drug use and prolonged, frequent offending, it comes as no surprise that drug use was one of the background characteristics used as a predictor of future criminality. Indeed prediction scales developed in research on incapacitation allowed indicators of prior drug use to count heavily in labeling an inmate high-risk (see Table 1). Because these prediction scales assigned such weight to drug use, they had the effect of converting drug use and drug sales into much more serious crimes than they had been previously (U.S. Sentencing Commission, 1995). In fact, these prediction scales were assigning greater weight to drug use in the1980s even as drug use levels were plummeting (Bachman, Johnston and O'Malley, 1990). Based on the aforementioned assumptions about the drug-crime link, drug use became an increasingly important factor in understanding criminal careers as use seemed to be tied to the frequency of offending and to the prolonging of criminal careers.

Because a history of drug use became an important predictor of future high-rate criminal activity, being sentenced to prison for a nonviolent drug law violation like heroin use took on new meaning. Depending on the nature of a heroin user's prior criminal career, they could be deemed to be as high risk as someone in prison for robbery and could get an equally long sentence. For example, an individual convicted for the crime of heroin *use* could be labeled high-risk if they had a particular type of history that indicated they had been unemployed for much of the prior 2 years, had juvenile convictions before age 16, had been committed to a juvenile institution and had begun heroin use as a juvenile (see Table 1). Since heroin users with these traits were seen as very likely to recidivate, the incapacitation literature suggested that such persons, convicted for the nonviolent crime of heroin use, should be punished severely because their heroin use was a portent of future criminal activity.

Yet many of the same problems that make it difficult to use prior criminal history as a predictor of future crime also make it difficult to use a prior history of drug use as a predictor of recidivism. Once again, because criminal careers do not proceed along a predictable path, it is difficult to distinguish those offenders who are most likely to offend at a high level in the future from those who are not. And much like before, a prior record that includes serious violent crimes is not a sure predictor that an individual offender will persist in serious violent crimes on release. Conversely, an offender with a history of minor, nonviolent crimes may or may not escalate into serious violent crime on release (Visher, 1995, Walker, 1994).

In short, knowing that an inmate with a history of prior bad acts has used drugs adds nothing to current understanding regarding the dynamics of a criminal career. A history of drug law violations cannot be seen as an indicator that an inmate will commit serious violent crimes, property crimes or indeed any predatory crimes at all upon release. Hence, prediction scales that include background characteristics like a prior history of drug use are likely to produce the same types of false positive and false negative errors that emerge when prior criminal history is used as a predictor of recidivism.

As noted previously, it is also difficult to develop accurate career trajectories because criminologists simply do not know how many years of criminal activity are left for any given offender who enters prison; this makes it impossible to say how much crime will be averted while they are in prison. Since much of the literature suggests that adult criminal careers last six years on average, it is conceivable that by the time an offender enters prison, much of his criminal career may be over. If drug involvement can potentially prolong the criminal career of predators, as some of the literature linking drugs and crime suggests, there is no way of knowing by how much. There simply is a dearth of research on whether drugs actually extend criminal careers. This means that for those inmates with convictions for nonviolent drug law violations and/or predatory crimes, there is no way of knowing if their careers in drug-related offending are likely to end during their stint in prison.

The Drug/Crime Link and Changing Drug Markets

The fact that the irregular progression of criminal careers defies all efforts at accurate prediction means that using background characteristics like prior criminal acts or prior drug use to predict recidivism is likely to lead to a good deal of error. As noted, false positive errors occur when these background characteristics predict that some inmates will recidivate and these inmates fail to recidivate as predicted. In fact, a case could be made that false positive error may have worsened in recent years as the prison population has shifted to include a larger proportion of nonviolent drug law violators. In 1980, a mere 6% of those admitted to prison had violated drug laws (use or sale of illegal drugs).

Yet, by 1998, fully 30.8 percent of those admitted to state prisons were drug law violators (Lindesmith Center, 1999, Beck, 2000). Not only do prisons now incapacitate many more nonviolent drug law violators than they did 20 years ago, they also include many more inmates who used or sold cocaine and crack-cocaine. By contrast, inmates imprisoned for drug violations 20 years ago were much more likely to include those who used and/or sold heroin. This may present a problem as prediction scales in the incapacitation literature suggested that there were strong links between heroin use and predatory crimes. Hence, it is not entirely clear whether crack and cocaine users and sellers who are now in prison will be more, less or equally likely to turn to crimes as the heroin using inmates that were measured in traditional prediction scales (see Table 1).

If it is assumed that crack and heroin use are about equally likely to amplify or prolong criminal activity, then it is possible to use traditional incapacitation research to argue that the imprisonment of numerous cocaine and crack-involved offenders in today's prisons would lead to reductions in crime. On the face of it, this argument seems reasonable as daily use of heroin or binge use of crack can both be very expensive. Hence, both drugs would seem to have the potential to cause an amplification of offending.

However, it is conceivable that crack-involved offenders might not be as inclined to commit numerous instrumental crimes like robberies or burglaries to support their habits as the heroin-involved offenders of yore. After all, in its heyday, the crack market was a much larger market with many more users than the heroin market (Johnston, O'Malley and Bachman, 1997, SAMHSA, 1996). The crack trade was also a higher volume business at its peak than the heroin trade as unit doses of crack last less time than unit doses of heroin. This means that a crack buyer would have needed to rely on more sellers than a heroin buyer (Riley, 1997). Because the crack market was larger, it would have provided crack involved offenders with more job opportunities within the market.

Furthermore, the profits to be realized from selling crack at the height of its popularity were higher than profits for heroin or any other drug (Reuter, MacCoun and Murphy, 1990). In fact, the profits to be realized from crack selling compared favorably to those to be realized from predatory crimes like personal robberies or residential burglaries.

Indeed some career criminals may actually have cut back on their predatory crimes and turned to nonviolent crack selling since the profits to be realized might have been greater than those for non-drug crimes.

In light of all this, the large and highly profitable crack market might have absorbed many offenders in nonviolent, consensual drug transactions, thereby turning them away from their predatory crimes. For these reasons, the relationship between crack and instrumental crimes like robbery and burglary might not be as strong as was true with heroin and instrumental crimes. This raises questions about assuming that crack has the capacity to amplify involvement in instrumental crimes like robbery and burglary, based on research that was conducted on the link between heroin and predatory crime.

In fact, there is evidence to suggest that the crack epidemic of the late 1980s and early 1990s did not lead to more instrumental crime. According to national victimization data, property crime rates actually fell during the late 1980s and early 1990s during the peak of the crack epidemic—particularly crimes like burglary and theft (Bursik, 2000, Chaiken, 2000). Because cocaine and crack users had many more opportunities to turn to nonviolent crack and cocaine selling than the heroin users of two decades ago, the link between drugs and crime may actually be weaker than it was in the past. Hence the already questionable utility of drug history as a predictor of criminal recidivism may actually have declined over the years with the rise in a larger and more profitable drug market. Because a larger and more profitable drug market might actually have contributed to a de-escalation in criminal careers as criminals turned from robberies and burglaries to nonviolent drug transactions, the link between drugs and predatory crime may be weaker with crack than it was with heroin. Hence, over the years, the potential for false positive error may actually have increased.

The Potential for an Inflated Drug/Crime Link

Even if many of today's crack and cocaine users have more opportunities to choose nonviolent drug transactions over less profitable instrumental crimes, there is still evidence of a strong drug/crime link among those who are actually incapacitated. For example, a 1997 survey of state prisoners indicates that fully 83 percent reported lifetime use of some illegal substance and 69.6 percent reported weekly use of drugs in at least one period in their lifetimes (Mumola, 1999). More to the point many inmates actually reported that they were using drugs at the time they committed the crimes for which they were incarcerated. For example, 39.9 percent of robbers and 38.4 percent of burglars reported that they were under the influence of an illegal drug at the time they committed their offense (Mumola, 1999). Hence, the fact that so many of the robbers and burglars in prison have used drugs may mean that policies that focus on imprisoning drug law violators could result in the incapacitation of the most likely recidivists even in the absence of accurate prediction scales.

Auerhahn (1999) makes this argument as she claims that the most active criminals commit so many crimes that their chances of being arrested and imprisoned rise accordingly. This means that high rate robbers and burglars are most likely to end up in prison simply because they are so criminally active. That so many of these robbers and burglars in prison also use drugs seems to offer support for the notion of a strong link between drug use and frequent offending.

However, there are reasons to question this seemingly strong correlation between drugs and high-rate offending. For while criminal predators in prison report very high levels of drug use, they may not be the most active of offenders. It is conceivable that their overrepresentation in prison populations is due to their greater tendency to get caught. Because their drug use undermines their ability to commit crime in ways so that they avoid getting caught, many of them may end up in jail or prison populations. Indeed because their regular drug use and frequent intoxication may limit their ability to get away from a crime scene, they may be arrested at a much higher frequency than 'true' high rate non-using criminals. Hence their extensive criminal records may be a better measure of their penchant for committing crime while intoxicated rather than their actual offending patterns.

The fact that frequent intoxication may make drug involved offenders look like high rate offenders raises the possibility that too much may have been made of the drug-crime link in the captive samples where this link has been tested. The notion that there is a strong drug-crime link because drugs amplify criminal behavior may need further testing in a sample that does not rely upon captive populations. After all, if regular drug use increases the chances of being arrested and imprisoned or forced into treatment, then there is a possibility that the drug-crime link will be inflated in a captive population whose drug use makes them more subject to capture (i.e., prison, arrestee and treatment samples).

In fact, when surveys are conducted with users that are not a part of captive populations, the drug/crime link is actually weak to nonexistent. Indeed a survey conducted with a nationally representative sample of youth indicated that fewer than 5% of the respondents reported involvement in both frequent drug use and serious crime (White and Gorman, 2000). This suggests that the strong drug/crime link, routinely cited in the incapacitation literature, might well reflect a tendency of this research to rely on captive samples of prisoners, arrestees and treatment clients mandated to treatment by the criminal justice system. The fact that a strong drug/crime link depends on the sample is especially troubling given recent trends in the prison population. For while prisons still include a large number of persons locked up for predatory crimes who are also found to use drugs, they also include many more persons today who are locked up solely for nonviolent drug crimes. It is possible that many of these new nonviolent prisoners who have been imprisoned for drug law violations, do not have the same level of commitment to predatory crimes as traditional populations of robbers and burglars who also use drugs. Because many more nonviolent drug law violators with less commitment to criminal careers are being locked up, it may mean that prisons now offer less crime prevention than ever, even as prison populations have swelled.

All of this suggests that it is simply not possible to use existing prediction scales to distinguish high rate recidivists from those whose recidivism rates are likely to be lower. As one of the predictors of future high rate offending, illicit drug use has not been very helpful in indicating which inmates are likely to do the most harm if left in the community. Hence, when it comes to drugs, it would be difficult to argue that a 20-year experiment in incapacitating larger and larger numbers of drug law violators has brought about aggregate reductions in instrumental crimes like robbery and burglary.

Still there is reason to think that the practice of locking up so many drug law violators in recent years has brought about a reduction in drug-related violence (Chaiken, 2000, Blumstein and Rosenfeld, 1998, Moran, 1997). After all, homicide rates have fallen even as more and more drug users and sellers have been incapacitated. For that reason, the link between the rise in the incapacitation of drug law violators and the decline in the homicide rates will be explored in the next section.

Can Incapacitation of Drug Offenders Bring Down the Homicide Rates?

On its face, the notion that incapacitating more drug offenders could bring down homicide rates is a reasonable one. There is longstanding evidence of a relationship between drugs—especially heroin and cocaine—and homicides (Bureau of Justice Statistics, 1992). Crack, in particular, has been found to have an especially strong relationship to homicide as one study on homicides in New York City indicates that crack was associated with 60 percent of all drug-related murders (Goldstein, Brownstein, Ryan and Belluci, 1997). Moreover, homicides rose in a number of cities with the outbreak of the crack epidemic in the mid-1980s and then proceeded to tumble as crack's popularity declined in the 1990s (Golub and Johnson, 1997).

Presumably drug use is related to homicides because many disputes in illegal drug markets are settled with violence (Goldstein et al., 1997). For example, violence can be used to settle disputes over territory between rival drug dealers or to discipline employees who cheat dealers out of drugs or money. Dealers may also use violence to retaliate against those who rob them of drugs. However, violence is not merely confined to conflicts between drug dealers as buyers may retaliate against dealers who sell them adulterated or bogus drugs. Violence may also arise in the course of drug transactions as users fight among themselves when one user steals drugs from another or refuses to share drugs (Goldstein et al. 1997, Bureau of Justice Statistics 1992). Since all of these conflicts involve illegal transactions, the disputants are not able to go to the police. Hence they must resolve disputes themselves. And because drug disputants actively avoid the police there is no interest in reporting even violent victimizations to the police. This means that much of the violence in the drug market does not get reported to the police unless there is a homicide or serious injury.

In light of this link between drugs and homicide, crack use levels and homicide rates should have risen and fallen in tandem. This was certainly true for adolescents whose crack use and homicide rates rose together in the late 1980's and then fell in the early 1990s (Blumstein and Rosenfeld, 1998, Golub and Johnson, 1997). However, adolescents typically do not end up in prisons, so the fact that so many adult drug law violators have been locked up since the 1980s does not explain these trends in youth homicides (Blumstein and Rosenfeld, 1998). A more likely explanation for the decline in youth homicides that began in the early 1990s is the waning of crack's popularity rather than incapacitation.

Crack's declining popularity may also account for the rise and fall in homicide rates for the traditionally murder-prone 18–24 year old age group. Their homicide rates rose in the late eighties, as crack became more popular in a number of cities. Their homicide rates then fell in the early and mid-nineties as crack became less popular in those same cities (Golub and Johnson, 1997).

Yet even though the waxing and waning of the crack epidemic seems to be the most likely explanation for the recent rise and fall in homicides for this murder-prone age group, an alternative hypothesis has been suggested. It has been argued that the surge in incapacitation that occurred in the late 1980s may have taken so many of these murder-prone 18–24 year olds out of circulation that a number of homicides were averted (Chaiken, 2000, Moran, 1997, Blumstein and Rosenfeld, 1998).

Hence, in this view, incapacitation may have served some useful purpose in preventing drug-related murders. However, any effort to assess how many drug-related homicides were averted due to a rise in the incapacitation of 18–24 year old adult drug law violators would likely be doomed to failure. The reasons why it is so difficult to evaluate whether incapacitation of drug law violators prevents homicides will be discussed in the following sections.

Homicide has no career trajectory.—Traditionally, the notion that incapacitation can prevent crime has rested on an accurate prediction scale. If a propensity for high-rate offending can be accurately predicted and those identified as high-rate can be incapacitated, then it is possible to assert that crime has been prevented. Efforts to assess whether incapacitation has actually prevented crime can then be conducted by following those predicted to be high risk and seeing how many actually commit the anticipated crimes.

While this type of thinking at least seems logical when applied to robberies and burglaries, it is difficult to see how it applies to homicide. Prediction scales can be used with career crimes such as robbery and burglary because inmates may commit many such crimes each year. For these crimes, a prior record of robberies and burglaries is used to make predictions about how many such crimes will be averted while the offender is in prison. However, unlike most robbers and burglars, murderers only commit one homicide; therefore, there is no way to look at prior criminal history and predict who is most likely to kill in the future. Because there is usually no such thing as a career in murder (except for serial killers), there can be no career trajectory. The 'best' predictor of future homicides might be a history of aggravated assaults. However, even a history of aggravated assaults cannot be considered an especially good predictor since so few of them end in murder.

Even if a history of violence were taken to be a predictor, there would be no reason to believe that the massive rise in the incapacitation of drug law violators brought down the murder rates. This is because so few of those actually imprisoned for drug crimes seem to have violent prior records. For example, a mere 15.6 percent of those in state prisons for drug law violations had violent prior records in 1991 as drug-related homicide rates neared their peak and only 23.6 percent had violent records in 1997 after drug-related homicide rates had begun their decline (Lynch and Sabol 1997, Mumola 1999).

It is impossible to incapacitate a violent behavior setting.—It is also difficult to demonstrate that locking up more drug law violators can prevent drug related homicides because the rise and fall of drug related homicides has more to do with the size of a disputatious drug market rather than individual propensities. Incapacitation works when *individual* high rate offenders are accurately identified and then put in prison longer. Yet the rise in homicides that accompanied the crack epidemic might be better understood in terms of changes in a behavior setting rather than changes in the violent propensities of individuals. This is because drug-related murders are tied more to situations rather than to the propensity to kill in any individual inmate.

Put differently, the emergence of an epidemic of heroin or crack use may be associated with a rise in disputes that end in severe injury or death because the increased popularity of these illegal drugs has the capacity to temporarily change the behavior setting in a community. Perhaps this can be illustrated by comparing behavior settings in epidemic years to those that exist in non-epidemic years.

In non-epidemic years when drugs like heroin, crack and cocaine are not popular, disputes that end in homicide or assault typically occur over trivial issues such as insults or perceived threats to honor (Luckenbill and Doyle, 1989, Oliver, 1994, Felson, Baccaglini and Gmelch, 1986, Messerschmidt, 1993, Covington, 1999, Covington, forthcoming). However, during the years of a heroin or cocaine epidemic, conflict over drugs is likely to be more serious and intense than the everyday disagreements that mark the non-epidemic years. There may be more at stake when conflicts occur over drug related profits or when disagreements arise about the sharing or theft of an expensive, addictive commodity like drugs than there is when conflicts occur over everyday insults. The epidemic in crack-cocaine certainly seems to have been accompanied by a rise in disputatiousness as indicated by the parallel rise in homicides among adolescents. By contrast, as an epidemic ends and drugs decline in popularity, it may also signal the decline in the number of serious issues that are likely to generate such heated disputes.

Because the propensity for violence lies in the intensity of the situation or the setting and not the individual, the incapacitation of drug-involved *individuals* is not likely to have much effect on drug-related violence. After all, incapacitation involves picking off individuals involved in violence one by one. Yet even as violent individuals are picked off, violent crime rates in the community can remain high as long as the highly disputatious behavior setting remains intact.

Drug-related violent disputes are the property of a market and not an individual; hence violence declines when markets decline.—While the incapacitation of violent individuals can do little to reduce aggregate levels of violence, the waning of a drug epidemic can send aggregate homicide rates into a nosedive. When drug epidemics go on the wane, markets contract as fewer new users enter the market. This means that there are fewer buyers and sellers. Thus there are fewer people available to get involved in drug-related disputes. It is this decline in the epidemic and the number of potential disputants in the market, then, which accounts for the drop in drug-related violence. Because drug-related disputes are the property of a market, and not of an individual, picking off violent individuals one by one and putting them in prison is not likely to have much effect on a violent drug market.

Separating violent propensities of individuals from neighborhood effects.—The incapacitation argument is also flawed because it assumes that individuals with an ongoing propensity for violence can be identified and locked up to reduce homicides. However, drug related homicides may frequently not be committed by those with an ongoing identifiable propensity for violence. In fact, many drug users incarcerated for homicides that grow out of drug-related disputes may have no appetite for violence. Their involvement in disputes that end in homicides is likely to have an almost accidental quality making it impossible to predict their likely involvement *before it occurs.* For them, assaults, homicides and gun possession may be *defensive* acts to protect themselves when they encounter those who would precipitate violence in the course of buying and selling drugs. The fact that such individuals are likely to have a prior record of involvement in serious violent crimes, then, may have more to do with their residence in a neighborhood with a violent drug market rather than their own propensity for violent behavior. (See Covington, 1999 for a more general discussion of this topic.) In short, it is the individual user's need to act defensively in the face of constant exposure to drug-related disputes that explains violent acts in his career.

Hence a nonviolent person in a neighborhood with a violent drug market could be expected to be involved in more assaults than similarly nonviolent individuals who buy and sell drugs in a neighborhood with a less violent drug market. The former would have more assaults simply because of the disputatious nature of the neighborhood drug market. However, the involvement in drug related violence would not be an indicator of a greater propensity for violence relative to that of a person living in a neighborhood with a peaceful market. Indeed because it is impossible to separate neighborhood effects from individual propensities, a criminal record for drug-related assaults cannot distinguish those who routinely precipitate disputes from those who only seek to defend themselves. This means that simply locking up those involved in drug related violence in violent neighborhoods may not prevent violence. In such cases, homicides and assaults are simply responded to after the fact rather than averted. There is no evidence that homicides and assaults are prevented while they are in prison since their involvement in violence is a product of chance. If there is no evidence of a career in homicide, then locking them up cannot be said to prevent homicides.

In sum, because reductions in violence can only come about if a neighborhood's drug markets become less violent, a policy that locks up individuals without changing the neighborhood context cannot be expected to have much effect on violence reduction. This points up broader problems with a policy such as incapacitation that can only work with crimes where an identifiable individual violent career criminal or chronic offender commits a lot of crimes. Such a policy cannot reduce crimes that are the product of interactions in a violent setting. After all, whole violent behavior settings cannot be incapacitated. In light of the obvious limits of incapacitating individuals, it may be time to shift the focus to policies that can reduce violence that is the product of a setting.

Summary and Conclusions

In the late 1970s, the U.S. had just experienced a drug revolution and illegal drug use levels were near their peak. At that point, very few people were actually in prison for drug use and drug sales. However, by the 1980s, even as drug use levels began to tumble, conservative policymakers began to urge a crack down on drugs. Hence the incarceration of drug law violators began a steep upward climb even as drug use levels went into freefall.

In part, drug policy became unhinged from actual trends in drug use in the 1980s because the notion that locking up some drug law violators (especially minority drug law violators) could reduce drug-related crime and violence was gaining currency. After all, the evidence clearly showed that drug use and drug sales were both linked to crime and violence in the ghettos. Hence, it was easy to conclude that "get-tough" policies that ended in the incarceration of a growing number of minority drug law violators over the last 20 years had prevented predatory acts of drug-related crime and violence. If these drug users and sellers had not been locked up, the reasoning went, they would have been at large in the community to commit drug-related crimes and foment drug-related violence. Presumably by incapacitating more and more of them, we have made them incapable of preying on the law abiding public. Hence, in this view, the declines in crime and violence that occurred in the 1990s can, in part, be attributed to this massive surge in the incapacitation of drug offenders that began in the 1980s.

In this paper, I have reviewed and critiqued the research on incapacitation that encouraged these notions and bolstered some of the draconian drug policies that have been put in place in the past two decades. Because there is little reason to believe that the imprisonment of so many minority drug law violators has had an effect on crime and violence, it is difficult to explain why we continue to fill our prisons with these nonviolent drug users and sellers. Perhaps these policies will change if more attention is paid to the limits of this punitive and costly approach to grappling with the nation's drug problem.

In fact, the need to re-examine drug policy could not be more urgent, for by the year 2000, there were 2 million people incarcerated in U.S. jails and prisons out of a total of 8 million persons incarcerated worldwide. This means that the U.S., with less than 5 percent of the world's population, has 25 percent of the world's prison population. Because nearly one-quarter of our now very large inmate population consists of nonviolent drug users and sellers, many think we are wasting expensive prison space on persons who cannot help us effect the promised reduction in serious and violent crime. Nearly all the research reviewed in this paper casts doubt on the crime-reducing potential of locking up nonviolent drug law violators and thereby supports initiatives that might lead to a reversal of these cruel and costly policies.

References

Auerhahn, K. (1999). Selective Incapacitation and the Problem of Prediction. *Criminology,* 37 (4):703–734.

Bachman, J., L.D. Johnston, and P. O'Malley (1990). Explaining the Recent Decline in Cocaine Use among Young Adults. *Journal of Health and Social Behavior,* 31:173–184.

Bachman, J., K. Wadsworth, P. O'Malley, L. Johnston and J. Schulenberg (1997). *Smoking, Drinking and Drug Use in Young Adulthood.* Mahwah, NJ: Lawrence Erlbaum Associates.

Beck, A. (2000). Prisoners in 1999. Bureau of Justice Statistics Bulletin, August 2000.

Blumstein, A. and R. Rosenfeld (1998). Assessing the Recent Ups and Downs in US. Homicide Rates. *National Institute of Justice Journal,* (October 1998): 8–11.

Bureau of Justice Statistics (1992). *Drugs, Crime and the Justice System.* Washington, D.C.: US Department of Justice, Office of Justice Programs, Bureau of Justice Statistics.

Bursik, R. (2000). Property Crime Trends. In J. Sheley (Ed.), *Criminology: A Contemporary Handbook, Third Edition.* 215–231 Belmont, CA: Wadsworth, 2000.

Chaiken, J. (2000). Crunching Numbers: Crime and Incarceration at the End of the Millennium. *National Institute of Justice Journal* (January 2000): 10–17.

Covington, J. (1999). African American Communities and Violent Crime: The Construction of Race Differences. *Sociological Focus* 32 (1): 7–24.

Covington, J. (2001). Round Up the Usual Suspects: Racial Profiling and the War on Drugs. In D. Milovanovic and K. Russell (Eds.) *Petit Apartheid in the U.S. Criminal Justice System: The Dark Figure of Racism.* 27–42 Durham, N.C.: Carolina Academic Press, 2001.

Covington, J. (forthcoming). The Violent Black Male: Conceptions of Race in Criminological Theories. In D. F. Hawkins (Ed.) *Violent Crime: The Nexus of Race, Ethnicity and Class.* New York: Cambridge.

Felson, R., W. Baccaglini and G. Gmelch (1986). Bar-Room Brawls. In A. Campbell and J. Gibbs (Eds.) *Violent Transactions.* Oxford: Basil Blackwell.

Gentry, C. (1991). Drugs and Crime. In J. Sheley (Ed.) *Criminology: A Contemporary Handbook.* Belmont, CA: Wadsworth.

Goldstein, P., H. Brownstein, P. Ryan and P. Belluci (1997). Crack and Homicide in New York City: A Case Study in the Epidemiology of Violence. In C. Reinarman and H. Levine (Eds.) *Crack in America: Demon Drugs and Social Justice.* Berkeley, CA: University of California Press.

Golub, A. and B. Johnson (1997). Crack's Decline: Some Surprises Across US Cities. Research in Brief, Washington,D.C.: US Department of Justice, National Institute of Justice, July 1997.

Greenwood, P. and A. Abrahamse (1982). *Selective Incapacitation.* Santa Monica, CA: Rand.

Human Rights Watch (2000). *Punishment and Prejudice: Racial Disparities in the War on Drugs* (accessed online: hrw.org/reports/2000/usa/Rcedrg00.htm)

Johnston, L.D., P. O'Malley and J. Bachman (1997). *Drug Use Among American High School Seniors, College Students and Young Adults, 1975–1995, Volumes I, II.* Rockville, MD: National Institute on Drug Abuse.

Justice Policy Institute (2000). *Poor Prescription: The Costs of Imprisoning Drug \Offenders in the United States.* (accessed online: cjcj.org/drug/pp.html)

Lindesmith Center (1999). *Research Brief: Drug Prohibition and the U.S. Prison System.* (accessed online:lindesmith.org/cites-sources/brief13.html)

Lynch, J. and W. Sabol (1997). Did Getting Tough on Crime Pay? *Crime Policy Report.* Washington, D.C.: Urban Institute.

Luckenbill, D. and D. Doyle (1989). Structural Position and Violence. *Criminology* 27 (3):419–436.

Messerschmidt, J. (1993). *Masculinities and Crime.* Lanham, MD: Rowman and Littlefield.

Moran, R. (1997). The New York Story: More Luck Than Policing. *Washington Post National Weekly Edition*, February 17–23, 1997.

Mumola, C. (1999). *Substance Abuse and Treatment, State and Federal Prisoners, 1997.* Washington, D.C.: Bureau of Justice Statistics, Special Report.

Nurco, D. T. Kinlock and T. Hanlon (1998). The Drugs—Crime Connection. In J. Inciardi and K. McElrath (Eds.), *The American Drug Scene.*

Office of Applied Studies, Substance Abuse and Mental Health Services Administration, U.S. Department of Health and Human Services (2000). *Summary of Findings from the 1999 National Household Survey on Drug Abuse.* Washington, D.C.: SAMHSA.

Oliver, W. (1994). *The Violent Social World of Black Men.* New York: Lexington.

Reuter, P., R. MacCoun, and P. Murphy (1990). *Money from Crime: A Study of the Economics of Drug Dealing in Washington,D.C.* Santa Monica: Rand

Riley, K.J. (1997). *Crack, Powder Cocaine and Heroin: Drug Purchase and Use Patterns in Six US Cities.* Washington, D.C.: Office of National Drug Control Policy and National Institute of Justice.

SAMHSA (1996). National Household Survey on Drug Abuse: Population Estimates. Rockville, MD: SAMHSA, Office of Applied Studies.

Steffensmeier, D. and E. Allan (1995). Criminal Behavior: Gender and Age. In J. Sheley (Ed.), *Criminology: A Contemporary Handbook.* 83–113 Belmont, CA: Wadsworth.

U.S. Sentencing Commission (1995). *Cocaine and Federal Sentencing Policy.* Special Report to Congress.

Visher, C. (1995). Career Offenders and Crime Control. In J. Sheley (Ed.), *Criminology: A Contemporary Handbook.* Belmont, CA: Wadsworth.

Walker, S. (1994). *Sense and Nonsense About Crime and Drugs: A Policy Guide.* Belmont, CA: Wadsworth.

White, H.R. and D. Gorman (2000). Dynamics of the Drug-Crime Relationship. In G. LaFree (Ed.), *The Nature of Crime: Continuity and Change. Criminal Justice 2000, Vol.1* Washington, D.C.: National Institute of Justice.

Winick, C. (1962). Maturing Out of Narcotic Addiction. *Bulletin on Narcotics* 16: 1–11.

"The Wide and Unreasonable Reach of California's Three Strikes Law"

Doug Kieso J.D.,
University of California, Irvine

Gilbert Geis,
University of California, Irvine

Introduction

Supporters of California's Three Strikes law claim that it is being used to keep "professional thieves," "career criminals," and "violent criminals" out of circulation (Lungren, 1996; Westerman, 1999). This claim was used when the law was passed in 1994, and is still used today to support the law. That support seems to be waning, however, as the reality of what has happened is contrasted to what voters believed they were approving (Ricciardulli, 2001).

This chapter looks at four Three Strike stories and offers comments that are based on hundreds of letters received from prisoners, as well as official statistics, case files, appellate court opinions, news articles, and interviews with defense attorneys, prosecutors, government officials, and family members and friends of prisoners who have been sentenced under the state's Three Strikes law.

The results paint a picture contrary to that presented by the supporters of the Three Strikes law. Although we did not have access to the records of the entire population of Three Strikers and our sample is not random, many of the cases we reviewed demonstrate that there are a significant number of people sentenced under the Three Strikes law who are not "professional" thieves in terms of making a living from crime, but rather can be characterized as committing small-time property offenses to support their drug addiction. In addition, contrary to being "violent" episodes, a significant number of cases we reviewed show an offender who has never been convicted of a crime that has physically harmed another person.

California's Three Strikes Law

On March 7, 1994, California Governor Pete Wilson signed into law AB (that is, Assembly Bill) 971. On November 8 of the same year, California voters by a referendum decision endorsed Proposition 184. AB 971 became encoded in the statutes as part of California Penal Code Section 667, and proposition 184 became Penal Code Section 1170.12. Both Three Strikes laws are virtually identical.

More than 28 states and the federal government have enacted "Three Strikes" laws since the State of Washington first did so in November of 1993 (Clark et al., 1997). California, the second state to pass such a law, stands out because of notably draconian elements of its statute (Vitiello, 1997:397). While the vast majority of jurisdictions require that their Strikes law can be triggered only by a "serious" or "violent" felony, California allows the last strike to be "*any* felony." The California law has drawn criticism from the promoter of Washington's Strikes Law, David La Course, who has stated that California's broad approach "has hurt the movement" (Litvan, 1998).

On close examination, one realizes that the California Three Strikes law is actually two different statutes or sentencing schemes. One part states that any person who has one prior "serious" or "violent" felony and then commits another felony will have the sentence doubled. Many observers call this the "two-strike" part of the law. The other, more publicized, element of the law states that any person who has two or more prior "serious" or "violent" felonies and then commits another felony will receive a minimum sentence of 25 years to life. This is generally referred to as the "three-strike" part of the law. "Serious" and "violent" overlap in many areas, and range from the more heinous crimes of murder, rape, and assault causing serious bodily harm, to robbery, arson, and burglary of a residence, even if the dwelling is unoccupied.

Both parts of the law are controversial, though for different reasons. The two-strike part is seen by some as having the greatest impact on the rapidly escalating number of people incarcerated in California prisons. As of March 31, 2001, there were 59,975 prisoners who had been convicted and were serving a sentence under the two-strike provision (California Department of Corrections, 2001). Combined with the decrease in allowable good-time credits spurred by the "Truth-in-Sentencing" legislation passed by the U.S. Congress in 1994, the average term served by two-strikers is more than three times what they would have had to serve prior to 1994.

The three-strike part of the law, on the other hand, has not materially increased the prison populations—yet—but it is controversial because of what many consider to be sentences that can be mercilessly out of line with the seriousness of the current felony. As of March 31, 2001, there were 6,700 people sentenced under the three-strike provisions who were serving a minimum term of 25 years to life (California Department of Corrections, 2001). Of that total, 332 had committed a third felony of petty-theft with a prior. For 634 people, the sentencing offense was the possession of a controlled substance, for 154, it was receiving stolen property, and for 380, it was the possession of a weapon. Aggregated numbers indicate that 1,234 of the 6,700 offenses were drug-related (possession, manufacturing, and sale) and only 42.15 percent were "crimes against persons" (See Table 1).

Table 1. Second and Third Strike Cases*
by Offense Group, March 31, 2001

	Second Strike Cases		Third Strike Cases	
	Frequency Count	Percent of Total Frequency	Frequency Count	Percent of Total Frequency
Missing	843	1.7	67	1.0
Murder 1st	108	0.2	117	1.7
Murder 2nd	221	0.4	93	1.4
Manslaughter	138	0.3	25	0.4
Vehicular Manslaughter	44	0.1	6	0.1
Robbery	4,034	8.1	1,229	18.3
Assault Deadly Weapon	2,095	4.2	320	4.8
Other Assault/ Battery	2,617	5.2	396	5.9
Rape	165	0.3	113	1.7
Lewd Act with Child	451	0.9	182	2.7
Oral Copulation	57	0.1	42	0.6
Sodomy	18	0.0	16	0.2
Penetration with Object	43	0.1	15	.2
Other Sex Offenses	1,300	2.6	134	2.0
Kidnapping	134	0.3	69	1.0
Burglary 1st	2,534	5.1	722	10.8
Burglary 2nd	3,594	7.2	439	6.6
Grand Theft	1,343	2.7	100	1.5
Petty Theft with Prior	4,551	9.1	332	5.0
Receiving Stolen Property	1,443	2.9	154	2.3
Vehicle Theft	1,912	3.8	203	3.0

Forgery/Fraud	871	1.7	60	0.9
Other Property Offenses	266	0.5	32	0.5
Cont. Sub. Possession	10,182	20.3	634	9.5
C. S. Poss. for Sale, Etc.	2,877	5.7	273	4.1
Cont. Sub. Sales, Etc.	1,513	3.0	182	2.7
Cont. Sub. Manuf.	196	0.4	24	0.4
Cont. Sub. Other	548	1.1	89	1.3
Hashish Possession	11	0.0	–	–
Marij. Possess. for Sale	489	1.0	6	0.1
Marijuana Sales	224	0.4	25	0.4
Other Marijuana Offenses	42	0.1	1	0.0
Escape	275	0.5	34	0.5
Driving Under Infl.	529	1.1	35	0.5
Arson	123	0.2	22	0.3
Possession of Weapon	3,149	6.3	380	5.7
Other Offenses	1,135	2.3	129	1.9
Total	50,075	100.0	6,700	100.0

*Source: California Department of Corrections—Data Analysis Unit.

In many ways, the story of the California Three Strikes law is symptomatic of the social and political "lock 'em up and throw away the key" attitude across the United States (National Criminal Justice Commission, 1996; Baum, 1997; Parenti, 1999). But the story of the California Three Strikes law has some differences. It is being applied to people who have committed a current felony that can be as petty as stealing a pair of jeans from a store, or having possession of less than a tenth of a gram of cocaine.

Usually the California Three Strikes law is not mandatory. Under *People v. Superior Court (Romero)*, judges have limited discretion in regard to the application of the law, though they tend to be extremely wary of appearing to the electorate as being tough enough on criminals by exercising such discretion. Also, the political scenery is different in California than in most states because the prison guard union has grown into a powerful force that will deliver millions of dollars to politicians who favor the union's policy of increasing the prison population.

Passage of California's Three Strikes Law

The impetus for California's Three Strikes law was the kidnapping and murder of Polly Klaas. Prior to Polly's death, the legislative sponsor of the Three Strikes law, Mike Reynolds, whose daughter had been murdered by a purse snatcher, had failed to get the Three Strikes bill out of committee in the spring of 1993 and had been able to obtain only about 15,000 signatures for his proposed ballot initiative during the first month of solicitation (Vitiello, 1997). Within a few days of the highly publicized death of Polly Klaas in the fall of 1993, Reynolds obtained an additional 50,000 signatures, and the Three Strikes initiative became the fastest qualifying ballot in California history (Vitiello, 1997). Reynolds, now able to argue that the public was strongly behind him, convinced the California legislature to enact the Three Strikes law. Politicians, fearful of appearing "soft on crime," managed to pass the "Three Strikes" law as an emergency statute, making it effective immediately. They also incorporated a provision requiring a two-thirds legislative vote or a public initiative to delete or amend the statute. Reynolds, perhaps pressured by politicians running for election who wanted to use it as a campaign issue, or perhaps fearful that the appellate courts would nullify the emergency statute, decided to put his initiative on the ballot anyway. It was passed by a 72 percent majority on November 8, 1994.

The public's emotional outrage and desire to keep another "Polly" from being murdered was the most significant reason for approval of the Three Strikes law. But such a response did not occur in a vacuum. California, and the United States in general, had been marching towards tougher laws and longer sentences for almost two decades, ever since the Nixon administration initiated the "War on Drugs" (Baum, 1997). Political rhetoric, combined with the media's increasing coverage of "true crime" stories, had helped fuel and distort the public's fear of crime (Patterson, 1994; Shuster, 1998). Politicians who might have been inclined to stand up against the "tough on crime" groups instead have tried to outdo them by pushing forward their own "punitive" statutes. In California, the Democrats helped to get the Three Strikes law through the legislature in hopes that it would not become a campaign issue for the incumbent Republican governor to use in the upcoming state elections. After twelve years of a Republican governor, Democrats desperately wanted a change. They were wrong in their gamble, however. Despite the Democrats effort to demonstrate that they could be just as tough on crime, Republican Governor Pete Wilson won another four-year term (Richardson, 1996).

Who Is Locked Up Under the Three Strikes Law?

In interviews with friends and family members of Three Strikers, we found many who voted for the law, but had no idea that it would be so easily applied to a family member or a friend of theirs. Sam Clauder, a subcontractor who employed people to gather signatures for the Three Strikes initiative, said that he had not, himself, looked at the details of the initiative and that he had been told by its promoters that it would be for "violent offenders only." This was the pitch that his employees used when seeking signatures. Michael J. Moore's video documentary, "The Legacy," shows that California politicians running for election in 1994 strongly endorsed the Three Strikes law, and that most of the time they talked about the law's application to "violent" offenders. Marc Klaas, Polly's father, stated: "That was the only message that was ever given out—that Three Strikes was a way to get violent offenders off the streets." (Moore, 1998).

Several years later, the supporters of the Three Strikes law still try to paint the people who have been locked up under the law as "evil," "violent," and "professional criminals." At a debate on the Three Strikes law at Chapman University on October 6, 1999, John Bacin, a deputy district attorney in Orange County, told the audience that it was "evil people," who were targeted by Three Strikes laws. In a column published in the *Los Angeles Times*, Ted Westerman stated: "Because few criminals specialize in only violent crimes, the majority of those going to prison under the three-strikes law are professional felons. Many have committed violent crimes in the past and, if surprised or confronted, would do so again."

Is this true? Are Three Strikers really all "professional" criminals? Have they really all "committed violent crimes in the past?" If surprised or confronted, would they "do so again?"

California's Three Strikes law's broad language allows people to talk about it in a way that can stigmatize everybody sentenced under the law. Murderers and rapists are "averaged" together with burglars, petty thieves, and drug users. The *Sacramento Bee* analyzed a random sample of 233 cases and reported that the "average" person sentenced under the Three Strikes law has had five prior felony convictions (Favre, 1996). Gregg McClain, the deputy district attorney who supervises Three Strikes cases in San Diego County, claimed in a 1999 televised debate on KCET-Los Angeles that the "average" person sentenced in San Diego County as a third striker has had "six prior felony convictions, four to six misdemeanors, and four prior prison commitments." But should the "average" be the factor when the major controversy revolves around the law's being too far-reaching? Is the Three Strikes law an "all-

or-nothing" concept? Or, are there parts of the California law that can be amended to make it more equitable and fair to society and to those who are subjected to incarceration under it?

The question of who is locked up under California's Three Strike law is not an easy one to research and answer. Judges, attorneys, administrators, and others see only a small portion of the criminal justice system and do not have the time or the means to investigate the whole picture. The best overall statistics available are breakdowns by the last felony only (see Table 1).

Methodology of Our Investigation

Our inquiry is not concerned with the overall picture of the Three Strikes law. Instead we focus on that part that allows nonviolent and non-serious offenders to receive what are grossly disproportionate sentences in terms of the crime committed.

The first author has worked with an organization called Families to Amend California's Three Strikes (FACTS) and thereby has been able to interview many family members, friends, and attorneys of people incarcerated under the Three Strikes law. He also has been able to review letters sent to FACTS by prisoners. The letters include waivers by the prisoners allowing media disclosure of what is written. We have not indicated the names of the public defenders, deputy district attorneys, and other government employees who were interviewed as they were apprehensive about having supervisors attach their identities to their comments.

The stories set forth below were verified by discussions with family members, attorneys, review of case files, probation reports, court opinions, and/or newspaper articles. They are not necessarily "typical" Three Strike stories. Instead, they represent cases that might be considered the more unjust. Once again, our concern is not with finding the "typical" or "average" striker, but rather learning how far the law reaches into the realm of what might reasonably be considered unjust or draconian sentences.

Shane Reams

On May 22 1996, Shane Reams, who is half white and half Hawaiian, was found guilty by an Orange County jury of aiding and abetting the sale of a controlled substance (crack cocaine with a street value of $20). The evidence against Shane was that he was standing thirty feet away from the transaction; the prosecutor painted him as the "lookout." Prior to the trial, his private defense attorney had assured Shane and his family that he probably would get only a year in prison. This was the first Three Strikes case to be handled by this attorney who, after the trial, said she wished she had known more about the law. Because Shane had two prior burglaries on his record, and a dozen or so minor felonies and misdemeanors, Judge Richard Luesebrink said he was going to refuse to invoke his discretionary power. He sentenced Shane to 25 years-to-life under the Three Strikes law. Shane acquired his prior "serious" felonies in 1990, at the age of 21, when he broke into his mother's and a couple of neighbors' homes and stole items of cash and jewelry worth less than $1,000. Upon hearing the neighbor's complaints, Shane's mother suspected her son and confronted him with her suspicions. When he admitted that he had done it, his mother practiced "tough love"—something she had learned from an organization she had joined. She asked him to turn himself in to the police. She now deeply regrets that decision.

His mother had hoped that Shane would be able to get into some type of government rehabilitation program so he could overcome his addiction to drugs. Shane, however, received no treatment in prison for his drug problems. The only time he had gotten any help with his drug use was in 1984 when his family took out a second mortgage on their home and paid $30,000 for one month to a local treatment program that didn't work. His mother says that instead of being treated, her son learned more about drugs from the other kids there.

The co-defendant in Shane's case, who was found guilty of the actual sale of the controlled substance, was not subject to the Three Strikes law and received a four-year sentence and was free from prison after serving two years. Not until the year 2021, when he is 53, will Shane be eligible for parole.

Doug Rash

Like Shane, Doug Rash also was sentenced to 25 years-to-life in an Orange County case. In October of 1994 Doug was in a hotel room with several friends when the police entered after having been given permission by the renter of the room. Seeing drugs and drug paraphernalia in plain view, the police searched everybody and found a little more than (four-tenths) of a gram of cocaine in the pocket of Doug's pants, pants that Doug alleges he had just borrowed from someone else.

Like Shane, Doug's "serious" priors also involved two burglary charges. In 1985, at the age of 19, he had been found guilty of burglary of his dad's home—a place where he often was allowed to shower, sleep, and store his clothes. The theft involved a keyboard that belonged to Doug's brother. Doug was found guilty of burglary because he took the keyboard to a pawnshop.

Then in 1987, Doug was found guilty of another burglary when he and a friend entered his friend's girlfriend's house to retrieve some compact disks.

The girlfriend's father chased them away and called the police. Doug and his friend were charged and convicted of burglary.

Doug, who is white, started using drugs when he was 14. His family paid to put him in a four-day detoxification program, but the clean-up did little to solve his drug problem. He did not receive any treatment while serving time in jail or prison.

Doug will not be eligible for parole until 2019 when he is 53 years old.

Gregory Taylor

At the age of 35, Gregory Taylor, an African-American, was a homeless person who often received free dinners at St. Joseph's Catholic Church in Los Angeles (see *People v. Taylor*, 1999; Bellisle, 1999). About 4 a.m. on July 11, 1997, allegedly too hungry to wait for the meal to be served the next day, Gregory was seen by two guards working a 2-by-4 into a crack in the church door. An arresting police officer later testified that Taylor said he "was trying to go in the kitchen to get something to eat."

Gregory's prior "serious" felonies were two robbery charges. The first was a purse snatching committed in 1982; the purse contained $10 and a bus pass. A year later, he and a buddy were arrested while attempting to rob a man on the street. They were not armed.

Gregory grew up in South Central Los Angeles and was one of nine boys born to a nurse who quit work and went on welfare to care for her children. Gregory left school in the 12th grade and had some run-ins with the police while in his late teens. He has suffered from heroin and cocaine addiction.

Father Allen McCoy, a Franciscan priest at St. Joseph's church where the third strike incident occurred, considers the sentence unjust and describes Gregory "as a peaceful man, a man who helped at the center with the feeding of the street people." Father McCoy has known Gregory for almost a decade and they now exchange letters.

In a dissenting California appellate opinion, Justice Johnson compared Gregory's case to a situation in Victor Hugo's novel *Les Miserable* in which the protagonist, Jean Valjean, is imprisoned for stealing bread. Gregory will be eligible for a parole hearing in 2022, the year he turns 60.

Luciano (Chano) Orozco

In 1996, Chano Orozco, a Latino, was found guilty in San Diego County of possessing five-hundredths of a gram of heroin and was sentenced to 25 years-to-life under the Three Strikes law. His prior "serious" felonies were two counts of burglary. He was convicted of the first burglary in 1988. According to his appellate attorney, Fred Uebbing, his law-breaking act was not classified as a "serious" burglary when his client was convicted. In addition, Uebbing describes the burglary as one in which Chano simply went along with an acquaintance. Chano was convicted of his second burglary in 1992. That offense involved an unusual series of events. Chano's car had broken down and he needed to call a service station or tow truck for help. As luck (obviously "bad" luck it turned out) would have it, Chano was close to his mother's home and decided to telephone from her house. Unfortunately, she was not at home. Instead of attempting to break into his mother's home, which had bars on the windows and was locked up tight, Chano decided to take the easier route and enter into the dwelling of his mother's tenant and make the call from there. While he was on the phone, the tenant came home and Chano said to him, "I'm sorry, brother. I won't do it anymore." Chano then ran past the tenant and out the front door, but he forgot to leave behind the cordless phone. The tenant called the police, and eventually Chano was caught and convicted of residential burglary. There are strong arguments that he should have been convicted instead of trespassing, an offense which does not count as a "strike."

According to Uebbing, Chano was a heroin addict—and, as so often with addicts having little means of support, he had other property and drug offenses on his record. The probation report when Chano was facing his third strike told the story this way:

> The 38-year-old defendant, who is a heroin addict of long standing (20 years), is before the Court for sentencing on a charge of possession of heroin. Such possession is a requirement for a practicing heroin addict. It is sad that the defendant has had numerous chances in the past 15 years or so, to clean up his act, but has not done so. Now, he faces 28 years to life for what could be considered a relatively minor felony charge.
>
> However, the defendant's prior record shows he is a danger to the property of others because he must feed his addiction. However, since the defendant is relatively unemployable because of his long history of criminal involvement and state prison commitments, it is most likely that the defendant would have to resort to property crimes to support his habit. Thus, sadly, the longer the defendant is incarcerated, the safer will be society. It is impractical to believe that at this date, the defendant will, "cure" his drug addiction.

Uebbing and Chano's wife dispute the statement that Chano had "numerous chances..to clean up his act." They point out that he had neither the means nor the opportunity to receive treatment in a decent substance abuse program. Chano will not be eligible for parole until 2021 when he is 61 years old.

No Typical Cases

We found when studying the histories of people who have been convicted under the Three Strikes law that rarely could we describe a case as "typical." Claims of innocence, ineffective assistance of counsel, plea bargaining to a different crime than the one actually committed, allegations of police and prosecutorial misconduct, pleading guilty to help a friend or relative who was the actual perpetrator, and many other issues seemed to be factors in at least one of the strikes in the cases we looked into.

As people involved in the criminal justice system are well aware, many "robberies" and "burglaries" do not match nicely with the public perceptions of the offenses. The Reams, Rash, Taylor and Orozco cases demonstrate that "burglary" can involve dwellings of acquaintances or family members of the alleged offender. In some "burglary" cases we investigated, ex-boyfriends or ex-spouses would break into an ex-lover's home to regain disputed property. These were not episodes of premeditated plans by a "professional burglar," but rather the result of an emotional domestic dispute in which the identity of the burglar was not even necessarily meant to be secret.

In other cases we reviewed, "robbery" included a drunk person snatching a twenty dollar bill out of a person's hand in a store after the victim had been holding it out, waiting to pay for something. In another case, it involved a couple of drunk people getting into a fight and the person who ended up in the hospital noticing that he no longer had a gold chain around his neck. "Assault with a deadly weapon" includes any object that can cause serious damage to another person, including a skate board in one case we investigated.

Characteristics of Strikers

While there may not be any "typical" Three Strike stories, the characteristics of those who fall under the Three Strikes law are somewhat easier to define. Generally, those sentenced under Three Strikes are low income, substance-addicted males, who are people of color.

According to the California Department of Corrections, of the 50,007 Second Strikers sentenced through March 31, 2001, 47,779 (95%) were male, 18,334 (37%) were black, 16,394 (33%) were Hispanic-Mexican, 2,062 (4%) were "other," and 13,285 (27%) were white. Of the 6,700 Third Strikers who received a minimum of 25 years-to-life through March 31, 2001, 6,632 (99%) were male, 2,972 (44%) were black, 1,719 (26%) were Hispanic-Mexican, 293 (4%) were "other," and 1,716 (26%) were white. Blacks make up only 6.0% of the California population, and 31% of the California prison population—but 44% of the Third Striker population (Baraback, 2001; California Department of Corrections, 2001).

California does not keep statistics regarding the income level of prisoners, but based on the letters we read and the interviews we conducted, we believe that the vast majority of letter writers were from lower to lower-middle class backgrounds. The letters conveyed an inability to obtain an attorney, or to obtain rehabilitation, employment, or housing, all indicators of low income.

Very rarely did we find a case where a striker could be identified as not having a substance abuse problem. Statistics indicate that about 80 percent of California prisoners suffer from drug abuse (Little Hoover Commission Report, 1998), and our review of Three Strike cases indicate that strikers have at least that high a rate.

Rehabilitation (or Lack Thereof)

In almost all of the cases we reviewed, persons known to be suffering substance abuse had received little or no rehabilitative treatment from the state of California, despite having been imprisoned or jailed prior to their Three Strike sentence. The lack of treatment programs available to the poor and incarcerated has often been cited as a problem that is particularly pronounced in California (Little Hoover Commission Report, 1998). Using the 80 percent estimate, this indicates that currently, of the 162,000 prisoners in California, about 129,600 suffer from substance abuse. Of these 129,600, only about 3,000 to 4,500 of them are receiving treatment. Politicians sometimes brag about treatment facilities, pretending that they are really doing something significant about drug treatment needs. In a 1998 bi-partisan report analyzing the California prison system, the lack of drug treatment for prisoners was cited as the major reason that in 1995, 60 percent of those admitted to California prisons were parole violators, whereas in New York, the figure was only 22 percent and in Texas only 29 percent (Little Hoover Commission Report, 1998:69).

Given that the Three Strikes law is targeting people who were previously part of a system that might have been able to assist them to control their substance abuse problems, it appears especially indefensible for the California system to turn around and impose 25 years-to-life sentences for what, in so many instances, are drug related crimes and property crimes to support addiction.

Prosecuters' and Judges' Use of Discretion

The Three Strikes law allows prosecutors to use their discretion "in the interests of justice." In June of 1996, the California Supreme Court extended this discretion to judges in the *Romero* decision (*People v. Superior Court (Romero)*, 1996). The use of such discretion by judges, however, is subject to attack on the ground that it is an abuse of their powers, and can be reversed on appeal (*People v. Williams*, 1998). In addition, while the rights against "cruel and unusual" punishment under the United States Constitution and "cruel or unusual" punishment under the California Constitution are available for Three Strikers on a case-by-case basis, only one appellate court has been bold enough to rule in favor of this type of claim in a Three Strikes case. In that case, the trial court had imposed a 25-years-to life sentence on someone whose last offense was failure to register as a sex offender (*People v. Cluff*, 2001).

The result is that a career-minded judges will probably not exercise their discretion because in that way they can avoid the possibility of a reversal on appeal or the chance of a "Willie Horton" type of scenario that could result if the media were to publicize an incident in which an ex-convict who benefitted from judicial discretion ended up committing a heinous crime. Even if the judge may have used discretion in hundreds of other cases, this will likely be ignored as the media and political opponents focus on the one "bad" decision. From a risk-analysis perspective, judges have little to risk when imposing a longer sentence, and much to lose if they choose to mete out shorter sentences. Many of the attorneys we spoke with believed this to be a major factor in how judges employ discretion. Defense attorneys tended to prefer some of the older judges who were nearing retirement because these judges did not have to worry about their careers as much as the younger judges, and therefore were more likely to use their discretion to correct obvious injustices.

District Attorneys generally have to balance their available resources to respond satisfactorily to the pressures and expectations to be "tough on crime." While they are supposed to seek "justice," in practice they "advocate" for the higher charges and longer and harsher sentences. Prosecutors also appear to worry about the "Willie Horton" scenario and their careers often are tied to their win-loss ratio.

The use of prosecutorial and judicial discretion under the Three Strikes law appears to vary widely by county. In some counties it differs within the particular courthouse, the floor of the courthouse, and even with the particular prosecutor or judge assigned to the case. Several attorneys have described the likelihood that a defendant will benefit from the use of discretion as "pure luck" or "capricious and arbitrary." Statistics from the California Department of Corrections and interviews with attorneys show that San Francisco and Alameda Counties have District Attorneys who rarely resort to the Three Strikes law for nonviolent and non-serious current offenses, while Kern, San Bernardino, and Orange counties use the Three Strikes law to a significantly greater degree for nonviolent and non-serious offenses than the average prosecutors. Interviews with public defenders in Los Angeles County, which is responsible for about 42 percent of all third strike cases, indicate that certain courthouses were known to enforce the Three Strikes law more strictly than others. As we note subsequently, these matters changed with the election of a new Los Angeles district attorney in 2000.

In 1996, the *Los Angeles Times* documented discrepancies by showing that the Van Nuys courthouse sentenced 33 percent of third strikers to at least 25 years-to-life, while the San Fernando branch sentenced only 14 percent of third strikers to the same penalty (Krikorian et al., 1996). The difference was said to be due to the varying views of the supervising head deputy district attorneys. According to one public defender we interviewed, in the downtown criminal courts building of Los Angeles, where there was a different prosecuting supervisor on each floor, the floor of the courthouse a defendant was sent to made a big difference in regard to whether discretion to waive a strike was employed or not. In some jurisdictions, juries will on occasion "nullify" the charge; that is, despite what the law stipulates, they will find the offender innocent rather than see imposed what they regard as a too harsh penalty for the offense committed (Dodge & Harris, 2000).

Interviews with attorneys indicate that prosecutors and judges sometimes try to push each other into using their discretion to reduce the charge or penalty because they do not want it to be placed on their own record. Sometimes, it is claimed, the two sides end up giving a striker a harsh sentence in order to call each other's bluff.

A Superior Court judge noted in an interview that prosecutors can often systematically try to manipulate the discretion process by getting certain cases removed from certain judges. This is a power that defense attorneys cannot use as effectively because there are so few judges who are known to be liberal about waiving prior strikes.

Plea Bargaining

The Three Strikes law technically does not allow plea bargaining, but according to interviews, there are tactics to "agree" to plead guilty if a strike or strikes are waived. Public defenders in Los Angeles County say that about every second strike case involving a nonviolent or non-serious current offense results in an automatic plea offer of 32 months. Defendants face six years or more if they take their case to a jury trial and are found guilty.

In third strike cases, the dilemma facing the defendant is sometimes so severe that public defenders say that they will strongly advise a client to take a plea even if the defendant adamantly professes innocence and the public defender suspects this to be true. Dan Johnson of Orange County was offered a sentence of four years, refused to take it, and after the jury's guilty verdict he received a sentence of 78 years-to-life, though it was reduced on appeal to 28 years-to-life. Michael Robles, also of Orange County, facing a third strike for an attempt to purchase an imitation controlled substance (actually a macadamia nut) for $20 had an offer of nine years, and turned it down. Following the jury's guilty verdict, he received a sentence of 25 years-to-life. After an effective appeal based on the issue of ineffective assistance of counsel and tried before a different judge, who waived some prior strikes, Robles ended up with a five-year term.

Many of the people in the criminal justice system we interviewed said that they see the Three Strikes law currently being used for two types of offenders. The first one is the dangerous "violent" offender that the public voted to enact the law against, while the second is the nuisance recidivist whom many of the law and order types in the criminal justice system have become tired of seeing again and again. But this second category of offender is not the type people had in mind when they voted for the law.

Imbalance of Political Power

Another major factor in California's administration of criminal justice is the pressure put on politicians by special interest groups. Increasing sentences is a relatively easy task for office-holders because rarely are there opposition groups to speak against such moves. Generally the only opposition comes from concerned defense attorneys and altruistic individuals or organizations that recognize a problem that will affect unknown others. Unfortunately, for society, defense attorneys are usually too busy with individual cases to take the time to campaign against more punitive laws, and altruistic individuals and organizations are few in number.

The other side of the picture is very different. There are many special interest groups whose members make a great deal of money as more prisons are being built. In the process, these groups become increasingly powerful.

In 1980 there were only a couple thousand California prison guards and they were guarding 23,511 prisoners and earning an annual salary of about $21,000.

By 1998, there were 24,314 full-time guards for about 160,000 prisoners, with veterans receiving an average salary of $51,000 (Morain & Vanzi, 1998).

In 1994, the California Correctional Peace Officer's Association (CCPOA) contributed more than $100,000 to the Mike Reynolds group that spearheaded the Three Strikes initiative, and provided additional sums to victims' rights groups that fought for approval of the Three Strikes initiative (Roemer, 1996; Vitiello, 1997). In the 1990 and 1994 gubernatorial campaigns, the CCPOA's contributions to Governor Pete Wilson, a Republican, totaled more than $1.5 million. The head of the CCPOA, Don Novey, boasted that it was his union that put Wilson over the top and gave him his victories.

During the 1998 election for governor, the CCPOA switched parties, but was able to stick with the winner as it supplied $2 million in campaign contributions and television ads to Democrat Gray Davis (Salladay, 1999). Since being elected, Governor Davis said: "In this business you have to be strong enough to accept contributions and then vote against the people who contribute the money" (Hoge, 1999). However, the CCPOA and the criminal enforcement agencies have rarely seen a Davis move go against them. Davis consistently has voted against paroling prisoners (Warren, 1999), vetoed a bill that would have allowed reporters to interview prisoners with recording equipment (reporters are not even currently allowed a pencil and paper) (Jacobs, 1999), vetoed a bill that would have limited police seizure of assets (Egelko, 1999), vetoed a bill that would have required police to keep tallies by race of the people they pulled over and detained (Ingram, 1999), and even vetoed a bill that would have funded a study of the Three Strikes law ("Davis Vetoes Study of Three Strikes Law," 1999).

Victim Rights groups also became a powerful lobbying force in California in the 1980s and 1990s, and there has been a symbiotic relationship between the "tough-on" crime politicians and crime victims. Not all victims, however, promote Three Strikes. Disturbed at the use of Polly Klaas's image to justify "draconian" sentences, Marc Klaas and Joe Klaas, Polly's father and grandfather respectively, have spoken out strongly against the Three Strikes law and advocated amending it so it will not be applicable to nonviolent and non-serious offenders.

Other special interests supporting Three Strikes are made up of individuals who do business with prisons and are involved in the construction of prisons. Prison construction requires the purchase of land, materials, and the use of great amounts of labor and is usually financed by the government selling special interest bonds. The sale of the bonds requires lawyers, underwriters, investment brokers, and buyers. The maintenance of prisons involves multimillion dollar contracts for suppliers of food, clothing, utilities, guns, ammunition, supplies, and all of the other materials needed to operate a city behind walls and fences. These people profit from, and are in a position to contribute to politicians who see things as they do.

Prisoners, on the other hand, cannot vote until after they are off parole and they generally come from communities where the voter turnout is very low. The prisoners' friends and family members, generally from lower income levels, are estimated to be less inclined to vote than others even within their communities (Maharidge, 1996).

Recent Trends

On March 7, 2000 California voters passed Proposition 21 that proposed a "tough on crime" approach to juvenile offenders by allowing prosecutors greater discretion to charge some juveniles as adults. Hidden amongst the 43 pages of juvenile and penal code changes in the Proposition were enhancements of the Three Strikes statute in regard to both juveniles and adults. The Proposition broadened the definition of crimes that can be regarded as "violent" or "serious" to include such offenses as "terrorist threats," "conspiracy to commit a serious crime," and "any felony committed by a gang member on behalf of a gang-related activity." Once again, it is difficult to discern the true beliefs of the voters who supported the measure as there was minimum news coverage of specific changes to the Three Strikes law.

In the fall of 2000, however, California voters demonstrated an awakening awareness that the trend to "lock 'em all up" might have gone too far. They passed Proposition 36 that directs first- and second-time drug offenders to rehabilitation programs rather than to incarceration. In addition, in Los Angeles county a new district attorney was elected whose platform advocated a reduced use of the Three Strikes law is an important gesture, though he probably won not because of this position but as a reaction to scandals in the police department that tainted his predecessor.

Proposition 36 benefits people who could be subject to the Three Strikes law, though it can only be used if they have not been convicted or incarcerated during the previous five years, and had not committed a misdemeanor in connection with the current drug offense. Unfortunately, both of these conditions will probably result in the elimination from the drug rehabilitation route most persons who fall under the Three Strikes law. As we have shown, most Three Strikers are drug addicts who often were caught because of petty drug and property offenses.

Steve Cooley, Los Angeles county's newly-elected district attorney, has established a policy built on his pre-election promise that he would ease up on use of the Three Strikes law, but his efforts have received mixed reviews from defense attorneys. Some report great progress toward more humanitarian actions (Riccardulli, 2001), but others insist that little of much significance has changed. And, of course, Cooley's views have no effect on persons already serving out desperately long terms based on a relatively trivial third offense.

Conclusion

The California Three Strikes law differs from the vast majority of other state's Three Strikes laws because it embraces nonviolent and non-serious offenders in regard to the last, or triggering strike. The California Three Strikes law also differs from most mandatory minimum sentencing laws because judges are allowed some discretion.

Our look at some of the nonviolent and non-serious offenders who have been sentenced under the California Three Strikes law demonstrates that supporters exaggerate when they claim that the people being locked up under the law are "professional thieves" or "violent" criminals. Statistics and a review of numerous cases indicate that a significant number of those persons sentenced under the Three Strikes law are small-time property and drug offenders who are suffering from substance abuse, and the state has often been negligent on earlier occasions in regard to offering them an opportunity to overcome their drug problems.

References

Barabak, Mark Z. (2001). "Blacks See a Shrinking Political Role in California." *Los Angeles Times*, May 20.

Baum, Dan. (1997). Smoke and Mirrors: The War on Drugs and the Politics of Failure. Back Bay Books, Boston.

Bellisle, Martha. (1999). "Les Miserables Revisited: Three-Strikes Law Lands Food Thief in Corcoran." *Los Angeles Daily Journal*, July 19.

Clark, John, James Austin, and D. Alan Henry. (1997). " 'Three Strikes and You're Out': A Review of State Legislation." *NCJ 165369*, National Institute of Justice, Washington DC.

"Davis Vetoes Study of Three-Strikes Law." (1999). *San Francisco Gate*, October 10.

Dodge, Mary, and John C. Harris. (2000). "Calling a Strike a Ball: Jury Nullification and Three Strikes Cases." Pp. 354–363 in G. Larry Mays and Peter R. Gregare, eds., *Crime & Justice: A Reader*. 2nd ed. Prospect Heights, IL: Haveland

Egelko, Bob. (1999). "Davis Veto Preserves Car Seizures in Drug, Prostitution Cases." *The San Francisco Gate*, October 5.

Favre, Gregory. (1996). "Three Strikes: The Verdict Is In." *Sacramento Bee*, March 31.

Hoge, Patrick. (1999). "Indians Lead in Legislative-Race Donations: 3 Tribes Topped $3.6 Million, Says Common Cause." *Sacramento Bee*, September 8.
Ingram, Carl. (1999). "Davis Vetoes Racial Data Legislation." *Los Angeles Times*, September 29.
Jacobs, John. (1999). "Davis Says 'No' to Open Government." *San Jose Mercury News*, September 15.
Krikorian, Greg, et al. (1996). "Front-Line Fights Over 3 Strikes." *Los Angeles Times*, July 1.
Little Hoover Commission. (1998). "Beyond Bars: Correctional Reforms to Lower Prison Costs and Reduce Crime." Sacramento (January).
Litvan, Laura M. (1998). "Can 'Three Strikes' Reduce Crime?" *Investor's Business Daily*, November 30, pp. A1 and A26.
Lungren, Daniel E. (1996). "Three Cheers for 3 Strikes." *Policy Review: The Journal for American Citizenship*. 80:34.
Maharidge, Dale. (1996). *The Coming White Minority: California, Multiculturalism, and America's Future*. Vintage Books, New York.
Moore, Michael J. (1998). "The Legacy." Video-Documentary, San Francisco.
Morain, Dan, and Max Vanzi. (1998). "Wilson Agrees to Pay Raises for Prison Guards." *Los Angeles Times*, August 25.
Parenti, Christian. (1999). *Lockdown America: Police and Prisons in the Age of Crisis*. Verso, London.
Patterson, Thomas E. (1994). *Out of Order*. Vintage Books, New York.
People v. Cluff, 87 Cal. Rptr. 2d (991 Cal. Ct. App. 1st Dist. 2001).
People v. Superior Court (*Romero*), 13 Cal. 4th 497, 917 P.2d 628 (Cal. 1996).
People v. Taylor, 71 Cal. App. 4th 693, 83 Cal. Rptr. 2d 919 (Cal. Ct. App. 2d Dist. 1999).
People v. Williams, 17 Cal. 4th 148, 948 P.2d 429 (Cal. 1998).
The Real War on Crime: The Report of the National Criminal Justice Commission. (1996). S. A. Donziger, ed. HarperPerennial, New York.
Ricciardulli, Alex. (2001). "Voters Get Their Way in Three-Strikes Law," *Los Angeles Times*, August 26.
Richardson, James. (1996). *Willie Brown: A Biography*. University of California Press, Berkeley.
Roemer, John. (1996). "Taking Three Strikes Outside the Wall." *California Lawyer*, 40.
Salladay, Robert. (1999). "Prison Guard Union, Davis Cozy Pairing." *San Francisco Examiner*, September 14.
"Second and Third Strike Cases—June 30, 1999." (1999). Data Analysis Unit, California Department of Corrections, Sacramento.
Shuster, Beth. (1998). "Living in Fear." *Los Angeles Times*, August 23.
Vitiello, Michael. (1997). "Three Strikes: Can We Return to Rationality?" *Journal of Criminal Law and Criminology*, 87(2):395–481.
Warren, Jennifer. (1999). "State Slams Door on Hopes for Parole." *Los Angeles Times*, October 3.
Westerman, Ted. (1999). "Three Strikes Law Does Serve the State Well." *Los Angeles Times*, September 28.

Section 7

Justice in a Postmodern Society

"Law, Crime, and Social Control: Making Sense of Conflict, Radical, and Postmodern Criminology"

Bruce A. Arrigo, Ph.D.,
University of North Carolina at Charlotte

Abstract

One way to assess whether the system of law, as a mechanism of social control, advances the common good is to turn to criminological theory. In this chapter, I consider the relationship between three criminological orientations. These include the perspectives of conflict, radical, and postmodern theory. I argue that radical and postmodern criminology respectively tell us something more, or something other, about the forces of control lodged within law and crime beyond what the conflict paradigm describes. Thus, I demonstrate how each perspective uniquely extends our awareness of law's ideological and repressive dominance in social life and civic affairs, mindful of how it undermines or thwarts prospects for advancing the common good.

Introduction

Conflict criminology is represented by many theoretical perspectives (e.g., Sellin, 1938; Simmel, 1950, 1955; Vold, 1958; Dahrendorf, 1959; Turk, 1969; Quinney, 1979; Chambliss and Seidman, 1982; Pepinsky, 1976). Each of these perspectives is a unique attempt to explain how certain groups in society maintain power sufficient to govern and control the operation of the state

(Vold, Bernard, and Snipes 1998: 235, 257–259). Thus, according to conflict criminologists, the values and interests of these formidable collectives, rather than society in general, are predominantly reflected in all institutional arrangements, all expressions of human social interaction.

Radical or Marxist criminology (Lynch, Michalowski, and Groves, 2000) is a specific type of conflict theory (e.g., Bernard, 1981; Bohm, 1982; Groves and Sampson, 1986; MacLean and Milovanovic, 1991; Guzy, 1994), and it functions as a "strategy for analyzing crime and justice [utilizing] theories and practices grounded in a materialist framework (Lynch and Groves, 1989: vii). There are varieties of radical criminology just as there are several conflict theory positions [1] of radical thought (see, Bohm, 1982). Despite differing degrees of support for and conviction over various criminogenic precepts, radical theorists are critical of the traditional and positive criminologies which fail to account for the devastating and demoralizing effects of the capitalistic economic system.

While radical criminology shares some affinities with conflict theory, the two are not synonymous (Bernard, 1981: 370–379; Bohm, 1982: 566–569; Lynch and Groves, 1989: 45–50). Conflict theory, for example, assumes that power is at the root of social organization. Radical criminology, however, maintains that economic greed is at the root of social organization (Beirne, 1979: 375–377; Plat, 1975: 98–99). Further, conflict theorists assert that stratification best accounts for the manifestation of crime. Radical criminologists, though, argue that the political economy of late capitalism is the explanatory variable (Keller, 1976: 283; Lynch and Groves, 1989: 51–71). These and other differences tend to confound and confuse the conflict/radical distinction, making it difficult to ascertain the relationship of one to the other.

Complicating this comparison is the emergence of a new, and somewhat different, criminology ostensibly embracing an even more critical agenda than radical theory. This new frame of reference is called postmodern[2] criminol-

---

1. Radical criminology has alternatively been defined as *new* criminology (Taylor, et al., 1973), *critical* criminology (Sykes, 1974), *materialist* criminology (Beirne, 1979), *socialist* criminology (Young, 1975), *dialectical* criminology (Quinney, 1979), and *left realist* criminology (Young, 1987; MacLean, 1991).

2. By "postmodern" I refer to that epistemological shift and historical break in which reality was no longer understood to be dominated by foundational truths, cause-effect relationships, linear thought processes, syllogistic reasoning, global assumptions, objective analyses and other conventions of modernist science. The postmodern agenda rejects these essential and absolute notions because of the intervening variable of *language*. Language conditions, shapes, modifies, and defines all social relationships, all institutional practices, all methods of knowing. For a macro application of postmodern thought to law and criminology see, Arrigo, 1995: 447–472.

ogy. Similar to both conflict theory and radical thought, there are several versions of postmodern analysis[3] exploring specific applications of affirmative postmodern criminology (see Arrigo, 1994, Arrigo and Schehr, 1998). Some critics of postmodern criminology suggest that it is a variation of radical thought best positioned at its extreme outer edge (Schwartz and Friedrichs, 1994: 221–222). Other commentators question if all radical criminologies are not themselves differing expressions of postmodern discontent (Henry and Milovanovic, 1993:1; Einstadter and Henry, 1995: 402–405). As a result of this disagreement, the relationship between radical and postmodern criminology remains largely amorphous.

There is also some debate about how best to interpret postmodern criminology in relationship to conflict theory (Arrigo, 1995: 452). According to postmodernism, language structures thought; that is, the words and phrases we use to convey meaning and the particular sequencing of these words and phrases we select to construct a coherent narrative are not neutral endeavors (Milovanovic, 1994: 143–145, 155–184; Arrigo, 1993a: 27–75). Both activities, knowingly or not, support dominant views of the world. Others have examined the marginalizing, alienating, and oppressive effects of this process. Selected works include the dilemmas of jailhouse lawyering (Milovanovic, 1988), psychiatric patients petitioning for institutional release (Arrigo, 1996a), police officers responding to 911 calls (Manning, 1988), and female attorneys seeking gendered justice and ways of knowing in courtrooms (Arrigo, 1992). In each instance, one view of reality (e.g., prison inmates, the mentally ill, patrol officers, women) is replaced by another (e.g., the legal, the medical, the correctional systems) thereby affirming and re-legitimizing the status quo.

While the preceding comments on postmodern thought point to a "conflict" of sorts between prevailing modes of speech and unique methods of expression silenced or oppressed in everyday interaction, conflict theory per se, does not take a position on the variable of language. Thus conflict theory's relationship to postmodern criminology is also unclear. In sum then, our understanding of postmodern criminology, while related to radical criminology

---

3. Broadly speaking, we can place postmodern views into one of two explanatory categories. On the one hand, there is the nihilistic, fatalistic, and relativistic version embracing deconstructive inquiry and oppositional sensibilities (e.g., Derrida, 1973, 1978; Baudrillard, 1981, 1983). On the other hand, there is the reconstructive, affirmative, and prospective version incorporating constitutive methods and productive outcomes (e.g., Giddens, 1984; Borgmann, 1992). For applications to criminology highlighting these differences see, Henry and Milovanovic, 1996: ix–xi, 1–15. For studies exploring specific applications of nihilistic postmodern criminology see Arrigo, 1997a.

in particular and conflict theory in general, remains largely undefined. In both instances, the absence of greater specificity contributes to the pervasive isolation which postmodern criminology experiences within the academy today (e.g., Handler, 1992: 697–731).

This chapter, then, represents an effort at clarifying the association between radical and postmodern criminology through the lens of conflict theory. In this way, I contend that the foregoing analysis offers a viable method by which to assess prospects for law's common good. I recognize that this conceptual foray is not the only way by which to distinguish between radical and postmodern criminology. However, given their apparent conflict sensibilities, I regard this approach as one, useful strategy. The chapter begins with an overview of conflict theory, emphasizing its essential criminological (and legal) tenets. I then present and discuss the radical and postmodern position on these fundamental principles. I conclude by comparing and contrasting radical and postmodern criminology in light of their respective views on conflict theory, law, and crime.

Conflict Theory: Outline of Core Principles

My position on conflict theory and its assorted criminological tenets is derived from Vold's (1958) theory of group conflict, Quinney's (1979) theory on the social reality of crime, Chambliss and Seidman's (1982) critique on the functioning of the criminal justice system, and Bernard's (1981:366–369; see also, Vold, Bernard, and Snipes 1998: 253–254) position on a unified conflict theory of crime. For purposes of clarity and simplicity, I first list the basic principle and then offer a brief description of it.

Conflict Theory is a Structural Theory

Complex societies are composed of segments or quasi-groups (Quinney, 1979: 38; Dahrendorf, 1959: 167–168). All of these groups possess values and interests[4] cultivated through life experiences. The values and interests of these

4. As used here "values" refer to the normative beliefs, attitudes, sentiments one engenders in relation to others and events which give rise to behavior. "Interests" refer to the monetary, status, and power concerns which underscore the values of individuals thereby producing conduct (Bernard, 1981: 368).

groups tend to be varied and, at times, incompatible. In general, however, people behave in ways that are consistent with their values and interests. This consistency provides some predictability for how various institutional aspects of social life (e.g., the family, education, religion, the economy, politics, crime) are or will be stably structured.[5]

Various segments within a given society struggle over the accumulation and social definition of money, status, and power. These are identified as quasi-group interests.

Conflict theorists recognize that there is some valued good (or goods) over which different groups compete. The specific "prize" may vary depending on the society; however, the ends of group interests are what all segments struggle to acquire or capture. In capitalistic cultures, money, status, and power are the goals of conflict. Further, wealth, position, and authority are different expressions of quasi-group interests differentially valued by various segments within a given society. Each segment, though, endeavors to promote and to achieve its version of interests within the larger community of quasi-group interests.

The presence of group conflict in society, then, is a means to achieving some greater end. The presence of group conflict in relationship to crime is about achieving definitions of law and crime based upon the interests of those segments with the most economic influence, social standing, and political power.

Conflict is a social process essential to the routine functioning of society (Vold, Bernard, and Snipes 1998: 253; see also Coser, 1967:37–51). The aim of group conflict is to maximize the segment's position in relation to the other quasi-groups. The better the segment's location among the throng of groups, the greater the likelihood that the segment's defined interests will be embodied within society. One constellation of interests includes definitions of crime and enactment of laws. Those segments well positioned within the web of conflicting groups will determine what definitions of law and crime will prevail in society. Segments best positioned to ensure that their interests are represented in these definitions are those collectives with the most money, status, and power.

Based on the continuous and ongoing conflict over prevailing definitions of crime, violations of human rights and acts of wrong doing are never absolute.

---

5. The structural stability of these institutional expressions of social life is more specifically about an uneasy adjustment. This adjustment is realized following conflict and, eventually, compromise between opposing groups embodying their respective interests (Vold, Bernard, and Snipes 1998: 236–237).

Given that conflict is so ubiquitous in and central to everyday life, various quasi-groups will inevitably define crime differently. These varying definitions will be consistent with the interests and values of the assorted segments. The segment(s) possessing the most wealth, position, and authority will determine which definitions of crime will prevail. The presence of such diverse explanations indicates that there is no behavior that is intrinsically harmful to others and, therefore, no definition of crime that is, in itself, universal.

Conflict criminology explains the distribution of crime rates among various segments in society. The definition of crime offered by conflict criminology is a probability statement.

The enactment of laws and the definitions of crime in a given society are generally a reflection of the values and interests of those quasi-groups (and their membership) leveraging the most economic influence, social standing, and political power. The higher the position of the segment, the lower the probability that its members will be found to have broken the law. The lower the position of the segment, the higher the probability that its members will be found to have violated the law.

Conflict criminology identifies the essential problem of crime to be the probability statement itself understood as a function of human nature.

Conflict criminology links the distribution of money, status, and power among quasi-groups to the official crime rates within that society. Those segments whose values and interests are abundant have both a higher quasi-group standing and a lower chance of being identified as law violators. Those segments whose values and interests are scarce have both a lower quasi-group standing and a higher chance of being identified as law violators. Further, the source of conflict and, thus, the probability statement itself are products of human nature (Bernard, 1983). In other words, the greed of quasi-groups (and their memberships) are responsible for the antagonisms that plague society and these segments are, as well, accountable for the distribution of the crime rate.

Conflict criminology seeks as its goal crime rates that are more evenly distributed among all segments of society.

Conflict criminology not only identifies how the distribution of crime works but ventures to change or ameliorate this allocation. Conflict criminology does not wish to replace one hierarchical distribution of crime rates with another. This dynamic would merely redistribute the interests of wealth, position, and authority from some social segments to others thereby creating new criminal groups. Rather, conflict criminology attempts to equalize interests among various segments of society. Ultimately, this helps to ensure a pluralistic society, the stabilization of power, and the compatibility of values among quasi-groups.

Applying Conflict Theory to Radical and Postmodern Criminology: Reassessing the Core Principles

My position on radical criminology is heavily influenced by Lynch, Groves' (1989) eclectic orientation, encompassing key insights contained in critical, materialist, dialectical, Marxist, left realist, socialist, and feminist criminologies (see also, Lynch, Michalowski, and Groves, 2000; Schwartz and Milovanovic, 1999). My assessment of postmodern criminology is largely adopted from Henry and Milovanovic's (1996, 1999) constitutive criminology (see also Arrigo, 1997b, 1997c), Milovanovic's (1992) psychoanalytic semiotics (see also Arrigo, 1994, 1996b) and Arrigo's (1995) macro-sociological analysis (see also Arrigo, 2000a; Arrigo and Young, 1998). For purposes of simplicity and clarity, I concisely present both the radical and postmodern position on each conflict theory principle first. Following the brief reassessment of each tenet, a more detailed explanation based on the respective insights of radical and postmodern criminology is supplied.

Radical criminology is a structural theory.

Postmodern criminology is a theory of the human subject.—Radical criminology focuses on social class and class structure to ultimately account for and explain crime (e.g., Bernard, 1981: 372; Lynch and Groves, 1989: 32–39, 51–71). By social class I refer to the position one assumes in relation to the means of production (e.g., master vs. slave, owner versus worker). By class structure I mean the extent to which the distribution of interests (e.g., money and power) are disproportionately concentrated in the hands of a few, thereby producing structural inequalities and a stratified social system. The variables of social class and class structure represent key determinants by and through which radicals draw inferential and causal relationships between the prevailing economy and its influence on routine social life (e.g., Lynch, 1988; Reiman, 1995).

Postmodern criminology is not a structural theory. It is a theory of the subject or person. Postmodern criminology examines the relationship between human agency and language in the creation of meaning, identity, truth, justice, power, knowledge, etc. (Henry and Milovanovic, 1996: 8–11, 26–44). This relationship is studied through the process of discourse analysis.[6] Dis-

6. Discourse analysis is a method of investigating how meaning and sense are constructed. Specific attention is paid to the values and assumptions implied in the language used by the author of speech or of a text (e.g., Lacan, 1977; Foucault, 1970, 1972). For re-

course analysis does not analyze the sociological roles or statuses people occupy; but, rather, considers the *discursive subject positions* that inform and contribute to the way people speak. The structure of lawyering, counseling, policing, and offending are discursive subject positions. These structures are historically mediated and, thus, experience changing definitions over time (Goodrich, 1984).[7] The decentered subject is crucial to postmodern criminology and is explored more depthfully in this chapter. Subjects who assume these positions, however, speak, think, act, feel, and know through the language embodying these structures (Arrigo, 1995: 453–455).[8]

The fundamental and inextricable connection between the subject and the person's grammar tells us something more or something other about whose voice and ways of knowing *speak through* the one communicating. Another way to describe this is to understand the place of *desire* in every act of speech production (Lacan, 1977, 1981).[9] By desire I mean all the longings, fears, dreams, joys, doubts, despairs, and hopes that saturate our being, that permeate our selves (e.g., Lacan, 1977:146–175, 1981: 211–213; Lemaire, 1977: 67–77; Silverman, 1983: 170–172, 200). These are the qualities of our lives that often go unspoken. These attributes fail to find fulfillment in the language through which we are compelled to speak as lawyers, correctional administrators, judges, police officers, etc. In short, desire in language (Kristeva, 1984) is reduced to certain anchored communication patterns consistent with the discourse in use (e.g., legalese). It is the discourse in use, then, with its

---

cent law and crime applications see Milovanovic, 1992; Arrigo, 1993a, 1996a; Arrigo and Williams, 1999.

7. We might also think of the person, then, as a subject-in-process or as an emergent subject (Kristeva, 1980; Moi, 1985) This is a reference to the subject as *decentered* (Lacan, 1977); that is, as someone who is less in control of his/her own thoughts, less in control of the discourse that one employs when speaking through discursive subject positions.

8. The various languages through which one occupies discursive subject positions have been alternatively referred to as language games (Wittgenstein, 1958), language regions (Pitkin, 1971), discursive formations (Foucault, 1972), linguistic coordinate systems (Milovanovic, 1986), rhetorics (Goodrich, 1987).

9. Although the social theory of Lacan is significant to postmodern thought, I do not include a detailed assessment of his seminal contributions. This project is decidedly beyond the scope of the present study. However, several references to Lacan's work and the insights of his psychoanalytic and criminological successors are utilized in my analysis. For more on the relevance of Lacan's work for the development of a postmodern criminology see Henry and Milovanovic, 1996: 28–34; Milovanovic, 1992; Arrigo, 1996a). For a more targeted exposition highlighting the essentials of Lacanian theory in a law-society context see Arrigo, 1996c: 159–187, Arrigo, 2000b.

own specialized and circumscribed desire, which is understood to represent both narrative coherence and interpersonal meaning (Jackson, 1988; Arrigo, 1997a: 15). Lost in this process, however, is that deeply felt desire which uniquely encodes and singularly expresses our understanding of that human social interaction constituting our given realities.

As postmodern criminologists remind us, because the relationship between human agency and the person's speech represents an incomplete desire consistent with the discourse in effect, the subject is *decentered.* That is, the person who speaks is never really who s/he claims to be and is always pretending to be someone else as the language system in use demands or expects (Henry and Milovanovic, 1996: 27). Thus, we are not so much in charge of the words, phrases, and sentences we employ to convey meaning. Again, *language speaks through us*! In order to communicate effectively we invoke specialized ways of knowing, thinking, acting, feeling (e.g., the language of law, medicine, sports, computer science, prison inmates, juvenile gangs, mental patients), and situate ourselves and/or are inserted within these designated codes or language systems. This process indicates that we are not really the ultimate arbiters and determiners of what we say. We are not so much centered, in control, purposive, autonomous as we are determined, dependent, controlled, and regulated.

Further, depending on the discourse in effect, the decentered subject may contribute, knowingly or not, to the re-legitimation of entrenched ideologies thereby reaffirming one's experience of personal alienation (Lacan, 1991).[10] Rape survivors, for example, when turning to the criminal courts, find that they must re-present their harrowing experiences to be consistent with what the courtroom determines is justiciable speech (i.e., acceptable, credible testimonial evidence). Deviations from this language may subject the survivor's testimony to objection by opposing counsel and a sustainable ruling by the judge, resulting in the defendant's eventual acquittal (Arrigo, 1993b). As postmodernists remind us, however, the subtleties and nuances of meaning that would otherwise uniquely embody the woman's fear, frustration, pain, rage (i.e., her desire) are sanitized or otherwise cleansed and made compatible with the speech coordinates representing the discourse of law. Thus the language

---

10. Lacan's (1991) work on *the four discourses* is relevant here. These grammars include those of the *master, university, hysteric, and analyst* (see also Bracher, 1993; Milovanovic, 1992; Ragland-Sullivan, 1988; Salecl, 1993; Lee, 1990; Melville, 1987). The *four discourses* are different structuring mechanisms by and through which interpersonal communication occurs. In short, the *four discourse* represent unique ways in which domination, education, rejection, and revolt are effected in speech production (Arrigo and Young, 1998: 229–232).

which speaks through us may also be the language which marginalizes and oppresses us.

Radical criminology identifies the conflict over which various segments of society struggle to be about the acquisition and accumulation of economic power. This is defined as the quasi-group interest.

Postmodern criminology identifies the conflict over which various segments of society struggle to be about languaging reality/existence through multiple voices and ways of knowing. This is defined as the quasi-group interest.—According to radical criminologists, the interests at stake in the conspicuous consumerism of late capitalism are wealth and income, (Lynch and Groves, 1989: 52–3; Taylor, Walton and Young, 1973: 270–271). These interests must be understood in relation to the larger political economy (macro-level analysis) and its capacity to condition more local and immediate events (micro-level analysis). The interactive effects of both levels are said to cause crime. The greater the disparities of income and wealth among the classes, the greater the level of perceived social inequalities. As the inequalities among the classes intensify, conflict (i.e., crime) is produced. Criminal behavior, then, is directly linked to the economic structure of a given society (e.g., Blau and Blau, 1982; Michalowski, 1985; Groves and Frank, 1987; Frank and Lynch, 1992; Reinman, 1995).

The interests at stake in postmodern society address the inclusion of various ways of expressing (i.e., languaging) and living reality, as illustrated in all institutional aspects of social life. One facet of social life is crime. Postmodern criminologists maintain that there is a conflict which underscores our understanding of crime, law, order, justice, victimization, etc. In short, only certain definitions are used to convey society's meaning for these constructs. These are the socially acceptable explanations. All other denotations are not included in the definitions. These are the socially unacceptable explanations.

Postmodern criminologists therefore ask whose grammar and way of communicating is reflected in theories and policies on gang delinquency and youth violence, white-collar and corporate crime, serial killing and mass murder, sexual assault and domestic abuse, drug use and distribution, and every classification upon which definitions of crime are articulated and enacted as law (Arrigo and Young, 1998; Arrigo and Schehr, 1998). According to postmodern criminologists, there are dominant languages (e.g., medicine, law), oppositional languages (e.g., prison inmates, mental patients), and pluralistic languages (e.g., sports, commercialism) (Milovanovic, 1994: 144). Oppositional or insurgent ways of communicating are often not reflected in definitions of crime. Thus, according to postmodern criminologists, entire ways of understanding are dismissed. By dismissing these oppositional languages, certain versions of how to think, act, feel and *be* are, indirectly, de-valued. It is this devaluation which postmodernists identify as the source of conflict in society. Accordingly, what is profoundly at stake is the right to voice and affirm, rather than to quiet and exclude, one's reality, regardless of how different it might be.

Radical criminology identifies the greater ends of conflict to be determined by those who own the means of economic production. Those segments in society owning the means of economic production are responsible for the prevailing definitions of law and crime.

Postmodern criminology identifies the greater ends of conflict to be determined by those who own the means of linguistic production. Those segments in society owning the means of linguistic production are responsible for the prevailing definitions of law and crime.—In advanced economic systems, those who own the means of production (e.g, sophisticated technology, heavy duty machinery) are corporate figures or capitalists contracting middle management, white collar employees to supervise salaried laborers or line staff personnel (Lynch and Groves, 1989: 8; Lynch and Stretesky, 1999: 18–20). Given their relatively high economic standing, business leaders can and do exercise their authority to shape definitions of law and crime which effectively insulate them from potential charges of criminal wrongdoing (Frank and Lynch, 1992; Friedrichs, 1995). Thus, according to radical theorists, as the economic clout of the entrepreneur increases, so, too, does his/her capacity to influence prevailing definitions of law and crime (Lynch, 1988).

Postmodern criminologists identify the ownership of the means of linguistic production as pivotal to current definitions of law and crime (e.g., Rossi-Landi, 1977, 1983; Milovanovic, 1986; Arrigo, 1997b). Language is a commodity; that is, words and phrases, whether written or spoken, possess both a use- and an exchange-value. The use-value of language is the ability to express, to convey meaning. This expression and conveyance of meaning is unique; that is, the language used has intrinsic significance for the one writing or speaking it. When interacting with others, our language takes on exchange-value. The exchange-value of language is its shared, common, or equivalent meanings created among the marketplace of speakers or writers. These meanings are more universal, more abstract. Potentially lost in our communication with others, however, are the subtleties and shadings of significance, informing our understanding of what we say or what we write.

According to postmodernists, not only is language a commodity but so, too, is it fetishized. Where Marx and radical criminologists identify money as the universal form, postmodernists identify speech as the universal form. As Marxists tell us, we create the abstraction, money, to establish an artificial ratio of exchange (e.g., three dollars can buy either a basket of fruit or four boxes of candy). However, postmodernists maintain that we do the same with language. For example: the phrase "the mentally ill" conveys an *equivalent* meaning for people whether identified as "touched by God," "psychiatrically diseased," "mental health system users," "in need of treatment," "incompetent," "differently abled," "disordered," or "invaded by Satan." Just as Marxists (and radicals) claim we reduce everything to a money value, postmodernists claim we reduce everything to a language value (Arrigo, 1997b). The inherent use-values (significances) for the words or phrases mentioned above disappear or are masked through a more universal, more abstract, linguistic form (i.e., the mentally ill).

The fact that language is a commodity and that it is fetishized, brings postmodernists to a fundamental question: who controls what language we can use and the contexts in which we can use it? Another way to put this query is: who controls the means of linguistic production? According to postmodernists, in advanced capitalistic societies those segments exercising a monopoly of political power, social standing, and/or economic influence are the enactors of the dominant discourse. Returning to the illustration above, the dominant discourse regarding definitions of mental illness relies heavily upon the lexicon of law and psychiatry, criminal justice and mental health (Arrigo, 1993a; Williams and Arrigo, 2001). We seldom hear of references to such citizens as "competent," "differently abled," "mental health consumers," "psychiatric survivors," etc. Instead, both criminal and civil statutory and case law consistently refer to the mentally ill as "diseased," "sick," "in need of treatment," and "dangerous" (Arrigo, 1996a). Thus it follows, that those segments in society owning the means of linguistic production (e.g., corporate leaders, politicians, judges, doctors), are the regulators of prevailing definitions of law and crime.

Radical criminology asserts that violations of human rights and social acts of wrongdoing are absolute.

Postmodern criminology asserts that violations of human rights and social acts of wrongdoing are not absolute.—Radicals assert that there is an objective basis to harm or behaviors defined as harmful (Bernard, 1981: 369; Lynch and Groves, 1989: 48). Reiman (1995: 43–47), for example, claims that "crimes should be crimes because their consequences are dangerous and undesirable." The radical position finds support in its use of impartial criteria which operationalize definitions of crime. Such criteria have been the basis for several empirical and related studies (e.g., Lynch, 1987; Chambliss, 1988; Friedrichs, 1995). Consistent with the radical position, behaviors that would otherwise be considered violations of human rights or social acts of wrongdoing are not defined as crimes by the official criminal justice system if committed by capitalists (Bernard, 1981: 370). Again, this is because such quasi-groups have the economic power to protect themselves from most forms of criminal sanction.

Postmodernists question the existence of *any* foundational, certifiable truths (Arrigo, 1995: 452–454, 458–460), including explanations of social harm. Such skepticism stems from the conviction that language structures thought in ways that are consistent with dominant views of the world. These principal perspectives (e.g., law, medicine, science) do not demonstrate that such ways of knowing and experiencing are, in and of themselves, the "correct" way of knowing and experiencing for all citizens. Postmodernists accept that there are violations of human rights and socially harmful behaviors (Henry and Milovanovic, 1996). However, they fundamentally examine the language that is used to define such phenomena. For these critics the question to be answered is: whose languaged (and therefore social) interests are valued and de-valued in prevailing (or alternative) definitions of crime (Arrigo, 1995: 466)?

Postmodern criminologists contend that the explanations and meanings excluded from definitions of crime represent the voice of various, disempowered collectives. The postmodern psychoanalytic approach of Arrigo and Young (1998), for example, shows how criminology has essentially, though unwittingly, failed to make sense of gender, race, and class differences within the discourse of its own theory. As they ponder, whose languaged point of view finds embodiment in criminological discourse (*Ibid.*: 220–1, 225–228)? Those viewpoints that are consistent with the discourse encompassing the criminological sciences are the only acceptable positions (Arrigo, 1997b). Again, according to postmodernists, these are limited explanations. Indeed, different definitions for crime often go unspoken or are dismissed and the users of these grammars are, on occasion, even disciplined.[11] According to postmodernists, related to the issue of race is *how* Mr. Jackson communicated to the patrol officer and how Mr. Jackson's language was interpreted by the arresting agent. Mr. Jackson opted for a method of speech that was not consistent with what the officer took to be the discourse of a "docile, good citizen/suspect." Such citizens do not repeatedly, though politely, ask officers to

11. The harrowing experience of Don Jackson, a former Long Beach California police officer, is a useful illustration. Jackson, a Black man, was thrown into a plate glass window by an patrol officer following Mr. Jackson's unwillingness to obey the requests and, then later, the demands of the arresting officer. Mr. Jackson hypothesized that by driving late at night in areas pocketed by high crime perpetrated by African Americans, he would be stopped and questioned without adequate cause.

justify their behavior. Good citizen/suspects do not insist that patrol officers explain their intentions. Mr. Jackson attempted to resist the conventional citizen/suspect discourse and was punished for it.

Radical criminology explains crime by focusing on the capitalistic economic system. Definitions of law and crime are rooted in the capitalistic political economy.

Postmodern criminology explains crime by focusing on the hegemony of dominant discourses. Definitions of law and crime are rooted in dominant languages.—According to radicals, the social structure of capitalism and the inequitable distribution of interests (i.e, money and wealth) produce crime (e.g., Quinney, 1979; Quinney and Wildeman, 1991; see also Engels, 1845; Marx, 1868; and Bonger, 1916 for the development of this concept). The radical model argues that in capitalistic cultures class is based on the private ownership of property where a few citizens (the bourgeoisie) own a large percentage of the interests and many citizens (the proletariat) own only their labor (Henry and Milovanovic, 1996: 141). Thus crime is a rational response to class-divided systems, featuring the disproportionate acquisition and/or accumulation of capital (Lynch and Groves, 1989: 64). Explanations for law and crime take on meaning through and are an expression of such class-based inequalities.

Postmodern criminology identifies the official power and authority of dominant grammars as the source of definitions on law and crime. The linguistic hegemony perpetrated through prevailing discourses is significant to postmodernists (Milovanovic, 1986; Arrigo, 1997b). This concept refers to how (criminological) reality is constructed.[12] In so doing, criminal defendants, knowingly or not, help re-legitimize the power that legal discourse has in their lives.

Linguistic hegemony is that process in which agents of the dominant language in use transform, channel, or re-present the speech of non-agents to be consistent with the language system in effect (Milovanovic, 1994:145–150). Criminal defense lawyers, for example, listen to their clients' stories and then re-package and re-construct the events so that the "what happened" in the case is conveyed through the argot of law. In this scripted process, however, much is lost in the attorney's well-intended translation. The nuances of meaning

12. A related feature of the postmodernist construction of (criminological) reality is linguistic reification. Linguistic reification is that process in which non-agents of the dominant discourse in use nevertheless turn to it for the recognition of their own desire. But in turning to the principal grammar, non-agents speak through and embody the desire of that language system; a grammar which is often the source of the non-agent's oppression, alienation, and marginalization.

contained in the client's grammar are often cloaked or sanitized when re-presented to the criminal court (Bourdieu, 1987: 831–32). The visibility and admissibility of the client's linguistic reality is denied while the language structuring lawyering is reinforced.

Radical criminology identifies the essential problem of crime to be greed as embedded in the social structure of society. Thus the problem of crime can be solved by overthrowing the capitalistic economic system.

Postmodern criminology identifies the essential problem of crime to be linguistic domination as prevalent in various situations or encounters. Thus the problem of crime can be solved by developing replacement discourses.—Radical criminology seeks an end to the capitalist economic system because, as it is ingrained within the socio-political structure of society, a series of class-based inequalities are routinely perpetuated (Bernard, 1981: 375–76). As previously stated, these class inequalities create greater disparities in the acquisition and accumulation of segment interests, and, thus, those quasi-groups receiving fewer economic rewards will increasingly experience marginality and will, consequently, be more likely to engage in criminal behavior.

Postmodern criminology seeks to neutralize the power of privileged grammars which regulate, normalize, and discipline the lives of alienated collectives. This neutralization process entails the cultivation of replacement discourses. Replacement discourses are ways of communicating that embody both one's meaning and one's desire at the same time (Henry and Milovanovic, 1991: 305–307; Henry and Milovanovic, 1996: 185–213). Replacement discourses substitute methods of control with languages of possibility (Henry and Milovanovic, 1996: 214–243). This activity encompasses the interdependent effects of the *dialectics of linguistic struggle and control* and the *reversal of hierarchies.*

The dialectics of linguistic struggle and control refers to the subtle requirements imposed on both our speech and our manner of communicating. Speaking within the coordinates of certain grammars is a necessary and sufficient condition if appropriate and intended meaning is to be transmitted to others. Explaining the "penalty kick" in soccer, for example, forces us to utilize the terminology of soccer to make our meaning exact and, hopefully, clear. But the language of athletics is neither a dominant nor an oppositional discourse. It is a pluralistic grammar. If one fails to communicate the meaning of the "penalty kick" in soccer without utilizing the argot of this sport, one is not punished.

Postmodern criminologists point out, however, that there are instances in which people are disciplined when resisting the use of the discourse demanded of them. Sustained membership in a juvenile gang often includes strict adherence to the code of speech representing the attitude, point of view, and focal concerns of the delinquent association (Miller, 1958; see also Arrigo and Schehr, 1998 for related analysis). A successful insanity defense plea entails some assessment of the defendant's speech-thought-behavior, at the time of the commission of the crime, based upon clinicolegal definitions of wellness, pathology, and the like (Arrigo, 1993a, 1994, 1996a). A proper prison write-up filed by a correctional officer involves some professional, procedure-driven description of the inmate infraction. In each instance, the person who speaks, acts, or writes is compelled to do so from within definite linguistic boundaries of meaning. The juvenile who refuses to speak through the code may be ostracized. The disordered defendant whose speech-thought-behavior is consistent with psychological wellness may be convicted. The correctional officer whose writing deviates from facility procedures may be reprimanded and, eventually, fired. According to postmodern criminology, this is how the dialectics of linguistic struggle and control function in every day contexts.

Postmodernists are also concerned about how to address the dilemma described above. They do not believe that the solution resides in the substitution of the dominant grammar with that of oppositional grammars. Thus the notion of "privileging" voices and ways of knowing is antithetical to the postmodern project. Creating new standards for saying things and construing events can be just as oppressive as the given system of communication, especially if hierarchical, though new, arrangements are maintained. This is why reversing or rearranging the significance of various perspectives is resisted by postmodernists.

According to postmodern criminology, the problem of crime (and law) can be solved by establishing replacement discourses. Replacement grammars entail the intercession of transpraxis (Henry and Milovanovic, 1991: 295–299). Transpraxis is the stance we assume in relation to our *spoken* connection to the institutions and social phenomena which constitute our lives. Through transpraxis we "are made continuously aware of the interrelatedness of our agency and the structures it reproduces through constitutive productive work such as talking, perceiving, conceptualizing, and theorizing" (Henry and Milovanovic, 1996: 204). Thus the structure of policing, lawyering, adjudicating, punishing, etc., shapes the people who engage in these endeavors. Moreover, these endeavors are shaped by the language we use to converse about them, particularly when engaged in these criminal justice activities. Postmodern criminology seeks the discovery of communication and interactional styles that help liberate subjects from the limiting (and therefore alienating and distancing) meanings implied in the conventional discourse on these structures. These alternative, more authentic, speech codes do not function as a substitute for the old ones. They are designed to provide different, hopefully greater, inclusiveness, especially for those whose voices would not otherwise find embodiment in the dominant discourse.[13]

Radical criminology seeks as its goal the elimination of class-based inequalities, endemic to a capitalistic economic system, through the creation of a socialist society.

Postmodern criminology seeks as its goal the equalization of linguistic power and authority through the elimination of competitive grammars.—Radicals contend that the only meaningful response to the problem of crime generated by capitalistic social and economic structures is the transition to socialism (Lynch and Groves, 1989: 127). Quinney (1979: 67) has even suggested that resolving patterns of crime through capitalistic methods "will solve *none* of the internal contradictions of the capitalist mode of production" (emphasis added). Radicals note that the substantial change they propose within the economic sphere requires macro-structural transformation.

Recognizing its limited scope of influence within the larger socio-political sector, radical criminology agitates for mid-level and intermediate policy solutions. Recommendations by radicals are extensive and include such initiatives as the prosecution of white collar criminals (Friedrichs, 1995), the abolition of repressive incarcerative practices (MacLean and Pepinsky, 1993), and the establishment of community-oriented and peace-directed crime control strategies (Pepinsky and Quinney, 1991). The radical policy agenda asserts that these and other mid-range responses will decrease the rampant economic marginality, social alienation, and political oppression symptomatic of class-based, capitalistic societies.

Postmodern criminologists maintain that the goal of replacement discourses and multiple ways of knowing is greater inclusivity, diverse communication, and a pluralistic culture. To achieve these ends, postmodernists listen carefully and incorporate the otherwise excluded points of view in the constitution of crime definitions and acts of social harm. In order not to silence or dismiss other grammars, postmodern criminologists consider the reconstitutive effects of their own speech regarding the discourse on crime. In other words, people's attitudes on crime are shaped by the dominant language

13. Others have examined how replacement discourses can be cultivated in various institutional settings. The work of Freire (1972, 1973) on education and pedagogy, Unger (1987) on empowered democracies, Cornell (1991, 1993) on woman and law all offer transformative possibilities. For more on the creation of replacement discourses within criminal justice practice see Henry and Milovanovic, 1996:215–235.

used to convey meaning about crime. At the same time, people co-shape the crime discourse through the words and phrases they utilize to describe it. As postmodern criminologists conclude, creating a society in which multiple desires can find embodiment in alternative discourses not only liberates citizens from the dictatorial constraints of prevailing speech patterns, but legitimizes their role in the project of reducing crime in society and harm to others. By affirming the significance of different, previously excluded, voices in the articulation of criminological notions, linguistic hegemony is neutralized and social power is equalized.

Radical Versus Postmodern Criminology: A Conflict Theory Analysis

Based on the radical and postmodern reassessment of the core criminological principles contained within conflict theory, I am now prepared to examine the relationship between radical and postmodern criminology. Table 1 summarily lists the following: 1) the theoretical issue previously under consideration; 2) the core conflict principle on that issue; 3) radical criminology's position on the core conflict principle; and 4) postmodern criminology's position on the core conflict principle. For purposes of simplicity and clarity, responses identified in the radical and postmodern category are stated as "consistent" or "inconsistent" with conflict theory.

Table 1. Analysis of Radical and Postmodern Criminology in Relation to Core Conflict Theory Tenets

Issue Under Review	Conflict Principle	Radical Criminology	Postmodern Criminology
1. Type of Theory	Structural	Consistent	Inconsistent
2. Nature of Conflict	$, status, power	Consistent	Inconsistent
3. Ends of Conflict	Control Crime Definitions	Inconsistent	Inconsistent
4. Nature of Crime	Crime Not Absolute	Inconsistent	Consistent
5. Definition of Crime	A Probability Statement	Inconsistent	Inconsistent
6. Crime Problem Source	Human Nature	Inconsistent	Inconsistent
7. Goal of Conflict	Equalize Power	Inconsistent	Consistent

In what follows, I more closely examine the findings presented in Table 1. These findings are of two types. The first set of observations address the relationship between radical and postmodern criminology in light of conflict theory. The first clustering of comments attempts to succinctly clarify the association between these two criminologies by comparing their respective positions on each conflict theory principle. The second set of observations examines the relationship between postmodern criminology and conflict theory. The second clustering of comments broadly considers how conflict-focused postmodern criminology is and what utility the conflict model offers for understanding this criminology. Some observations on radical criminology's conflict basis are also examined.

Clarifying the Relationship Between Radical and Postmodern Criminology: A Conflict Theory Explication

A brief comparative review of the radical and postmodern responses to the seven core tenets of conflict theory and crime, indicates that these two criminologies are mostly dissimilar. Radical and postmodern criminology differ dramatically in four conflict categories. These include distinct points of view on issues 1, 2, 4, 7. Further, in the remaining three categories (issues 3, 5, 6), radical and postmodern criminology both offer responses that are inconsistent with the conflict position. However, in each instance, the two criminologies disagree for vastly different reasons.

Similar to conflict theory, radical criminology is a structural theory. Postmodern criminology however, is a theory of the subject. Radical criminology also identifies the nature of the conflict to be about interests. These interests fundamentally include economic and political power. Social standing is important to radical criminology; though, it is regarded as an indirect effect of both the acquisition and accumulation of capital. Postmodern criminology offers an entirely different conception on the nature of the conflict. What is at stake is neither money, status, nor power. Instead, postmodern criminology identifies the conflict to be waged over reality and how our very existences are defined and lived through language and prevailing discourses.

Similar to conflict theory, postmodern criminology maintains that violations of human rights and acts of social harm are not absolute. Radical criminology, however, asserts that the nature of crime is such that there is some consensus on what constitutes harm and, thus, certain acts are categorically wrong and/or unequivocally criminal. The goal of conflict in postmodern criminology is the equalization of power and a pluralistic, participatory democracy. These ends are achieved through the elimination of competitive grammars and the inclusion of replacement discourses. Postmodernists argue that these activities will effect a reduction in crime. Much like postmodern criminology, conflict theory does not believe that substituting one hierarchical arrangement of segment interests will reduce crime. Although conflict theory does not emphasize the role of language per se, it, too, seeks to foster a more evenly distributed crime rate. Conflict theory argues that this end can be achieved by equalizing interests among the various segments of society. Radical criminology, however, identifies as its primary goal the establishment of a socialist society.

The preceding analysis pointed out where either radical or postmodern criminology was consistent with a conflict tenet and then explored the differences between the two criminologies. There are also conflict principles upon which both radical and postmodern criminology disagree. Although these are shared areas of inconsistency, the explanations offered by the two criminologies differ immensely in each case.

According to conflict theory, the end of conflict, in relation to law and crime, is to determine what definitions will prevail. Those segments in society with the most economic influence, social standing, and political power will be best positioned to shape such definitions. Radical criminology is not interested in establishing crime definitions per se. Rather, it sees the essential conflict to be waged over control and ownership of the means of economic production. Postmodern criminology is likewise disinterested in the definitions of crime as a fundamental end of conflict. Instead, postmodern criminology regards the crucial conflict to be about determining the control and ownership of the means of linguistic production. As I have shown, economic production (radical criminology) is not the same as linguistic production (postmodern criminology).

Conflict theory contends that definitions of crime are expressed through a probability statement. Certain segments of society (quasi-groups with broadly recognized and legitimized interests) establish laws and define crime while certain other segments of society (quasi-groups with under recognized or legitimized interests) yield to such expressions of power. As groups increase their interests (i.e., money, status, and power) they increase their ability to determine the crime agenda. As groups decrease their interests, they decrease their ability to determine the crime agenda.

Radical criminology asserts that definitions of crime are directly linked to and influenced by the political economy. The class structure of capitalistic societies produces massive divisions among citizens best reflected in the unequal distribution of interests (i.e., capital). The greater the disparities, the greater the likelihood that those with less wealth and/or income will engage in behavior that those with more income and/or wealth define as criminal behavior. Postmodern criminology maintains that definitions of crime are a function of the dominant language in use. In capitalistic cultures, those who control and regulate the discourse, in effect, are entrepreneurs. They are also lawyers, doctors, police personnel, correctional administrators, and all group members insisting that a specialized way of communicating be adopted when interacting with representatives of these collectives. Crime, then, is related to the frequency, intensity, and duration of the oppositional language employed by non-users while resisting the dominant discourse in use. As I have demonstrated, rooting definitions of crime in the capitalistic economic system (radical criminology) is not the same as rooting them in privileged grammars (postmodern criminology).

Conflict theory contends that the source of the crime problem is traceable to human nature. The competitive greed of individuals assuming membership in various segments of society accounts for conflict—not the least of which would be the dilemma of crime. In order to neutralize harm and victimization, quasi-group interests need to be equalized. Radical criminology claims that the origin of crime is embedded in the structure of capitalistic economic systems. In order to solve the problem of crime, radicals call for the overthrow of the prevailing system. Postmodern criminology alleges that the source of crime is found in language and the marginalizing and alienating effects of dominant grammars. According to postmodernists, crime and harm can be reduced, but only through the creation of replacement and more authentic discourses. These are codes that embody the voices of and ways of knowing for disenfranchised collectives. As I have demonstrated, overthrowing the capitalistic political economy (radical criminology) is not the same as cultivating new language systems (postmodern criminology).

Postmodern Criminology and Conflict Theory: Reconsidering the Relationship

Based on the findings presented in Table 1, several statements can also be made about the degree to which postmodern criminology is truly a conflict theory. Related to this matter is the extent to which it is useful to conceptualize postmodern criminology through the conflict frame of reference.

Postmodern criminology is consistent with conflict theory on issues 4 and 7. Both agree that violations of human rights and definitions of crime are not absolute. Further, both agree that the goal of conflict is to produce a more inclusive, less crime-ridden society. The equalization of power is fundamental to both perspectives. Generally speaking, however, postmodern criminology is inconsistent with most of the conflict principles reviewed. This inconsistency suggests that postmodern criminology and conflict theory are fundamentally different. They are different as to: type of theory; nature of the conflict; ends of conflict; nature of crime; and source of crime problem.

It is also instructive to consider how conflict-focused postmodern criminology is in comparison to radical criminology. Radical criminology is consistent with conflict theory in two categories. These include type of theory (issue 1) and the nature of the conflict (issue 2). On all other conflict theory principles, the two are dissimilar. In terms of points of consistency versus inconsistency, postmodern and radical criminology are equally conflict-oriented. Although they are conflict-focused in different areas, both criminologies are consistent with conflict theory in two of the seven categories.

From my analysis of postmodern criminology and its relationship to conflict theory, it is best to *not* conceptualize postmodern criminology as a type of conflict theory. As described in the introduction, there is some confusion regarding where best to position postmodern criminology in relation to both radical thought and the conflict model. This investigation indicates that it is wise to think of postmodern criminology as an independent orientation and method of analysis, providing insight on where and how the discourse of law and crime fail to represent the common good. While there are certainly some points of convergence between it and conflict theory, postmodern criminology is a very different perspective from which to engage in social science research. The same is true about postmodern criminology's association with radical thought. While there are some approximate areas of agreement, the two orientations are mostly different. Thus they, too, should be viewed as conceptually distinct in all future criminological endeavors addressing matters of import for theory, method, and practice.

Conclusions

Theoretical advances in criminology abound. Many of these innovative conceptual models ostensibly share some affinities with conflict analysis and radical thought. One of these novel perspectives is postmodernism. Each of these models (conflict, radical, and postmodern inquiry) is useful for comprehending the operation of law and crime as forces of ideological and repressive control. This investigation emphasized the importance of distinguishing between radical and postmodern criminology by exploring their respective positions on several core conflict theory principles. We discovered that postmodern thought is very different from radical criminology. Further, we found that conceptualizing postmodern criminology as a type of conflict theory is a misnomer. In sum, although there are some points of convergence between: 1) radical criminology and conflict theory; and 2) postmodern criminology and conflict theory, it is generally better to recognize these three perspectives as unique and distinct approaches to the study of crime and its control.

These conclusions are significant. Questions concerning the functioning of law and its capacity to advance the interest of the common good must principally proceed from theoretical inquiries. Indeed, as this chapter makes clear (and as this book endeavors to explore), the problems plaguing the criminal justice system (including the oppression promulgated by law), necessitate critical evaluation. Conflict theory, radical thought, and postmodern criminology are, in the main, three distinct conceptual prisms that help us understand how forces of marginalization, victimization, and oppression are enacted through systems such as the law.

References

Arrigo, Bruce A. 1992. Deconstructing Jurisprudence: An Experiential Feminist Critique. *The Journal of Human Justice* 4(1):13–30.

Arrigo, Bruce A. 1993a. *Madness, Language, and the Law*. Albany, NY: Harrow and Heston.

Arrigo, Bruce A. 1993b. An experientially-informed feminist jurisprudence: Rape and the move toward praxis. *Humanity and Society* 17(1): 28–47.

Arrigo, Bruce A. 1994. Legal Discourse and the Disordered Criminal Defendant. *Legal Studies Forum* 18(1): 93–112.

Arrigo, Bruce A. 1995. The Peripheral Core of Law and Criminology: On Postmodern Social Theory and Conceptual Integration. *Justice Quarterly* 12(3): 447–472.

Arrigo, Bruce A. 1996a. *The Contours of Psychiatric Justice: A Postmodern Critique of Mental Illness, Criminal Insanity and the Law*. New York: Garland.

Arrigo, Bruce A. 1996b. The Behavior of Law and Psychiatry: Rethinking Knowledge Construction and the Guilty But Mentally Ill Verdict. *Criminal Justice and Behavior* 23(4): 472–592.

Arrigo, Bruce A. 1996c. Desire in the Psychiatric Courtroom: On Lacan and the Dialectics of Linguistic Oppression. *Current Perspectives in Social Theory* 16: 159–187.

Arrigo, Bruce A. 1997a. Media Madness as Crime in the Making: On O.J. Simpson, Consumerism, and Hyperreality. In Gregg Barak (ed.), *Representing OJ: Criminal Justice & Mass Culture*, (pp. 123–136). New York: Harrow and Heston.

Arrigo, Bruce A. 1997b. Marxist Criminology and Lacanian Psychoanalysis: Outline for a General Constitutive Theory of Crime. In Jeffrey I. Ross (ed.), *Cutting the Edge: Current Perspectives in Critical and Radical Criminology*, (pp.40–62). New York: Praeger.

Arrigo, Bruce A. (1997c). The constitution of constitutive theory: A review essay of Alan Hunt's *Explorations in Law and Society: Toward a Constitutive Theory of Law* and Stuart Henry and Dragan Milovanovic's *Constitutive Criminology: Beyond Postmodernism. Theoretical Criminology: An International Journal,* 1(3): 392–396.

Arrigo, Bruce A. 2000a. Social Justice and Critical Criminology: On Integrating Knowledge. *Contemporary Justice Review* 3(1): 7–37.

Arrigo, Bruce A. 2000b. Ed. *Law, Society, and Lacan.* Special Issue of the *International Journal for the Semiotics of Law.* The Netherlands: Kluwer Press, 13(2): 127–250.

Arrigo, Bruce A. and T.R. Young. 1998. Theories of Crime and Crimes of Theorists: On the Topological Construction of Criminological Reality. *Theory and Psychology* 8(2): 219–253.

Arrigo, Bruce A. and Robert Schehr, 1998. Restoring Justice for Juvenile: A Critical Analysis of Victim Offender Mediation. *Justice Quarterly* 15(4): 629–666.

Arrigo, Bruce and Christopher Williams. 1999. Law, Ideology, and Critical Inquiry: The Case of Treatment Refusal for Incompetent Prisoners Awaiting Execution. *New England Journal on Criminal and Civil Confinement* 25(2): 367–412.

Baudrillard, Jean. 1981. *For A Critique of the Political Economy of the Sign.* St Louis: Telos Press.

Baudrillard, Jean. 1983. *Simulacra and Simulations.* New York: Semiotext(e).

Beirne, Piers. 1979. Empiricism and the Critique of Marxism on Law and Crime. *Social Problems* 26: 373–385.

Bernard, Thomas J. 1981. The Distinction Between Conflict and Radical Criminology. *The Journal of Criminal Law and Criminology* 72(1): 362–379.

Bernard, Thomas J. 1983. *The Consensus-Conflict Debate: Form and Content in Social Theories.* New York: Columbia University Press.

Blau, Julia and Peter Blau. 1982. The Cost of Inequality: Metropolitan Structure and Violent Crime. *American Sociological Review* 47: 114–129.

Bohm, Robert M. 1982. Radical Criminology: An Explication. *Criminology* 19(4): 565–589.

Bonger, Wilhelm. 1916. *Criminality and Economic Conditions.* Boston, MA: Little, Brown.

Borgmann, Anthony.1992. *Crossing the Postmodern Divide.* Chicago: University of Chicago Press.

Bourdieu, Pierre. 1987. The Force of Law: Toward a Sociology of the Juridical Field. *The Hastings Law Journal* 38: 814–853.

Bracher, Mark. 1993. *Lacan, Discourse, and Social Change: A Psychoanalytic Cultural Criticism.* Ithaca, New York: Cornell University Press.

Chambliss, William J. and Robert B. Seidman. 1982. *Law, Order, and Power (2nd).* Reading, MA: Addison-Wesley.

Chambliss, William. 1988. *On the Take: From Petty Crooks to Presidents.* Bloomington, IN: Indiana University Press.

Cornell, Drucilla. 1991.*Beyond Accommodation: Ethical Feminism, Deconstruction and the Law.* New York: Routledge.

Cornell, Drucilla. 1993. *Transformations: Recollective Imagination and Sexual Difference.* New York: Routledge.

Coser, Lewis A. 1967. *Continuities in the Study of Social Conflict.* New York: The Free Press.

Dahrendorf, Ralph. 1959.*Class and Conflict in Industrial Society.* Stanford, CA: Stanford University Press.

Derrida, Jacques. 1973. *Of Grammatology.* Baltimore: Johns Hopkins University Press.

Derrida, Jacques. 1978. *Writing and Difference.* London: Routledge and Kegan Paul.
Einstadter, Werner and Stuart Henry. 1995. *Criminological Theory: An Analysis of its Underlying Assumptions.* Fort Worth, TX: Harcourt Brace.
Engels, Friedrich. 1845. *The Condition of the Working Class in England.* New York: International Publishers.
Foucault, Michel. 1970. *The Order of Things.* New York: Vintage Books.
Foucault, Michel. 1972. *The Archeology of Knowledge.* A. Sheridan (trans.). New York: Pantheon.
Frank, Nancy and M. J. Lynch. 1992. *Corporate Crime, Corporate Violence.* Albany, New York: Harrow and Heston.
Freire, Paolo. 1972. *Pedagogy of the Oppressed.* New York: Herder and Herder.
Freire, Paolo. 1973. *Education for Critical Consciousness.* New York: Seabury Press.
Friedrichs, David O. 1995. *White Collar Crime in Contemporary Society.* Bellmont, CA: Wadsworth.
Giddens, Anthony. 1984. *The Constitution of Society: Outline for a Theory of Structuration.* Oxford: Polity Press.
Goodrich, Peter. 1984. Law and Language: An Historical and Critical Introduction. *Journal of Law and Society* 11:173–206.
Goodrich, Peter. 1987. *Legal Discourse: Studies in Linguistics, Rhetoric, and Legal Analysis.* London: MacMillan.
Groves, W. Byron and N. Frank. 1987. Punishment, Privilege and the Sociology of Structured
Choice. In W. Byron Groves and Graeme R. Newman (eds.), *Punishment and Privilege.* New York: Harrow and Heston.
Groves, W. Byron and Robert J. Sampson. 1986. Critical Theory and Criminology. *Social Problems* 33(6): 58–80.
Guzy, Myer. 1994. Foundations of Western Marxism. Ph.D. dissertation, The Pennsylvania State University.
Handler, Joel. 1992. Postmodernism, Protest, and the New Social Movement. *Law and Society Review* 26(4): 697–731.
Henry, Stuart and Dragan Milovanovic. 1991. Constitutive Criminology: Maturation of Critical Theory. *Criminology* 29(2): 293–315.
Henry, Stuart and Dragan Milovanovic. 1993. Back to Basics: A Postmodern Redefinition of Crime. *The Critical Criminologist* 5(2/3): 1–2, 6, 12.
Henry, Stuart and Dragan Milovanovic. 1996. *Constitutive Criminology: Beyond Postmodernism.* London: Sage.
Henry, Stuart and Dragan Milovanovic. 1999. Eds. *Constitutive theory at Work: Applications in Crime and Justice.* Albany, NY: SUNY Press.
Jackson, Bernard. 1988. *Law, Fact and Narrative Coherence.* Merseyside, U.K.: Deborah Charles.
Kristeva, Julia. 1980. *Desire in Language.* New York: Columbia University Press.
Kristeva, Julia. 1984. *Revolution in Poetic Language.* New York: Columbia University Press.
Keller, Ronald L. 1976. A Sociological Analysis of the Conflict and Critical Criminologies. Ph.D. dissertation, University of Montana.
Lacan, Jacques. 1977. *Ecrits: A Selection.* A Sheridan (trans.). New York: Sheridan.
Lacan, Jacques. 1981. *The Four Fundamental Concepts of Psycho-Analysis.* New
York: W.W. Norton.

Lacan, Jacques. 1991. *L'Envers de la Psychanalyse.* Paris, France: Editions du Seuil.

Lee, S.L. 1990. *Jacques Lacan.* Amherst, MA: University of Massachusetts Press.

Lemaire, A. 1977. *Jacques Lacan.* D. Macey (trans.). New York: Routledge and Kegan Paul.

Lynch, Michael J. 1987. Quantitative Analysis and Marxist Criminology. *Social Justice* 15(1):173–185.

Lynch, Michael J. 1988. Surplus Value, Crime and Punishment: A Preliminary Examination. *Contemporary Crises* 12:329–344.

Lynch, Michael and W. Byron Groves. 1989. *A Primer in Radical Criminology.* Albany, New York: Harrow and Heston.

Lynch, Michael and Paul Stretesky. 1999. Marxism and Social Justice. *Social Justice/Criminal Justice: The Maturation of Critical Theory in Law, Crime, and Deviance,* B. Arrigo (Ed.), (pp. 14–29). Belmont, CA: West/Wadsworth.

Lynch, Michael, Raymond, Michalowski, and W. Byron Groves. 2000. (3rd Ed.). *A Primer in Radical Criminology.* New York: Willow Tree Press.

MacLean, Brian D. 1991. In Partial Defense of Socialist Realism. *Crime, Law, and Social Change* 15: 213–254.

MacLean, Brian D. and Dragan Milovanovic. 1991. *New Directions in Critical Criminology.* Vancouver, Canada: Collective Press.

MacLean, Brian and Harold, Pepinsky. 1993. *We Who Would Take No Prisoners: Selections From the Fifth International Conference on Penal Abolition.* Vancouver, BC: Collective Press.

Manning, Peter K. 1988. *Symbolic Communication: Signifying Calls and the Police Response.* Cambridge: MIT Press.

Marx, Karl. 1868. *Capital (3 vols.).* New York: International Publishers.

Melville, S. 1987. Psychoanalysis and the Place of Jouissance. *Critical Inquiry* 13: 349–370.

Michalowski, Raymond J. 1985. *Order, Law, and Crime: An Introduction to Criminology.* New York: Random House.

Miller, Walter B. 1958. Lower Class Culture as a Generating Milieu of Gang Delinquency. *Journal of Social Issues* 14(3):5–19.

Milovanovic, Dragan. 1986. Juridico-linguistic Communicative Markets: Towards a Semiotic Analysis. *Contemporary Crises* 10: 281–304.

Milovanovic, Dragan. 1988. Jailhouse Lawyers and Jailhouse Lawyering. *International Journal of the Sociology of Law* 16: 455–475.

Milovanovic, Dragan. 1992. *Postmodern Law and Disorder: Psychoanalytic Semiotics, Chaos and Juridic Exegeses.* Liverpool, UK: Deborah Charles.

Milovanovic, Dragan. 1994. *A Primer in the Sociology of Law.* Albany, New York: Harrow and Heston.

Moi, Terri. 1985. *Sexual/Textual Politics.* London: Methuen.

Pepinsky, Harold and Richard Quinney. 1991. *Criminology as Peacemaking.* Bloomington, IN: Indiana University Press.

Pepinsky, Harold E. 1976. *Crime and Conflict.* New York: Academic Press.

Pitkin, Howard. 1971. *Wittgenstein and Justice* Berkeley: University of California Press.

Platt, Anthony. 1975. Prospects for a Radical Criminology in the USA. In Ian Taylor, Paul Walton, and Jock Young (eds.), *Critical Criminology.* Boston, MA: Routledge and Kegan Paul.

Quinney, Richard and J. Wildeman. 1991. *The Problem of Crime: A Peace and Justice Perspective (3rd Ed.).* London: Mayfield.

Ragland-Sullivan, Elizabeth. 1988. *Jacques Lacan and the Philosophy of Psychoanalysis.* Chicago, IL: University of Illinois Press.
Reiman, Jeffrey. 1995. *The Rich Get richer and the Poor Get Prison: Ideology, Class, and Criminal Justice.* Needham Heights, MA: Allyn & Bacon.
Rossi-Landi, F. 1977. *Linguistics and Economics.* Netherlands, Mouton.
Rossi-Landi, F. 1983. *Language as Work and Trade: A Semiotic Homology for Linguistics and Economics.* South Hadley, MA: Bergin and Garvey.
Quinney, Richard. 1979. *Criminology.* Boston, MA: Little, Brown.
Schwartz, Martin D. and David O. Friedrichs. 1994. Postmodern Thought and Criminological Discontent: New Metaphors for Understanding Violence. *Criminology* 32: 221–246
Schwartz, Martin D. and Dragan Milovanovic. 1999. *Race, Gender, and Class in Criminology: The Intersections.* New York: Garland.
Salecl, Robert. 1993. Crime as a Mode of Subjectivization: Lacan and the Law. *Law and Critique* 4(1): 2–20.
Sellin, Thornsten. 1938. *Culture, Conflict, and Crime.* New York: Social Science Research Council.
Simmel, George. 1950. *The Sociology of George Simmel.* Kurt H. Wolff (trans.). Glencoe, ILL: The Free Press.
Simmel, George. 1955. *Conflict and the Web of Group Affiliation.* Rinehard Bendix (trans). Glencoe, Ill: The Free Press.
Silverman Kaja. 1983. *The Subject of Semiotics.* New York: Oxford University Press.
Sykes, Gresham. 1974. The rise of Critical Criminology. *the Journal of Criminal Law and Criminology* 65: 206–213.
Taylor, Ian, Paul Walton, and Jock Young. 1973. *The New Criminology: For A Social Theory of Deviance.* New York: Harper and Row.
Turk, Austin T. *Criminality and Legal Order.* Chicago: Rand McNally.
Unger, Roberto. 1987. *False Necessity.* New York: Cambridge University Press.
Vold, George B. 1958. *Theoretical Criminology*, New York: Oxford University Press.
Vold, George B., Thomas J. Bernard, and Jeffrey B. Snipes 1998. *Theoretical Criminology* (4th). New York: Oxford.
Williams, Christopher and Bruce Arrigo (2001). *Law, Psychology, and Justice: Chaos Theory and the New (Dis)Order.* Albany, NY: SUNY Press.
Wittgenstein, Ludwig. 1958. *The Blue and Brown Books.* New York: Harper and Row.
Young, Jock. 1975. Working-class Criminology. In Ian Taylor, Paul Walton, and Jock Young (eds.), *Critical Criminology.* Boston, MA: Routledge and Kegan Paul.
Young, Jock. 1987. The Task Facing a Realist Criminology. *Contemporary Crises* 11: 337–356.

The Jury and the Common Good: Synthesizing the Insights of Modern and Postmodern Legal Theories

Andrew E. Taslitz,[1]
Howard University School of Law

Introduction

The institution of the jury has a powerful grip on the popular legal imagination. (*See generally* Bergman and Asimow, 1996: 232–69).[2] Despite media coverage critical of the jury, it remains a symbol of American democracy. Trial by jury is:

> [a]bout the best of democracy and about the worst of democracy.... Juries convicted women as witches in Salem, but they resisted witch hunts for communists in Washington. Juries in the American South freed vigilantes who lynched African-Americans, but in the North they sheltered fugitive slaves and the abolitionists who helped them escape.... The names of John Peter Zenger, John Hancock, Angela Davis, Father Philip Berrigan, and the Oakland Seven mark the courage of jurors willing to protect dissenters from the orthodoxies of the day. In short, the drama of trial by jury casts ordinary citizens as villains one day, heroes the next, as they struggle to deal justly with

---

1. Andrew E. Taslitz, Visiting Professor of Law, Duke University Law School of Law, 2000–01; Professor of Law, Howard University School of Law; J.D., University of Pennsylvania Law School, 1981; former Assistant District Attorney, Philadelphia, PA. Professor Taslitz thanks his wife, Patricia V. Sun, Esq., for her comments on earlier versions of this essay, and Carla Bedrosian and Amy Pope for their outstanding research assistance. Professor Taslitz also thanks Delphyne Bruner and Ann McCloskey for superb secretarial assistance and the Howard University School of Law for its financial support of this project.

2. Bergman and Asimow have collected in the cited portion of their work reviews and analysis of a wide range of popular films involving the jury. These films illustrate the popular fascination with the jury, as do the many high-profile trials covered by the media, and the daily fare on Court T.V. (*See generally* Schrager, 1999; Sherwin, 2000).

> the liberties and properties—sometimes even the lives—of their fellow men and women.
> (Abramson, 1994: 1).

Even in more mundane cases—from petty theft to automobile accidents—the jury involves the ordinary citizen in profound decisions of legal morality. The jury must find facts—for example, did Johnny pull the gun's trigger, ending his wife's life, or was Johnny framed by the wife's jealous ex-lover?—that determine whether a man lives or dies. (*See* Damaska, 1997: 26–57). And, despite public protestations to the contrary, the jury also creates law everyday. (*See generally* Brown, 1998; Conrad, 1998).[3] A judge will tell jurors that they may mitigate murder to manslaughter if the defendant killed under an "extreme emotional disturbance" for which there is a "reasonable explanation or excuse." (MPC §210.3). But does killing another because he ridiculed the killer's sexual orientation or "foreign" accent count as a "reasonable explanation"? (Judge Draws Protests After Cutting Sentence of Gay Man's Killer, N.Y. Times, Aug. 17, 1994: A15.) (*Cf.* Taslitz, 1998a). In applying vague legal standards to concrete facts the jury necessarily gives those standards a new meaning. Juries deal with issues of money, power, sex, revenge, greed, anger, and jealousy enacted in the trial theater. (*See generally* Schrager, 1999). Jury deliberations are the subject of legend, and jury verdicts, followed closely by the media, evoke praise or outrage, catharsis or frustration. Because juries deal with the messy stuff of life in vivid narratives, jury tales enliven novels, movies, television shows, comic books, plays, and, gambling. (*See generally* Bergman and Asimow, 1996). Jury images shape popular perceptions of justice and mold the public's sense of the justice system's legitimacy. (*See, e.g.*, Lehman, 1997.) Although few cases actually result in a jury trial, all other legal tasks—negotiation, contract drafting, mediation, counseling, and arbitration, among others—take place in the jury's shadow. (*See generally* Mauet, 1995). The *fear* of an uncertain jury verdict is indeed what motivates parties and lawyers to seek alternative means for resolving their disputes. All this high drama is at its greatest in a criminal trial.

---

3. Professor Darryl K. Brown reviews empirical data demonstrating that jurors necessarily interpret criminal statutes in the act of applying them to a specific case. (*See generally* Brown, 1998). For Professor Brown, the dichotomy between "law" and "facts" is misleading, each interacting so extensively as really to be part of a single process. Professor Conrad offers a rousing historical and theoretical defense of the idea that the jury, not the judge, is the ultimate source of the law, so-called "jury nullification." (*See generally* Conrad, 1998). On the history of the jury, *see* Levy K. (1999). The Palladium of Justice Chicago: I.R. Dee.

For all these reasons, the jury serves as a gripping paradigm for examining differing modern and postmodern conceptions of the common good in the law. And novels and films serve as particularly illuminating ways to illustrate these differing conceptions.

This essay will critique four novels, later made into films, about jury trials, using them as windows into contrasting modern and postmodern notions of the common good. By "modernism," I mean legal theories that draw on the key teachings of the Enlightenment project as a search for a pre-existing truth using the neutral inquiry tools of legal "science." (*See* Litowitz, 1997: 8–18; Brooks, 1998: 28–30; Minda, 1995: 5–6, 13–62). By postmodernism, I mean legal theories that reject many or all enlightenment teachings, instead viewing reality as a social construct, the outcome of politically-charged negotiations among radically different groups. (*See* Litowitz, 1997: 8–18; Brooks, 1998: 28–30; Minda, 1995: 224–57).

Part one analyzes *To Kill a Mockingbird* and *Twelve Angry Men* as classic examples of the modernist view of law. Part two contrasts that view with the postmodern ones, using *A Jury of Her Peers* and *A Time to Kill* as a way to highlight the two movement's differences.[4] Part three explains why modernism and postmodernism are not necessarily mutually exclusive. To the contrary, if law is ever to serve the common good, a fusion of the insights of both movements is needed. Part four applies the tools crafted in Parts one through three of this essay to analyze other essays in this volume, exploring some shared themes that synthesize the individual authors' work to show us some possible gateways to a fairer and more rational legal future.

Modernism and the Law

To Kill A Mockingbird

To Kill a Mockingbird recounts defense lawyer Atticus Finch's representation of Tom Robinson, a young African-American man falsely accused of beating

---

4. Neither *A Jury of Her Peers* nor *A Time to Kill* is likely to be classified as "postmodernist" in style by literary or film studies scholars nor would many philosophers unconcerned about legal issues find postmodern ideas in these works. My focus, however, is on the message sent by these works about the nature of law generally and of juries specifically, messages that, even if not by design, are strikingly consistent with aspects of *legal* postmodernism—postmodernism as understood and expressed by many legal scholars. Through film and popular novels, elite postmodern legal ideas filter their way into popular consciousness.

and raping Mayella Ewell, a young white woman, in Depression Era Maycomb, Alabama (Lee, 1960).[5] Mayella testifies at trial that Tom attacked her when she invited him into her house to do chores. Mayella's father, Bob, a "racist and alcoholic redneck," (Bergman and Asimow, 1996: 139), testifies that he came home to find Tom on top of Mayella, so Bob chased Tom away. The prosecution offered no medical evidence or third party eyewitness testimony.

Tom told a very different trial tale. He said that Mayella often invited him in to do chores, which he did for free "because he felt sorry for her." (*Id.* at 140). On this occasion, she grabbed and kissed him just as her father came home. Mayella did suffer facial injuries, but Atticus demonstrates that only a left-handed person—such as Mayella's father—could have caused those injuries. Bob's left arm was, however, useless. Atticus' blistering cross-examination indeed quickly destroys Mayella's composure, and it is "apparent to everyone except the jury that her injuries came from a beating by her father." (*Id.* at 142). Nevertheless, based on minimal circumstantial evidence from obviously lying witnesses, the all-white jury convicts Tom. When Tom later tries to flee, he is killed by the sheriff's deputy.

Bob Ewell later attacks Atticus' two children, Scout and Jem, as they are walking home from a school pageant. The quiet and odd Boo Radley suddenly appears, killing Ewell in defense of the children. The sheriff falsely asserts that Ewell fell on his knife, thus protecting Boo "to atone for... [the sheriff's] terrible mistake in having believed the Ewells' false story." (*Id.* at 140). Atticus initially opposes the sheriff's lie but finally relents because "[e]ven to him, some values are of greater importance than the truth." (*Id.* at 142).

Atticus' tale reflects a number of assumptions and tensions in what I will call the market-based strand of modernist Enlightenment philosophy.[6] The

---

5. A useful summary of Harper Lee's novel, on which the film was based, and an excerpt from Atticus Finch's closing argument from the novel, appear in Shapiro, F. & Garry, J. (Eds.), (1998). Trial and Error: An Oxford Anthology of Legal Stories (pp. 330–346). New York: Oxford University Press. on which I partly here rely. I cite to this anthology or to Harper Lee's novel only where I quote from one of those sources. Otherwise, the plot summary offered here comes from my own reading of these texts, and of the analysis of the film by Bergman, P., and Asimow, M. (1996). Reel Justice: The Courtroom Goes to the Movies (pp. 139–142). Kansas City: Andrews and McMeel, which I also cite where appropriate. I make no distinction between the novels and the corresponding film versions discussed in the essay unless there is a difference of significance to a point I am trying to make.

6. Excellent summaries of modernist Enlightenment legal thinking can be found in Minda, G. (1995). Postmodern Legal Movements: Law and Jurisprudence at Century's End (pp. 1–80). New York: New York University Press and Litowitz, D. E. (1997). Postmodern Philosophy & Law: Rorty, Nietzsche, Lyotard, Derrida, & Foucault (pp. 1–19). Lawrence,

tale's author, Harper Lee, makes clear her view that there is a single, objective truth to be found "out there": there was no rape.[7] Tom Robinson told the truth, and the Ewells lied. This assumption reflects Enlightenment empiricism, in which there is a sharp distinction between subject and object, observer and observed. (*See* Taslitz, 1998b: 8–11, 12–28; and nn. 20, 32–33; Cammack, 1995: 411–15). The "truth" about what happened between Maya and Tom is not even partly in Tom's eyes, or Maya's, or the jury's. These observers' and participants' preconceptions do not combine with physical events to create a reality. There *is* a reality separate from our minds, and "truth" exists if our statements about the world accurately reflect that reality, "if they accurately depict the world as it really is." (Cammack, 1995: 414). Moreover, reason—a universal faculty of the mind held by all persons—can be applied to articulate a set of rational, true beliefs about the world, beliefs separate from the contingent and distorting features of tradition and emotion. (Litowitz, 1997: 10). The jury was perfectly capable of seeing the truth about what happened, even though they were not present at the scene of the alleged

---

Kan.: University Press of Kansas. Professor Minda describes the "first generation" of law and economics scholars (those applying the rational actor theories of classical economics to the law) as a "jurisprudence of conceptualism," Minda, 1995, *supra*, at 8B, "not unlike legal formalism." *Id.* at 90. "Conceptualists" and "formalists" are part of modernist legal thinking, the core tenets of which are developed later in Part I of this essay. *See* Id. at 14–19, 24. While writers of fiction like Harper Lee did not think in these terms, their visions of the courtroom and the justice system as ideally about rational exchange of ideas and verdicts in a free market, resulting in "correct" discovery of pre-existing or logically derivable truths, is quite consistent with this "first generation" of law and economics scholarship. Harper Lee, of course, recognized that the system often falls short of this idea, but the problem is not merely the system's its distortion by bias, as we will soon see. Thus I label tales like *To Kill a Mockingbird* part of a "market—based strand" of Enlightenment philosophy.

Minda goes on to argue that there is a "second generation" of law and economics scholars who are more diverse than the first generation scholars but still connected to modernist thinking. *See id.* at 95–101. But the newer wave, the "post-Chicago" law and economics scholars, says Minda, reject many modernist assumptions, moving closer to postmodernism's shared ambivalence toward reason and skepticism of law's autonomy from other social institutions. *See* id. at 101–05. Whether Minda is right or not about post-Chicago thinkers, judges and legal practitioners at jury trials tend to be dominated by modernist, first-generation, rational actor, free-market thinking. *See* Taslitz, 1999b: 103–109; *accord*, Cammack, M. (1995). In Search of the Post-Positivist Jury, 70 Ind.L.J. 405–489, (pp. 411–415) (making similar point in the context of jury selection).

7. For a critique of the modernist assumption that trials always search for a pre-existing truth "out there," *see* Taslitz, A. (1998). A Feminist Approach to Social Scientific Evidence: Foundations, 5 Mich. J. Gender & L 1–80.

crime when it happened. Indeed, in his closing argument Atticus urges the jury to "review without passion the evidence you have heard, come to a decision, and restore this defendant to his family." (Sharpio and Garry, 1998: 334). Later, Atticus explains to his son the importance of reason:

> "If you had been on that jury, son, and eleven other boys like you, Tom would be a free man," said Atticus. "So far nothing in your life has interfered with your reasoning process. Those are twelve reasonable men in everyday life, Tom's jury, but you saw something come between them and reason. You saw the same thing that night in front of the jail. When that crew went away, they didn't go as reasonable men, they went because we were there. There's something in our world that makes men lose their heads—they couldn't be fair if they tried. In our courts, when it's a white man's word against a black man's, the white man always wins. They're ugly but those are the fact of life.
> (*Id.* at 346).

What ensures that reason will ordinarily be applied fairly to relevant, relatively complete and accurate information? The answer: the free market for justice, that is, the adversary system. (Taslitz, 199b: 103–09). The adversary system is based on a market metaphor. In the market for justice, lawyers sell persuasive discourse to jurors in exchange for a verdict. The free clash of opposing ideas achieves truth as each side competitively seeks to prove its case while pointing out the weaknesses of the opponent's case. The battle of equally matched adversaries is the way to justice. (Taslitz, 1999c: 188–91). Cross-examination, "the greatest engine for the discovery of truth ever invented," (Wigmore, 1983: § 1:18, at 608), by a well-prepared zealous advocate is one central tool to ensuring a properly-functioning market. (*See, e.g.*, Taslitz, 1999b: 81–82, 103–05; Strier 32–33, 54–55). Atticus was such an advocate, so this portion of the market system seemed to work well.

But the market metaphor continues in the jury room. The exchange of ideas among dispassionate, reasoning individuals, rooted in the evidence, is supposed to lead to truth. The image is akin to that of the ""free and robust market of ideas" in first amendment free speech law in which the clash of opposing views is seen as leading to the correct result. (*See* Weinstein, 1999: 11–50). The market result both defines truth and ensures that the pre-existing objective truth will be found via the market process. (Taslitz, 1999c: 188–91). But that process can work only if the jurors act as *individuals*, another aspect of this strand of Enlightenment thinking. (Mercuro and Medema,

1997: 57–60; Minda, 1995: 88–101).[8] Law, this strand maintains, is separate from culture, as is the true "self," a transcendent entity separate from any false or "contingent" self immersed in a particular culture, language, or history. (Litowitz, 1997: 11–12; Taslitz, 1999c: 179–80). Jurors, therefore, must put aside their self-interest, their group affiliations, and their biases to examine evidence with objective reason. (*See* Cammack, 1995: 422–28). Moreover, the exchange of views in the jury helps one person's passion to cancel another's, so that the transcendent self can come out and truth can prevail. (cf. Abramson, 1994: 123). The flaw in Tom Robinson's jury was that group-think replaced individual reasoning. The jurors sat not as a debating body of twelve individual citizens but as a white mob.

The film's rejection of group-think generally is clearest in a scene in which a white mob appears at the jailhouse bent on lynching Tom Robinson. Atticus intervenes, and it seems that he too will suffer at the mob's hands. But Atticus' daughter, Scout, then appears, and she begins to address a member of the mob *as an individual.* "Hey, Mr. Cunninghman, hey; don't you remember me?" declared Scout. "You brought me some hickory nuts one morning. I meant to thank you," she said. "I go to school with your boy, Walter," she continued. By directly addressing Mr. Cunningham, a figure near the front row of the mob, Scout slowly and concretely reminded all of the men gathered at the jailhouse of their individuality. As a result, the mob, at first psychologically, then literally, broke up into neighbors and citizens. These *individuals* listened to Scout and to Atticus, and reason prevailed.

Atticus knows that the same mob mentality might infect the jury room. He understands that the jurors will want to help Mayella hide her own crime: "She knew full well the enormity of her offense," he told the jury, "but because her desires were stronger than the code she was breaking, she persisted in breaking it. She persisted, and her subsequent reaction is something all of us have known at one time or another...she tried to put the evidence of her offense away from her." (Shapiro and Garry, 1998: 332). Atticus continued: "What was

---

8. Professors Mercuro and Medema explain that the Chicago School of Law and Economics, whose teachings I argue match those in Harper Lee's novel, assumes that: "(1) *individuals* are rational maximizers of their satisfactions in their nonmarket as well as their market behavior; (2) *individuals* respond to price incentives in nomarket as well as market behavior...." Mercuro, N., & Medema, S.G. (1997). Economics and the Law: From Posner to Postmodernism. Princeton, N.J. : Princeton University Press: 57. Similarly, Gary Minda describes even most second generation law and economics thinking as "structured by behavioral assumptions about economic motivations of *homogenous individuals....*". Minda, 1995, *supra* note 5, at 101.

the evidence of her offense? Tom Robinson, a human being. She must put Tom Robinson away from her. Tom Robinson was her daily reminder of what she did. What did she do? She tempted a Negro. She did something that in our society is unspeakable: she kissed a black man. Not an old Uncle, but a strong young Negro man. No code mattered to her before she broke it, but it came crashing down on her afterwards." (*Id.*). Atticus knew that racism might unite the jury into a mass bent on protecting Mayella and sacrificing Tom. That mass would justify its actions by "the evil assumption—that *all* Negroes lie, that *all* Negroes are basically immoral beings, that *all* Negroes are not to be trusted around our women...." (*Id.* at 333). Atticus' fears were realized. Perhaps some group-think is unavoidable, but a racially mixed jury might "cancel..out the competing [individual] biases built into identity in America," letting individuals' reason things out, as some theorists have argued. (Abramson, 1994: 123). But that could not happen on an all-white jury of the 1930s South. Group-think, mobocracy, undermines the individualist assumptions of market-based faith, and markets fail, as they failed Tom Robinson.

The power of objective reason also applies not only in fact-finding but in law-finding. The two processes cannot, of course, be entirely separate, each informing the other, as the beginning of this essay explained. Nevertheless, most legal reasoning generally begins with an assumption that the two processes are distinct—the former to be done by the jury, the latter by the judge, with the initial assumption often being abandoned as the jury sits down to deliberate. (*See* Taslitz, 1995: 419–24; Brown, 1998: 1205–38). In much Enlightenment thinking, there are objective legal rules that exist apart from the interpreters of those rules, and a combination of experience and reason can lead the interpreters to the right result. (Minda, 1995: 5). A unique form of reason—"legal method"—based on "deduction, analogy, precedent, interpretation, social policy, institutional analysis, history, sociology, and scientific method" brings Legal Truth to light. (*Id.* at 5–6).[9] This assumption is

9. For first generation law and economics scholars, the "correct" legal result is the most efficient one. *See* Mercuro and Medema, 1997, *supra* note 7, at 59–74. "Public choice" theorists of the second generation of law and economics scholars frequently intimate that the "correct" legal result is instead what a majority would vote for, as they often critique the legislative process as generally being incapable of articulating and reflecting the majority's will. *See, e.g.*, Minda, 1995, *supra* note 5 at 97–99 (on public choice as second generation); Taslitz, A. (1995). Interpretive Method and the Federal Rules of Evidence: A Call for a Politically Realistic Hermeneutics, 32 Harv. J. Leg. 329–401 (pp. 355–357) (explaining public choice theory's common argument that "[l]egislation often reflects the will not of the people but of small, rent-seeking groups."). But many other modernist scholars outside the law and economics fold—what Gary Minda calls "modern normative jurisprudence"—

at work in three ways in *To Kill A Mockingbird* First, author Harper Lee leads us to believe that the law defining rape is clear, that the beyond a reasonable doubt standard is clear, and that no rape has been proven by that standard upon the prosecution's "merely circumstantial" evidence. Second, there is a higher law—whatever its source—that must guide judge and jury; for Atticus, that higher law demands equality in the courtroom, if nowhere else. That commitment to equality must guide judge and jury, as Atticus again explained in his closing argument:

> [T]here is one human institution that makes a pauper the equal of any college president. That institution, gentlemen, is a court. It can be the Supreme Court of the United States or the humblest J.P. court in the land, or this honorable court on which you serve. Our courts have their faults, as does any human institution, but in this country our courts are the great levelers, and in our courts all men are created equal.
>
> I'm no idealist to believe firmly in the integrity of our courts and in the jury system—that is no ideal to me, it is a living, working reality. (Shapiro and Garry, 1998: 334).

A commitment to the higher law of equal respect would break the mobocracy and clear the clouds of prejudice from the skies of reason. But the jury ignored that higher law and fled from truth. Atticus' son, Jem, in response to his father's explanation that racism breeds wrong, expresses his protest: "doesn't make it right," said Jem stolidly. He beat his fist softly on his knee. 'You just can't convict a man on evidence like that—you can't.' (*Id.* at 346). Atticus agrees, pronouncing sentence: "[Y]ou'll see white men cheat black men every day of your life, but let me tell you something and don't forget it—whenever a white man does that to a black man, no matter who he is, how rich he is, or how fine a family he comes from, that white man is trash." (*Id.*).

Third, if truth is denied, then often so is justice, and the higher law, perhaps a law of nature and "of nature's God," (*cf.* Jefferson, 1776: para. 1) will have its due, for justice overrides all else.[10] Atticus again explains to his son: "There's nothing more sickening to me than a low-grade white man who'll

---

look to some higher law, whether found in basic moral principles describing an "objective moral reality," natural law (though most current modernist theories shy away from natural law language), shared community values, or some other source that lends objectivity and autonomy to the law. *See* Minda, 1995, *supra* note 5, at 44–61.

10. *See* Patterson, D. (1996). Law & Truth. New York: Oxford U. Press.

take advantage of a Negro's ignorance. Don't fool yourselves—it's all adding up and one of these days we're going to pay the bill for it. I hope it's not in your children's time." (*Id.*). Justice indeed did not await Atticus' apocalyptic vision. The enigmatic Boo Radley, an often meek and sad creature, acted as the instrument of God's vengeance, ending the life of Bob Ewell, whose lies and abuse of his daughter ultimately led to Tom Robinson's unjust conviction and death. Atticus' zeal for justice initially prompted him to reveal the truth about Boo's actions, but he feared another injustice—perhaps another angry jury unable to hear the truth or the destruction of the ordinarily timid Boo even if acquitted, who, by nature never uttering a word, would be destroyed by being made a public figure. Justice demanded suppressing one truth to serve others. (Bergman and Asimow, 1996: 140–42).

The "common good" in *To Kill A Mockingbird* is thus embodied not in the majority's will but in the community's noblest aspirations as contained in its higher law.[11] Indeed, the majority may delude itself as to its own long-term

---

11. *See supra* note 9. There, I noted three particularly significant modernist views of when a legal result is "correct" *or,* loosely stated, "true": (1) when it is the efficient result; (2) when it reflects majority will; and (3) when it complies with higher law. But each of these three conceptions implies a corresponding notion of the common good. Thus "efficiency" is often justified on the theory that it maximizes a society's total wealth, that wealth is an essential positive good, and that wealth-maximization creates the possibility, if not always the actuality, of making all members of society better off. *See* Mercuro and Medema, 1997, *supra* note 7, at 59–60; Seidenfeld, M. (1996). Microeconomic Predicates to Law and Economics (pp. 49–60); *see generally* Posner, R. A. (1981). The Economics of Justice. Cambridge, Mass.: Harvard University Press (defending the justice of wealth-maximization, even where the increased wealth is not redistributed to make everyone better off). The majority's will is equated by some to justice because a democratic society is by definition committed to the idea that the good of the many rules over the good of the few. *See e.g.*, Merrill, T.W. Chief Justice Rehnquist, Pluralist Theory, and the Interpretation of Statutes, 25 Rutgers L.J. 621, 637 (1994). Higher law dictating a correct result is considered just because those discernible dictates are by definition moral, or God's will, or whatever sense of right is implicit in the particular higher law theory, *see* Minda, 1995, *supra* note 5, at 44–61, and the "right" matters more than the power of the many. Real modernist legal systems, of course, combine all three notions of the common good, for example, often trying to serve majority will but not concerning certain core values for which higher law demands viewing the majority's will as oppression, *cf.* Bickel, A. (1986). The Least Dangerous Branch, 2d ed. New Haven, Conn.: Yale University Press (pp. 16–23) (describing the "countermajoritarian difficulty"), or favoring efficiency where not radically inconsistent with higher law notions of fairness, Calnan, A. (1998). Tobacco Litigation and Regulation: The Settlement and Beyond Litigation and Compensation: Distributive and Corrective Justice Issues in Contemporary Tobacco Litigation. 27 Sw. U. L. Rev. 577–672 (pp. 608–612).

interest or, by imposing its will in service of its perceived self interest, may forfeit any right to declare its views as serving any "common good."[12] What serves white self-interest at the expense of black self-interest in Maycomb, Alabama, what exalts the many over the one, serves no broader community interest. But Atticus serves the greater good, for he speaks on behalf of equal respect, uniform rule application, and objective decisionmaking as commanded by higher law. For Atticus, the higher law is a happy and reciprocal obligation of individual to community and community to individual. Higher law is empowering and sacred, and its service is what ties us together in a common bond. Higher law is salvation.

Twelve Angry Men

I will deal more summarily with the film, *Twelve Angry Men*, which teaches many of the same lessons as does *To Kill A Mockingbird*. In the former, unlike the latter, however, the jury proves to be an assemblage of reason, reaching a just verdict. But the jury's success can be seen as due either to the sound workings of the market or to the deliberative, democratic process, thus enabling us to explore another strand in Enlightenment thinking that I will call "communitarian justice" (defined below).[13]

---

12. *Cf.* Ackerman, B. (1996). We, The People: Foundations. Cambridge, Mass.: Belknap Press of Harvard University Press (arguing that values embraced by the people during "constitutional moments" guide long-term constitutional principles, unlike the short-term rules resulting from more self-interested "normal politics"); Taslitz, A. (1999). What Feminism Has to Offer Evidence Law, Sw. U. L. Rev. 171–219 (Even some modernist, liberal thinkers recognize that individuals can be deluded about their own self-interest).

13. I choose the term "communitarian justice" to emphasize that there is a modernist strand of Enlightenment thinking that has long stressed the important role of the individual in his broader community. The term does not here identify any particular political or intellectual movement beyond this broad stress on community. Communitarian thinking, as here defined, is still modernist in its embrace of "objective" or "correct" (albeit not necessarily only one) answers to legal questions arrived at by universal methods of reason. Furthermore, the individual, not the group, remains the basic unit of analysis, or at least the starting point for discussions. It is individuals in communities, and the relationship between the two, that matters. Nevertheless, communitarian thinking's stress on how individuals in communities "create" correct answers and on how the community helps to craft the individual and vice-versa contains shades of the postmodern social constructionist thinking to be discussed shortly or, more precisely, points of connection that make a conversation between the two movements easier than between more 'liberal" (individual-centered) modernist thinkers, such as market—oriented scholars, and the postmoderns.

Twelve Angry Men recounts the deliberations of a jury in a seemingly open and shut murder one case brought against an 18-year-old teenager accused of stabbing his father.[14] The weather is hot and the jury mostly eager to resolve the matter quickly and move on. But an architect forces the others to pause and examine the evidence more carefully. Ultimately, he changes everyone's mind, and all twelve jurors unanimously vote to acquit.

The evidence against the defendant is straightforward. A woman living near elevated train tracks testifies that she saw the defendant do the dirty deed from her bedroom window and through the windows of a passing train. An old man living downstairs from the victim testified that, around midnight, he heard the defendant say, "I'll kill you," followed by the sound of a body falling. The old man ran to his front door, where he saw the defendant running down the stairs. The knife used in the killing was much like one shown to have been recently bought by the defendant. The defendant's alibi, furthermore, seemed weak. He claimed to have been at the movies from 11:00 p.m. until 3:00 a.m., but he did not even remember the movie's name.

The almost all-white, all male jury (one juror is "perhaps Hispanic") votes eleven to one to convict on a first quick round of many rounds of voting. At one point, a bigoted juror complains that "these people"—referring to the defendant's apparent Puerto Rican ethnicity—are animalistic, fight all the time, have too many children, lie, and have no respect for life. (Washington). Another juror has, because of his estrangement from his own son, "deepened his bitterness toward young people." (Bergman and Asimow, 1996: 267). But, in the end, the architect "forces them to put down their prejudices and expose each piece of evidence to the cold light of logic." (Twelve Angry Men, 1957).

For example, the shopkeeper who had sold the defendant the switchblade testified that "he had never seen one like it." (Bergman and Asimow, 1996: 266). Yet the architect dramatically produces an identical one that he purchased at a pawnshop the night before. Similarly, the architect points out that the old man could not have heard the defendant yell over the noise of a passing train nor have traveled from his bed to his apartment door in the fifteen seconds needed to watch the defendant fleeing. The architect's efforts eventually prove infectious as other jurors begin to pick apart the evidence. Thus one juror points out eyeglass indentations on the female witnesses' nose, indicating her wearing glasses that could not have been on her face when she awakened from sleeping in bed. An older juror suggests that the elderly eyewitness

14. Most of this plot summary is drawn from Bergman and Asimow, 1996, *supra* note 3, at 265–69, and my own recent viewing of the film.

exaggerated his account to gain much-needed attention. Still another juror concedes that he, like the defendant, could not remember the details of a recently-watched movie. The bigot's rantings also backfire, stirring other jurors' commitment to equal justice. In the end, none truly believe in the defendant's innocence, but all find reasonable doubt that obligates them to acquit.

The story can be read as an example of the justice market's working. The free exchange of ideas purged prejudice in the fire of debate. Passionless individuals remained committed to reason and higher law. While this is a fair and perhaps a sensible interpretation, it seems in some ways strained. The architect is indeed an individual, an initial lone wolf crying out against the cold wind of majority oppression. However, justice does not result from competing prejudices canceling one another out, for only one or two jurors display such prejudices. Moreover, emotion plays as much a role as does logic, as other jurors react against the bigot's diatribe and as empathy for witnesses enables the jurors to better assess those witnesses by standing in their shoes. Furthermore, the jury inexorably moves toward a sense of commonality, not simply of agreement, of being a "jury" rather than a collection of twelve separate, distinct persons coldly debating the matter before them. This growing sense of commonality is not the group-think of mobocracy but "the conscience of the community, as one final protection against the risk that the criminal law machine may grind up an innocent person." (Bergman and Asimow, 1996: 269).

This picture is closer to what Professor Jeffrey Abramson calls the "deliberative ideal." He explains:

> Deliberation is a lost virtue in modern democracies; only the jury still regularly calls upon ordinary citizens to engage each other in a face-to-face process of debate. No group can win that debate simply by outvoting others; under the traditional requirement of unanimity, power flows to arguments that persuade across group lines and speak to a justice common to persons drawn from different walks of life. By history and design, the jury is centrally about getting persons to bracket or transcend starting loyalties. This is why, ideally, voting is a secondary activity for jurors, deferred until persons can express a view of the evidence that is educated by how the evidence appears to others.
> (Abramson, 1994: 8).

Indeed, the architect in *Twelve Angry Men* promises to vote with the majority on a second vote if no one else then joins the architect's vote for acquittal. An older juror does join the architect, not because he is persuaded by the latter's argument about reasonable doubt but because he wants to keep the conversation going. The conversation—an open embrace of ideas in good faith among trusting participants working toward a shared goal (Pineau 18–19)—replaces the free market metaphor. As Professor Abramson further explains, jurors must "clearly understand that their goal is not to represent, to protect, or to assert the interest of their own groups." (*Id.* at 195). Rather, it is "to join with others in search of the truth and shared justice, making a positive contribution to that search by drawing on their own backgrounds when necessary but also listening to what others know better by virtue of their experiences." (Abramson, 1994: 196). Jurors thus contribute to an "ongoing discussion" that achieves "collective wisdom through deliberation, rather than collapsing into a body where jurors behave as if their function were to represent the preconceptions and interests of their own kind." (*Id.*)

The deliberative ideal is an instance of the communitarian strand in Enlightenment thinking. While the market strand viewed the common good as a freely negotiated result among isolated individuals, communitarians do not so clearly link individual choice and benefit to the common good. Instead, individuals are viewed as joining in a public space to create something new that did not exist before. The New Republicans—one prominent branch of communitarian thinking, for example—emphasize that debate resulting from "civic virtue" can alter pre-existing preferences and promote consensus among political equals, a process of "deliberation" rather than simple interest-bargaining.[15] Their emphasis on political equality leads them to believe in the possibility of eliminating disparities in political participation and asymmetrical influences among individuals or groups. They remain committed to universalism, believing that an atmosphere of political equality conducive to deliberation mediates among differing views to yield substantively correct answers. The answers are "correct" in the sense that they reflect a "common good" created by the very process of deliberation, an aspiration distinct from the mere self-interested motivations of the individual participants.[16] Furthermore, they

---

15. My summary here of New Republican thinking is drawn from fusing ideas in Kalman, L. (1996). The Strange Career of Legal Liberalism. New Haven : Yale University Press (pp. 143–163); Mercuro and Medema, 1997, *supra* note 7, at 97–100; Sunstein, C. (1988). Beyond the Republican Revival, 97 Yale L. J. 1539–1590.

16. New Republicans sometimes "rejected Kantian premises that political deliberation provided one right answer." Kalman, 1996, *supra* note 14, at 159. But there were nevertheless 'right" and "wrong" answers, that is, answers embodying a "common good" and those that did not. New Republicans thus "avoided pluralism's tendency to interpret political outcomes as inevitably and entirely subjective." *Id.* at 159. The "common" good had an objective, real, and independent existence apart from mere individual self-interest and will. Frank Michelman explained:

emphasize citizenship as definitionally involving broad rights of participation. These rights enable the people to monitor their representatives' behavior, while instilling in individual citizens empathy, virtue, and other qualities that promote community. New Republicans, therefore, favor decentralization, local self-determination, citizen involvement in control of national institutions, and other devices to encourage active citizen involvement in government, values all well-served by the jury. While a narrow self-interest rules the private sphere, private interests can be and are subordinated to the common good in the public sphere. Spirited, ongoing public debate is necessary to craft a common good, and that vigorous process enables government to serve as a creative force and moral teacher.

New Republican and other communitarian thinking differs from market-based reasoning primarily in emphasis. Most of the tenets of new republicanism—rooted, of course, in the Republicanism prevailing at this nation's founding and revived during and shortly after the Civil War (Taslitz, *Racist Personality*)—reflect classic Enlightenment principles: universal reason allows the testing and mutation of ideas to discover an objectively real truth, here about the common good. But the importance in republican thinking of governmental and other institutions cultivating "citizen virtue" is ambiguous in its commitment to the idea of the individual self as prior to the society.[17] While the individual is given a key role in such thinking, law's role in changing the

---

> [R]epublicanism affirms, while liberalism denies, the notion of a statewide, substantive common interest or good. Accordingly, the special mark of republican constitutional thought is affirmation of "an autonomous public interest independent of the sum of individual interests, a common interest existent and determinable not just within the confines of a particular social group.... but at the encompassing level of the sovereign or law-making state.

Sunstein, C. (1983). Interest Groups in American Public Law, 38 Stan. L. Rev. 29–87.

17. These sorts of ambiguities might indeed arguably support the idea of placing New Republicans into the postmodernist camp, much in the way that Professor Minda surprisingly but convincingly labeled some law and economics scholars as postmodern. *See supra* note 5. I reject that move. First, New Republicanism is rooted in our Founders' ideas and classical republicanism, ideas long preceding postmodernism. Furthermore, while New Republicans talk of a broadly defined "community," legal postmoderns stress the role of contextualized group identity over the individual in a way that New Republicans do not. *See infra* note 19. Additionally, the created reality of New Republicans includes the objective, shared "common good" and the instilling of "virtue" in individuals. But postmoderns purport to stress subjectivities, difference, and a far greater degree of social constructionism—of group as well as individual identity, of social institutions, and of our entire sense of what is "real." *See infra* text accompanying notes 23.

individual smacks of more than a mere instrumental function. Political institutions depend on but also create virtuous citizens. The sharp line between the self and the social is muddied, especially because the interaction of individuals helps to create, and make them a part of, something that cannot exist at the individual level: a common good. While the meaning of this "common good" is rarely clearly explained, it seems to be an abstraction about the noblest ideals of a society, something true as well in the version of market-based thinking reviewed here. But while the injustice of *To Kill a Mockingbird* stemmed from the submersion of the individual into the whole, blunting the power of the market, the justice of *Twelve Angry Men* stemmed from their eventual partial fusion into a public, a "jury," reflecting not a community's power but its conscience.

Postmodernism and the Law

Jury of Her Peers

The feminist novella, A Jury of Her Peers, involves the investigation of a farmer's murder.[18] The farmer was strangled to death by a rope. His wife is the chief suspect. The story opens with the murder being investigated in the farmer's home by the sheriff, a neighbor, and a prosecutor. These three men have brought two women with them: the sheriff's and the neighbor's wives. The two women chat in the kitchen while their husbands search the house looking for evidence of a motive. The men ignore the kitchen, concentrating their search on what they see as more likely places, such as the bedrooms and the barn. The women end up finding evidence in the kitchen.

> [Their] attention is drawn to domestic items, such as sewing; they quickly notice that the woman's usually careful stitching went terribly awry at some point, as if she had suffered some shock. Eventually, their affinity with a homemaker's world leads them to a sewing box, in which they find a dead canary, its neck broken in quite the same way as the husband's.
> (Abramson 120 n.*).

To the women, the evidence reveals a severely disturbed and abusive marital relationship. The women view this evidence, however, as exculpatory, not

18. The plot summary here comes from my reading of the novella. *See* Susan Glaspell, *A Jury of Her Peers*, *in* Shapiro and Garry, 1998, *supra* note 3, at 139–156.

*in*culpatory. In the women's view, the murder was justified or excused. This metaphorical jury of the wife's peers acquits her, hiding the evidence to ensure against a less well-informed body's missing the truth.

A Jury of Her Peers can be read as a postmodern tale. For postmodernists, reason is local rather than universal. (Taslitz, 1998b: 7–10 and n.28; Taslitz, 1999c: 173–77, 196–203). Reason is socially constructed, situated in existing practices and discourses. (Taslitz, 1999c: 173–77, 209–17). Those practices reflect current power arrangements, so what legal authorities dub "reasonable" may only be the reason of the powerful. (*See* Taslitz, 1998a: 1056–59). Multiperspectival reason is at work both in making factual and legal judgments. (*See id.* at 1059–65). Indeed, judgments about what happened and about what rules govern, as sorts of reasoning, are socially constructed and thus reflect the perceived realities of the persons and groups making these decisions. (*Id.*). Law and fact are not easily severable, and reasoning about both is necessarily bound up with, and not radically distinct from, power, self-interest, ideology, and emotions. (*See* Taslitz, *Patriarchal Stories* 404–33; Taslitz, 1999c: 192–96, 213–19).

The men in the story indeed exalt a very different sort of reason than do the women. The men search the bedroom and the barn, dismissing the kitchen as but a woman's world: "Nothing here but kitchen things," the sheriff says, "with a little laugh for the insignificance of kitchen things." (Glaspell, 1998: 144). Women, moreover, say the men, are "used to worrying about trifles." (*Id.* at 145).

But in these trifles and "insignificant" kitchen things the women see a troubled relationship and the husband's murder of a beloved pet (a canary) as motives for the wife's crime. The women see what the men cannot: a shabby, cheerless kitchen with a "bad stove" as the sign of a barren life and a troubled marriage; a half-wiped table and a change from careful to sloppy quilting blocks as signs of nervousness and tasks suddenly interrupted; and a bird cage without a bird as a sign of strife where the woman had little beauty but the bird. The men scoff at the women's focus on whether the suspect knotted or quilted her stitching, condescendingly and laughingly instructing the women to look for evidence, and ignoring all that the women examine intently. But what the men see as irrelevant the women see as the crime's solution.

Postmoderns also view the self as "de-centered," the product of language and discourse. (Taslitz, 1998b: 18–23; Taslitz, 1999c: 209–11; Minda, 1995: 240–43). This notion goes beyond the Enlightenment republican idea of a self situated in, interacting with, and partly created by, the community. For postmoderns, the self cannot be understood as apart from the society that created it. (Taslitz, 1999c: 209–10). Moreover, that society consists of groups, and each of us defines ourself partly by our affiliations with certain salient groups, especially those based on race, gender, sexual orientation, and class. We must, therefore, understand the experiences of such groups to understand the individual. (Taslitz, 1998b: 23; Brooks, 1998: 28–30).[19]

The *Jury of Her Peers* women are decidedly defined significantly by their gender. The men certainly view their wives' conversations as but the chatterings of idle gossips. They see the center of the female home, the kitchen, as a way to occupy the women with women's tasks while the men do more important things. When one of the women protests at a man's description of the wife's dish towels as dirty, the man expresses his perception of female solidarity: "Ah, loyal to your sex, I see," he laughed. (Glaspell, 1998: 145). The women, of course, felt precisely such a sense of loyalty, not entirely trusting the men. Indeed, the women felt an affinity, an empathy, for the wife that the men simply could not feel. The women had shared experiences unknown to the men. One woman, Mrs. Hale, remembered that the wife, when younger, had worn pretty clothes, now replaced in her life with her husband by the humiliation of shabby ones. The women understand the pain of what it must be like to live with a man like the dead husband, "Like a raw wind that gets to the bone." (*Id.* at 151). They understand that a life with such a man and without children would be a life of dark pain to which a bird would bring light. "If there had been years and years of nothing, then a bird to sing to you, it would be awful—still, after the bird was still," said Mrs. Hale. "I know what stillness is," replied Mrs. Peters, "when homesteaded in Dakota, and my first baby died—after he was two years old—and me with no other then...." (*Id.* at 153). The women's experiences, their lives *as* women, define who they are, and they hide the broken-necked canary partly as a gesture of solidarity, a way of protecting one of their own.

---

19. At its most extreme, postmodernism might seem to imply a rejection of groups. Thus postmoderns often reject "essentialism"—the idea of an inherent or authentic view of group members. *See* Brooks, R.L. (1998). Critical Procedure. Durham, N.C.: Carolina Academic Press, (pp. 28–30). For some anti-essentialists "legal analysis is highly contextualized and subjective, so much so that it can properly be described as 'personal.' "*Id.* at 29. Nevertheless, the postmodern stress on anti-essentialism most often manifests itself as intersectionality, that is, a plea for recognizing the worldview of each subgroup, "for instance, black women, Asian disabled lesbians, and perhaps even poor white men...." This manifestation, combined with its stress on social constructionism, places analysis of group identity at the core of much (though by no means all) current postmodern legal writing. Importantly, postmodernism "presents equally legitimate claims of reality and, hence, truth for each subgroup. *Id.* at 29. But postmodernism also stresses that individual and subgroup identities can change. *Id.*

Postmodernists are also skeptical about the idea of a fixed truth. Truth is, once again, socially constructed, affected by context and reflecting the distorting influences of class, race, and gender. (Taslitz, 1999c: 209–17, Brooks. 1998: 28–30). These women, because of their different experiences, see a truth that the men cannot. For the men, understanding the motive for the killing would justify labeling the farmer's wife a murderer. After all, she strangled him, apparently while he slept, and with little if any reasonable provocation. But for the women the wife acted in self-defense. Mrs. Hale explained: "No, Wright [the husband] wouldn't like the bird—a thing that sang. She used to sing. He *killed that too*." (Glaspell, 1998: 153). The reference to the husband as killer is ambiguous, but the "that" seems to be not only his wife's singing but her essence. He killed her song and her bird's song and thus killed her or, what is the equivalent, killed her soul. The women understand that the men will see this as murder, and the law as clear: "The law has got to punish crime, Mrs. Hale," said Mrs. Peters. (*Id.*). But ultimately the women apply their own law and their own truth. Justice for them requires the wife's acquittal, protecting her from further abuse and the indifference of others that denied her earlier aid. The women wordlessly understand their mutual agreement to hide the evidence from the men, to serve women's truth in solidarity with "the third woman—that woman who was not there, and yet who had been there with them through that hour." (*Id.* at 155). Only peers (in-group members), not men, can do justice.

The women's actions can, however, also be viewed in a different light. Perhaps they sought not their own truth but *the* truth. What they feared was that male prejudice would blind a jury to that truth. Susan Glaspell, the novella's author, obviously intended for us to sympathize with the women's choice, sensing the "rightness" of their actions. They should not be viewed, therefore, as striking a blow for a group right (a right of women to kill abusive husbands) but for an individual right to equal and fair judgment by unbiased decision-makers. Such an interpretation moves us a step back toward Enlightenment ideas but despairs of the chance that the legal system can discern truth given our inability to get beyond group biases (the men, in short, can never be trusted).

A Time to Kill

John Grisham's *A Time to Kill* searches for a more optimistic vision of this Enlightenment-Postmodern middle ground. The plot is spare: after learning of the arrest of two men who kidnapped, beat, and attempted to lynch his ten year old daughter by two white men, Carl Lee Hailey, an African-American Vietnam Vet, shoots and kills the two men with an M-16 rifle as they leave the courthouse after a bail hearing.[20] In doing so, Hailey also unintentionally shoots Sheriff's Deputy Looney, who, as a result, has one of his legs amputated below the knee.

Hailey's technical defense is insanity, requiring jurors to believe that he suffered from a mental disease or defect that rendered him incapable of knowing the nature and quality of his actions or from knowing they were wrong or that subjected him to an irresistible impulse to kill.[21] His implicit defense was jury nullification—asking the jury to ignore the law as stated by the judge, instead applying the jury's own version of the law.[22]

Grisham shows a sensitivity to postmodern insights that our perceptions are shaped by our social position and that, at least to this extent, ourselves and our understandings are socially constructed. He contrasts prevailing images of "pure" whiteness and "stained" blackness with the contrary truths of his character's lives. The white rapists are "rednecks," one a stupid drug dealer who cannot hold a job, the other an ex-con, having served three years for his similar efforts at drug dealing. The African-American Hailey by contrast is hard-working, honest, and law-abiding, a brave Vietnam Veteran and devoted family man. Hailey rejects his lawyer, Jake Brigance's, entreaties to plead guilty in exchange for life imprisonment instead of the death penalty. In doing so, Hailey explains that he needed the white defense lawyer's help precisely because he will have access to a world Hailey cannot understand:

> You white and I'm Black. Ya see, Jake, you think just like them. That's why I picked you. You one of them, don't you see? Oh you think you ain't cuz you eatin' claws and you out there tryin' to get me off on TV talkin' 'bout Black and White. But fact is, you just like all the rest of them. When you look at me, you don't see a man. You see a Black man.... We ain't no friends, Jake. We on different sides of the line. I ain't never seen you in my part of town. I bet you don't even know where I live. Our daughters, Jake, they ain't never going to play to-

---

20. This plot summary is based on my own recent reading of the novel, Grisham, J. (1989). A Time to Kill. New York : Doubleday, and of the summary and analysis of that plot at Baynes, L.M. A Time to Kill, the O.J. Simpson Trials, and Storytelling to Juries. (1997). 17 Loy. L. A. Ent. L.J. 549–569, (pp. 553–56).

21. The book is fuzzy on the law involved, but my text states a common version of the insanity defense. *See* Dressler, J. (1995) Understanding Criminal Law, 2nd ed. New York, NY: Matthew Bender & Co.

22. For a detailed explanation, analysis, and history of the concept of jury nullification, *see* Duncan C. (1999). Jury Nullification: Evaluation of a Doctrine.

> gether.... America is at war, and you on the other side. How a Black man ever gonna get a fair trial with the enemy on the bench and the jury box—my life in White hands? You, Jake, that's how. You my secret weapon because you one of the bad guys. You don't mean to be, but ya are. It's how you's raised. Nigger. Negro. Black. African-American. No matter how you see me, you see me as different. You see me like the jury sees me. You are them. Now throw out your points of law, Jake. If you was on that jury, what would it take you to set me free? That's how you save my ass. That's how you save us both.
> (A Time to Kill, 1996).

Brigance takes Hailey's advice to heart, leading to a hopeful ending. In his closing argument the next day, Brigance asks the jury to imagine that Hailey and his daughter were white and only then to judge Hailey. Some commentators have seen this gambit as recognizing that whites give value only to white lives. (Baynes, 1997: 552–553, 557–558). But empathy—standing in another man's shoes—always requires drawing on your own experience in a way that makes you feel some commonality to the other. (Taslitz, 1998a: 1054–56). The jury never intellectually forgot that Hailey was Black. But emotionally their thought experiment enabled them to feel his pain. What emerged was a single and higher truth—the limitless value of anyone's children, the unendurable pain of their loss. Grisham paints for us a picture of universal truths (at least some) found via common bonds of inquiry but informed by postmodern insights about the importance of context, perspective, and the social self. This middle way is a cure for the nihilism of extreme postmodernism and the destructive naivete and oppressive universalism of the Enlightenment. In the next and penultimate section of this chapter I examine at a slightly higher level of abstraction how postmodern legal thinking about the common good is indeed evolving toward this middle way.

Postmodernism and "Hypertruths"

Extreme postmodernists do not seem to recognize the possibility of a common good. What these thinkers stress is unmasking the many ways that law covertly serves the private good of the powerful.[23] This unmasking is done to

---

23. *See, e.g.*, Brooks, L. (1998) Critical Procedure Durham, N.C.: Carolina Academic Press (pp. 28–30) (implying similar point). Professor Minda summarized the critique of extreme postmodernism by a leading traditionalist scholar, Owen Fiss:

> Fiss argued that CLS [Critical Legal Studies] practitioners critique without a vi-

provoke powerless groups from complacency and to confront the powerful with their hypocrisy.[24] Postmodern analysis of this sort sees group identity as important, that is, there may be local truths for particular groups in the narrow sense that each group's members share a consensus about the good and the nature of reality. (*See* Brooks, 1998: 28–30). "Group-based" analysis can reveal commonalities among the local truths of seemingly disparate groups, thus spurring coalitions against the elite. (*See* Delgado, 1998: 109–122). But because there are no absolute or universal truths, there is no broader ideal common even to the dominant group to which these postmoderns appeal to guide action.

This singleminded emphasis of these extreme postmoderns on what serves group interests thus smacks of self-interest as a primary rationale for legal change, even if such narrow, self-interested appeals are not necessarily the messages that these thinkers intend to send.[25] But the perceived message of group self-interest as *the* justification for political action leads these postmoderns to be labeled the avatars of a destructive "identity politics." (*See* Gitlin, 1995: 126–65, 200–37; Farber and Sherry, 1997: 78–84; Jacobs and Potter 5, 130–32). Because these postmoderns reject notions of foundational truths or texts with determinate meanings, they also eschew the quest for "rights" as meaningless fictions. (Hunt 227–28; Brooks, 1998: 10–11). Some postmoderns, notably the Critical Legal Studies movement in its heyday, see unending change, the constant unsettling of legal meanings so that no one dominant meaning can take hold, as the only way to break the stranglehold of the elites and to attain political sanity in a world without foundations.[26] Thus endless agitation is the only "truth" worth having.

---

sion of what might replace that which is destroyed—a form of critique Fiss found "unappealing and politically irresponsible." Fiss claimed that the indeterminacy claims that Crits assert about law are suspect because the assertions have not been empirically established or defended. Fiss then argued that the "law is politics" creed of CLS is threatening to both law and public morality because there is no way of confining the "law is politics" criticism. His primary objection was that the CLS movement generated a dangerous form of legal nihilism that threatened the ability of law to sustain or generate a public morality. Minda, 1995, *supra* note 5, at 214.

24. *See*, e.g., Kelman, M. (1987) A Guide to Critical Legal Studies. Cambridge, Mass.: Harvard University Press.

25. *See* Gitlin, T. (1995). The Twilight of Common Dreams. New York: H. Holt.

26. *See* Belliotti, R. (1992). Justifying Law: The Debate Over Foundations, Goals, and Methods (pp. 170–72). Philadelphia: Temple University Press. Mark Tushnet, an early and leading Critical Legal Studies theorist, outlined what he saw as CLS' inherently oppositional nature.

Racial and Feminist Realists go further, combining skepticism about rights with pessimism about either coalition-building or hypocrisy-exposure as achieving any long-term good for women and minorities. These groups will benefit only when it serves majority interests to do so. (Brooks, 1998: 4 and n.8). Otherwise, legal scholars and lawyers can at best strive for documenting racial and gender oppression, (*id.*), a noble but losing battle.

A more optimistic strain in postmodern jurisprudence displays shades of republicanism. This strain defines political "truth" as whatever emerges from processes that give all salient groups an "effective voice" concerning outcomes. An "effective voice" is one that has a real chance of making a difference in a result. (Taslitz, and Rape and Culture 137–41 and nn. 12–22). As with republicanism, the emphasis shifts to process, but there are no unifying ideals involved. So long as all have their say and enough power to at least sometimes win, results must be accepted.[27] But this sounds as well in the logic of iden-

---

> Instead of having political positions flow from social theory, the dominant CLS project simply takes political positions. But not just any political positions. *The politics of the dominant position is the politics of decentering, disrupting whatever understandings happen to be settled, criticizing the existing order whatever that order is.* Some CLS proponents are attracted to small-scale decentralized socialism. But that attraction must be understood as the embodiment of a critique of large-scale centralized capitalism. It cannot set forth a permanent program, the realization of which would be the end of politics. In fact, in a socialist society, the critical legal scholar would criticize socialism as denying the importance of individual achievement, and decentralization as an impediment to material and spiritual achievement.

Tushnet, M. (1996). Critical Legal Studies: An Introduction to Its Origins and Underpinning, 36 J. Leg. Educ. 505–517 (p 515). *But see* , 1995, *supra* note 5, at 123–27 (summarizing recent growth of CLS scholarship away from "trashing" and in response to charges of nihilism).

27. The idea of "effective" voice need not be rooted in postmodernism, but the postmodern justification for voice-representation is unique: there is no "truth," so the only outcomes entitled to respect are those in which all competing and equally epistemically valid voices have had a chance to be heard. *See* Taslitz, A. (1998). Abuse Excuses and the Logic and Politics of Expert Relevance, 49 Hastings L.J. 1039–1068 (pp. 1060–1061) (on the "hyperskeptic's" insistence on voice in an anti-realist world). Mark Kelman, in addressing whether battered women who kill their abusers and racist subway vigilantes raising self-defense should both equally be allowed to submit evidence of their unusual perceptions of danger to a jury, noted that:

> the essential political task is to insure that each subculture's voice is adequately heard. Thus, we might see multiculturalists demand corporatist, proportional representation schemes. In the context of jury trials, the context we are most concerned with here, the notion would presumably be that the subway killer will get an adequately sympathetic hearing without the aid of expert testimony or cau-

tity politics and suggests the absence of a substantive notion of the public good beyond interest-bargaining. The chance to be heard matters more than the chance to create a new, unifying good.

The rejection of any objective or universal truths puts these thinkers in an awkward position, as Professor Bartlett has explained: "[Criticalists] influenced by postmodernism are left in the awkward position of maintaining that [racial or] gender oppression exists while challenging their capacity to document it." (Bartlett, 1990: 879). Moreover, the perceived obsession with identity politics is arguably likely to lead to more, not less, misery for the oppressed. Sixties radical Todd Gitlin explains:

> To develop a political majority requires more than occasional coalitions knitted together by overlapping interests. It requires also, and urgently, a *culture* of commonality. If groups spend Monday through Saturday turned inward, separately, cultivating their differences, consolidating their internal unities, practicing cordiality to the exclusivists in their midst, it will not do for them to gather together on Sunday morning to speak of commonalities. To be active citizens of the whole, they must also spend time Monday through Saturday fraternizing across the lines, cultivating cultural hybrids, criticizing the narrowness of the tribe, working up ideas that people "unlike" themselves might share. One may respect the democratic rights of distinct groups to organize as they choose and still argue vigorously against the aggrandizement of difference.
> (Gitlin, 1995: 217–18).

Many other postmodern sympathizers who may be less derisive than Gitlin of identity politics and less trusting of coalition-building nevertheless share his commitment to fusing the best of Enlightenment and postmodern think-

---

> tionary instructions, while the battered woman's claims will be unduly discounted and marginalized unless we make special efforts to bolster them. There may be no ultimately objective view of risk determined by evidence; given, though that a political body (the jury) exists with the power to validate certain views, it must be manipulated to treat each inevitably partial understanding as equally weighty.

Kelman, M. (1994) Reasonable Evidence of Reasonableness. In J. Chandler, A. I. Davidson, & H. Harootunian (Eds.) Questions of Evidence: Proof, Practice, and Persuasion across the Disciplines (pp. 169–188). Chicago: University of Chicago Press (p. 178). My own ideas about effective voice have offered both postmodern and substantive-good justifications for voice as a guiding principle. *See* Taslitz, 1999b, *supra* note 5: 137–41, 204 n.13.

ing. Critical legal scholar Roy L. Brooks labels this growing viewpoint "positionality." Positional thinkers acknowledge the existence of at least some empirical truths, values, and knowledge. But they recognize that each person or group's understanding of these truths at any given time is partial and perspectival. Culture and life experience shape how much we perceive of a truth and the way in which we understand it. Thus it is perfectly consistent with the idea of there being "a" truth to acknowledge that each of us may have access to portions of the truth that others do not. (Brooks, 1998: 30–31). The situation is much like a circle of observers surrounding an enormous globe. The globe is so huge that each observer sees only a portion of it. If one half of the globe is blue and one half red, the entire globe will seem blue to those on one side, while the whole globe seems red to those on the other side. Both are right. A constant process of struggle, respectful exchanges of views, critical evaluation, and new experiences lead to constantly changing perspectives, and the incorporation of one person's truth into another's may yield new truths that were previously unknown.[28] Truth is thus generally a state of becoming rather than a state of being. A variant on positional thinking posits that there are indeed some sorts of "hyper-truths" we can discover, but there are also some questions for which there are no objective answers to be found. (Brooks, 1998: 30–31). But once we concede there to be even a limited number of hyper-truths, we have the basis for the sorts of "common dreams" of which Gitlin wrote.

Richard Delgado, perhaps the leading jurisprude in critical legal postmodernism, has indeed moved toward, or always implicitly embodied, positional thinking in a way that illustrates its advantages. In his book, The Rodrigo Chronicles, he outlines a series of stories involving, or debates between, Rodrigo, a fictional young law teacher, and his fictional mentor, the Professor. In one of these debates , Rodrigo bemoans the kind of coalition-building in which a smaller or less cohesive minority group, rather than forming its own organization, works within a larger, relatively more powerful minority group's institutional framework. Rodrigo makes this argument partly on narrow grounds of the smaller group's self-interest and pride: not sacrificing what is most dear to it, nor heading in a direction that on its own it would never seek. (Delgado 106–34). But Rodrigo next explains why separatism is in the larger group's self-interest as well:

---

28. For a detailed exposition of a similar epistemological position, though not labeled "positionality," *see* Rourke, N. E. (1997). A difference of reason. Lanham, Md.: University Press of America, which inspired my use of the globe example in text.

> But it's also bad for the larger group [if the smaller does not break off] because dissenters who agree to remain in the larger movements become coopted and alienated from their own position, with the result that the larger group loses an important source of criticism, a kind of early warning signal by which they could learn something.
> (*Id.* at 123).

But this discussion takes place as part of a larger dialogue. Rodrigo has spent much of his preceding conversation time with the professor documenting the dominant Western culture's long-run educational, economic, environmental, and social decline. Rodrigo portrays a western civilization mired in a linear way of thinking that blocks finding real solutions to worsening social problems, even though band-aid fixes may sometimes ameliorate some short-run pain. Yet he worries about the postmodern suggestion that the ruling group can never get past its own vision. (Id. at 10–15, 90–105). While at the same time rejecting Enlightment thought as hierarchical and suffering from a limited, linear vision, he also rejects nihilism. (*Id.* at 143–63). Radical dissent can save the West:

> If the United States is to save itself, it must incorporate ideas and people from non-Western sources—and yet these are the very sources they've constructed...to seem unworthy, ridiculous, lazy and morally debased... [Minorities must thus reject the image of their own inferiority and make their voices heard, for there is] no reason why all persons cannot have equal levels of dignity and respect.
> (*Id.* at 33–34).

The fusion of Enlightenment and postmodern thinking here is striking. Like postmoderns, Rodrigo stresses differing group perspectives. But like Enlightenment thinkers (despite his protestations to the contrary), he appeals to a transcendent objective good: saving "the West" by recognizing everyone's objectively real and inherent "dignity." Moreover, in echoes of Republican thinking, he seems to suggest that the "West" or the "United States" exists as a body politic that can continue to exist while being changed and improved by real deliberation. He sees minorities as empowered and best situated to promote such deliberation. But he appeals to classic, dare we say universal, Enlightenment values: equal dignity and respect for all persons.[29] This is an expression

29. Rodrigo indeed expressly criticizes republican thinking, but his criticism's tone is, in a sense, more about how to make republican thinking more truly "republican," that is, both more inclusionary and more action-oriented so that the "deliberation" so prized by republicans is not an excuse for complacency or a perhaps inadvertent silencing of outsider

of a concrete notion of the common good as a way both to justify political action and to seek pragmatic support for it from minority and majority. Delgado's appeal, through the personality of Rodrigo, is both to personal interest and principle. He never veers from the task of using postmodern insights to uncover the fact of, and mechanisms of, oppression. But once oppression is exposed, he argues for its end by appeal to universal "hypertruths." In a feedback loop, however, once those values establish the need for change, postmodern teachings help in crafting more effective change mechanisms. For Delgado, this means avoiding solutions that require submerging one group's identity in another's, for that would mute the loud, diverse dissent needed to promote universal dignity. Thus the apparent inconsistency with which positional thinkers comfortably live: group solidarity and difference furthers a common understanding and a common good.

Conclusion

Each of the papers in this anthology implicitly touches on the themes that I have raised in this essay. The attitude taken by several of the authors of this anthology toward the problems that they respectively address is one of primarily optimistic modernism, seeing an objectively real and achievable common good.

Gordon Knowles also seems to embrace an optimistic modernism. Knowles' study of the street sex market in Honolulu's Chinatown concluded that the sex trade raises many social concerns. Drug and alcohol addiction accompany the trade, and the risk of HIV transmission is high. Although feminists have often derided the criminalization of prostitution as a "capitalistic construction that is merely patriarchal in nature," Knowles sees this judgment as ill-informed by the objectively true fact that "studies have noted, just as many men [are] exploited by the sex trade as women for over the last thirty years." There is also an objectively true reality, "an accurate depiction of the individuals, behaviors, and activities of a population over time" that Knowles sees to be revealed by his study. That reality of drug use and high risk sex behavior, Knowles suggests, may require continued criminalization of street prostitution to serve the objectively determinable common good of both the prostitutes and the broader society:

> [T]his research contends from a public health perspective or a common good the law may attempt to restrict behaviors strongly associated

---

perspectives. *See* Delgado, R. (1995). The Rodrigo Chronicles. New York: New York University Press (pp. 138–163).

> with fostering a strictly epidemiological concern. Thus, laws restructuring the behavior of sex workers are not merely used to persecute those involved in socially unacceptable behavior, but rather the laws may be conceived as attempting to prevent a public health issue.

Steven F. Cohn and Steven E. Barkan's essay is harder to characterize yet is modernist in its feel. They thoroughly document evidence of racial prejudice as a factor explaining a wide array of punitive measures against crime yet are not unrelenting in their criticism. They acknowledge, for example, that the public has "legitimate reasons, including a fear of crime, a concern for public safety, and even a desire for retribution" for favoring harsh treatment of criminals. These are concerns that reach across race, class, gender, and ethnic background. Furthermore, the authors agree that public opinion should influence policy in a democracy. Nevertheless, they condemn the portion of public opinion based on race as rooted "to some degree in antidemocratic sentiment." By "antidemocratic," they seem to mean that some values—such as judging another's merit based on his or her race—are objectively wrong. Greater voice for minority groups would not solve this problem. For example, if the majority voted based on racial bias despite hearing critiques of such bias from minority groups who also had this right to vote, that would not render laws based on bias either just or consistent with democratic principles. Racial bias is wrong. While the public may not be willing to acknowledge its bias, the public as a whole would concede that the bias is wrong. These authors hope by their work to help the public to see the light of day.

Other authors, however, adopt positionality, seeing worth in both modernist and postmodernist ideas and expressing an optimistic belief that the law can sometimes serve the common good, while recognizing the obstacles to its doing so. Rebecca Katz and Amy Kelley adopt a similar attitude. They place their study of the feminization of poverty in rural Kentucky into a broader stream of empirical and theoretical work demonstrating that crime control strategies serve the interests of elites. In postmodern fashion, the authors see the elites as in part creating a category they label crime for social control purposes rather than because there is some objectively determinable criminal conduct that society can agree must be punished to serve a common good. Their study concludes that white and black males are both subjected "to more criminal justice system control as the result of capitalist exploitation and the subsequent poverty that ensues." However, they continue, "among both black males and females the threat hypothesis also operates by increasing their conviction rates as they become a larger percentage of the population relative to whites." Furthermore, "among white women, being poor translates into a greater likelihood of conviction." Yet, in modernist fashion, they embrace both the existence of objectively real standards for justice and the possibility of their being applied in service of the commons, not merely the elites:

> We argue that the impact that the system has on poor women and minorities clearly violates the 8th amendment to the Constitution and our equal protection laws. Thus, both policy makers and the public must be made aware of the disparate impact with which the criminal justice [system] exerts on both poor women and minority populations. Such awareness should lead to the creation of an equitable system of justice, such as restorative justice and social policies that prevent poverty and the capitalist exploitation of workers.

Other positional authors focus much more heavily on postmodernist ideas of the social construction of knowledge to serve dominant groups. Yet the tone of even these author's papers is sometimes one hopeful of finding a higher truth as a common ground. Kellina Craig, in her essay on hate crimes laws, for example, acknowledges the postmodern insights of critical race theorists, who worry that hate crimes laws may be used against the very minorities whom they were designed to protect. Other criticalists, Ms. Craig notes, worry that courts, not understanding the pain that hate speech inflicts on minorities, will invalidate hate speech laws as violative of rights to free speech. As an empirical matter, however, Ms. Craig finds little evidence that hate crimes laws are being used as a club against minorities. She concedes that the concern of abuse is wise, however, given similar tendencies in other parts of the legal system. But a "certain degree of vigilance... [in] monitoring such patterns" should adequately address this concern. Moreover, she recognizes, as have other positional thinkers, that free speech and equality are not in conflict. To the contrary, both are interdependent because both are necessary to creating the sort of community to which the American polity aspires. She effectively sees this aspiration as a "hypertruth," an objectively real standard that can enable "judges and lawmakers... [to] construct hate laws which work for all."

Kathleen Burke and Lisa Crooms similarly optimistically embrace postmodernist conceptions of knowledge as consistent with hypertruths. These authors differ from Craig and Katz and Kelley, however, in demonstrating a greater emphasis on the oppressed's sympathizers and the oppressed themselves changing their own ways of seeing the world. New eyes are, to these authors, a prerequisite to social change. Both see dominant images of masculinity as causing much injustice. For Burke, sexual abuse of young boys, especially when male-on-male, is hidden or ignored, and, when exposed, often given insufficient therapeutic attention by the state. The state may also seek to label male victims homosexual as a way of assigning implicit blame.

The reasons for these practices are that "images of masculinity as omnipotent, self-commanding, and aggressive" abound, the "resulting notion that the categories of victim and offender are gender specific... [thus] compounding the reticence of some men to disclose the abuse." Accordingly, "the state is [also] less likely to perceive boys [as] in need of protection or seriously traumatized as a result of sexual abuse." Male sexual life is, furthermore, meant to be heterosexual, and "Heterosexual prowess, physical potency, and invulnerability are among the defining characteristics currently associated with hegemonic masculinity.

Liberation lies in exposing the assumptions in this "discourse of masculinities," helping to jettison "essentialized understanding of both victim and gender." But Burke is hopeful that consciousness raising will change both treatment practices and the willingness of the powerful to promote change, that "continued work in the area of masculinities and victimization will yield more detailed insight not only into how men negotiate victimization, but also how police, lawyers, judges, jurors, and victim services variously respond to men as victims and victims as men."

Lisa Crooms is far more skeptical that the state's institutions can be "enlightened" into serving a broader good by exploding the flawed world-views implicit in our language practices. Instead, Crooms sees exploding assumptions, thereby raising the consciousness of the vulnerable, as a way of exposing shared interests among them. That exposure in turn encourages coalition-building in service of a common justice. Crooms implicitly appeals to such commonality rather than to mere group self-interest because, for Crooms, "oppressor and oppressed are highly situational statuses."

For Crooms, much of the injustice stemming from the law's treatment of sexual violence focuses on the varying gender of the victim. It is more useful to focus on the perpetrator's gender, which is usually male. Doing so reveals that much sexual violence grows from our culture's definitions of masculinity. Black Feminist Thought (BFT) and Critical Race Feminism (CRF) reject simple dualistic notions of identity. Gender identity is multiple, intersectional, and shifting, turning on race, class, ethnicity, and sexual orientation. Moreover, forms of oppression interlock, working together. Our society's acceptance of a narrow, uni-dimensional notion of masculinity thus supports racial, sexual orientation, and other forms of oppression. By focusing on the masculine "gender" (a social construct), not the male "sex" (a biological trait) of the perpetrator, we can see how masculine images promote sexual and related forms of violence. That insight is revealed in the stories of real people, in the elderly Grace Edwards' death from street violence because "respect and manhood remain[ed] central to the [masculine] code that rules on 10th Place, S. E.," a code that "no longer exempts elders from its violence"; and in the thronging of women in Central Park at New York's National Puerto Rican Day Parade because in Puerto Rican communities a real man "pursues, punishes, repudiates, or devalues those women who reject him or pay no attention to his demands."

Yet, if male oppression of these women is met by increased criminal penalties, argues Crooms, history shows that the result will simply be greater oppression of African-American and Puerto-Rican communities, given the "reality of the racially disparate treatment of people of color by law enforcement officials...." Nevertheless, argues Crooms, revealing the masculinist assumptions at work in our language and practices concerning sexual violence encourages "political alliances between those who are relatively devalued and dispossessed in a system organized to serve the interests of white, heterosexual, middle class men." Exposing assumptions gets us beyond "polarized identity politics" that divides the oppressed. The male victimizers must be held responsible, but they too are victimized by the ideology of masculinity. Coalitions of the enlightened can "combat oppression under the 'matrix of domination' and counter the law's tendency to see identity and oppression as one-dimensional." In the act of struggle, the oppressed create their own "common good," appealing to higher principles of justice that pressure a legal system that serves elites to change its ways.

Kathleen Gale is a third optimistic postmodern author stressing ways of seeing. Gale, unlike Crooms and Burke, is interested solely in the vision of the oppressed themselves and not that of their purported sympathizers. Gale interviewed two women victimized by male violence. Her interviews explored why these women generally did not respond with their own violence. Gale apparently rejects simple self-control as an explanation. Nor does she see patriarchy as serving to "control" what would otherwise be these women's expression of explosive rage.

These women explained their own actions as based on their own view of what is "normal." Patriarchy may play a role in defining normalcy, but this is not the same sort of psychological process as "control." These women's view of their acting as "just folks" superceded gender, argues Gale. "Just folks" do not react with violence.

Patriarchal oppression and flawed institutions, however, add their own forces and may keep a non-violent terrorized woman from fleeing. One interviewee, Katy, illustratively explained that her abuser maintained economic power by keeping Katy from accumulating her own money and possessions. His violence also kept her submissive to preserve her own life. To focus solely on these factors demeans and misunderstands the women, however, who have a right in the first instance to define themselves. Gale explains:

> In a feminist perspective and a humanist perspective, our questions should be how we can reduce harms to those who are dominated by domestic terror. A first step is to make known those harms, and tell the stories of those silenced—giving them agency to define what is "normal" and good action.

Furthermore, argues Gale, once we allow women to express their own vision, we can better see how institutions designed to reduce domestic violence may increase it. Our institutions should and can take into account the oppressed's voices when crafting social policy. Gale sees her essay as contributing to that goal.

Bruce Arrigo, rather than analyzing a particular social problem, examines at a higher theoretical level the advantages for criminology of viewing the world through an optimistic postmodern lens. Like Burke and Crooms, Arrigo stresses postmodernism's focus on language. Crime is defined not by those who control the means of production, as argue the radical criminologists, or by those individuals and groups who have the most power on particular issues, as argue the conflict theorists. Rather, crime is defined by those who control the means of *linguistic* production because language defines our reality. The crime problem is, therefore, for postmodernists, really a problem of voice:

> The policy implications for postmodern criminology include the equalization of power and a pluralistic, participatory democracy. These ends are achieved through the elimination of competitive grammars and the establishment of replacement discourses. Postmodernists argue that these activities will effect a reduction in crime.

Because Arrigo sees postmodernism as questioning the existence of "*any* foundational, certifiable truths," and believes that language "structures thought in ways that are consistent with dominant views of the world," he does not believe that there are absolute violations of human rights. Conflict theorists adopt a similar view. Only radicals assert "that there is an objective basis to harm or behavior defined as harmful." But this skepticism by postmoderns does not blind them to the possibility of achieving higher, shared principles of justice. Thus, the author explains that "the nature of crime is such that there is some consensus on what constitutes harm and, thus, certain acts are categorically wrong and/or unequivocally criminal." In an achievable, more pluralistic world respectful of competing linguistic visions of reality, consensus on a commonly-held notion of the good is possible and worthy of respect.

Debra S. Emmelman is also an author stressing ways of seeing. But Emmelman is a pessimistic, rather than an optimistic, postmodern. Emmelman does not consider whether exposing narrowed vision alone presses legal institutions to change. Nor does she see such exposure as helpful in coalition-building. Unlike Burke and Crooms' vision, Emmelman merely marks law as in service to the elites. Emmelman's focus is on the blinders worn by the apparent friends of the oppressed: lawyers representing impoverished criminal defendants.

Poor criminal defendants are convicted at higher rates than wealthier defendants. Criminal defense lawyers mold their entire representation, however, to what will appeal to middle class judges and juries as decisionmakers, the "common sense" or "shared values, beliefs, and norms of the status quo...." Thus, defenders assume that lack of a permanent residence, job, or stable family relationship, which may be true of many of the poor, will be seen as making the defendant a poor bail risk. By seeking to stress whatever few sorts of middle-class ties the defendant may have to the community, and downplaying the seriousness of the offense, the defender sends the message that the poor lack the "integrity and moral fortitude to show up at court hearings." Similarly, a defender might judge a defendant's case to be weak because it will not convince a jury. A defendant charged with theft but protesting his innocence may be disbelieved by juries because he "has no job and therefore more reason to have committed the theft." Correspondingly, if, of two suspects, one has a job and one does not, the prosecutor is more likely to drop charges against the employed one and proceed against the jobless one, as happened in one case documented by Professor Emmelman.

Such common sense judgments affect plea bargains too. A well-educated, employed ex-military man with little criminal record until a family crisis (an amalgam of her example) is likely to get a better deal than a jobless offender who dropped out of high school with a record of a number of thefts. Indeed, argues Emmelman, at *every* step in the criminal process defenders play into assumptions that favor the status quo, assumptions that often discriminate based on race and ethnicity as well as class.

The major cause of the problem is that "due to their different experiences of the social order, the dominant group cannot understand or appreciate fully situations of racial oppression in their own society." For example, "most whites in this country cannot actually fathom why contemporary minority groups proclaim discrimination, and find minority experiences of police exploitation especially difficult to believe." Defenders, therefore, "acknowledge some complications in portraying the cases of their minority clients in a manner which is consistent, not simply with common sense, but with what is the same thing, the cultural understandings of the *white* status quo." Emmelman's depressingly unqualified conclusion: "The use of 'common sense' in the adjudication of criminal cases does *not* imply that the legal system safeguards the *common* good. Instead, it means that the sensibilities of the powerful are sustained (at the expense of less powerful groups.)" Note yet again, however, that Emmelman does expect her readers to bemoan this observation, seeing it as violative of some higher truth, namely, the wisdom of a social commitment to equality. That assumption suggests an underlying belief in widely shared values to which an appeal can be made, even if Emmelman is skeptical of our purported commitment to those values enabling us to get beyond the constraints of "commonsense" justice.

Randel Shelden, William Brown, and Shelley Listwan are, however, even more pessimistic than Emmelman, They carefully document how the combined effects of the War on Drugs and Welfare Reform have decimated segments of the African-American community. They document the high percentages of African-American men in prison or jail, the growing numbers of Africa-American women suffering a similar fate, and the feminization of poverty. Furthermore, they explore case studies that make palpable the resulting feelings of despair as many African-American families disintegrate, despite the best efforts of struggling parents. To these authors the policies causing these effects are a "new apartheid," a "systematic attack on African-Americans." The social system creates a "surplus population" as the search for corporate profits shrinks the available pool of semi-skilled and unskilled jobs. To "manage" the superfluous, the prison system expands and the welfare system turns mean.

The authors bluntly describe the War on Drugs and the War on Gangs as "intentionally target[ing] the most marginalized Americans," "a form of slow genocide," a "disenfranchisement of ethnic minorities," and a "form of ethnic cleansing." The picture painted is an unrelenting one of an elite majority ravaging a vulnerable minority, then portraying the minority as the "dangerous classes" and "predators" who bring their suffering on themselves.

These authors suggest that their paper does little more than document suffering unlikely to be relieved. They embrace postmodern notions of the "social construction" of knowledge by emphasizing the importance of language, labeling the oppressed in such a way as to free the oppressor from responsibility. Yet even this unremittingly pessimistic vision embraces a belief in objective truths. The oppressed have real, objective value, both by virtue simply of being human and by having valuable labor, love for family, and a commitment to struggle, all assets to offer the larger society. The current system is to be condemned because it obscures the real worth of the oppressed classes. If Shelden, Brown, and Listwan do not see law as currently embracing a common good, they at least hold forth the insistence that it should and implicitly the faint hope that it could.

Ann Lucas' paper represents a final viewpoint, which I will label "postmodern agnosticism." Lucas' interviews with ten indoor male prostitutes explore their feelings about, and motivations for doing, their work. Many expressed disappointment at the social stigma associated with a career that the prostitutes often saw as socially useful and professional. The work was better than some other sorts of tasks that the prostitutes had done for a living and offered higher pay and more autonomy. Lucas' impression is not viewed as "real" prostitution by society. Most people define prostitution largely as women exchanging sex for money with men. People object to male prostitution not when it involves gigolos but rather when both partners are men. It is the homosexuality, and not the marketing of sex, that bothers heterosexuals about male prostitution. Yet, says Lucas,

> [W]hat turns sex into prostitution is precisely the money. And this is why I think male prostitution *is* technically prostitution, but not viewed as the social evil female prostitution is—because most people who are objecting aren't really objecting to the commercialization of sex when both parties are men. Nor, of course, are they quite as judgmental of male customers of female prostitutes as they are of the prostitutes themselves. So it seems that buying and selling sex is a behavior expected, or at least understood, in men, while for women it's a sign of larger problems. And so in terms of the social construction of gender, I believe that female prostitution and its criminalization are highly significant, but male prostitution and its criminalization are not.

In her stress on the social construction of gender, Lucas is obviously postmodern in her approach. She is agnostic in that she does not seek to characterize her observations as either good or evil based on some objective standard. Although she may hold such views, she does not express them. That may reflect a "pure" postmodernism, an embrace of the view that *all* reality is socially constructed and there are no foundational "truths" to which we can turn for guidance. Her observations could, of course, support an argument that there are good reasons to legalize prostitution generally, or to treat male and female prostitution the same, regardless of the gender of the "john." Lucas does not make or hint at that argument, however, and that may reflect as well an agnosticism about whether policy prescription can accomplish any real change. If there is a definable, achievable common good, Lucas is unwilling to say so. Rather, she merely highlights the workings of social power, again suggesting a purer postmodernism than expressed by other authors and one that is for that reason the most discouraging of the essays in this anthology.

Doug Kieso and Gilbert Geis, in their essay on the California Three Strikes Law, also seem at first blush to adopt a pessimistic postmodernism. They thus stress the data suggesting that the California law, which "embraces nonviolent and non-serious offenders in regard to the last or triggering strike," is based on exaggerated claims that the "people being locked up under the law are 'professional thieves' or 'violent' criminals." Instead, the authors find, many of those sentenced are small-time property and drug offenders suffering from substance abuse. Many have reached that stage because "the state often has been negligent on earlier occasions in offering them an opportunity to overcome their drug problems." The authors further stress that the law came about in part because of the public's emotional outrage at the high-profile murder of Polly Klaas and partly because of political rhetoric and media coverage that fueled the public's fear of crime. Yet notice that while the authors recognize that the empirical assumptions that led to the law—a belief in widespread violent crime by repeat offenders whom this law would isolate—were socially constructed and reflected unreasoning fear, the basis for the author's criticism of those assumptions is that there are objective truths. The objective truths that they assert are that the law was based on an inaccurate picture of crime overall and that the law reaches petty thieves for whose misconduct society is partly responsible. By making these claims, the authors apparently hope to stir the public conscience. While the authors do not excuse petty criminality, they do question the enormity of some of the punishments under this law for offenders who do relatively little harm and whom society failed to aid. The authors thus implicitly appeal to higher principles of proportionality and fairness that they hope can be seen by the public as reflecting common ground.

All the authors in this anthology but Lucas at least implicitly recognize the existence of hypertruths to which they can appeal, with some hope of success, even if they sometimes seem to stress the contrary. There is a common good, and the law can at least sometimes serve it. Nevertheless, though the authors differ in their assessment of the likelihood of that happening, these authors hope to move society toward that goal by exposing and critiquing the ways that it presently fails in this aspiration.

References

Abramson, J. (1994). *We, the Jury: The Jury System and the Ideal of Democracy*. New York, NY: BasicBooks.

Ackerman, B. (1996). *We, The People: Foundations.* Cambridge, Mass.: Belknap Press of Harvard University Press.

Bartlett, K. (1990). Feminist Legal Methods. In *Harv. L. Rev.*, 103:829–889.

Baynes, L.M. (1997). A Time to Kill, the O.J. Simpson Trials, and Storytelling to Juries. In *Loy. L. A. Ent. L.J.*, 17:549–569.

Belliotti, R. (1992). *Justifying Law: The Debate Over Foundations, Goals, and Methods* Philadelphia: Temple University Press

Bergman, P., and Asimow, M. (1996). *Reel Justice: The Courtroom Goes to the Movies.* Kansas City: Andrews and McMeel.

Bergmann, A. (1992). *Crossing the Postmodern Divide.* Chicago: University of Chicago Press.

Bickel, A. (1986). *The Least Dangerous Branch, 2d ed.* New Haven, Conn.: Yale University Press.

Brooks, R.L. (1998). *Critical Procedure.* Durham, N.C.: Carolina Academic Press.

Brown, D. K. (1998). Plan Meaning, Practical Reason, and Culpability: Toward a Theory of Jury Interpretation of Criminal Statutes. In Mich. L. Rev, 96:1199–1268.

Cammack, M. (1995). In Search of the Post-Positivist Jury. In *Ind.L.J.*, 70:405–489.

Caudill, D. S. (1997). *Lacan and the Subject of Law: Toward a Psychoanalytic Critical Legal Theory.* Atlantic Highlands, N.J.: Humanities Press.

Conrad, C. S. (1998). *Jury Nullification: The Evolution of a Doctrine.* Durham, N.C.: Carolina Academic Press.

Damaska, M. (1997). *Evidence Law Adrift.* New Haven: Yale University Press.

Delgado, R. (1998). *When Equality Ends.* Boulder, Colo.: Westview Press.

Delgado, R. (1995). *The Rodrigo Chronicles.* New York: New York University Press.

Dressler, J. (1995.) *Understanding Criminal Law, 2nd ed.* New York: Matthew Bender/Irwin.

Farber, D. A. & Sherry, S. (1997). *Beyond All Reason: The Radical Assault on Truth in American Law.* New York: Oxford University Press.

Gitlin, T. (1995). *The Twilight of Common Dreams.* New York: H. Holt.

Glaspell, S. (1998). A Jury of Her Peers. In F. Shapiro & J. Garry (Eds.) *Trial and Error: An Oxford Anthology of Legal Stories* (pp. 139–156). New York: Oxford University Press.

Grisham, J. (1989). *A Time to Kill.* New York : Doubleday.

Hunt, A. (1993). *Explorations in Law and Society: Toward a Constitutive Theory of Law.* New York, N.Y.: Routledge.

Jacobs, J. B., & Potter, K. (1998). *Hate Crimes: Criminal Law and Identity Politics.* New York: Oxford University Press.

Jefferson, T. (1776). *Declaration of Independence.*

Judge Draws Protests After Cutting Sentence of Gay Man's Killer, *N.Y. Times*, Aug. 17, 1994 A15.

Kalman, L. (1996). *The Strange Career of Legal Liberalism.* New Haven : Yale University Press.

Kelvin, M. (1994). Reasonable Evidence of Reasonableness. In J. Chandler, A. I. Davidson, & H. Harootunian (Eds.) *Questions of Evidence: Proof, Practice, and Persuasion across the Disciplines* (pp. 169–188). Chicago: University of Chicago Press.

Kelman, M. (1987). *A Guide to Critical Legal Studies.* Cambridge, Mass.: Harvard University Press.

Lee, H. (1998). To Kill a Mockingbird. In F. Shapiro & J. Garry (Eds.) *Trial and Error: An Oxford Anthology of Legal Stories* (pp. 330–346). New York: Oxford University Press.

Lee, T. M. L. (1997). *Politics and Truth: Political Theory and the Postmodernist Challenge.* Albany: State University of New York Press.

Lehman, G. D. (1997). *We the Jury: The Impact of Jurors on Our Basic Freedoms.* Amherst, N.Y.: Prometheus Books.

Levy, L. (1999). *The Palladium of Justice.* Chicago: I.R. Dee.

Litowitz, D. E. (1997). *Postmodern Philosophy & Law: Rorty, Nietzsche, Lyotard, Derrida, & Foucault.* Lawrence, Kan.: University Press of Kansas.

Maier, P. (1997). *American Scripture: Making the Declaration of Independence.* New York: Knopf.

Mauet, T., (1995). *Fundamentals of Pretrial Techniques, 3rd ed.* Boston: Little, Brown.

Mercuro, N., & Medema, S.G. (1997). *Economics and the Law: From Posner to Postmodernism.* Princeton, N.J. : Princeton University Press.

Minda, G. (1995). *Postmodern Legal Movements: Law and Jurisprudence at Century's End.* New York: New York University Press.

Pineau, L. (1996). Date Rape: A Feminist Analysis. In L. Francis (Ed.) *Date Rape: Feminism, Philosophy, and the Law.* University Park: Pennsylvania State University Press (pp. 1–26).

Posner, R. A. (1981). *The Economics of Justice.* Cambridge, Mass.: Harvard University Press.

Rourke, N. E. (1997). *A Difference of Reason.* Lanham, Md.: University Press of America.

Rue, L. (1994). *By the Grace of Guile: The Role of Deception in Natural History and Human Affairs.* New York : Oxford University Press.

Schrager, S. (1999). *The Trial Lawyer's Art.* Philadelphia : Temple University Press.

Seidenfeld, M. (1996). *Microeconomic Predicates to Law and Economics.*

Shapiro, F. & Garry, J. (Eds.), (1998). *Trial and Error: An Oxford Anthology of Legal Stories.* New York: Oxford University Press.

Sherwin, R. K. (2000). *When Law Goes Pop: The Vanishing Line between Law and Popular Culture.* Chicago: University of Chicago Press.

Strier, F. & Greene, E. (1990). *The Adversary System: An Annotated Bibliography.* Littleton, Co: Fred B. Rothman & Co.

Sunstein, C. (1988). Beyond the Republican Revival, *Yale L. J.*, 97:1539–1590.

Sunstein, C. (1983). Interest Groups in American Public Law, *Stan. L. Rev.*, 38:29–87.

Taslitz, A. (1998). *Abuse Excuses and the Logic and Politics of Expert Relevance, Hastings L.J.*, 49:1039–1068 [hereinafter Taslitz, 1998a].

Taslitz, A. (1999). *Condemning the Racist Personality: Why the Critics of Hate Crimes Legislation Are Wrong, B.C.L. Rev*, 40:739–785 [hereinafter Taslitz, 1999a].

Taslitz, A. (1998). *A Feminist Approach to Social Scientific Evidence: Foundations, Mich. J. Gender & L*, 5:1–80 [hereinafter Taslitz, 1998b].

Taslitz, A. (1996). *Patriarchal Stories I: Cultural Rape Narratives in the Courtroom, S. Cal. Rev. L. & Women's Stud*, 5:387–500.

Taslitz, A. (1995). *Interpretive Method and the Federal Rules of Evidence: A Call for a Politically Realistic Hermeneutics, Harv. J. Leg*, 32:329–401.

Taslitz, A. (1999). *Rape and the Culture of the Courtroom* [hereinafter Taslitz, 1999b].

Taslitz, A. (1999). *What Feminism Has to Offer Evidence Law, Sw. U. L. Rev.* 171–219 [hereinafter Taslitz, 1999c].

A Time to Kill. (1996). Warner Brothers.

Twelve Angry Men. (1957). United Artists.

Tushnet, M. (1996). *Critical Legal Studies: An Introduction to Its Origins and Underpinning, J. Leg. Educ,* 36:505–517.

Twinning, W. (1994). *Rethinking Evidence: Exploratory Essays.* Evanston, Ill.: Northwestern University Press.

Washington, Julie E., *Reaching a Verdict on Jury-Room Play, 12 "Angry Men" Actors Discuss Case, The Plain* Dealer, Cleveland, Ohio, 1 E. (Nov. 14, 1998), 1998 *WL* 4163755

Weinstein, J. (1999). *Hate Speech, Pornography, and the Radical Attack on Free Speech Doctrine.* Boulder, Colo.: Westview Press.

Wigmore, J. H. (Tillers rev. 1983). *Evidence in Trials at Common Law.* Boston: Little, Brown.

Biographical Statements

Bruce A. Arrigo is Professor and Chair of the Department of Criminal Justice at the University of North Carolina at Charlotte, with Adjunct Professor appointments in the Public Policy Program and the Psychology Department respectively. Formerly the Director of the Institute of Psychology, Law, and Public Policy at the California School of Professional Psychology-Fresno, Dr. Arrigo began his professional career as a community organizer and social activist for the homeless, the mentally ill, the working poor, the frail elderly, the decarcerated, and the chemically addicted. Dr. Arrigo received his Ph.D. from Pennsylvania State University, and he holds a master's degree in psychology and in sociology. He is the author of more than (100) monographs, journal articles, academic book chapters, and scholarly essays exploring theoretical and applied topics in critical criminology, criminal justice and mental health, and socio-legal studies. He is the author, coauthor, or editor of nine (9) books; including, *Madness, Language, and the Law* (1993), *The Contours of Psychiatric Justice* (1996), *Social Justice/Criminal Justice* (1998), *The Dictionary of Critical Social Sciences* (with T.R. Young, 1999), *Introduction to Forensic Psychology* (2000), *Law, Psychology, and Justice* (with Christopher R. Williams, 2001), *The Power Serial Rapist* (with Dawn J. Graney, 2001), *Punishing the Mentally Ill: A Critical Analysis of Law and Psychiatry* (2002), and *Criminal Competency on Trial* (with Mark C. Bardwell, 2002). Dr. Arrigo is the past Editor of *Humanity & Society* and founding and acting Editor of the peer-reviewed quarterly, *Journal of Forensic Psychology Practice.* He was recently named the Critical Criminologist of the Year (2000), sponsored by the Critical Criminology Division of the American Society of Criminology.

Steven E. Barkan is Professor of Sociology at the University of Maine. His current work focuses on racial prejudice and punitive attitudes toward criminals and on the correlates of participation in voluntary organizations. He is the author of *Criminology: A Sociological Understanding, 2nd edition* (Prentice Hall, 2001).

Marian J. Borg is Associate Professor in the Department of Sociology at the University of Florida. She teaches courses in the sociology of social control, criminology and deviance. Her research focuses on examining various processes of social control including mediation, capital punishment, monitoring, violence and police response to criminal behavior.

William B. Brown is an Associate Professor in the Department of Criminal Justice at Western Oregon University. Essentially, my research has centered on inner-city African American Youth Gangs, Human Rights, and Comparatice Criminal Justice. I am currently making travel arrangements in preparation to conduct research in Southeast Asia (Thailand, Vietnam, Cambodia), Latin America (Nicagragua, Costa Rica, Guatemala, Columbia), and Europe (Germany, France, Poland). The focus of this research is two-pronged: First, comparing crime and responses to crime in these geographic regions, and to analyze U.S. influence to crime responses in each of these regions. Naturally, human rights issues shall be a mainstay of concern during this study.

Sandra Lee Browning is an associate professor of criminology at the University of Cincinnati. She has published extensively in marriage and the family, law and social control, and race and the criminal justice system. Her first two books: *Till Death Do Us Part: a Multicultural Anthology on Marriage* (1999) and *With This Ring: Divorce, Intimacy and Co-habitation from a Multicultural Perspective* (2000) she co-edited with R. Robin Miller. She can be reached at the Department of Criminology, 600 Dyer Hall, University of Cincinnati, Cincinnati, Ohio 45221-0389.

Kathleen M. Burke is currently an instructor in the School of Criminology at Simon Fraser University. She received her Ph.D. in Criminology from Simon Fraser University in 1999 and spent the 1999–2000 academic year as a visiting Assistant Professor in the Department of Criminal Justice at Indiana University. Her research interests include gender, victimization, ethics in criminal justice and critical theory. She has co-authored an article on masculinities and crime with Brian Burtch and is currently writing articles from her dissertation "*Take it like a man: The silencing of men's experiences of male child sexual abuse.*"

Steven F. Cohn is Professor of Sociology at the University of Maine. His current research interests are in social movements, criminology, and urban poverty. In addition to his continued work on the relationship between racial prejudice and punitive attitudes towards criminals, he is conducting research on the social conditions of homeless youth.

Jeanette Covington is an associate professor of criminology at Rutgers University. She has worked extensively in such areas as race, ethnicity, and the drug wars.

Kellina Craig-Henderson teaches in the Department of Psychology at Howard University. Her research interests include work in hate crime legislation, crime and social control.

Lisa Crooms teaches criminology, sociology and law at Howard Law School. Her research includes work in gender studies, law and violence.

Debra Emmelman is an Associate Professor at Southern Connecticut State University and is currently writing a book on justice for the poor. She may be reached at the Department of Sociology and Anthropology, Southern Connecticut State University, 501 Crescent Street, New Haven, CT 06516.

Kathleen Gale (Ph.D. Victoria University of Manchester, England) is an Associate Professor of Sociology and Criminal Justice at Elmira College, Elmira, New York. She has numerous publications and presentations in the sociology of law, criminology and women's studies. At Elmira she has developed a program in Social Science: Criminal Justice that gives students grounding in sociological and legal theory and methodology, while encouraging them to give their time and skill to the communities in which they live. She has applied her training in social anthropology and the sociology of law to fieldwork and research in women and justice. She is primarily devoted to teaching and has involved undergraduate and graduate students in field research on sentencing, criminal victimization, fear of crime, and juvenile justice. She is inspired by the peace seeking, humanism and sense of justice of students she has taught and people she has observed, listened to and interviewed over the past twenty five years as a College teacher.

Gilbert Geis is Professor Emeritus, Department of Criminology, Law and Society, University of California, Irvine. He is a former president of the American Society of Criminology and recipient of its Edwin H. Sutherland Award for research achievement. Correspondence can be addressed to 970 Poppy Lane, Corona del Mar, CA 92625.

Gail Hurst in an assistant professor of criminology at Xavier University. Her research includes studies in gender, race and the criminal justice system.

Rebecca S. Katz is an Assistant Professor of Sociology and Criminology at Morehead State University in Morehead Kentucky. Her research interests include developmental theories of crime, critical theories of crime, and the white supremacy movement. Rebecca spent thirteen years as a mental health professional prior to receipt of her Doctorate in Sociology from the University of Oklahoma in 1995. She has worked in a variety of settings including state and federal prisons and psychiatric hospitals. She has recently authored or co-authored publications in "Violence Against Women" and "Sociological Focus". She is currently working on a book with Paul Becker on women's involvement in the white supremacy movement.

Amy Kelly is currently a senior at Morehead State University with a double major in government and criminology. She is in the process of making applications to a variety of graduate schools. She plans on pursuing a masters degree and a Ph.D. Her research interests include local, national, and international forms of social control. Correspondence to her may be addressed to 401 1/2 N. Maysville Road, Mt. Sterling, Kentucky 40353.

Douglas W. Kieso is currently a Ph.D. candidate at the University of California-Irvine in the Department of Criminology, Law and Society.

Gordon James Knowles received his Ph.D. in Sociology with an emphasis in Criminology from the University of Hawaii and also holds an M.S. in Criminal Justice Administration with an emphasis in Law Enforcement and Corrections Management from Chaminade University of Honolulu. His main interests include urban ethnography, applied sociology, criminology, criminal justice, and law. Interested readers may contact him at voice/fax (808) 566-9933 or via E-mail at GordonKnow@aol.com.

Shelley Johnson Listwan received her Ph.D. from the University of Cincinnati with a focus on criminological theory and corrections. Previous research projects include: an evaluation of Georgia's cognitive skills programming for offenders, an evaluation of Ohio's juvenile and adult drug courts, and a national needs assessment of juvenile and adult drug courts around the country. She has served as a consultant to several state, local, and national agencies with regard to case classification and assessment as well as improving the effectiveness of correctional interventions. Current research interests also include an exploration of psychological classification systems and their impact on treatment effectiveness.

Ann Lucas is an associate professor in the Department of Sociology at the University of Texas, El Paso. Her research includes work in gender studies, prostitution, and social control of populations.

R. Robin Miller is an associate professor of sociology at Drury University. Her first two books *Till Death Do Us Part: a Multicultural Anthology on Marriage* (1999) and *With This Ring: Divorce, Intimacy and Co-habitation from a Multicultural Perspective* (2000) she co-edited with Sandra Lee Browning. Her most recent work has been on incarceration and the black community, and she soon expects a third book to be released, entitled *Impacts of Incarceration on the African American Family*. She can be reached at Drury University 900 North Benton Avenue, Springfield, Missouri 65802.

Karen F. Parker is Assistant Professor of Sociology in the Center for Studies in Criminology and Law at the University of Florida. Her current research interests include examining the effects of labor market conditions and racial competition on disaggregated homicide rates, exploring violence in the urban context and the evaluation of recidivism among Florida inmates. Her most recent publications appear in *Social Forces, Social Science Quarterly,* and *Journal of Quantitative Criminology.*

Randall G. Shelden is a Professor in the Department of Criminal Justice, University of Nevada-Las Vegas. He is the author or co-author of four books, including the award-winning *Girls, Delinquency and Juvenile Justice* (co-author, Meda Chesney-Lind, winner of the Hindelang Award) and lead author of *Youth Gangs in American Society* (both published by Wadsworth and each in their second edition). His most recent book is *Controlling the Dangerous Classes: A Critical Introduction to the History of Criminal Justice* (Allyn and Bacon). His current book project is a history of the American prison system, tentatively titled: *The American Gulag: The Emergence and Growth of the Prison Industrial Complex.* He can be reached at the Department of Criminal Justice, University of Nevada, Las Vegas, NV 89154-5009. Phone: 702-895-0251, fax: 702-895-0252. e-mail: shelden@nevada.edu.

Andrew E. Taslitz is a Professor of Law at the Howard University School of Law and has also taught at the Duke University and Villanova University Law Schools. A former prosecutor, he now teaches Evidence, Criminal Procedure, Criminal Law, and Professional Responsibility. He has written numerous articles and books in the areas in which he teaches, focusing much of his work on issues of racial and gender discrimination in the criminal justice system. His most recent work has emphasized the areas of sexual assault, hate crimes, hate speech, group-bias in searches and seizures, and postmodern and other feminist approaches to evidence law. His work draws heavily on the intersections of law and social science and law and constitutional history. His most recent books include *Evidence Law and Practice* (2001) (co-authored); *Rape and the Culture of the Courtroom* (1999); and *Constitutional Criminal Procedure* (1997) (co-authored) (second edition forthcoming 2002). He has a forthcoming book with N.Y.U. Press entitled, *Law on the Street: Search and Seizure, Race and Respect in American Life* (expected publication 2003). He is the current Chair of the Association of American Law Schools' Criminal Justice Section and Chair-Elect of its Evidence Section; current Chair of the American Bar Association's (ABA's) *Criminal Justice* periodical Editorial Board and a member of its Advisory Board for the annual publication, *The State of Criminal Justice*; a former consultant for the ABA Council on Racial and Ethnic Justice; and a former member of a National Research Council Committee on bomb-blast terrorism, appointed in the wake of the Oklahoma City bombing. He has sought in his writings on the jury to reach a synthesis between modernist and postmodernist approaches to factfinding in his own optimistic quest for the common good.

Alberta Thrash is an associate professor and administrator at Central State University. Her research interests include work and occupations, drug testing, and civil liberties.

Name Index

Subject Index